# Living and Dying in England
## ⊰ 1100–1540 ⊱
### *The Monastic Experience*

# Living and Dying in England

## ⚜ 1100–1540 ⚜

## *The Monastic Experience*

*by*

## Barbara Harvey

*The Ford Lectures*
*Delivered in the University of Oxford*
*in Hilary Term 1989*

CLARENDON PRESS · OXFORD

1993

Oxford University Press, Walton Street, Oxford OX2 6DP

Oxford  New York  Toronto
Delhi  Bombay  Calcutta  Madras  Karachi
Kuala Lumpur  Singapore  Hong Kong  Tokyo
Nairobi  Dar es Salaam  Cape Town
Melbourne  Auckland  Madrid
and associated companies in
Berlin  Ibadan

Oxford is a trade mark of Oxford University Press

Published in the United States
by Oxford University Press Inc., New York

British Library Cataloguing in Publication Data
Data available

Library of Congress Cataloging in Publication Data
Harvey, Barbara F.
Living and dying in England, 1100–1540 : the monastic experience /
by Barbara Harvey.
p.     cm.
"The Ford lectures delivered in the University of Oxford in Hilary
Term 1989."
Includes bibliographical references and index.
1. Westminster Abbey—History.  2. Monasticism and religious
orders—England—History—Middle Ages, 600–1500.  I. Title.
BX2595.W47H37   1993
271'.1042132—dc20                                          92–21141

ISBN 0–19–820161–3

Typeset by Graphicraft Typesetters Ltd, Hong Kong

Printed in Great Britain
on acid-free paper by
Bookcraft Ltd, Midsomer Norton, Bath

# Preface

THE first version of this book was given as the Ford Lectures in the University of Oxford in Hilary Term 1989. I owe a debt of a special kind to Jennifer Loach and Joanna Innes, my colleagues in the History School at Somerville, who ensured in unobtrusive ways, but not without cost to themselves, that I had sufficient time in which to prepare. In revising the lectures, I have added substantially to each. Nevertheless, much of the original text survives, unchanged, and in consequence the sound of the human voice can sometimes be heard in the book. I hope that readers will not find this a difficulty.

The book will, I hope, shed light, as its title implies, on monastic life in England. But its purpose is quite as much to illumine the life of secular society to which monastic, and particularly Benedictine, life was, at many points, closely assimilated. I have tried to bring as large a number of monasteries as possible under contribution. Yet in each chapter the monks of Westminster have provided the principal case-study. I gratefully acknowledge the permission of the Dean and Chapter of Westminster to use, and cite, their muniments, and I am also indebted to Dr Richard Mortimer, Keeper of the Muniments, who has facilitated my work in this exceptionally rich archive in every possible way. Dr Mortimer, Mrs Enid Nixon, and Miss Christine Reynolds have ensured that my visits to the Muniment Room at the Abbey have been not only useful in scholarly terms, but also exceedingly enjoyable. I think also with gratitude of the welcome which I received from the late Mr Howard Nixon, formerly Librarian of Westminster Abbey, and the late Mr Nicholas MacMichael, formerly Keeper of the Muniments.

In writing the book, I have needed many different kinds of help and at every juncture have been fortunate enough to enjoy exactly the kind that I most needed. Dr Paul Slack has assisted at many points, but particularly as Chapter I, on charity, took shape. He has also read a substantial part of the final draft of the book. Professor David Conning, Director-General of the British Nutrition Foundation, spared time to discuss various aspects of nutrition with me. Miss Anne Halliday, also of this Foundation, made the first analysis of the data relating to the diet of the monks of Westminster that are summarized below, in Table II.4, and has readily answered many questions from me about nutrition. I have benefited from Professor Christopher Dyer's unrivalled knowledge of medieval diet and of the archaeological evidence that is now essential for an understanding of this subject. Mr Jim Oeppen, of the Cambridge Group for the History of Population and Social Structure, and Miss Ros Walley analysed the mortality data relating to the monks of Westminster which are indispensable to Chapter

IV. Mr Oeppen also prepared the figures for this chapter and for Chapter III and has written one of the appendices to the book. He has been unfailingly helpful with advice on demographic and statistical problems as these chapters took shape. I have drawn frequently on Mrs Susan Hall's knowledge of medieval medical and surgical texts. Dr Alan Loach and Dr John Walker have helped me with medical problems in general.

I owe a great deal to Dr John Blair's expert knowledge of ecclesiastical and secular buildings of the medieval period, and their uses, and of much else in the history of that period. He and Mrs Sarah Blair have drawn the maps for the book and undertaken time-consuming research as a preliminary to this task. Books come and go. Maps sometimes have greater staying-power, and I am confident that these maps, if not destined to be quite as long-lasting as some of the buildings they serve to locate, will be found useful by anyone interested in Westminster Abbey and its medieval environs for many years to come.

I have benefited greatly from Dr Gervase Rosser's profound knowledge of the medieval town of Westminster and its inhabitants; and Dr Rosser has provided some essential information for the maps. Professor Marjorie McIntosh has been kind enough to comment on several chapters of the book, and I have tried to take full advantage of her suggestions. From Mrs Loach and Dr Richard Smith I have received unstinted help at every stage: it is hard—indeed, impossible—for me to express adequately my debt to each.

Dr Roger Schofield, Director of the Cambridge Group for the History of Population and Social Structure, has generously permitted the use of the period estimates relating to the population of England that are illustrated in Figure IV.3. I am grateful to Dr John Hatcher and the Editors of the *Economic History Review* for permission to use the estimates relating to the monks of Christ Church, Canterbury, in the same figure.

To Dr Anthony Morris, Miss Sophie MacCallum, and Miss Anne Gelling, of Oxford University Press, I owe timely encouragement to finish the book and invaluable help when it was finally on its way. At the copy-editing stage Mrs Dorothy McCarthy eliminated many errors and inconsistencies and made other suggestions for the improvement of the book for which I am extremely grateful.

I wish also to thank Dr Susan Brigden, Dr David Carpenter, Dr Clive Burgess, Dr Pierre Chaplais, Dr Brian Golding, Dr Joan Greatrex, Dr Diana Greenway, Mr John Henderson, Dr Margaret Howell, Dr Richard Hoyle, Dr. Trevor Hughes, Dr. Colin Michie, Dr. Margaret Pelling, Dr Jocelyn Russell, Mrs Dale Serjeantson, Dr. Larry Usilton, Dr Nancy Waugh, Professor Michael Winterbottom, and Professor Joyce Youings: each has helped in general or specific ways.

BARBARA HARVEY

*Somerville College, Oxford*
*August 1992*

# Contents

# List of Figures

# List of Maps

The maps have been drawn by John and Sarah Blair.

# List of Tables

# Abbreviations

## I. ABBREVIATED REFERENCES

| | |
|---|---|
| *Abbot's House at Westminster* | J. Armitage Robinson, *The Abbot's House at Westminster* (Cambridge, 1911) |
| *AHR* | *Agricultural History Review* |
| *Annales, ESC* | *Annales, Économies, Sociétés, Civilisations* |
| BAR | British Archaeological Reports |
| *Bath Cartularies* | *Two Cartularies of the Priory of St Peter at Bath*, ed. W. Hunt (Somerset Record Society, vii, 1893) |
| Beaven, *Aldermen* | A. B. Beaven, *Aldermen of the City of London, temp. Henry III to 1912* (2 vols., London, 1908–13) |
| *BIHR* | *Bulletin of the Institute of Historical Research* |
| BL | British Library |
| *BRUO* | A. B. Emden, *A Biographical Register of the University of Oxford to AD 1500* (3 vols., Oxford, 1957–9) |
| *BRUO 1501–40* | A. B. Emden, *A Biographical Register of the University of Oxford AD 1501 to 1540* (Oxford, 1974) |
| *Cal. Ch. R.* | *Calendar of Charter Rolls* (HMSO, London, 1903– ) |
| *Cal. Cl. R.* | *Calendar of Close Rolls* (HMSO, London, 1892– ) |
| *Cal. Papal Reg., Petitions,* i | *Calendar of Entries in the Papal Registers relating to Great Britain and Ireland. Petitions to the Pope,* i *(1342–1400)* (HMSO, London, 1896) |
| *Cal. Papal Reg., Letters,* xiii | *Calendar of Entries in the Papal Registers relating to Great Britain and Ireland. Papal Letters,* xiii *(1471–84)* (2 pts., HMSO, London, 1955) |
| *Cal. Pat. R.* | *Calendar of Patent Rolls* (HMSO, London, 1891– ) |
| *Cal. Plea and Mem. R. 1323–1364* | *Calendar of Plea and Memoranda Rolls preserved among the Archives of the Corporation of the City of London at the Guildhall, AD 1323–1364,* ed. A. H. Thomas (Cambridge, 1926) |

| | |
|---|---|
| *Cart. Ram.* | *Cartularium Monasterii de Rameseia*, ed. W. H. Hart and A. P. Lyon (3 vols., Rolls Series, 1884–94) |
| *CCM* | *Corpus Consuetudinum Monasticarum* |
| *Chapters of English Black Monks* | *Documents Illustrating the Activities of the General and Provincial Chapters of the English Black Monks, 1215–1540*, ed. W. A. Pantin (3 vols., Camden 3rd ser. xlv, xlvii, liv, 1931–7) |
| *Chron. Abingdon* | *Chronicon Monasterii de Abingdon*, ed. J. Stevenson (2 vols., Rolls Series, 1858) |
| *Chron. Evesham* | *Chronicon Abbatiae de Evesham ad annum 1418*, ed. W. D. Macray (Rolls Series, 1863) |
| *Chron. Melsa* | *Chronica Monasterii de Melsa*, ed. E. A. Bond (3 vols., Rolls Series, 1866–8) |
| *Close Rolls, Henry III* | *Close Rolls of the Reign of Henry III, 1227–1272* (14 vols., HMSO, London, 1902–38) |
| *Councils and Synods* | *Councils and Synods, with Other Documents relating to the English Church*, vol. i, AD *871–1204* (2 pts., ed. D. Whitelock, M. Brett, and C. N. L. Brooke, Oxford, 1981); vol. ii, AD *1205–1313* (2 pts., ed. F. M. Powicke and C. R. Cheney, Oxford, 1964) |
| CUL | Cambridge University Library |
| *Customary* | *Customary of the Benedictine Monasteries of Saint Augustine, Canterbury, and Saint Peter, Westminster*, ed. E. Maunde Thompson (2 vols., Henry Bradshaw Society, xxiii, xxviii, 1902–4) |
| *Customary of Bury St Edmunds* | *Customary of Bury St Edmunds in Suffolk*, ed. A. Gransden (Henry Bradshaw Society, xcix, 1973 for 1966) |
| *Customary of Eynsham* | *Customary of the Benedictine Abbey of Eynsham in Oxfordshire*, ed. A. Gransden (*Corpus Consuetudinum Monasticarum*, ii, 1963) |
| CYS | Canterbury and York Society |
| *DB* | *Domesday Book, seu Liber Censualis Willelmi Primi Regis Angliae*, ed. A. Farley, H. Ellis, *et al.* (4 vols., Record Commission, 1783–1816) |
| *Decretum* | *Decretum Gratiani*, in *Corpus Juris Canonici*, ed. E. Friedberg (Leipzig, 1879–81), i |
| DH 41 | Department of Health, *Dietary Reference Values for Food Energy and Nutrients for* |

| | |
|---|---|
| | *the United Kingdom* (Report on Health and Social Subjects 41, HMSO, London, 1991) |
| Dyer, *Standards of Living* | C. Dyer, *Standards of Living in the Later Middle Ages: Social Change in England c.1200–1520* (reprint, 1990, of 1st edn., Cambridge, 1989) |
| Econ. Hist. Rev. | *Economic History Review* |
| EEA | *English Episcopal Acta*: i, *Lincoln 1067–1185*, ed. D. M. Smith (London, 1980); ii, *Canterbury 1162–1190*, ed. C. R. Cheney and B. E. A. Jones (London, 1986); iii, *Canterbury 1193–1205*, ed. C. R. Cheney and E. John (London, 1986); iv, *Lincoln, 1186–1206*, ed. D. M. Smith (London, 1986) |
| EHR | *English Historical Review* |
| Flete | *The History of Westminster Abbey by John Flete*, ed. J. Armitage Robinson (Cambridge, 1909) |
| Foedera | *Foedera, conventiones, litterae et cujuscunque generis acta publica etc.*, ed. T. Rymer (20 vols., London, 1704–35) |
| Gesta Abbatum | *Gesta Abbatum Monasterii Sancti Albani*, ed. H. T. Riley (3 vols., Rolls Series, 1867–9) |
| Gilbert Crispin | J. Armitage Robinson, *Gilbert Crispin, Abbot of Westminster* (Cambridge, 1911) |
| GL | Guildhall Library, London |
| Harvey, *Estates* | B. F. Harvey, *The Estates of Westminster Abbey in the Middle Ages* (Oxford, 1977) |
| HBS | Henry Bradshaw Society |
| HMSO | Her Majesty's Stationery Office |
| JEH | *Journal of Ecclesiastical History* |
| Knowles and Hadcock | D. Knowles and R. N. Hadcock, *Medieval Religious Houses, England and Wales* (2nd edn., London, 1971) |
| Land, Kinship and Life-Cycle | R. M. Smith (ed.), *Land, Kinship and Life-Cycle* (Cambridge, 1984) |
| L & P Henry VIII | *Letters and Papers, Foreign and Domestic of the Reign of Henry VIII*, ed. J. S. Brewer, J. Gairdner, and R. H. Brodie (21 vols. in 35, HMSO, London, 1862–1932) |
| Lanfranc's Constitutions | *The Monastic Constitutions of Lanfranc*, ed. and trans. D. Knowles (Nelson's Medieval Texts, 1951) |
| Lincoln Visitations, *1517–1531* | *Visitations in the Diocese of Lincoln, 1517–1531*, ed. A. Hamilton Thompson (3 vols., Lincoln Record Society, xxxiii, xxxv, xxxvii, Hereford, 1940–7) |

| | |
|---|---|
| LNQ | Liber Niger Quaternus (a cartulary of Westminster Abbey) |
| *MO* | D. Knowles, *The Monastic Order in England* (2nd edn., Cambridge, 1963) |
| *Mon. Ang.* | W. Dugdale, *Monasticon Anglicanum*, ed. J. Caley, H. Ellis, and B. Bandinel (6 vols., London, 1817–30) |
| *Monks* | E. H. Pearce, *The Monks of Westminster* (Cambridge, 1916) |
| *MPME* | C. H. Talbot and E. A. Hammond (edd.), *The Medical Practitioners in Medieval England: A Biographical Register* (London, 1965) |
| NMT | Nelson's Medieval Texts |
| *Norwich Visitations* | *Visitations of the Diocese of Norwich*, AD *1492–1532*, ed. A. Jessopp (Camden Society, NS xliii, 1888) |
| OMT | Oxford Medieval Texts |
| *OV* | *The Ecclesiastical History of Orderic Vitalis*, ed. and trans. M. Chibnall (6 vols.: i and iii–vi, Oxford Medieval Texts, 1972–86; ii, corrected reprint, 1991, of 1st edn., 1969) |
| *P & P* | *Past and Present* |
| *PBA* | *Proceedings of the British Academy* |
| Peter the Venerable, *Statutes* | *Statuta Petri Venerabilis abbatis Cluniacensis IX (1146/7)*, ed. G. Constable *et al.*, in *Consuetudines Benedictinae Variae (Saec. XI–Saec. XIV) (Corpus Consuetudinum Monasticarum*, vi, 1975) |
| *PL* | *Patrologia Latina* |
| PRO | Public Record Office |
| *Reg. Malm.* | *Registrum Malmesburiense*, ed. J. S. Brewer (2 vols., Rolls Series, 1879–80) |
| *Rites of Durham* | *Rites of Durham, being a Description or Brief Declaration of all the Ancient Monuments, Rites and Customs belonging or being within the Monastical Church of Durham before the Suppression, written 1593*, ed. J. T. Fowler (Surtees Society, cvii, 1903) |
| *RO* | D. Knowles, *The Religious Orders in England* (3 vols., Cambridge, 1948–59) |
| Rosser, *Medieval Westminster* | G. Rosser, *Medieval Westminster, 1200–1540* (Oxford, 1989) |
| RS | Rolls Series |
| *Rule* | *The Rule of St Benedict*, ed. and trans. J. McCann (London, 1952) |

| | |
|---|---|
| Sawyer | P. H. Sawyer, *Anglo-Saxon Charters: An Annotated List and Bibliography* (London, 1968) |
| SCH | Studies in Church History |
| *SR* | *Statutes of the Realm* |
| SS | Surtees Society |
| Stouff, *Ravitaillement et alimentation en Provence* | L. Stouff, *Ravitaillement et alimentation en Provence aux xiv<sup>e</sup> et xv<sup>e</sup> siècles* (Paris, 1970) |
| Thompson, 'Corrody' | A. H. Thompson, 'A corrody from Leicester Abbey, AD 1393–4, with some notes on corrodies', *Transactions of the Leicestershire Archaeological Society*, xiv (1925), 113–34 |
| Tout, *Chapters* | T. F. Tout, *Chapters in the Administrative History of Medieval England* (6 vols., Manchester, 1920–33) |
| *TRHS* | *Transactions of the Royal Historical Society* |
| VCH | *Victoria History of the Counties of England* |
| *VE* | *Valor Ecclesiasticus temp. Henrici VIII, auctoritate Regia Institutus*, ed. J. Caley and J. Hunter (6 vols., Record Commission, 1810–34) |
| *Visitations of Religious Houses* | *Visitations of Religious Houses in the Diocese of Lincoln*, ed. A. Hamilton Thompson (3 vols., Canterbury and York Society, xvii, xxiv, xxxiii, London, 1915–27) |
| *Walter de Wenlok* | *Documents Illustrating the Rule of Walter de Wenlok, abbot of Westminster, 1283–1307*, ed. B. F. Harvey (Camden 4th ser. ii, London, 1965) |
| WAM | Westminster Abbey Muniments |
| WD | Westminster Domesday (a cartulary) |
| Westlake, *Westminster Abbey* | H. F. Westlake, *Westminster Abbey: The Church, Convent, Cathedral and College of St Peter, Westminster* (2 vols., London, 1923) |
| *Westminster Abbey Charters* | *Westminster Abbey Charters, 1066–c.1214*, ed. E. Mason (London Record Society, 1988) |
| *Westminster Chronicle* | *The Westminster Chronicle*, ed. and trans. L. C. Hector and B. F. Harvey (Oxford Medieval Texts, 1982) |
| Widmore, *Enquiry* | R. Widmore, *An Enquiry into the Time of the First Foundation of Westminster Abbey* (London, 1743) |
| Wilkins, *Concilia* | D. Wilkins, *Concilia Magnae Britanniae et Hiberniae* (4 vols., London, 1737) |
| *Wills*, ed. Nichols | *A Collection of all the Wills now known to be extant of the Kings and Queens of England etc.*, ed. J. Nichols (London, 1780) |

Wills, ed. Sharpe                    *Calendar of Wills proved and enrolled in the*
                                     *Court of Husting, London, AD 1258–AD 1688,*
                                     ed. R. R. Sharpe (2 vols., London, 1889–90)
Yorks. Arch. Jnl.                    *Yorkshire Archaeological Journal*

## II. OTHER ABBREVIATIONS

i. *Weights*
   cwt.     hundredweight
   g.       gram
   kg.      kilogram
   lb.      pound
   mg.      milligram
   oz.      ounce
   µg       microgram

ii. *Dry and liquid measures*
   bus.     bushel
   gall.    gallon
   qu.      quarter

iii. *Measures of length*
   cm.      centimetre
   ft.      foot
   m.       metre

iv. *Energy values etc.*
   DRV      Dietary Reference Value
   kcal.    kilocalorie
   kJ       kilojoule
   MJ       megajoule
   RNI      Reference Nutrient Intake

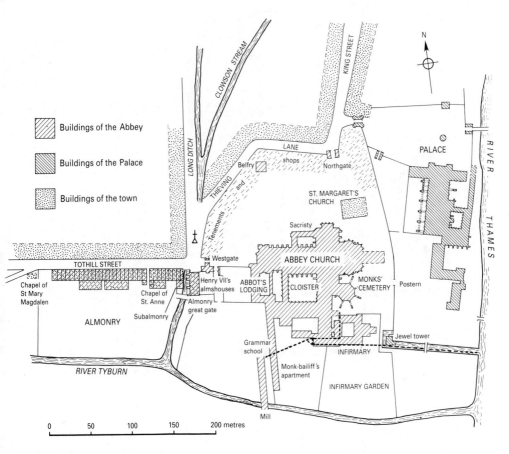

MAP I. Westminster Abbey and its environs in the later Middle Ages

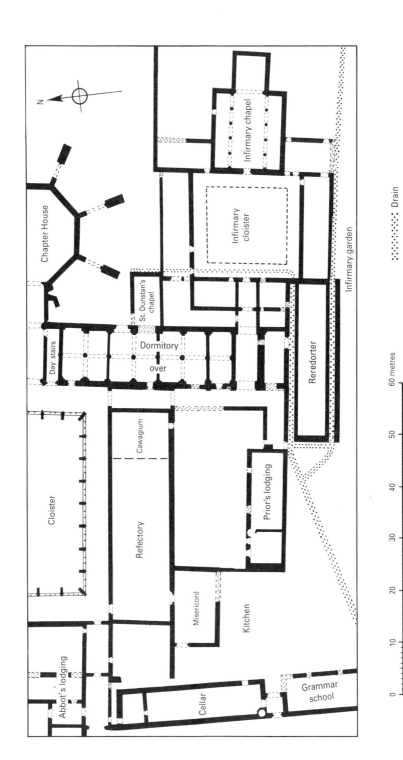

MAP II. Westminster Abbey: the central monastic buildings

Chapter House

Cloister

Abbot's lodging

Refectory

Cawagium

Misericord

Cellar

Kitchen

Prior's lodging

Grammar
school

Day stairs

Dormitory

over

St. Dunstan's
chapel

Reredorter

Infirmary
cloister

Infirmary garden

Infirmary chapel

N

0    10    20    30    40    50    60 metres

∶∶∶∶ Drain

# Introduction

EARLY in the period covered by this book, the Benedictine monks, to whom it will devote a good deal of attention, passed into the background of religious life: wherever the spiritual action was after the mid-twelfth century, it was not in their choirs and cloisters. Released from the burden of spiritual leadership, which passed to new orders and eventually to the friars, the Benedictines achieved a remarkable degree of identification with the secular life of their times, and particularly with upper-class life. Considered as an expression of human frailty, the extent to which this came about occasions no surprise. But given the fact that the monks continued to have liturgical duties which were not shared by secular society, and a distinctive *horarium*, or timetable for the day, to accommodate these, the extent to which they were not in fact separated from the society around them was indeed remarkable.[1]

Benedictines were able to live like the nobility or gentry, and, in the circumstances of the time, were almost obliged to do so, because, in common with these others, they owned a great deal of property. St Anselm told a monk whose conscience was troubled on the point that he might, without sinning, leave the monastery to transact secular business if ordered to do so by his abbot: in these circumstances, he would be absenting himself from the monastery under obedience.[2] This passage in Eadmer's *Life* reminds us that the cares of property were already perceived as a threat to monastic observance at the beginning of the twelfth century. These cares, however, were multiplied at the end of the century, when monks, like other landowners, reclaimed their manors from the hands of the lessees to whom they had been committed earlier, and began to administer them directly for market profits. Later still, in the fifteenth century, when leasing was once again the preferred arrangement, there was not the same need to ride to the manors or see to paper-work at an obedientiary's desk, instead of participating in the daily office and liturgy and other features of the common life. But the monks of this period found a return to a more observant way of life hard to contemplate and impossible to execute. Indeed, a common life in which monks had no possessions of their own, and subordinated every personal desire to a shared routine, was a thing of the past. Even the modified form

[1] For the classic account of Benedictine decline, see R. W. Southern, *Western Society and the Church in the Middle Ages* (Harmondsworth, 1970), 233–40; and for the *horarium*, below, pp. 154–9.

[2] Eadmer, *Life of St Anselm, Archbishop of Canterbury*, ed. R. W. Southern (OMT 1962), 74–7.

which now obtained was not regarded by many as a lifelong commitment: on the contrary, it was treated as a stage in a career which a monk would leave behind as soon as he could demonstrate that he was too busy or distinguished, or too senior, to be held to its demands. In wealthy monasteries—and many Benedictine houses were wealthy in relation to the number of monks which they supported—standards of living were comparable to those found at similar income levels outside the cloister. The monks were as well housed and well fed as their social equals in secular society; and, within the constraints imposed by the need to wear clothes of a certain cut and colour, many were probably as well dressed too.

Reformers inside and outside the cloister deplored these developments. Historians, on the other hand, must surely welcome them, for they mean that from the twelfth century onwards Benedictine communities reflect very clearly the status quo in secular society and the direction of change, when it occurred, in that society. Secular society, however, has left records which are, in some important areas of life, inferior to monastic records. In this book, as in the lectures in which it originated, I have tried to identify some fundamentally important aspects of medieval life where the monastic experience can add substantially to our understanding of trends in society as a whole. I hope that the discussion of charity in Chapter I, for example, will shed light not only on the Benedictines' own practice and, in particular, their moves, from the twelfth century onwards, in the direction of discrimination and systematic almsgiving, but also on such moves in society more generally and when these occurred. The book has a wide chronological range and draws on a variety of case-histories. Its main focus, however, is on the later Middle Ages, and on the experience in that period of the Benedictine community at Westminster Abbey. As a preliminary, I shall describe the complex situation of the Abbey, which had as neighbours the Palace of Westminster and the town of Westminster.

It is likely that the first church at Westminster was a minster church, dating from the early eighth century and serving an area stretching as far north as present-day Oxford Street.[3] Every great church needed water, and the proximity of the River Thames and the streams later known as Long Ditch and Tyburn helps to explain the choice of the site for the new minster. But one could have too much water for domestic use. The site also had commercial potential, and this was perhaps a more important consideration. In the 960s or very early in the 970s St Dunstan, assisted by King Edgar, planted a Benedictine community here, and, a century later, Edward the Confessor, having chosen the church as his place of burial, rebuilt it in the new Romanesque style, and augmented its endowments, thus enabling it to support about eighty monks, a much larger community than the twelve of

---

[3] Rosser, *Medieval Westminster*, 12–15.

St Dunstan's foundation.[4] His burial in the Abbey, and the growth of his cult as a saint, ensured that the Abbey became, from 1066 onwards, the coronation church of the kings of England. But no other king was buried there until the thirteenth century. Then, Henry III, who was intensely devoted to the cult of the Confessor, rebuilt the Abbey church in the Gothic style, as a mausoleum where he and his successors could lie near the shrine of that saint.[5]

On the map (Map I) the Palace of Westminster, situated as it is on the edge of the site, looks like an afterthought,[6] and it was in fact a late arrival in comparison to the church. The first palace here was probably that built by Edward the Confessor in the mid-eleventh century.[7] No one could be unimpressed by a complex of buildings which included, as this one soon did, William Rufus's great hall. But the existence of the Palace of Westminster may not have affected the ordinary daily lives of the monks of Westminster until the second half of the twelfth century, for only then did the palace become the permanent seat of royal government in England and a frequent place of residence of her kings. In due course, part of the royal treasure and some government records came to be housed in the Abbey, and for this and other reasons royal ministers and clerks were often—too often for the monks—in and about the claustral area. They disturbed the peace of the monastery and sometimes damaged its property.[8] Relations between the monks and the king, and between the monks and those who served the king in the Palace of Westminster, were sometimes tense. Thus, to the indignation of the monks, Edward III appropriated Abbey land for his Jewel Tower;[9] and at the end of Edward's reign, and continuing in that of his successor, the monks were involved in a hard-fought dispute with the king about the Abbey's claim to jurisdiction in certain cases over residents in the palace.[10]

Such disputes were of the very essence of medieval ecclesiastical life. In the present case, they did not impede relationships of a quite different kind, which flowed naturally from the proximity of the church and palace to each other and from the status of the former as the coronation church and principal royal mausoleum. Henry II's attendance at Mass in the Abbey is recorded on one famous occasion and may have been a common event.[11] By

[4] R. Gem, 'The Romanesque rebuilding of Westminster Abbey (with a reconstruction by W. T. Ball)', *Proceedings of the Battle Conference on Anglo-Norman Studies*, iii (1980), 33–60; Harvey, *Estates*, 26–8.
[5] H. M. Colvin (ed.), *The History of the King's Works* (6 vols., HMSO 1963–82), i. 130–57.         [6] A point which I owe to John Blair.
[7] Rosser, *Medieval Westminster*, 14; and for the subsequent architectural history of the Palace, Colvin (ed.), *History of the King's Works*, i. 45–7, 491–510.
[8] Below, p. 88 and n.
[9] A. J. Taylor, *The Jewel Tower, Westminster* (HMSO 1965), 7.
[10] *Westminster Chronicle*, 378–80 and n.
[11] *The Chronicle of Battle Abbey*, ed. E. Searle (OMT 1980), 156, 200.

the end of his reign, however, a chapel existed in the palace, and the king could attend Mass here if he preferred.[12] The monks may not have regretted this development, for a Mass attended by Henry was sometimes the occasion for the brisk transaction of royal business, even while the liturgy was in progress. After this time, the common practice may have been that of Richard II, who apparently came to services in the Abbey on some major feast days and on other special occasions, but not habitually.[13] The monks had also to expect visits of a more social kind by the king or a member of his family, and they were not always given much notice of these. In 1386 Richard II entertained Leo VI of Armenia by taking him on an evening visit to the church, where they viewed the relics and the coronation regalia. It was an impromptu event, which Richard arranged at the last moment on hearing that the king of Armenia was to pass through London on his way to Pleshey.[14]

It goes almost without saying that where the monarch was, there the nobility and gentry liked to be too. The Abbey's Customary, compiled *c*.1270, permits the sacrist to speak in a natural voice when showing visitors of the highest status round the church, but requires him to drop his voice for lesser persons.[15] Behind that rule, we may suspect, lay a long experience of minimizing the disturbance caused by talkative visitors of noble rank.

The status of the Abbey as a royal mausoleum explains the scale of its initial endowment and its great wealth in the later Middle Ages. Kings and their consorts in fact paid handsomely for the assurance of the monks' prayers when they should die. In 1535, with a net income of £2,800 per annum, the Abbey was second in wealth only to Glastonbury Abbey by this measure, and £560 of this sum (20 per cent) represents the surplus income of the major royal foundations, after the costs of the necessary anniversaries and chantry masses had been met.[16] The Abbey's wealth, in turn, explains how it was that the community of monks here remained relatively large— about fifty in numbers—to within a few years of the Dissolution in 1540: it was always possible to clothe and feed this number.[17] Moreover, the royal connection may have assisted numbers in more particular ways—as, for example, in attracting recruits from the ministerial and clerical families who were employed in the palace and resided in the town of Westminster.[18] It left its mark on the Abbey's office and liturgy, and on its calendar. On royal anniversaries, it was the means of involving the monks, willy nilly, in the distribution of alms to the poor on a scale probably unequalled in any other English monastery, however distinguished the anniversaries observed there.[19]

[12] Colvin (ed.), *History of the King's Works*, i. 493.
[13] *Westminster Chronicle*, 144, 206–8, 314, 450.     [14] Ibid. 154–6.
[15] *Customary*, ii. 51–2. The normal voice was permissible when talking to the king or queen, an earl related to the king, a bishop, or a Benedictine abbot.
[16] Harvey, *Estates*, 34, 63; *RO* iii. 473–4, where, however, the net income of Westminster Abbey in 1535 is said to be £2,409 p.a.     [17] Below, pp. 73–4.
[18] Below, p. 76; and for the prominence of this group in medieval Westminster, see Rosser, *Medieval Westminster*, 16–32.     [19] Below, pp. 24–7.

These are some of the ways in which the Abbey's royal associations affected the life of its monks. To some extent, of course, all wealthy Benedictine houses were vulnerable to the royal visitor; and, certainly, all were vulnerable to unwelcome demands on the part of their patrons, royal or aristocratic. Yet, for better and for worse, the Abbey's position was to some extent unique. If, however, the king and members of the aristocracy visited the Abbey and were buried there, they did not encourage their relatives to become monks of this house. Among all those who are known to have been professed at Westminster in the later Middle Ages, only a handful of such recruits can be identified.[20] In fact, in social origin, the monks of Westminster were quite as obscure as any other community of English Benedictines of this period, and their mode of life from day to day was probably very similar to that of any other wealthy Benedictine community. The retreat from the common life followed the same basic pattern here as elsewhere, and went on at much the same pace. Though splendid, their buildings followed, in essentials, the usual Benedictine plan (Map II). Their splendour did not avert trouble with the water supply of a mundane kind.[21] It is this ordinariness, as much as the unusual features of life at Westminster—as, for example, the scale of post-obit almsgiving—that I have tried to put to good use in the following pages.

Inevitably, when Westminster became the administrative capital of the kingdom, the importance of the monks in its affairs was diminished, for the Abbey was no longer the only large and powerful institution in the vicinity: it had a rival in this respect in the palace. To be precise, the monks became relatively less important in a town which became itself larger, and structurally more complex, as a result of its changed status. Yet they continued to exercise authority as lords of the manor of Westminster, and the town was never in fact enfranchised by charter in the medieval period.[22]

In the later Middle Ages, the town had 2,000 to 3,000 inhabitants.[23] It was a small town, but, for much of this period, a growing one. It would be misleading to say that the urban population invaded the Abbey precinct in this period, for the monks, in a sense, invited it in, by building dwellings and shops for occupation by townsmen in the almonry, on the west side of the Abbey church, immediately adjacent to the sanctuary, and in the sanctuary itself (Map I). Some of the monastery's custom as a consumer of huge quantities of fish, meat, and foods of all kinds was given to tradesmen in the City of London, and for cloth it sometimes went further afield.[24] Nevertheless, its custom must always have been important to the townsmen of

---

[20] The exceptions are Nicholas Litlyngton (professed +1333), Thomas Pomeray (1421–2), Thomas Clifford (1462–3), and Edward Bridgewater (1465–6), for whom see *Monks*, 84–6, 138–9, 159–60, 161. Litlyngton may have been of illegitimate birth, and Pomeray is known to have been. [21] Below, pp. 78–9.

[22] Rosser, *Medieval Westminster*, ch. 7.   [23] Below, p. 80.

[24] Below, p. 47; B. F. Harvey, *Monastic Dress in the Middle Ages: Precept and Practice* (William Urry Memorial Trust, Canterbury, 1988), 18–19.

Westminster: it was perhaps more important by 1500 than in 1300, for the abbot, who had to feed a large household of his own, was less peripatetic and in consequence less often at a distance from the monastery at the later date compared with the earlier. As an employer, as well as consumer, on a large scale, the monastery helped to fuel the urban economy.[25] It probably recruited some of its novices from the town of Westminster—and from the families of ordinary townsmen involved in trade and crafts, as distinct from those who served in the Palace of Westminster.[26] Moreover, the monks cultivated good relations with the townsmen and townswomen who counted, as the prior's dinner for 'wives of the town' in January 1511 suggests.[27] And they directed some of the alms which they administered to the poor of the town.[28]

If the monks of Westminster wished to provide a focus in the Abbey church for the religious life of the town, they failed to do so in this period. The townsmen seem to have been, on the whole, indifferent to the Abbey church as a place of worship or for burial, and resorted instead to the parish church of St Margaret's: the Abbey was now, it appears, too closely associated with the court and governmental establishment in the Palace of Westminster to be attractive to the independently minded population of the town.[29] Townsmen may have attended the sermons instituted by Henry VII for a popular audience on between fifty and sixty days in the year, but these occasions, which took place in the Lady Chapel, rebuilt at Henry's expense, had perhaps a touch of the establishment about them and attendance may have been disappointing.[30]

The remarkable fact is that the Abbey's relations with the town were rarely, if ever, contentious. In 1381 it was probably rebels from the City of London and further afield, not local residents, who violated the Abbey's sanctuary and laid hands on a royal servant hoping for sanctuary there.[31] In general, relations between the Abbey and the town were friendly. In this respect they may have been untypical of towns where, as in Westminster, a monastery claimed a measure of jurisdiction over economic life. In such a situation, dinner parties for local residents could only be makeweights. Did the secret lie in the monks' reasonableness as landlords, employers, and consumers? The following pages, though not addressed explicitly to this question, may shed some light on it.

---

[25] See Ch. V.        [26] Below, p. 76.

[27] WAM 33325, fo. 5ᵛ; and on the importance of women in the late medieval urban economy, see Rosser, *Medieval Westminster*, 196–201.        [28] Below, pp. 31–2.

[29] See, for this and other relevant considerations, Rosser, *Medieval Westminster*, 255–63.

[30] *Cal. Cl. R., Henry VII*, ii *(1500–9)*, no. 389 (p. 142).

[31] *Westminster Chronicle*, 9; and on the broader issue, Rosser, *Medieval Westminster*, 244–8.

# I

# Charity

## 1. Perceptions of Monastic Almsgiving

SIR THOMAS MORE, in his retirement, defended monks as almsgivers, and he singled out for this purpose the almonry at Westminster Abbey. To the 'dolehouse' at Westminster, he wrote, the poor came in such numbers 'that my self for the preace of them haue ben fayn to ryde another waye'. And he added: 'as farre as euer I harde, the munkes vse not to sende awaye many vnserued'.[1]

Four centuries and more later, and in a quantitative age, it has all looked rather different. 'The quality of monastic alms', wrote Professor W. K. Jordan in 1959, 'was even less impressive than the quantity', and few have disagreed with him.[2] Patchily useful, more useful in the north of England than in the south, and to the end obstinately old-fashioned—this, I suggest, is a fair summary of monastic almsgiving as perceived by most historians of the subject today.[3] I shall not attempt the hopeless task of demonstrating that, on the contrary, the monks did well. Quite simply, I suggest that monastic practice illumines, as nothing else does half as well, a fundamental problem in the development of charitable institutions and deserves fresh scrutiny for this reason. The problem is that of discrimination.

In the present context, discrimination may be defined as having regard to the character, age, physical strength, and capacity to work of the suppliant for alms, or to any of these considerations. It is widely agreed that medieval practice in general tended towards the unsystematic and undiscriminating arrangement. It is also widely believed that a perceptible change occurred in this respect in the later Middle Ages. Some historians—and they include Dr Miri Rubin, in her notable study of charity in Cambridge—have argued that

---

[1] *The Apology*, ed. J. B. Trapp (*Complete Works of St Thomas More* (Yale, 1963– ), ix, 1979), 104, where 'the dolys' is the almonry at Westminster Abbey. (I am indebted to Dr Philippa Tudor for this reference.) 'Dolhus' occurs as the popular, local name for the almonry at Westminster in a 13th-cent. source (*Customary*, ii. 179).

[2] W. K. Jordan, *Philanthropy in England, 1480–1660* (London, 1959), 59; cf. id., *The Charities of London, 1480–1660* (London, 1960), 280.

[3] See e.g. C. Haigh, *Reformation and Resistance in Tudor Lancashire* (Cambridge, 1975), 120–1; *RO* iii. 264–6; J. J. Scarisbrick, *The Reformation and the English People* (Oxford, 1984), 52–4. For much useful information about monastic obligations to give alms, and hospitality in a wider sense, in the later Middle Ages, see F. Heal, *Hospitality in Early Modern England* (Oxford, 1990), 228–46.

a growing scarcity of resources encouraged a more discriminating attitude on the part of donors towards the poor from the thirteenth century onwards.[4] Others, though taking note of earlier debates on the subject, have placed the important changes in the actual distribution of alms in the later Middle Ages. A new factor now, they argue, was the labour shortage brought about by a dramatic fall in population in the fourteenth century: this made it highly desirable to distinguish beggars who could work from those who could not. The change in attitude, whenever it made itself felt, inevitably brought casual and spontaneous almsgiving into a degree of disrepute with many of those in a position to give generously, if they would. However, the continuing cult of prayers for the dead, and the practice of including, if possible, a large distribution of alms in the commemorative rites—the funeral itself, the month's mind that followed, and, in subsequent years, the anniversary—with the direction that all coming on the right day should be eligible, ensured the persistence to the very end of the Middle Ages of indiscriminate almsgiving as a common form of charity. Since, even in the centuries of monastic decline—that is, all centuries after the twelfth—many testators still turned to monasteries for burial and for anniversary Masses, it fell to the monks to administer large numbers of these casual distributions and to be identified by posterity with the system. In the passage which I have cited, Jordan characterizes monastic alms at the end of the Middle Ages as, by and large, a matter of doles for casual beggars.[5]

This commonly accepted chronology of developments has one disconcerting feature. The Decretists, the commentators on canon law, discussed the problem of discrimination in almsgiving in the second half of the twelfth century: they were unwilling to leave the question as Gratian left it—that is, open.[6] One reason for their interest was their perception that an insufficiency

[4] M. Rubin, *Charity and Community in Medieval Cambridge* (Cambridge, 1987), 291; cf. ibid. 68–9. For the seminal treatment of discrimination in medieval charity see B. Pullan, *Rich and Poor in Renaissance Venice* (Oxford, 1971), 197–204. See also id., 'Support and redeem: charity and poor relief in Italian cities from the fourteenth to the seventeenth centuries', *Continuity and Change*, iii (1988), 177–208, at 180; and M. Mollat, *Les Pauvres au Moyen Age: Étude sociale* (Paris, 1978), 78–91, 147–91, trans. A. Goldhammer as *The Poor in the Middle Ages: An Essay in Social History* (Yale, 1986), 70–86, 135–57. (The belief that, already in the 12th cent., monasteries were failing to adapt to changing needs is important to Mollat's argument.) For an excellent short account of medieval perceptions of poverty, see Dyer, *Standards of Living*, 234–40; and for the suggestion that local attitudes to the idle poor were little changed by events in the 14th cent. but hardened in the later 15th cent., see M. K. McIntosh, 'Local responses to the poor in late medieval and Tudor England', *Continuity and Change*, iii (1988), 209–45, at 217, 224.

[5] For perceptive comment see P. Slack, *Poverty and Policy in Tudor and Stuart England* (London, 1988), 13, 166; and for the earlier current of ideas, M. Mollat, 'La notion de la pauvreté au Moyen Age: position de problèmes', *Revue d'Histoire de l'Église de France*, lii (1966), 5–23, at 18–19.

[6] B. Tierney, 'The decretists and the "deserving poor"', *Comparative Studies in Society and History*, i (1958–9), 360–73; id., *Medieval Poor Law: A Sketch of Canonical Theory and its Application in England* (Berkeley and Los Angeles, 1959), 54–67.

of resources must affect the destination of alms: if there is not enough to go round, it will be necessary to distinguish between claimants. Yet the first real growth of discrimination is always placed later, and by some very much later, than this discussion. It is as though we were to assume that the ingenious discussions of usury in the same period were unrelated to an actual contemporary practice of lending at interest.[7] I shall suggest that monastic practice in the twelfth century, which seems to place a high value on system and involves not a little discrimination, helps to bridge this gap between the early discussion of discrimination in almsgiving and the perceived arrival of that principle in codes of practice. And, secondly, I shall suggest that the system of post-obit almsgiving with which monasteries are so strongly identified in the later Middle Ages, was not, in the end, quite the blunt instrument it has appeared to some to be.

In the practice of monastic charity, the distinction between, on the one hand, the ordinary income of the house in question, and, on the other, special funds earmarked by their donors for particular purposes is fundamental. In the use of special funds, the monks were bound, always by moral, and often by legal, constraints, to use the income in the intended way. If, nevertheless, they wished to set aside the donor's wishes, they were obliged to wait until he had been some time in the grave. How long this time was is an under-explored subject. In the case of ordinary income, they enjoyed a quite different freedom of control. On the whole, the study of monastic charity directs our attention in the early Middle Ages to ordinary income, but in the later more to special funds.

## 2. Monastic Almsgiving from Ordinary Income

### (i) Resources

What, then, did the monks of this period give in alms from their ordinary resources, and how did they give it? I shall refer mainly to the Benedictines, sometimes known, after the colour of their habits, as black monks. At the beginning of the twelfth century, the Benedictines accounted for a very high proportion of all religious in England and owned an even higher proportion of the religious houses; a century later, they accounted for less than 50 per cent of the religious and owned fewer than 50 per cent of the houses.[8] For various reasons, however, they always had more to give than other Orders,

[7] T. P. McLaughlin, 'The teaching of the canonists on usury (xii, xiii and xiv centuries)', 2 parts, *Mediaeval Studies* (Toronto), i (1939), 81–147, and ii (1940), 1–22. See e.g. the work of Bernard of Pavia in this field (ibid. i. 96–8).

[8] Knowles and Hadcock, 489 ff. The above estimates take account of alien priories, Cluniac houses, and houses belonging to other Orders but affiliated to the Benedictines; they exclude houses in Wales, for which see ibid. 52, 53, etc. In 1216 the Benedictines, so defined, accounted for c.265 (44%) of c.600 houses for monks and canons then in existence, and for c.4,050 (43%) of c.9,450 such religious.

if they would but give it, and, unlike the Cistercians, the largest of the newer Orders, they tended to live in or near centres of population: they were accessible to the poor day by day.

In the course of the twelfth century, most Benedictine houses assigned a regular income to the almonry, the department where many of their charitable activities were carried on. Much of this income came from appropriated tithes which had been acquired explicitly for the maintenance—the word commonly used is *sustentatio*—of the poor. But was it intended that the revenues so assigned should provide a regular and stable basis, of a kind hitherto lacking, for unsystematic and undiscriminating almsgiving along traditional lines, or was some more profound change afoot? When, for example, in 1177, Archbishop Richard Dover gave the church of Meopham to the monks of Christ Church, Canterbury, for the maintenance of the poor of their almonry, did he and the monks, with whom the grant would certainly have been discussed, have in mind the general relief of the poor who should come to the gate of the almonry at Christ Church in search of alms, or the continuous support of a select number of poor—or, indeed, both kinds of arrangement?[9] The wording of this and many similar grants that could be cited lends itself to any of these interpretations: we have to reconstruct monastic practice in this period as best we can from other clues.

The litmus test of monastic values in almsgiving was always the fate of the monks' discarded clothing and the spare resources of the refectory, and I shall focus on the latter. In the refectory, however, there is a system to be mastered.

Dinner in a typical Benedictine house of this period was constructed around the two dishes of cooked food prescribed in the Rule of St Benedict and often known as 'generals' (*generalia*).[10] To these, however, it was now a common practice to add a third main dish and a number of extra dishes known as pittances. The contents of a dish of generals were the same for everyone present—hence the term. Pittances contained a variety of foods, with the consequence that neighbours at the same table might well find themselves eating different foods when such a dish was served; and pittances were normally of superior quality to generals. The number of pittances, and

---

[9] *EEA* ii, no. 87. The church was granted *usui et sustentationi pauperum* and was to be held, as the churches of Eastry and Monkton were already held by Christ Church, *ad usus . . . pauperum elemosinarie*. I am indebted to Dr Richard Sharpe for help in interpreting the phrase *sustentatio pauperum* in this and other 12th-cent. sources.

[10] In this book I have preferred the English word to the Latin, although the former, in the sense of 'common allowance or provision', is now obsolete. In post-medieval usage the term, whether in Latin or English, is sometimes applied to a monk's whole corrody of food and drink. Medieval usage seems normally to restrict it to the common dishes of cooked food in the refectory. For an example of the wider usage see the entry '*generale*, the single commons, or ordinary Provision of the religious in Convents' in N. Bailey, *An Universal Etymological English Dictionary* (17th edn., London, 1757).

indeed the quality, fluctuated according to the liturgical status of the day: was it a major feast, a minor feast, or just an ordinary day? The monks of Glastonbury Abbey under their abbots Thurstan and Herluin, who between them spanned the years 1077/8–1118, had three generals with two pittances and two generals with three pittances on alternate days.[11] William of Malmesbury, who notes these arrangements, would not have found them remarkable had they been very common, but some balancing of generals and pittances on ordinary days may have been quite usual. If, even in a wealthy house like Glastonbury Abbey, a mere handful of dishes could be considered appropriate for dinner on ordinary days, on festivals the number was sometimes large enough to attract critical comment from observant visitors. Gerald of Wales claimed that he counted sixteen dishes in the refectory at Christ Church, Canterbury, on Trinity Sunday 1179, when he happened to be present.[12] Gerald was not the most reliable of witnesses. Yet we need have no difficulty in believing that the monks of Christ Church dined particularly well on Trinity Sunday, a feast commended for observance by Thomas Becket, and the anniversary of his consecration.[13] Whatever the day, the larger the number of pittances, the smaller a monk's need of the less appetizing food served as generals, though the latter were always placed on the table at the appropriate point in the meal. On his visit to Christ Church, Gerald of Wales noticed that the monks had no appetite for the final dish of generals when it was brought to the table.[14]

As for the contents of the dishes at dinner, it was an unusually strict house where meat in some form was not, now, consumed quite frequently, in addition to the fish, eggs, cereal, and vegetables which made up the classic repertoire of monastic refectories. Tender consciences, however, were to some extent relieved by the practice of serving dishes in which meat was only one of the ingredients—as, for example, a pork fritter—instead of slices straight from the joint, or by serving dishes of offal, the latter being, arguably, not meat at all. Vegetables and cereal foods were served on occasion in addition to generals and pittances, on occasion as substitutes for the former, and dishes containing these foods were known as *pulmenta*. When

---

[11] William of Malmesbury, *De antiquitate Glastoniensis ecclesiae*, in Adam de Domerham, *Historia de Rebus Gestis Glastoniensibus* (2 vols., ed. T. Hearne, Oxford, 1727), i. 1–122, at 118–20. Cf. *Rule*, cap. xxxix. See also *Customary of Eynsham*, 190, where it is implied, as late as the 13th or early 14th cent., that a regime of 3 main dishes existed only in Lent, and not at all times. On the subject-matter of this paragraph and the next, see also below, pp. 43–5.

[12] *De rebus a se gestis*, in *Giraldi Cambrensis Opera*, ed. J. S. Brewer *et al.* (8 vols., RS 1861–91), i. 3–122, at 51; *The Autobiography of Giraldus Cambrensis*, trans. H. E. Butler (London, 1937), 71; see also *MO* 463.

[13] Gervase of Canterbury, *Historical Works*, ed. W. Stubbs (2 vols. RS 1879–80), i. 171; F. Barlow, *Thomas Becket* (1986), 73.

[14] The dish in question was actually a dish of vegetables, served, as Gerald notes, *loco generalis*, but the substantive point is not thereby affected.

served as substitutes, two such dishes were sometimes equated with one dish of generals.[15] At Abingdon Abbey, a later generation of monks attributed to Æthelwold himself, their tenth-century founder, the introduction of a daily regime of one dish of generals, two *pulmenta*, and one pittance. Whatever its origin, this regime may well have been normal on ordinary days in the twelfth and thirteenth centuries.[16]

On most days between Easter and mid-September, supper was served as well as dinner, and at this second meal a dish or two of cooked food, probably containing eggs, cheese, or offal, was specially provided, but monks made do with the remainder of the bread and of the ale, mead, or wine which had been served at dinner. The second meal was served much less frequently in winter, and none but a sick monk would have eaten it at all during the fast seasons of Advent and Lent—these comprised a total of about ten weeks. Moreover, during Lent, monks abstained not only from meaty dishes, where these had been introduced, but also from eggs and cheese; and observant monks gave up the meat, if not the eggs and cheese, at Septuagesima, the third Sunday before Ash Wednesday.[17]

For the poor, these dietary rhythms and varieties of practice were exceedingly important, because they affected the size of each meal and the amount of food that was available for them at the conclusion.

Every day, three portions of food and drink, said to be identical with those served to a monk, were set aside, in commemoration of the Maundy of Jesus, at which He washed the feet of the disciples, and in principle at least these were administered to three of the poor after a ritual washing of feet in some suitable place in the monastery—as, for example, the chapter house. Carried out to the letter, this practice would have earmarked a considerable quantity of food for the poor, especially on feast days. But whenever a monk's portion was given to anyone other than a monk—be the recipient a poor person, a servant, or a corrodian—the minimum definition applied: unless otherwise specified, it consisted of bread, ale, and generals, and pittances were disregarded. So it was with the Maundy portions. At Abingdon Abbey these portions included cut cheese, because—as it was believed— Æthelwold had so decreed, but even here no other kind of pittance is mentioned.[18]

---

[15] *Cart. Ram.* ii. 252, where *unum ferculum* is to be understood as a dish of generals. For *pulmentum* as a dish of vegetables and/or cereal, see *Chron. Evesham*, 218. However, on occasion this word denoted any dish of cooked food, and sometimes a main dish. For examples of the latter usage, which is analogous to that of *pulmentarium* in *Rule*, cap. xxxix, see *Lanfranc's Constitutions*, 75, and *Customary of Eynsham*, 190.

[16] *Chron. Abingdon*, ii. 279; cf. ibid. i. 346. On the authenticity of these passages, see M. Lapidge, 'Æthelwold as scholar and teacher', in B. Yorke (ed.), *Bishop Æthelwold: His Career and Influence* (Woodbridge, 1988), 89–117, at 106 and n.

[17] For a more rigorous practice, however, see *Consuetudinum saeculi x/xi/xii monumenta non-Cluniacensia*, ed. K. Hallinger (*CCM* vii(3), 1984), 386(6).

[18] *Chron. Abingdon*, ii. 148. The portion of cooked food at the Maundy here now consisted

Secondly, the poor had the leftovers of the monks' own portions of food and drink, and here, especially on ordinary days, human frailty was not without influence. Gilbert of Sempringham, the founder of the Order that bore his name, placed his own very large leftovers in a special dish which he called 'Lord Jesus' dish', and this was on the table in full view of the room—an example to others eating there to be equally generous.[19] Benedictines may sometimes have received similar encouragement from their abbots or priors to be generous. Nevertheless, the sources suggest that the quantity of leftovers was regulated as much by monastic appetite as by the absolute needs of the poor. Nor did the waste inseparable, then as now, from housekeeping on a large scale ensure a supply of food that was more or less steady from day to day for those waiting at the gate. On supperless days there was normally more bread to spare than at other times, but less cooked food, and on days when the two meals were served but a single loaf did duty at both, there was more cooked food but less bread. In Lent, however, monks consumed a great deal of bread at the one meal of the day, there being noticeably less cooked food than at other times of the year. But for the common practice of increasing the size of the monks' daily loaf in this season, the poor would have done very badly indeed at this time of the year. Nor was it always owing to the monks themselves that the worst was avoided. At Battle Abbey, where the Lenten loaf was 25 per cent larger than the ordinary one, the leftovers were given in alms for the king—a sure indication that William the Conqueror, the founder of Battle, or one of his successors, provided for the additional outlay so incurred.[20]

If ordinary leftovers fluctuated in quantity, so too did the food provided by the portions, often known as corrodies, of deceased monks. I refer to the universal practice of commemorating deceased monks by putting their portions of food and drink on the tables in the refectory at meal-times for a period after the decease, the whole to be given to the poor at the conclusion of the meal. Commonly, each monk was commemorated in this way for never less than thirty days after his death, and in some houses for a whole year; a deceased abbot was thus commemorated for never less than a year and in some houses in perpetuity. And where old traditions were still powerful, anniversaries were observed in the same way: a monk's portion of food was given to the poor on the anniversary of his decease each year. Moreover, down to the twelfth century, benefactors and others who had earned the

---

of 2 *pulmenta*, the equivalent of 1 dish of generals. For the decretists' view that delicacies should not be given to the poor, but only common food, see Tierney, 'The decretists and the "deserving poor"', 366–7.

[19] *The Book of St Gilbert*, ed. R. Foreville and G. Keir (OMT 1987), 63.

[20] *Chronicle of Battle Abbey*, ed. Searle, 69. For an increase of cooked food at the one daily meal in Lent, see n. 11 above.

prayers of the monks were enrolled in this system: hence the portions which commemorated Offa of Mercia, Henry I, and Pope Adrian IV in perpetuity at St Albans Abbey, and the year's portion commemorating Louis VII at Christ Church, Canterbury.[21] In fact, a sick year for the monks could be a good year for the poor, and some of the advantages could be long-lasting.

In these cases, too, the portion given to the poor was smaller than the monk's actual portion of food, for pittances were normally omitted. A portion for a deceased monk, decreed Lanfranc, should consist of bread, drink, and 'regular' food, and in this context the latter phrase signifies generals, the common main courses.[22] Even so, the practice of observing the anniversaries of deceased monks in this way was very costly in old-established houses where the deceased far outnumbered the living and grew in numbers every year: it proved to be a vulnerable part of the system. On the Continent, the economy of the Abbey of Cluny was in danger of collapse when Peter the Venerable took the matter in hand in the 1140s, and understandably so, for Cluny, which had been founded at the beginning of the tenth century, still commemorated every deceased member of its very large community, and a great many benefactors beside, with a portion for the poor on the anniversary of the decease. Peter's decree, limiting the number of daily portions for the poor to fifty, represented a great easing of the burden.[23]

A general anniversary, observed for all deceased monks on a single day in the year, with a strictly limited distribution to the poor, was a much cheaper arrangement than the individual anniversaries that so nearly proved fatal to Cluny. The anniversary of this kind instituted at Ramsey Abbey at the beginning of the thirteenth century exemplifies this point. It was agreed that this anniversary should be observed with a distribution to 100 poor persons. Ramsey Abbey, however, had been founded in the tenth century and housed a large community, if not one as large as Cluny's: by 1200 the obituary lists at Ramsey must have commemorated many more than 100 deceased monks.[24] Yet in England general anniversaries for deceased monks

---

[21] *Gesta Abbatum*, i. 203 (cf. *VCH Herts.* iv. 429); *EEA* ii, no. 164. In the case of England, the practice is a neglected topic. For comment on Continental practice, see J. Wollasch, 'Les obituaires, témoins de la vie Clunisienne', *Cahiers de Civilisation Médiévale*, xxii (1979), 139–71, at 159–64; and for the views on penance which underlay the system universally, H. E. J. Cowdrey, *The Cluniacs and the Gregorian Reform* (Oxford, 1970), 121–6. I am indebted to Mr H. M. Colvin for the reference to Wollasch's article.

[22] *Lanfranc's Constitutions*, 131; cf. ibid. 75.

[23] Peter the Venerable, *Statutes*, 66–7 and n.; *Recueil des Chartes de l'Abbaye de Cluny*, ed. A. Bernard and A. Bruel (6 vols., Paris, 1876–1903), v, no. 4132. For the *praebendae* given at anniversaries at Cluny as a monk's portion of bread, wine, and vegetables and generals, including, on occasion, flesh-meat, see Ulrich of Cluny, *Antiquiores Consuetudines Cluniacensis Monasterii* (PL cxlix), 766.

[24] *Cart. Ram.* ii. 218. This anniversary was endowed concurrently with his own by Abbot Richard (1214–16) and may represent a politic gesture on the abbot's part towards the community which was to pray for him after his own decease. For numbers at Ramsey, see Knowles and Hadcock, 73; and for the general anniversaries for monks observed in Cistercian houses from the late 12th cent., Wollasch, 'Les obituaires, témoins de la vie Clunisienne', 164.

are seldom mentioned: they were perhaps less common here than in Normandy, where they had attracted the attention of Orderic Vitalis at a much earlier date.[25] In many English houses the old practice of keeping individual anniversaries may have continued, but with a much reduced portion for the poor and in some cases with nothing except bread. At St Augustine's Abbey, Canterbury, in the second half of the thirteenth century, as much as 5s. was spent in bread for the poor on the first anniversary of the death—the sum was sufficient to provide a hundred large loaves and more for the distribution. In this house, however, it is unlikely that the poor received anything in subsequent years.[26] At Abingdon Abbey the anniversary portion now consisted, it appears, of a single loaf.[27]

Behind these developments lay more than a desire for economy. Cooked food is messy to administer, and, moreover, administering it to large numbers is a slow business. Ale, too, has its disadvantages in such a situation. To reduce the quantities of ale and cooked food in a poor man's portion and, on occasion, to eliminate the two altogether was in keeping with the strong desire of the Benedictines of this period for a well-ordered cloister and precinct. In the main, however, the changes reflect the growing scarcity of resources now afflicting the Benedictines. This scarcity is also reflected in the use of leftovers to feed the lower servants—a practice which became very common.[28] It is explained by several factors, but principally by the effects of a long-term rise in prices on the real income of monasteries and the turning away, towards the newer Orders, of many of the benefactors who might otherwise have rescued them. The price-rise was probably at its worst in the years around 1200.[29] By that date, however, competition from other Orders had been an unwelcome fact of life for the Benedictines for the greater part of a century. Yet the numbers of the poor, and especially the urban poor, were growing fast. We may think that in a great many houses a reduction in the number of pittances at meal-times would have had very beneficial effects on the funds available for the poor, and as a matter of fact Gerald of Wales made this very point at about the time in question.[30] Yet this was not the view from within the cloister. Though keenly aware of the existence and growing numbers of the poor, the monks themselves found it impossible to increase their ordinary almsgiving proportionately and, in

[25] *OV* ii. 115.
[26] *Customary*, i. 351. An identical distribution was made on the day of the death and at the month's mind. Cf. ibid. 369, where the *dies anniversaria* occurs at the end of the year subsequent to the death: it was a unique event.
[27] *Chron. Abingdon*, ii. 405. For the persistence of a full portion of food and drink as the norm or ideal at an anniversary distribution, see, however, *Customary of Eynsham*, 190. (This customary was written between c.1230 and the early 14th cent.)
[28] Below, pp. 173–4. And on the use of the portions of deceased monks to feed monastic corrodians, see below, pp. 191–2.
[29] P. D. A. Harvey, 'The English inflation of 1180–1220', *P & P* lxi (Nov. 1973), 3–30.
[30] *De rebus a se gestis*, 53; *Autobiography of Giraldus Cambrensis*, trans. Butler, 72.

some cases, even to maintain the existing level. In fact, by the second half of the twelfth century the monks were in precisely the situation envisaged by the Decretists at this very time: it was necessary to distinguish between deserving and undeserving poor because resources did not suffice for the needs of both.[31] Who, then, laid claim to monastic alms, and whom did the monks now prefer?

## (ii) Claimants, and the need to choose between them

In the Middle Ages, *pauperes*—'poor people'—was a word of very wide reference, and at first it did not denote a social or economic category but those who were at the opposite pole from the powerful (*potentes*).[32] When it is used by monks of those who might receive their alms, we have always to ask which poor are intended. In the late eleventh century and the twelfth century, the sources bring several different kinds to our attention.

The poor traveller, who was often a pilgrim, was the person to whom above all others monks living according to the Rule of St Benedict owed hospitality.[33] Although, by the end of the twelfth century, it was the fate of anyone arriving, as he did, on foot and not on horseback to be sent to the almonry instead of consorting with the better-off visitors in the guest-house, the supreme importance of accommodating him somewhere never faded. When, for example, we read that in the time of Odo, abbot of Battle from 1175 to 1200, the monastery's gates were open for all passing to enter, we should understand that Battle, under Odo, welcomed poor travellers as well as the rich.[34] And quite possibly poor pilgrims were favoured in the distribution of the daily portions commemorating the Maundy, for these are sometimes described as 'pilgrims' portions'.[35]

The poor traveller's need for alms might last only as long as his journey. The naked poor, or, as they were also called, the poor who begged from door to door, were the destitute, utterly dependent on alms for their livelihood. Abbot Sampson's account of how, as a young clerk, he was robbed

---

[31] Above, pp. 8–9.

[32] K. Bosl, 'Potens und Pauper: Begriffsgeschichtliche Studien zur gesellschaftlichen Differenzierung im frühen Mittelalter und zum "Pauperismus" des Hochmittelalters', in his *Frühformen der Gesellschaft im mittelalterlichen Europa* (Munich, 1964), 106–34.

[33] *Rule*, cap. liii.

[34] *Chronicle of Battle Abbey*, ed. Searle, 307. At the Abbey of Bury St Edmunds, a black monk, no less, was sent to the almonry if he arrived on foot (*Customary of Bury St Edmunds*, 26). Cf. Walter Map's strictures on the Cistercians' niggardly hospitality (*De Nugis Curialium: Courtiers' Trifles*, ed. M. R. James, rev. C. N. L. Brooke and R. A. B. Mynors (OMT 1983), 98–100).

[35] *Chron. Abingdon*, ii. 148; *Cartularium Abbathiae de Whiteby*, ed. J. C. Atkinson (2 vols., SS lxix, lxxii, 1879–81), ii. 519, where the *corrodium monachale ... quod unus peregrinus habere solitus [est] in Refectorio* is to be understood as one of the daily Maundy portions given in alms by the monks of Whitby. Cf. *Regularis Concordia*, ed. T. Symon (NMT 1953), 61–2, where poor pilgrims receive sustenance, though not the Maundy portions: these are for poor 'who are wont to receive their support from the monastery'.

near Rome and had, in consequence, 'to beg from door to door all the way back to England' reminds us that the second of these descriptions was now a term of art which is not to be taken quite literally.[36] Yet the phrase also described an actual way of life. Similarly, the words 'naked poor', though now also a term of art, powerfully evoked the actual condition of the destitute who shivered for lack of clothing.[37] Professor Georges Duby has suggested that many poor of this kind were driven towards the towns by a growing reluctance on the part of rural society to find room for them.[38] Some may have travelled, not once, from village to town, but frequently between towns. Many more, however, probably stayed in the same place for long periods. Characteristically, the naked poor were indeed urban poor, and in the towns the monastery gate was one of their regular pitches. At St Albans Abbey, Abbot William of Trumpington (1214–35) was in the habit of inviting into the monastery for refreshment the poor whom he found at the gate whenever he returned from a journey: they were always there.[39]

In addition to the naked poor and the poor traveller, poor persons living in institutions are frequently mentioned. Some of these claimants for alms were actually religious communities, and some of the communities in question had been founded by Benedictines—as Thetford Priory, for example, was founded for women in the mid-twelfth century by Abbot Hugh of Bury St Edmunds.[40] Other poor of this kind were inmates of hospitals, and in many cases of leper hospitals, of which *c.*100 were probably in existence by the end of the twelfth century.[41] And, finally, some poor were admitted as residents to monastic almonries. 'The poor of the almonry' (*pauperes elemosinarie*) is a phrase much used in the assignments of income to these institutions which survive in such numbers from the mid-twelfth century onwards, and even from that early date the phrase may in fact have denoted, among others, poor who lived in.[42] Early in the thirteenth century, a clear

---

[36] *Chronicle of Jocelin of Brakelond*, ed. H. E. Butler (NMT 1949), 49; translation from Jocelin of Brakelond, *Chronicle of the Abbey of Bury St Edmunds*, trans. D. Greenway and J. Sayers (Oxford, 1989), 44. The undertaking of the monks of St Augustine's, Canterbury, in 1251, to distribute anniversary alms for a benefactor '*pauperibus debilibus hostiatim mendicantibus in cimiterio Sancti Augustini*' illustrates the same point (*The Register of St Augustine's Abbey, Canterbury, commonly called the Black Book*, ed. G. J. Turner and H. E. Salter (2 vols., London, 1915–24), ii. 561).

[37] For a late 11th-cent. example of the appeal of the literal sense of this term, see *Chron. Evesham*, 93. This chronicle was compiled in the 13th cent. by Thomas of Marlborough. For the probability that at this point he used, but revised, an 11th-cent. source, see R. R. Darlington, 'Æthelwig, abbot of Evesham', *EHR* xlviii (1933), 1–22, 177–98, at 1–10; and J. Sayers, '"Original", cartulary and chronicle: the case of the Abbey of Evesham', *Fälschungen im Mittelalter* (Monumenta Germaniae Historica, xxxiii(4), 371–95, at 371–4).

[38] G. Duby, 'Les pauvres des campagnes dans l'Occident médiévale jusqu'au xiiiᵉ siècle', *Revue d'Histoire de l'Église de France*, lii (1966), 25–32.      [39] *Gesta Abbatum*, i. 303.

[40] Knowles and Hadcock, 266–7; S. Thompson, *Women Religious: The Founding of English Nunneries after the Norman Conquest* (Oxford, 1991), 64.

[41] Knowles and Hadcock, 313 ff.      [42] Above, p. 10.

reference to resident poor in the almonry at Reading Abbey puts the matter there beyond doubt, and it is unlikely that arrangements at Reading were unique.[43] Almonries, it may be suggested, were themselves becoming hospitals of a kind. Eventually, although it is unclear when this happened, some resident almsmen were brought under rule as lay brethren. By the mid-thirteenth century, Westminster Abbey had such brethren: they lived in the almonry, enjoyed the services of a secular priest who was himself an almsman, and performed the lowliest of domestic chores in the monastery.[44] The lay brethren at Westminster were sometimes called *conversi*, the name formerly applied to illiterate monks who were not in orders and this name was now used in the same sense elsewhere.[45]

Finally, there were the poor householders living in the vicinity of the monastery and having claims on its alms for that very reason. In his decrees, Lanfranc laid on the almoner the duty of visiting these, the poor of the district: the almoner was in particular to seek out the sick and the weak, who were to be regarded as especially suitable recipients of the monastery's alms.[46] Contrary to what has been suggested more than once, this duty to seek out the poor with addresses, who would not come to the almonry gate, or could not do so, was never forgotten, and Lanfranc's words were incorporated in some later Customaries, including those of Westminster Abbey and Eynsham Abbey.[47]

In the actual distribution of alms, the distinctions which I have mentioned were often blurred. This was inevitable, since vulnerable members of society often moved from one kind of predicament to another, if, indeed, they were not in more than one at the same time. In a bad year, for example, or when old age made it impossible to work, some of the poor of the district, who normally avoided this fate, might need to beg.[48] But the

---

[43] BL Harley MS 1708, 152ᵛ, 153ʳ, 142ʳ; calendared in *Reading Abbey Cartularies*, ed. B. R. Kemp (2 vols., Camden 4th ser. xxxi–xxxii, 1986–7), nos. 737, 739, 909. Harder to interpret is Reginald de Lisle's gift of the right to take wood for fuel, and an ass or horse for transport, to poor persons dependent on the alms of the Abbey of Holy Trinity, Vendôme, who are described as *pauperes in elemosina ejusdem abbatie commorantes* (*Cartulaire de l'Abbaye cardinale de la Trinité de Vendôme*, ed. Ch. Métais (4 vols., Paris, 1893–1900), iii, no. 655). Were these poor actually resident in the Abbey's almonry, or the poor of the district?

[44] *Customary*, ii. 176, 180. Cf. ibid. 179, a reference pointing to an origin before the time of Abbot Richard Crokesley (1246–58).

[45] For an example in a charter of the prior and convent of St Andrew's, Northampton, a Cluniac house, which may be as early in date as *c.*1230, see *Mon. Ang.* v. 192. (I am indebted to Dr Diana Greenway for advice on the dating of this charter.)

[46] *Lanfranc's Constitutions*, 89.

[47] *Customary*, ii. 178 (a passage exemplifying the mixture of conventional norms and actual practice which characterizes this source in general); *Customary of Eynsham*, 190.

[48] For 'life-cycle poverty', which can be of this temporary kind, see R. M. Smith, 'Some issues concerning families and their property in rural England 1250–1800', *Land, Kinship and Life-Cycle*, 1–86, at 68–85; T. Wales, 'Poverty, poor relief and the life-cycle: some evidence from seventeenth-century Norfolk', ibid. 351–404; and M. K. McIntosh, 'Local responses to the poor in late medieval and Tudor England', 219–20, and 230–1.

distinctions evidently existed in monastic minds, and, as resources became
scarce, they influenced actual arrangements. Increasingly, from the beginning of the twelfth century, it was the institutionalized poor who attracted
monastic alms, and the naked poor who suffered in consequence. Promises
were made which committed the monks to the long-term, even perpetual,
support of the first of these classes, and in some cases to support with the
most valuable resource of the refectory, a monk's portion of food and drink.
In the course of the century, portions of this kind, or other regular liveries
of food and drink, were, to our knowledge, promised by the Abbey of Bury
St Edmunds to the nuns of Thetford, by Reading Abbey to the hospitals of
St Mary Magdalen and St John Baptist, Reading, by Westminster Abbey to
the nuns of Kilburn, by St Albans Abbey to the nuns of St Mary de Pré,
and by Whitby Abbey to St Michael's Hospital, Whitby.[49] Evidently, the
practice was not localized. Nor is it at all likely that the assignments of this
kind which are mentioned in the surviving sources were the only ones to be
made. Indeed, circumstantial evidence shows that this was not the case. At
the end of the twelfth century, there was a queue at St Albans Abbey for
the portions commemorating Offa, Henry I, and Adrian IV mentioned above.
These formed part of the endowment of St Mary de Pré, but the nuns of this
house were told that they must wait for possession until the portions were
in fact vacant: evidently, each had been granted at an earlier date to some
deserving recipient.[50]

In all this, twelfth-century monks did little or nothing that had not been
anticipated in the actions of Lanfranc of Canterbury and Æthelwig of
Evesham, and probably many others, towards the end of the previous century. In that earlier period, monastic prelates exercised greater influence
over the whole range of their monastery's almsgiving than would be considered appropriate for most of their successors, and their actions, well
recorded by their biographers, shed some light on monastic practice more
generally. Neither Lanfranc nor Æthelwig was content merely to hand out
doles to the naked poor. When William the Conqueror harried the North in
1069–70, vast numbers of utterly destitute people, but especially old people
and women with children, came to Evesham in search of alms—the monks,
we are told, buried five or six every day. Æthelwig persuaded each of the
monastery's servants and officials, and some of the monks with means at
their disposal, to take in a child and feed him. In due course many of these

---

[49] Bury St Edmunds: *VCH Suffolk*, ii. 85–6; Reading: *Reading Abbey Cartularies*, ed. Kemp,
i. nos. 221, 224; Westminster: Appendix V, no. 2; St Albans: *VCH Herts.* iv. 429; Whitby:
*Cartularium Abbathiae de Whiteby*, ed. Atkinson, ii. 519. The portions granted by Westmin-
ster Abbey to the nuns of Kilburn included wine and pittances. For the assignment by Abbot
Osbern of St Evroul, in Normandy, of monks' corrodies to 7 lepers—a number later reduced
to 3—in the mid-11th cent., see *OV* ii. 117.
For later criticism at St Albans of the foundation of St Mary de Pré, see Thompson, *Women
Religious*, 59.                                                          [50] *VCH Herts.* iv. 429.

waifs made good and were themselves given employment in the monastery.[51] Lanfranc, on his arrival in England, instituted 'prebends' or pensions for poor people on the manors of the see of Canterbury—and whenever we read of an arrangement of this kind, we can probably conclude that many of the recipients were, or had formerly been, householders: they were the equivalent in the manors of the poor of the district near the monastery.[52] Moreover, Lanfranc founded not one hospital but two, and a church staffed by secular clergy that later became St Gregory's Priory at Canterbury.[53]

In the late eleventh century, however, it was possible to give selectively with one hand and be prodigally generous in undiscriminating ways—as was always expected of a prelate at this time—with the other, and precisely this feat is recorded of the two prelates who have been mentioned. In the twelfth century, when responsibility for almsgiving devolved, to a large extent, on obedientiaries having charge of departmental funds, it was more often necessary to choose between these two courses: there was not the means for both. It is a telling fact that in these circumstances monks so often preferred the systematic and long-term arrangement to anything more casual.

Moreover, it was not only the monastery as a body that now tended to discriminate: individual monks did so. From its first meeting in 1218 or 1219, the General Chapter of the Benedictine Order expressed concern lest the poor be defrauded of the leftovers of the refectory and other rooms where monks took their meals. The poor could be cheated at meal-times in several ways, and the Chapter clearly had more than one in mind. In the present context, however, one is of particular interest. Monks, it appears, were tempted to offend by giving leftovers to poor of their own choosing, instead of leaving them on the table for the almoner to collect at the end of the meal, and doing so without permission.[54] Of those who benefited from this

---

[51] *Chron. Evesham*, 90–1.

[52] *Vita Lanfranci*, attrib. Miles Crispin (*PL* cl), 46. (For the mid 12th-cent. date of this source, see M. Gibson, *Lanfranc of Bec* (Oxford, 1978), 196). For the poor to whom Gundulf of Rochester gave 'prebends', see *Vita Gundulfi episcopi Roffensis*, in H. Wharton (ed.), *Anglia Sacra* (2 vols., 1691), ii. 284, 289. Cf. the 150 widows and 60 clerks for whom the abbot of St Riquier provided in the 9th cent., in addition to 300 uncategorized 'poor' (Hariulf, *Chronique de l'Abbaye de Saint-Riquier (vᵉ siècle–1104)*, ed. F. Lot (Paris, 1894), appendix vii, p. 307; cited in R. McKitterick, 'Town and monastery in the Carolingian period', in D. Baker (ed.), *The Church in Town and Countryside* (SCH xvi, 1979), 93–102, at 100–1). The categories 'widows' and 'clerks' imply a degree of selectivity in these alms.

[53] Gibson, *Lanfranc of Bec*, 185–6. One of the hospitals was that of St John the Baptist. Eadmer's statement that Lanfranc *ordinavit etiam eis* [sc. the inmates of St John's] *de suo vestitum et victum quotidianum* refers to an assignment of actual portions of food and drink from the archbishop's table (Eadmer, *Historia Novorum in Anglia*, ed. M. Rule (RS 1884), 15). Twelve portions of food and drink in this hospital were later assigned to St Gregory's priory (*Cartulary of the Priory of St Gregory, Canterbury*, ed. A. M. Woodcock (Camden 3rd ser. lxxxviii, 1956), nos. 14–17).                      [54] *Chapters of English Black Monks*, i. 10, 36–7, 79.

individualism, we know only that they had ready access to the cloister—every monastic refectory opened off the cloister—and were thus able to forestall the naked poor who were detained at the gate. They were probably poor servants who had attracted the special attention of individual monks, or local residents who found it easy to slip in and out of the monastery; and some may have been relatives of the monks in question. At Durham Cathedral Priory under Prior Bertram (1189–1212/13), monks seem to have been permitted to choose recipients for the alms on Maundy Thursday: hence the provision that every monk should have five poor persons at this distribution.[55] These developments help us to make sense of a rebuke addressed to the monks of Bury St Edmunds by Sampson, who was abbot from 1182 to 1211: Sampson accused his monks of withholding their old clothes from the naked poor and giving even food and drink to them unwillingly.[56]

Eventually, to our knowledge, a number of houses abandoned the former daily distribution of the leftovers of the refectory to the poor at the gate, and this may have been a common development. Where the daily distribution was abandoned, a distribution two or three times a week, sometimes of bread or bread and ale, seems to have taken place. At Malmesbury Abbey, Abbot William Colerne (1260–96) considered two distributions a week—now evidently the established rule in this house—to be inadequate, increased the number to three, and assigned four bushels of grain per week to the almonry for the extra day.[57] Westminster Abbey, where Sir Thomas More remembered never to have seen the poor turned away unsatisfied, had abandoned its daily distribution, in favour of a distribution twice a week, by the mid-thirteenth century and may have done so at a considerably earlier date. Something, no doubt, was found for beggars who rang the almonry bell on the wrong day of the week, but, compared with earlier distributions, these were token alms. In this house, the ordinary daily leftovers of the refectory were now appropriated to the use of the lay brethren.[58]

Left to their own devices and disposing of their own resources, the Benedictines often showed a clear preference for stable and formal arrangements in almsgiving and dislike of the casual and the spontaneous; and they did so relatively early. But did they exercise real discrimination, or merely channel their alms with a new efficiency to the poor who happened to live among

[55] *Historiae Dunelmensis Scriptores Tres*, ed. J. Raine (SS ix, 1839), appendix, p. xxxv.

[56] *Chronicle of Jocelin of Brakelond*, ed. Butler, 110.

[57] *Reg. Malm.* ii. 368–9. The existing distributions occurred on Mondays and Thursdays, and at these the poor were to have the sum of 2 bus. wheat and 10 bus. barley (a small increase on the previous provision). For a distribution two or three times a week in an Augustinian house in the 13th cent., see *The Observances in Use at the Augustinian Priory of S. Giles and S. Andrew at Barnwell, Cambridgeshire*, ed. J. W. Clark (Cambridge, 1897), 179. (I owe this reference to Dr John Maddicott.)

[58] *Customary*, ii. 178–9. The priest, however, had one of the daily portions for the Maundy (ibid. 180). On the food of the lay brethren at Westminster see also below, pp. 67–9.

them or nearby? Discrimination is implied in many of the arrangements
which I have described, including the support of communities for women.
Writing *c.*1200, the biographer of Gilbert of Sempringham explained why
Gilbert had chosen to direct his alms to a community of women. The nucleus
of the Order of Sempringham was a group of seven young women whom
Gilbert brought under rule and to whom he made over his possessions.
This, to the writer, was a correct way of giving, for, in bestowing his goods
to support consecrated virginity, Gilbert had fulfilled the injunction, found
in Ecclesiasticus, 'Give to the good, do not harbour sinners'.[59] I have found
no considered apology for a discriminating use of alms in a Benedictine
source of this period, and indeed no explicit recognition at all that a shift
in practice was under way. But the apparent slowness of the Benedictines,
the black monks, to recognize what they were doing may owe much to the
thoroughness with which the Cistercians, the white monks, embraced the
principle of discrimination in almsgiving.

The code of practice used by the Cistercians of Beaulieu Abbey, in
Hampshire, in the second half of the thirteenth century is a remarkable and
illuminating document. In accordance with normal Cistercian practice, the
distribution of alms at Beaulieu was entrusted to the porter, and his instructions were precise: no alms for prostitutes at any time of the year, unless there
was a famine. As for other paupers: from the first day of the harvest in the
Abbey's granges to the last, only pilgrims, and the old, the young, and the
weak might receive alms—that is to say, only the unemployable might do so.[60]
The exclusion from alms of those of an infamous profession, the admission
even of these if there was a risk that they might die, the denial of alms to the
wilfully idle—each of these points occurring in the porter's instructions had
been taken up by the Decretists, the commentators on canon law, a century
before.[61] The Cistercians, however, were careful about such matters before
ever the Decretists published their views. When, for example, in 1154, the
General Chapter of the Order decreed that worthy matrons, if found outside the monastery at night, were to be taken to the village nearby and lodged
there, it meant that prostitutes were not to be so treated.[62] And when Walter
Daniel, in his Life of St Ailred of Rievaulx, distinguished the poverty of the
white monks from the penury of the idle, echoing as he did so a phrase of St
Bernard, it was surely with a glance towards the poor at the gate of Rievaulx.[63]
In fact, the Cistercians were explicitly discriminating from an early date.
How could they fail to be so, when their whole economy depended on a

[59] *Book of St Gilbert*, ed. Foreville and Keir, 30–2; Ecclus. 12: 5.
[60] *The Account-Book of Beaulieu Abbey*, ed. S. F. Hockey (Camden 4th ser. xvi, 1975), 174.
[61] Tierney, 'The decretists and the "deserving poor"', 364–9.
[62] *Statuta Capitulorum Generalium Ordinis Cisterciensis ab anno 1116 ad annum 1786*, ed.
J.-M. Canivez (6 vols., Louvain, 1933–8), i. 58.
[63] Walter Daniel, *Life of Ailred of Rievaulx*, ed. F. M. Powicke (NMT 1950), 11 and n.; cf.
St Bernard, *Sermones in cantica*, lxviii, in *Opera Omnia*, iv (*PL* clxxiii), 1111: *Perniciosa
paupertas, penuria meritorum; praesumptio autem spiritus, fallaces divitiae.*

capacity to persuade large numbers of the illiterate and poor to enrol as lay brethren and work under harsh conditions, and for no wages at all?

## 3. Monastic Almsgiving from Special Funds

### (i) The bias in favour of post-obit distributions

The special funds entrusted to monasteries for the purpose of almsgiving were devoted, with few exceptions, to distributions at funerals and anniversaries, and principally anniversaries. By the twelfth century, monks had been saying anniversary Masses for their benefactors for a very long time indeed: they had been founded in part to do this. But no sooner did the monks begin to count the cost of the traditional distributions associated with anniversaries—a change affecting their commemoration of benefactors as well as monks—than benefactors themselves began to express the desire for something a little more elaborate and—a vital point—offer funds to endow this. Their purpose in endowing a distribution of alms was as much to enlist the prayers of the recipients as to relieve their poverty, and the larger the number of recipients, the larger the number of prayers. Moreover, in the course of the thirteenth century, when these developments were well advanced, another equally important change made itself felt: distributions in cash instead of kind became much commoner than previously. This development seems to have ended an earlier restraint on the number of doles for the poor envisaged on each occasion—a perfectly natural consequence, since cash was, and is, easier to distribute on a large scale than food.

Whether made in cash or in kind, post-obit distributions of alms tended to be indiscriminate: they were normally for those who should come on the day in question, until the alms were exhausted. Thus indiscriminate almsgiving flew in at monastic windows just when, if I am right, it had been subjected to a degree of regulation and discouragement at the door. Since the doles distributed at funerals and anniversaries were known to be of this kind, the scramble for them was sometimes uncontrollable and could end in tragedy. On a day in July 1322, fifty-two people died in the crush of men, women, and children trying to enter the gate of the Dominican friary at Ludgate, where alms were to be distributed to mark the anniversary of Henry Fingrie, a wealthy fishmonger and former sheriff of the City of London, and other disasters could be cited.[64] But is it true that these distributions were to the end undiscriminating, and unaffected, therefore, by

---

[64] *Calendar of Coroners Rolls of the City of London*, AD 1300–1378, ed. R. R. Sharpe (London, 1913), 61; *Annales Paulini*, in *Chronicles of the Reigns of Edward I and Edward II*, ed. W. Stubbs (2 vols. RS 1882–3), i. 304. The chronicler gives the number of victims as 55. Henry Fingrie was sheriff 1299–1300 and died in 1318. For his will, see *Calendar of Wills proved and enrolled in the Court of Husting, London*, AD 1258–AD 1688, ed. R. R. Sharpe (2 parts, London, 1889–90), i. 278. For what was probably a similar incident in London in 1298, see *The Chronicle of Bury St Edmunds, 1212–1301*, ed. A. Gransden (NMT 1964), 149.

the contrary trends which have been perceived in almsgiving generally in the later Middle Ages? And were monks, who were so often charged with the duty of administering this kind of charity, content to the end with the old ways of doing things? I shall consider this kind of almsgiving at Westminster Abbey—that is, at the very dole-house which Sir Thomas More saw fit to praise.

## (ii) The case of Westminster Abbey

### (a) Royal anniversaries at the Abbey

The town of Westminster was now the legal and administrative capital of the kingdom, but it was, even so, small in comparison to its neighbour, London. At the beginning of the fifteenth century Westminster probably had c.2,000 inhabitants, and at the beginning of the sixteenth, 2,400 to 3,000. The population of London may have been c.35,000 at each of these dates, and a much higher figure is possible at the later one.[65] But the Palace of Westminster was the principal residence of the kings of England, and a number of other residences in the town belonged to members of the lay or ecclesiastical aristocracy, for occupation when duties at court or in parliament made this necessary. The comings and goings of great households, the cycle of law terms and vacations, the convening and adjournment of parliaments—all these circumstances must mean that the actual population of the town, as distinct from the resident core, fluctuated a great deal seasonally and even over quite short periods.

The focus of the religious life of the townsmen, formerly the Abbey church, was now the nearby parish church of St Margaret's. By the early sixteenth century, the parish could boast of at least nine religious gilds, some of them relatively wealthy and possessed of a well-developed social conscience which extended to the needs of many who were not actually members.[66] If, however, St Margaret's had the gilds, the Abbey had the alms. At the end of the Middle Ages, the monks of Westminster were spending c.£400 per annum—10 per cent of their gross income—on alms of one kind or another.[67] Of this sum, £185 per annum (46 per cent) was devoted to institutionalized forms of charity, old and new: to the lay brethren and the

---

[65] Rosser, *Medieval Westminster*, 168, 175; C. Barron, 'The later Middle Ages: 1270–1520', in M. D. Lobel (ed.), *The City of London, from Prehistoric Times to c.1520* (British Atlas of Historic Towns, iii, 1989), 42–56, at 56.

[66] Rosser, *Medieval Westminster*, 282–93, 310–24.

[67] 'Gross income' here includes income held in trust by the monastery for almsgiving, whether or not it was exempted from taxation in *VE*. My own figure for gross income as recorded in *VE* is £3,962 p.a.; cf. A. Savine, *English Monasteries on the Eve of the Dissolution* (Oxford Studies in Social and Legal History, i, 1909), 278, where a slightly lower figure is given. Of the sum of c.£400 p.a. mentioned in the text, c.£105 p.a. came from the ordinary or net income of the monastery and represented 3.7% of the latter: net income in 1535 was c.£2,830 p.a.

nuns of Kilburn, to the Abbey's grammar school and its song school, both of which could trace their origins to a school in the almonry first mentioned in the fourteenth century, and to the almshouses which Henry VII endowed and committed to the Abbey's supervision. But £215 per annum (54 per cent of the total) was distributed in doles, and mainly in doles commemorating the anniversaries of benefactors.[68] In the early sixteenth century, £215 per annum was not only a very large sum in the scale of almsgiving, but also a substantial sum by any standard. It exceeded, for example, the total income of a great many religious houses, including some that survived the lesser Dissolution of 1536: a condition of survival then was possession of an income of not less than £200 per annum.

The scale of post-obit almsgiving at the Abbey is explained by the status of the church, from the thirteenth century onwards, as the principal burial place of English monarchs and their spouses. Moreover, Margaret Beaufort, Henry VII's mother, was also buried there. In the Middle Ages, the place of burial was not necessarily the place chosen by the deceased before his demise, or by his executors subsequently, for the principal anniversary. However, Henry III, Eleanor of Castile, Edward I's consort, Richard II for himself and Anne of Bohemia, and Henry V all had anniversaries, and in most cases elaborate anniversaries, at the Abbey. As for Henry VII and his mother, they patronized the new age with a heavy testamentary investment in sermons, scholarships, lectureships, and even colleges at Oxford and Cambridge, but in the matter of anniversaries showed a great desire for the consolations of the old: they were commemorated quite as elaborately as any of their predecessors.[69] Moreover, in addition to a yearly anniversary, Henry VII endowed a weekly one, of lesser but still considerable ceremony, as Eleanor of Castile and Richard II had done earlier.[70]

The central features of all these anniversaries were the same. Some of the details, however, expressed the idiosyncrasies of the testator in question. On and around the tomb, 100 so-called tapers or cierges were lit; and if the tomb was not yet built, a temporary structure, known as a hearse, was used

[68] £165 p.a. on the royal anniversaries mentioned in the next paragraph, £30 p.a. on other anniversaries, and £20 p.a. on other occasions, such as Rogationtide and Maundy Thursday. For the detailed break-down of both kinds of almsgiving, see Appendix I.

[69] Henry III: Harvey, *Estates*, 391; Eleanor of Castile: *Cal. Ch. R.* ii *(1257–1300)*, 411, 424–6; Richard II and Anne of Bohemia: *Cal. Ch. R.* v *(1341–1417)*, 347–8, 375–80; Henry V: *Foedera*, xi. 90; Henry VII: *The Will of Henry VII*, ed. T. Astle (London, 1775), 1–47, *Cal. Cl. R., Henry VII*, ii *(1500–1509)*, no. 389; Margaret Beaufort: *Wills*, ed. Nichols, 356–88; *Cal. Cl. R., Henry VII*, ii *(1500–1509)*, no. 770. For Margaret Beaufort's dispositions see also M. K. Jones and M. G. Underwood, *The King's Mother: Lady Margaret Beaufort, Countess of Richmond and Derby* (Cambridge, 1992), 204–31, 239–50.

For a perceptive account of anniversaries etc. at lower, but still well-to-do, levels of English society in the later Middle Ages, see C. Burgess, '"By quick and by dead": wills and pious provision in late medieval Bristol', *EHR* cii (1987), 837–58.

[70] *Cal. Cl. R., Henry VII*, ii *(1500–1509)*, no. 389 (p. 144); *Cal. Ch. R.* ii *(1257–1300)*, 411; ibid. v *(1341–1417)*, 348, 375–6.

for this purpose.[71] Tapers were large candles, though not as large as the torches, each weighing 24 lbs. or more, which were used at several of the anniversaries. These were carried by poor persons especially recruited for the purpose. Normally, there were twenty-four torch-bearers, but this number might well be exceeded in the first two or three years of the existence of the anniversary in question, while interest in the occasion as a spectacle was at its height. At the anniversary of Edward III, which was in fact observed at the Abbey, though never fully endowed, 100 torch-bearers were employed in 1378, forty the following year, but eventually only twenty-four.[72] In addition to the black tunic, which he wore at the ceremonies and was allowed to keep, each torch-bearer received a money reward for his labours, the rate being prescribed for all time in the deed of foundation. Henry V's torch-bearers received 5*d.* on the vigil and 5*d.* on the anniversary; Henry VII prescribed 6*d.* per torch-bearer on the anniversary but apparently dispensed with their services on the vigil.[73] The vigil was kept with the funeral office of *Placebo* and *Dirige*, and nine lessons. On the anniversary, a Mass of Requiem was sung at the high altar, and the private Masses of the monks were said as Requiem Masses for the deceased. Monks who were not yet priests recited the psalter in its entirety. The lay brethren recited the Lord's Prayer, the Creed, and the Hail Mary as often as required by the abbot and convent, and at the weekly anniversaries for Eleanor of Castile and Richard II, the poor were expected to recite these three items before and after receiving their alms.

With all these liturgical duties to be ordered and carried to a conclusion, the monks no doubt considered that they had earned a reward, and a reward was in fact provided for in the endowment of each anniversary. Alone among the royal founders, Henry VII decreed that those monks who were absent from the ceremonies without good cause should forfeit their share, and this rule was observed.[74] In common with some other commemorative

[71] For hearse and tomb as alternatives, see *Cal. Cl. R., Henry VII*, ii (*1500–1509*), no. 389 (p. 143). The tomb was probably provided with a permanent structure of tapers. For a reference to the cleaning of Henry VII's hearse, see WAM 24241*. (I am indebted to Dr Richard Mortimer for help with the subject-matter of this note.)

[72] PRO E. 101/400/4, mm. 23–4; ibid. E. 101/401/6, mm. 20, 24. Each torch-bearer wore a gown, with hood, made from 3 'short' ells of black cloth. For draft schemes for perpetual anniversaries for, respectively, Edward III and Philippa of Hainault, and Thomas, duke of Gloucester, and Eleanor his wife, Thomas being the putative founder in each case, see WAM 6319–20. These envisaged 50 torches on the former anniversary and 20 on the latter, and a distribution of 2*d.* on the former and 1*d.* on the latter to every poor person coming to the monastery. See also Harvey, *Estates*, 397.

[73] *Foedera*, xi. 90; *Cal. Cl. R., Henry VII*, ii (*1500–1509*), no. 389 (p. 143); and for actual payments to the torch-bearers in each case in the early 16th cent., WAM 24183 ff., 24238 ff. Margaret Beaufort's will provided for the use of torches at her funeral but not at the subsequent anniversaries.

[74] WAM 24242, 24244, 24249, etc., where those assisting at the annual vigil and anniversary receive a reward, and the shares of absentees from the weekly anniversary are explicitly divided

occasions, a royal anniversary quickly lost its initial appeal, not least with the relatives of the deceased. Initially, however, some were very popular with others beside the poor seeking alms: for example, they attracted Londoners who were distinguished enough to be entertained to refreshments after the ceremonies.[75] The need to receive the quality in seemly fashion at the north entrance to the Abbey—the ceremonial entrance—whilst at the same time controlling the crowds gathered for the alms at the almonry outside the west entrance must have been a familiar problem for the monks of Westminster on every royal anniversary.

On Henry III's anniversary only a small distribution was normally made to the poor: a few quarters of wheat for bread, a few shillings, and eventually as little as 6s. 8d., for distribution in penny doles.[76] On the other anniversaries which have been mentioned, the sums available were on an altogether different scale. Even so, Eleanor of Castile's anniversary, observed from 1291, the year following her death, on or near 28 November each year, was in a class of its own. Edward I, the actual founder, directed that every poor person coming to the monastery on that day should receive one penny for food, and he added the rider, imitated in some later royal deeds of foundation at the Abbey, that the poor were always to receive the equivalent of a penny at the time of the foundation. Thus no limit was placed on the total amount to be disbursed. The foundation was wealthy, and within ten years of Eleanor's death £100 per annum, representing 24,000 penny doles, was available for alms.[77] In every other case a fixed amount was prescribed, and it was normally £20 per annum—a sum representing 4,800 penny doles. For a weekly anniversary the normal provision was a penny for each of 140 poor persons—a number quite frequently found useful in royal almsgiving more generally.[78]

## (b) Some practical problems

As far as we know, in the later Middle Ages the poor always received cash, not food or drink, at royal anniversaries. The provision that every poor

among those present. Cf. *Cal. Cl. R., Henry VII*, ii *(1500–1509)*, no. 389 (p. 145). For a similar provision in the case of a private anniversary, that of John Waltham, bishop of Salisbury, see WAM 5262A.

[75] WAM 18730, 18740–1. Londoners also attended on the feasts of SS Peter and Paul (29 June), St Peter in Chains (1 Aug.), and the translation of St Edward the Confessor (13 Oct.).

[76] WAM 19840 ff. An outlay of 6 qu. wheat, presumably in bread, is recorded in 1344, and in 1351 an outlay of 10s. 7d., representing penny doles for 127 persons (WAM 19845*, 19848). Exceptionally, in 1437, as much as £7, representing 1,680 penny doles, was distributed (WAM 23035*). For Henry's anniversary, observed on 16 Nov., see Harvey, *Estates*, 391.

[77] The total sums distributed on the anniversaries in 1300–3 inclusive averaged £104 p.a. (WAM 23631).

[78] e.g. PRO E. 101/369/11, fos. 24, 24ᵛ, 26ᵛ. Henry VII decreed that his weekly alms should be given to the 16 inmates of his almshouses and 124 others beside (*Cal. Cl. R., Henry VII*, ii *(1500–1509)*, no. 389 (p. 144)).

person should have the equivalent of a sterling penny at the date of the foundation meant that the royal distributions in question were, in a sense, index-linked. Nevertheless, circumstantial evidence suggests that the actual per capita rate was often a penny and rarely more than 2*d*. Henry VII, careful as ever, decreed that none of the poor was to receive more than 2*d*. on his anniversary; a year or two later, his mother specified 1*d*. per person on her own.[79] In a period when ¼*d*. would buy 2 lbs. of coarse bread, and 1*d*. food and drink for a day, these sums must have seemed highly desirable.[80] But how much was actually to be given *in toto* on each occasion? The monks always took the view that this sum should vary with need and circumstance, of which they were the judges. Their directive role in this respect is most clearly evinced in the dramatic alteration of the scale of the distribution on Eleanor of Castile's anniversary in the mid-fourteenth century. Down to the 1340s, the sum disbursed on this anniversary quite frequently exceeded £100. In the second half of the fourteenth century and the first half of the fifteenth, the largest sum recorded is £25 3*s*. 4*d*., and the average for this long period is as low as £16 10*s*.[81]

Distributions took place at or near the almonry, a complex of buildings on the west side of the monastery, and normally they began at 8 or 9 a.m. by clock-time.[82] Much bell-ringing on the vigil and on the day itself served to publish the fact that something out of the ordinary was about to take place.

The problems facing the monks at this point on a royal anniversary were directly proportioned to the size of the approaching distribution. To some extent the problem of sheer numbers may have been eased by a ready tolerance of multiple applications. Certainly, when alms were distributed in cash—much easier to hide in a pouch than a loaf of bread—and simultaneously at more than one station—a necessary arrangement where thousands were involved—only a ticket system could have eliminated such a practice. Yet when every allowance is made for multiple applications and some flexibility in per capita rates, it is scarcely possible to think that the monks

---

[79] *Cal. Cl. R., Henry VII*, ii *(1500–1509)*, no. 389 (p. 143), no. 770 (p. 291). However, Henry prescribed 4*d*. doles in the case of the alms totalling £1,500 that were to be casually distributed on the day of his decease (*Will of Henry VII*, ed. Astle, 9); and on his anniversary each inmate of his almshouses was to receive 12*d*. Only £10 p.a. was to be distributed at Margaret Beaufort's anniversary. In the late 14th cent., members of the monastic household, in the widest sense of the word, receiving 'rewards' from the elemosynary funds on the occasion of a distribution did so on a sliding scale, ranging from 1*d*. for a prisoner in the gatehouse prison, and 2*d*. for a lay brother, through 6*d*. for the master of the grammar school and 1*s*. for the master cook, to 3*s*. 4*d*. for some superior servants who were probably clerks (WAM 23712, 23716). In this list, the prisoner and the lay brother represent the poor.

[80] Dyer, *Standards of Living*, 253.

[81] WAM 23694 ff.; and for £25 3*s*. 4*d*. in 1439, see WAM 23798. The average relates to the period 1355–1444; the accounts of the wardens of Queen Eleanor's manors survive for 77 years in this period. From *c*.1444, the sum accounted for each year was a standardized £20.

[82] Expressed in the earlier anniversaries as the 3rd hour of the day. For the late medieval almonry, see Map I. The sub-almonry was the focal point for the distribution of doles.

dealt with fewer than 12,000 to 15,000 poor on some of Eleanor of Castile's anniversaries down to the mid-fourteenth century. Long after this date such numbers must have been familiar features of funeral distributions. Margaret Beaufort, though not a queen, directed that her executors should distribute £133 6s. 8d. (32,000 pence) on the day of her decease and an equivalent sum on the day of her burial.[83] A considerable proportion of these very large sums was probably distributed in penny or twopenny doles near the Abbey, where Margaret died and was buried. On many of the anniversaries when the total sum distributed was a modest £20 or thereabouts, we should probably envisage at least 2,000 to 3,000 poor.

On an ordinary, private anniversary, when the number of doles provided for by the testator was rarely more than 200 or 300 and often less, the almoner and his small staff saw to the distribution. For the royal occasions, it was usual to appoint two other monks to supervise the operations, and it is clear that in the early fourteenth century, when the crowds were great-est, they were assisted not only by lay servants of the Abbey but also by many other monks. This explains why the extra course served at dinner in the refectory to mark Queen Eleanor's anniversary was eaten a day or two after the event.[84] It would not do to allow the monks who were too frail or too senior to participate in the distribution to enjoy the pittance on the anniversary day itself, while the young and the strong were still engaged in holding back the crowds at the gate. Since in November the monastic din-ner was probably delayed, in this period, until some time after noon, this detail tells us that such a distribution, beginning as it did at 8 or 9 a.m., went on for several hours—and inevitably so. References to wand- or rod-bearers afford a glimpse of medieval methods of crowd control; canvas bags, specially made for the occasion, were used for the coins.[85]

If the monks had their problems on these days, so, too, did the poor. The comprehensive words 'to all who shall come', which were included in so many of the deeds of foundation, embraced the poor of the district, provided they came to the distribution point, as well as the naked poor, and among the latter, the transient beggar as well as the beggar who never left the neighbourhood: to be eligible, it was necessary only to be poor and at hand. But the system of post-obit almsgiving, like the monastery's ordinary dis-tributions, actually favoured the local poor—in this case, the local house-holder and the local beggar. Unlike the transient poor, they had ample

[83] *Wills*, ed. Nichols, 362; Jones and Underwood, *The King's Mother*, 237.
[84] For explicit references to this practice in 1301, 1302, and 1304, see WAM 23638.
[85] WAM 23667; and for a reference in 1500 to the reward of monks taking part in the anniversary distribution out of money in bags (*per bagas*), see WAM 23908. For the wand-bearers (*virgatarii* and *virgatores*), who are mentioned in the late 14th cent. but who were, no doubt, employed earlier as well, see WAM 23699–700. They always received money rewards. (I am indebted to Mrs L. P. Lyons, of the *Dictionary of Medieval Latin from British Sources*, for help with Latin vocabulary at this point.)

opportunity to master the calendar of anniversaries—and indeed to master the monastic calendar in a more general sense—as it unfolded year by year, nor did they need to master a large number of calendars to take full advantage of the system. It was much harder for the transient poor to be in the right place at the right time. In the case of funerals, the advantage of the local poor was even greater: by their nature, these events occurred at short notice, but never too short for them to attend.

But, of course, the locality in question was large and exceptional, for effectively it included the City of London and its environs: there, the Abbey was well known, on account of its extensive interests as a landlord, its fairs, and its shrine and relics. We must, I think, conclude that the vast numbers receiving alms at the Abbey on Queen Eleanor's anniversary in the early fourteenth century consisted, overwhelmingly, of the poor of London: only in this way can we explain the convergence on the Abbey of numbers far exceeding the entire population of the town of Westminster at this date, and, moreover, their convergence on the right day. A chance remark by one of the Abbey's obedientiaries, in the early fifteenth century, itself points to the conclusion that numbers were on occasion swollen by labouring poor from London and Westminster. In 1416 a larger sum than usual (£17 5s.) was disbursed in alms on Eleanor of Castile's anniversary, and the obedientiary in charge of the fund made a note in his account of the reason: the anniversary that year fell on a Sunday. The explanation of this, at first, puzzling remark is, almost certainly, that a considerable number of the poor who were in employment in London or Westminster found it easier to come to the monastery for alms on Sundays, when they did not work, than on other days.[86]

## (c) The growth of discrimination

What, then, explains the decline in the number of doles distributed on Queen Eleanor's anniversary after the mid-fourteenth century? Since the monks shared among themselves whatever surplus remained after the distribution of alms on royal anniversaries, we cannot exclude the simple factor of human greed: indeed, we should give it considerable weight. Yet the surplus of Queen Eleanor's foundation had always been dealt with in this way, and this had once been compatible with the distribution of very large sums in alms. For the main explanation of the change, we must look to other factors, and to two in particular. First, the numbers of the poor living in and around London declined in the second half of the fourteenth century, in the wake of great demographic catastrophe and the ensuing transformation of the labour scene. Secondly, however, in the same period—the period of the

---

[86] WAM 23761. Cf. the weekend comprising a 'domestic' Sunday and an 'outdoor' Monday suggested in M. Harrison, 'The ordering of the urban environment: time, work and the occurrence of crowds 1790–1835', *P & P* cx (Feb. 1986), 134–68. (I am indebted to Joanna Innes for this reference and for the explanation suggested in the text.)

labour laws, making it a statutory offence to beg if one was capable of labouring for hire—the attitude of society as a whole towards beggars and begging hardened, and the monks of Westminster were swept along by this new tide of feeling.[87] Even now they were still giving doles to many able-bodied people who would have been excluded from all such benefits in the sixteenth century, for it was only in the later period that the drive against sturdy beggars and indiscriminate almsgiving acquired irresistible momentum.[88] Yet the new climate of opinion encouraged them to administer Queen Eleanor's foundation, the largest to date of the special funds entrusted to them for the purpose of almsgiving, with some of the same caution which they and other Benedictine communities had long brought to almsgiving from their ordinary income.

It was against this background of a hardening of attitudes towards the able-bodied beggar that testators endowing anniversary distributions at the Abbey after the time of Queen Eleanor began to open the alms to others beside those who should actually come to the distribution points on the day in question: in some cases 'to anyone else in need'; in others, to poor residents of the district. In the context, each of these phrases actually signifies the established local poor, the respectable poor with addresses. The new wording legitimized a more discretionary use of funds than heretofore. It first occurs in the foundation deed of Richard de Chesterfield's anniversary in 1366: the small distribution of alms—only 6s. 8d. per annum—endowed by this very rich royal clerk was to benefit those who should come to the monastery on the day and others in need.[89] Since all details of this kind were a matter for preliminary treaty between the testator in question and the monks, we can be sure that the merits of directing post-obit alms more exactly towards others beside the begging poor were already being canvassed in the monastery at this date. At the end of the century, Abbot William Colchester directed that half the alms on his anniversary should go to the poor of the town of Westminster and half to parishioners of Aldenham, in Hertfordshire, where tithe had been appropriated to endow the observance: the transient poor were, it appears, to have nothing.[90] In 1445 Henry V's executors, belatedly establishing that monarch's chantry and anniversary, specified that his alms should go to the poor coming to the monastery and to others in need.[91] Fifty years later, Henry VII's directions for the

---

[87] 12 Richard II, cap. 7 (*SR* ii *(1377–1504)*, 56). On the customary law which anticipated some provisions of the labour laws, see E. Clark, 'Medieval labor law and English local courts', *American Journal of Legal History*, xxvii (1983), 330–53. For a mid 13th-cent. example of the restriction of the doles given on an anniversary to the *impotent* poor 'begging from door to door', see above, n. 36.

[88] Slack, *Poverty and Policy in Tudor and Stuart England*, ch. 6.

[89] LNQ 99'; Harvey, *Estates*, 396.

[90] Harvey, *Estates*, 397. Note also Abbot Colchester's practice of giving so-called 'corrodies' to the deserving poor of his manors in Worcs. and Glos.: these consisted of small cash pensions, reckoned on a daily or weekly basis (WAM 24411–26).     [91] *Foedera*, xi. 90.

distribution of alms on his anniversary were, it appears, designed to exclude
sturdy beggars from consideration. Henry required the abbot and convent
of Westminster to divide the total sum of £20 provided on each occasion
into two unequal parts. The greater of these (£16 13s. 4d.) was to be distributed among the blind, lame, impotent, and most needy persons among
those actually coming to the monastery on the day in question. The smaller
part (£3 6s. 8d.) was to be distributed among the residents of the almshouses
founded by the king in the precinct, and among the blind, lame, bedridden,
and most needy residents in the monastery itself, the town of Westminster,
or the city and suburbs of London who could not come for alms in person,
and among prisoners in Westminster and London.[92] Margaret Beaufort, who
was evidently less concerned than her son to avoid giving to the able-bodied,
gave priority, on her anniversary, to the claims of the poor who should
come to the monastery at the given time and may have had transient beggars
in mind; but the poor of Westminster and London who could not come to
the distribution point, and prisoners in either place, were to have the resi-
due, and Margaret specified at this point the blind, the lame, the bedridden,
and the poorest of the poor.[93]

In fact, after the mid-fourteenth century the naked poor lost ground to
other kinds of poor in the economy of almsgiving at Westminster, and the
monks themselves favoured this development. It was entirely in accordance
with their new outlook that some income entrusted to them for post-obit
distributions should have been deflected to their song school. By the 1520s,
the sum of £14 per annum formerly distributed in doles at Henry VII's
weekly anniversary had been assigned to this very different charitable purpose.[94] And it even came to seem appropriate that anniversary doles should
help to pay for the new work on the Abbey church: in 1521–3 the large sum
of £70 6s. 8d., which had probably been kept back from the distribution at
the weekly anniversary of Eleanor of Castile, was used for this purpose.[95]

When, therefore, in 1535–6, Thomas Cromwell's Injunctions instructed
monastic almoners to pay special attention to the needs of deserving

---

[92] PRO C54/365, m. 5. Cf. the inadequate summary in *Cal. Cl. R., Henry VII*, ii *(1500–1509)*, no. 389 (p. 143). The anniversary was endowed in 1504. The needy residents in the monastery mentioned in this passage were probably members of the monastic household, some of whom, to our knowledge, received alms on royal anniversaries; see n. 79 above. In his will, in 1509, Henry directed that £500 of the sum of £2,000 to be distributed in alms on the day of his death should be reserved for the lame, blind, bedridden, and other 'most needy' persons in London and Westminster who could not 'travaile to aske elemesse'—i.e. come to a distribution point—and for prisoners in those places. He also distinguished categories of deserving prisoners, *Will of Henry VII*, ed. Astle, 9.

[93] PRO C54/372, m. 23ᵛ; *Cal. Cl. R., Henry VII*, ii *(1500–1509)*, no. 770 (p. 291). Like Henry VII, Margaret included poor living in the monastery among those who might receive alms without coming to the distribution point.

[94] WAM 33301, fos. 7ᵛ, 10ᵛ, etc. The money, described as 'doles', was received by the sub-almoner for the song school in monthly instalments of £1 2s. 8d. from William Allowe, who was rent-collector for Henry VII's foundation.　　　　　　　　　[95] WAM 23024*.

householders—those who laboured with their hands for a living but could not 'fully help themselves for their chargeable household and multitude of children'—the almoner of Westminster Abbey may have reflected that he had been doing this for some time.[96] When, moreover, Henry VIII, on transferring the possessions of the dissolved monastery to the new cathedral and collegiate church at Westminster, directed that the sum of £100 per annum should in future be given, out of its income, to 'poor householders', he was not so much altering the character of almsgiving at the Abbey as giving the final push to a development long in the making.[97]

## 4. Conclusions

This survey of monastic charity has extended from the late eleventh century to the early sixteenth: from one period of painful transformation in the Christian life to another—the latter being, for monks, not only painful but also fatal. Throughout, I suggest, we need to distinguish much more clearly than is at present customary between what monks liked to do and what the tyranny of founders and benefactors often obliged them to do. Left to their own devices, and using their ordinary revenues, they evinced from a very early date a preference for systematic arrangements, which they administered with a marked degree of discrimination. If, in the years around 1500, monks did not share the new concern of charity more generally to rescue the outcasts of society, they perhaps anticipated its other, quite different, thrust towards the respectable poor. In administering casual doles at funerals and anniversaries—to many the rock of their offence—they were for the most part agents of benefactors, and above all of lay benefactors, who sought in this way to spread the good work of prayers for their souls as widely as possible. Monks could and to some extent did mould these benefactions to their own ideas, but the basic institution itself they could not change, even if they wanted to, without the concurrence of testators and executors—and the latter were even more difficult to handle than the former. It was not the case that monks were too old-fashioned or too soft-hearted to discriminate but that influential members of secular society liked the old way of doing things. Not for the last time in the history of the Church, the true conservatives were the laity.

---

[96] Wilkins, *Concilia*, iii. 790; J. Youings, *The Dissolution of the Monasteries* (London, 1971), 150. Relatives of monks were also to receive special consideration.

[97] In the several draft schemes for the new foundation, the sum of £100 for poor householders remained constant, although many other proposed allowances changed. See WAM 6478, fo. 4ᵛ; PRO E. 315/24, fos. 5ᵛ, 37ᵛ, 81–2. See also *L & P Henry VIII*, xvi (1540–1), no. 333. However, the funeral alms distributed for Henry VIII at Leadenhall and St Michael's, Cornhill, from noon to 6 p.m. on 7 Feb. 1547 evidently belonged to the old dispensation: one observer estimated that 21,000 men, women, and children received a groat (4*d.*) each (C. Wriothesley, *A Chronicle of England during the Reigns of the Tudors, from AD 1485 to 1559*, ed. W. D. Hamilton, i (Camden Soc. NS xi, 1875), 181. (I owe this reference to Jennifer Loach.)

# II

# *Diet*

## 1. The Problems

A RECENT notable work by a distinguished medievalist concludes with this testimony: 'I do not think that enquiry must be defeated by lack of material.' Many will recognize the source of this quotation: it is Professor Anne Hudson's *Premature Reformation*.[1] How much more do the historians of diet need the conviction it expresses than the historians of Lollardy, whose adherents so greatly esteemed the written word and did so much to procure its circulation! Historical sources on diet are at best reticent, and often fail us altogether. It will be clear that in what follows, and especially in what I shall say about quantities and the energy value of food, I make these words my own.

Monastic diet, my particular subject, was a form of upper-class diet[2], the equivalent within the cloister of the diet of the nobility, gentry, or urban élites outside. A monastic exemplar will, I hope, shed some light on knotty problems relating to the larger theme, and among these problems I distinguish three of outstanding importance.

First, what was, in general, the make-up of upper-class diet? An odd choice of question, it may be thought, given the past twenty or thirty years' study on the composition of diet at every level of late medieval society.[3]

---

[1] A. Hudson, *The Premature Reformation: Wycliffite Texts and Lollard History* (Oxford, 1988), 517.

[2] I have used the description 'upper-class' in this chapter, where others might prefer 'aristocratic'; both words beg questions, but in the present context the former begs fewer than the latter. It will be clear that the description is not used as a term of art.

[3] Among seminal works, see J. C. Drummond and A. Wilbraham, *The Englishman's Food*, rev. D. Hollingsworth (London, 1958); Stouff, *Ravitaillement et alimentation en Provence*; H. Neveux, 'L' alimentation du xiv^e et xviii^e siècle', *Revue d'Histoire Économique et Sociale*, li (1973), 336–79; and P. Charbonnier, 'La consommation des seigneurs Auvergnats du xv^e au xviii^e siècle', and other contributions to 'Histoire de la Consommation alimentaire du xiv^e au xix^e siècle' (a 'dossier' presented by B. Bennassar and J. Joy), *Annales, ESC* xxx (1975), 402–632. For a social-anthropological perspective, see J. Goody, *Cooking, Cuisine and Class, a Study in Comparative Sociology* (Cambridge, 1982).

For indispensable accounts of English diet at different levels of society, see Dyer, *Standards of Living*, 55–70, 151–60; id., 'English diet in the later Middle Ages', in T. H. Aston, P. R. Coss, C. Dyer, and J. Thirsk (edd.), *Social Relations and Ideas: Essays in Honour of R. H. Hilton* (Cambridge, 1983), 191–216; and id., 'Changes in diet in the late Middle Ages: the case of harvest workers', *AHR* xxxvi (1988), 21–37.

However, although we now possess many studies of expenditure in upper-class households, which show how much was spent per annum on each of the major food groups, we have very few showing the actual importance of the food groups themselves in the diet. Yet the two things are quite different: it is, for example, one thing to know that the households in question commonly spent on cereal foods 30 to 40 per cent of their total outlay on food of all kinds, but quite another to know what cereal foods contributed to the nutritious content of the diet or its energy value. As for differences of diet within the broad upper-class bracket, these are only now beginning to receive due attention from historians. Social anthropologists, by contrast, have long concerned themselves with social differentiation as one of the very purposes of eating and drinking.

Secondly, is it true, as is commonly said, that the upper classes neglected, and perhaps actually despised, some exceedingly important foods, namely dairy produce—important as a source of Vitamins A and D—and fruit and vegetables—sources of Vitamin C? Here too the argument from expenditure has been very strong: the appeal has been more to the amounts spent on these foods, which were always very small, than to any analysis of the dishes served day by day.[4] Yet some of the vital nutrients in question were needed only in very small quantities—milligrams per day: mere expenditure cannot settle the matter.

Finally, there is the problem of quantity; and this is a problem at every level of society where we encounter a formal allowance of food. Today, a rather heavy, moderately active, man needs a daily intake of 3,158 kilocalories (kcals.), and only one engaged in strenuous activity—as, for example, a soldier in the field—needs more.[5] Yet in the later Middle Ages, in widely differing social and cultural settings, allowances far exceeded this figure in their energy value. In his magisterial study of diet in Provence, Professor Stouff has valued the daily allowance of a member of the archbishop of Arles' household in the mid-fifteenth century at *c.*4,580 kcals.[6] Had it been possible to distinguish the food served at the high table in this household from the rest, the per capita share of the privileged few sitting there would certainly have exceeded this figure by a considerable margin, it being a universal assumption of the period that the quantity of food, as well as its

[4] Note, however, Stouff's cautious remarks (*Ravitaillement et alimentation en Provence*, 236–8).

[5] i.e. 13.2 megajoules (= 3,158 kcals.) (DH 41, p. 27). The likelihood that the monks of Westminster were, in general, obese, makes it appropriate to use the figure for a rather heavy man as a point of reference. A sedentary way of life is assumed. Cf. the intake of 4,200 kcals. per day deemed necessary for a British soldier in the field in the reassessment of needs which took place after the Falklands campaign of 1982 (*The Times*, 6 Aug. 1988).

[6] Stouff, *Ravitaillement et alimentation en Provence*, 246. Cf. F. Braudel, *The Mediterranean and the Mediterranean World in the Age of Philip II*, trans. S. Reynolds (2nd edn., London, 1972), i. 459.

quality, should vary directly with social status. 'How did people get through it all?' we are tempted to ask, and, in the case of the upper classes, the suggested explanation is normally the practice of leaving something for the poor, or sheer waste, itself a form of poor relief: their allowances were merely a means of getting a large amount of food into the public domain represented by the hall of a great house, where a considerable proportion would be channelled to other recipients. But how much was consumed by the privileged few, and how much was left?—that is the neglected question.

## 2. The Sample

The problems which I have outlined demand, for their solution, not only records of a particular kind but also defined groups of consumers, whose eating habits lend themselves to per capita analysis. My sample is provided by the monks of Westminster, and I shall consider the monks' diet principally in the years c.1495–c.1525. A Benedictine house of this period exemplified several different standards of living, and Westminster Abbey is no exception. The abbot of Westminster, who lived separately from the convent, affected a noble way of life. The convent, for its part, lived like the gentry, and it is the convent that provides my sample. In the later Middle Ages, it numbered about fifty monks—not a large number for a great household of this period, yet large enough to confer some of the advantages of economies of scale. With an annual outlay of c.£11 per monk per annum—that is, 7d. per day, or 4s. per week—on victuals alone, a large sum at the time, the monks achieved a genteel standard of living with something to spare: they are in fact to be compared to the greater gentry of the period. The convent's outlay on foodstuffs of all kinds, shown in Table II.1, represents c.37 per cent of its net income: this was now c.£2,100 per annum.[7] I shall draw on a variety of sources but especially on the accounts of the officials who shared the main costs of the monastic meals: the kitchener, who provided the main dishes of cooked food; the pittancer, who provided many of the extras consumed on feast days; the cellarer, who, together with his subordinates, the baker and brewer, provided the bread and ale; and, finally, the treasurers, who underwrote many of the expenses incurred by these officials and could be relied upon to provide supplementary funds from time to time.

The principal sources, however, will be the kitchener's day-books, which survive for a dozen or so years between 1495 and 1525: these record the main

---

[7] Harvey, *Estates*, 63. Cf., for per capita outlay, Dyer, *Standards of Living*, 70, where the expenditure on food of a number of the late medieval nobility and gentry and of one institutional consumer is expressed as a percentage of total expenditure.

TABLE II.1. Estimated Expenditure Per Annum of the Convent of Westminster on Foodstuffs, *c.*1495–*c.*1525[a]

| | £ | % |
|---|---|---|
| Bread | 75[b] | 13 |
| Oatmeal & flour | 2 | 0 |
| Eggs | 31 | 5 |
| Dairy produce | 19 | 3 |
| Fruit & vegetables[c] | 5 | 1 |
| Spices | 9 | 2 |
| Salt | 4 | 1 |
| Meat, meat products, & fish | 271 | 47 |
| Ale | 100 | 18 |
| Wine | 50[d] | 9 |
| Misc.[e] | 5 | 1 |
| TOTAL | 571 | 100 |

*Notes*: [a] The table relates to outlay on foodstuffs for the convent and others eating in the refectory and misericord; it does not include expenditure in the abbot's or prior's household or in any other separate household in the monastery.

[b] Of which sum £16 (21%) came from special funds and represents the cost of bread and buns etc. for endowed feasts and anniversaries.

[c] Including dried fruit, the major item.

[d] Of which sum £40 (80%) came from special funds and represents the cost of wine for endowed feasts and anniversaries.

[e] Including oil, used for cooking in Lent and the major item, and nuts.

*Sources*: Accounts of the cellarer (WAM 18903–40), kitchener (WAM 33317–18, 33321–3, 33327–9, 33330), pittancer (WAM 33336, 33339–44, 33347, 33350–1), treasurers (WAM 19987–99, 23001–25), and of other obedientiaries providing pittances.

items of cooked food served at every dinner and supper in the years in question, and frequently the form in which they reached the table.[8] A sample entry, that for Tuesday, 24 January 1503, will illustrate the conventions employed in these accounts:

[8] WAM 33318, 33321–3, 33327–9, 33330. These accounts cover the following periods: 29 Sept. 1497–11 Oct. 1498; 17 Oct. 1501–13 June 1503; 22 Oct. 1506–28 Nov. 1507; 23 Dec. 1507–13 Oct. 1509; 29 Sept. 1516–24 June 1517; 29 Sept. 1517–28 Sept. 1518; 4 Nov. 1520–3 Sept. 1522. WAM 33318, fos. 46ᵛ–114 and WAM 33321 represent different recensions of the account for the period 17 Oct. 1501–6 June 1503. The two derive from a lost original, the work of a scribe who believed that Oct. has 32 days. For further details, see Appendix II.

The kitchener also kept an account of bulk purchases: for an example, see WAM 33317.

For household accounts in the late Middle Ages, see J. M. Thurgood, 'Introduction' to *The Account of the Great Household of Humphrey, First Duke of Buckingham, for the year 1452–3*, ed. M. Harris, in *Camden Miscellany*, xxviii (Camden 4th ser. xxix, 1984), 2–5, and *Household Accounts from Medieval England*, ed. C. M. Woolgar, pt. i (Oxford, 1992), 18–65.

Item viij. messe of beffe xxd. Item viij messe of motton xvjd. Item pork to roste xvjd. Item motton to roste xijd. Item frowse flesches xvjd. Item motton to soper xijd. Item scheppys gadders iijd. Item brede ijd. Item eggs for frowse jC.iijᵃ quarteria xxijd. ob. Item eggs for leuerys iijC. iijs. iijd. Item a net tong jd. Item sawse for the K. vjd. Suma xiijs, vd. ob.[9]

We are to understand that on the day in question beef, boiled mutton, and roast pork and roast mutton were served at dinner in the misericord; and meat froise—a form of fritter—and umbles in the refectory. The ingredients of the umbles included sheeps' entrails and bread. At supper, mutton was served in the misericord, and neat's tongue with a sauce in the chamber normally known as the *cawagium* and here referred to as 'the K'. The entry relating to 'liveries' covers two uses for eggs: at dinner, monks eating in the refectory had an egg dish in addition to froise; and on this as on other meat days, some eggs, in lieu of cooked food, were distributed to the poor for the souls of deceased monks. Day-accounts in some other years mention the dish of pottage which was always served at dinner in the refectory.

Although the sources are exceptionally good for the period, much guess-work is nevertheless involved in their interpretation, and this element of conjecture is conspicuous in what I shall have to say about the quantities of food finding their way on to the monastic tables.

## 3. Benedictine Diet, Regular and Irregular

Although, by 1500, Benedictine diet was largely secularized, and, over much of the year, very similar to that eaten in genteel households outside the cloister, it still possessed some idiosyncrasies that were rooted in the past; and even when the monks of this period ate what any lay household of comparable income and geographical location might have eaten, their arrangements for dispatching it were a little strange, and for the same reason. First, therefore, I shall sketch in this institutional background.

The arrangement of meals in the Rule of St Benedict depends on the liturgical year, and especially on the so-called temporal cycle of feasts and fasts commemorating the life, death, and Resurrection of Christ. Two meals are provided for, though somewhat unequally.[10] Monks are to eat dinner every day of the year, but supper only from Easter to 13 September, and, after Pentecost, not on Wednesdays or Fridays. At dinner, each table in the refectory is to have two dishes, and a monk unable to partake of the food in the one can thus make his meal out of the other. Fresh vegetables and

---

[9] *Sic* MS: correctly, xiijs. ixd. ob. For this extract see WAM 33321, fo. 54; cf. WAM 33318, fo. 100, where the sums of money are different. For the rooms mentioned in the following explanation of the extract, see below, pp. 41–2.

[10] *Rule*, caps. xxxix–xli; and for comment, A. de Vogüé and J. Neufville, *La Règle de Saint Benoît* (7 vols., Paris, 1972–7), vi. 1125–1203; *MO* 456–65; *RO* i. 280–5.

fruit, if available, are to form a third dish. The daily ration of bread is normally to be a pound loaf—the Roman *libra* was equivalent to 11.5 oz. avoirdupois—and a third of it is to be saved for supper, if the day is a day for supper; and this is the only indication we receive of the food at the second meal. Flesh-meat is forbidden to all except the sick: to be precise, the flesh of quadrupeds is forbidden. Decisions about the daily allowance of wine, the beverage of sixth-century Monte Cassino—are left to the superior, and nothing is said about the occasions when it may be drunk. Above all, St Benedict was concerned with intangibles—with attitude and desire: his monks are to esteem moderation, avoid gluttony and excess, and endure a scarcity of wine, which seems to have been anticipated, without grumbling.

It is a truism to say that this regime, especially the lack of a second meal from mid-September to the end of Lent, between twenty-eight and thirty-two weeks later, was more easily supported in the Mediterranean world to which Monte Cassino belonged than in the colder climate of northern Europe. But more than a cold climate is needed to explain an elaboration of diet that became as conspicuous in southern Europe as in the north. A more potent influence was the cult of saints: this was allowed to disturb the primitive rhythm of feast and fast enshrined in the temporal cycle to an extent that St Benedict, despite his special provision for saints' days in his monks' office, could scarcely have foreseen.[11] When the long office was chanted for a saint, when copes were worn, and all the candles lit, some addition to the accustomed fare—an extra dish or an extra supper, or better still both—was only appropriate; and by the eleventh century it was a poor calendar that did not include more than one high-ranking saint's day every week. Nor could monastic life be uninfluenced by the rise in standards of living outside the cloister. Inevitably, even on ordinary days, St Benedict's two dishes at dinner became, not alternatives, but complementary to each other and to be served successively to everyone present; and, commonly, a third main dish was added.[12] As for flesh-meat, in the 1140s or 1150s Peter the Venerable himself testified to the consumption by Cluniac monks of every kind of quadruped and fowl reared for the table, and game beasts and birds as well, although he does not say in which rooms in the monastery they performed this feat.[13] At this date, few other monks may have been as uninhibited as the Cluniacs. Yet increasingly, for Benedictines in general, the question was becoming, not whether meat might be eaten, but where—at the abbot's table, or in a special room?—and by how many at a time? What was actually new in the twelfth century was the fundamentalism of the early

[11] *Rule*, cap. xiv; cf. ibid., cap. xi.
[12] *Lanfranc's Constitutions*, 75, implying a daily regime of three main dishes by the end of the 11th cent. See also above, pp. 10–11.
[13] *The Letters of Peter the Venerable*, ed. G. Constable (2 vols., Cambridge, Mass., 1967), i. 388–9.

Cistercians, later to be emulated by the curial reformers, in attempting to overthrow every irregular practice except the most ancient.

In the end, the Benedictines eased the problems of diet, and meat-eating in particular, as the Franciscans tried to ease the moral problems of property: by the use of fine distinctions. By the twelfth century, the consumption of fowl, two-legged creatures, had long been regarded as permissible in Benedictine houses: indeed, the practice may have been so regarded by St Benedict himself.[14] Twelfth-century monks applied their dialectical skills to the far more difficult problem of the flesh of quadrupeds. They distinguished between the muscle tissue of animals—'butcher's meat', as we should say—and the offal and entrails, which were not to be regarded as 'meat'; and between fresh meat cut from the joint, on the one hand, and salted, precooked, or chopped meat, on the other. A monk, they said, kept the Rule if all that he consumed was a pork fritter, for which the meat was precooked, or 'umbles'—sheeps' entrails cooked in ale and breadcrumbs—but he broke it if he ate fresh roast beef. These refinements were so well established by the end of the century that Jocelin of Brakelond could employ the distinction between flesh-meat (*carnes*) and meaty dishes (*carnea*) without pausing to explain his meaning.[15] Above all, the Benedictines learnt to distinguish between what went on in the refectory—the only room for eating known to St Benedict and therefore the only room mentioned in the Rule—and what went on elsewhere. Only regular food and meals, it was agreed, might be served in the refectory, but irregular food and meals—that is, what was not permitted by the Rule—might be served elsewhere, provided only that a proportion of the community stayed behind in the refectory to maintain a degree of observance there. It became usual to build a room, known as the misericord, to accommodate the irregular practices. Also useful was the distinction between a meal and the food consumed at it, for this opened the way, on supperless days, to the practice of adding to the food at dinner extra dishes representing what would have been consumed, on any other day, at the second meal.[16]

In 1336 Pope Benedict XII recognized and set bounds to these equivocal compromises. Benedict decreed that the proportion of monks eating in the refectory must never be less than half the total number in the community. Moreover, no monks at all were to eat irregular food on Wednesdays, Fridays, or Saturdays, or on any day during Advent—the four weeks preceding Christmas—or Lent; and he prescribed the long Lent of eight weeks,

[14] Vogüé and Neufville, *La Règle de Saint Benoît*, vi. 1140 and n.
[15] *Chronicle of Jocelin of Brakelond*, ed. Butler, 40; cf. *The Book of St Gilbert*, ed. Foreville and Keir, 62, and the complaint of Gerald of Wales that monks eat bacon yet claim that they abstain from flesh-meat (*Speculum ecclesie*, in *Giraldi Cambrensis Opera*, iv. 99).
[16] *Chapters of English Black Monks*, ii. 46 (recognizing, no doubt, a practice well established in some houses of the period).

beginning at Septuagesima.[17] Within a few years, these decrees were so widely accepted that the Provincial Chapter of the English Black Monks could refer to its own decrees in terms implying that they supplemented those of Benedict XII.[18] However, the Chapter had already mitigated Benedict's requirement that at least half the community eat in the refectory, by excluding from the reckoning the sick, office-holders detained elsewhere by business, and monks invited to the abbot's table: the half was to be half the number actually requiring the common meal on the day in question, and this was normally smaller, by a considerable margin, than the total number of monks in the community.[19]

## 4. Arrangements at Westminster Abbey

### (i) Rooms for eating

It will be clear that with two rooms a Benedictine community could evade many awkward restrictions on diet. With three, it could evade even more, and by the end of the Middle Ages the monks of Westminster were using three. The oldest of these was the refectory—a vast room, 130 ft. (40 m.) long and 37 ft. (11 m.) wide.[20] Unlike its counterpart at Durham and in many other monasteries, the refectory at Westminster had not become a white elephant but was still in daily use at meal-times. Its east end, however, was partitioned off, to make a two-storeyed chamber known as the *cawagium*, and the lower storey of this was used for meals. This chamber dated from the fourteenth century, and probably from the 1340s.[21] The misericord, the third room, was older: it was built in the mid-thirteenth century, in the very period when the controversies on diet in the Order as a whole were most bitterly pursued. The outer dates for the construction of this room are *c*.1230, when the infirmary is referred to as the alternative to the refectory for meals, and *c*.1270, when the Abbey's only surviving Customary was

---

[17] Wilkins, *Concilia*, ii. 609. The fast on Fridays is tacitly assumed.
[18] *Chapters of English Black Monks*, ii. 28, 230; cf. ibid. 46 and 86.      [19] Ibid. 11.
[20] *Royal Commission on Historical Monuments, London, i (Westminster Abbey)* (London, 1926), 84 and end plan, and for the location of the refectory, see Map II (above, p. xviii). The refectory had once been even longer. It was considerably altered *temp*. Nicholas de Litlyngton (1362–86) and in the early years of his successor, and unroofed soon after the Dissolution in 1540.
[21] For the first reference in 1375–6, see WAM 19504, and on the likelihood of an earlier date, below, p. 42. The prior existence of this chamber explains the failure to complete the sequence of windows inserted in the north wall in the late 14th cent. with a window at the east end for which there would otherwise have been room. For repairs in 1391–2 and rebuilding in 1408–9, see WAM 19508, 19523, and LNQ 146. By 1391–2 the chamber was of two storeys, of which the upper was used by the refectorer and his servants. Both storeys had windows, which were presumably on the south side (WAM 19508, 19513). (I am indebted to Mr John Field and Dr Richard Mortimer for help with the problems posed by the *cawagium*.)
For a reference to a so-called *cawagium* in the bakery in 1396–7, see WAM 19881.

finished: this refers explicitly to the misericord.[22] This room was at first-floor level and filled the space between the refectory and the kitchen, which was detached from the latter room. Food from the kitchen reached the misericord and the refectory via a passage under the former, and once, we are told, the behaviour of monk-servers navigating this passage, out of sight, as they thought, of the assembled diners, had not been *comme il faut*.[23] Whatever the behaviour of the servers, much of the food was no doubt rather cold when it reached the table.

Moving adroitly between these rooms, but remembering, when appropriate, that all must not move at once, the late medieval community managed to have supper as well as dinner on five or six days a week throughout the year, outside the fast seasons of Advent and Lent, and to eat meat on four days a week—Sundays, Mondays, Tuesdays, and Thursdays—outside these seasons.[24] On fasts, dinner was served in the refectory, and everyone ate fish. On meat days, it is probable, though not quite certain, that, to the end, the monks observed Benedict XII's constitution on the division of numbers between refectory and misericord, though with one or two convenient modifications. Accordingly, on these days, a rota assigned half the community to the refectory and half to the misericord.[25] Those eating in the misericord had flesh-meat; those eating in the refectory, offal or some other examples of the meaty dishes long deemed to be regular food. In summer, suppers were also served in these two rooms, and, again, flesh-meat was served in the misericord, but only regular food in the refectory. The real problem was where to seat everyone for supper in winter on days other than Sunday, when the meal was still deemed irregular and no one might eat it in the refectory. Yet, if Benedict's ruling meant anything, it meant that the misericord must never be used by the entire community at one and the same time. It was at this juncture that the *cawagium* was so useful: indeed, it had evidently been built with this very point in mind. This chamber, although in the refectory, was not of it. In winter, therefore, the rota assigned some monks to the misericord and others to the *cawagium*. Yet the situation of the *cawagium*, inside the refectory, could not be altogether ignored, and it was for this reason that the food at the irregular suppers eaten here was always, itself, regular: it included offal and meaty dishes but never flesh-meat.[26]

---

[22] WD 596; *Customary*, ii. 133–4. However, the sub-vault beneath the misericord has been dated *c*.1220–*c*.1245 (G. Black, 'Excavations in the sub-vault of the misericorde of Westminster Abbey, February to May 1975', *Trans. London and Middlesex Archaeological Soc.* xxvii (1976), 135–78, at 147, 154. The misericord was 46 ft. × 26.5 ft. (14 m. × 8 m.).

[23] *Customary*, ii. 133–4.

[24] By the late 15th cent., suppers were also eaten on Sundays in Advent and Lent and, in Advent, on Wednesdays as well. However, throughout the year 'supper' on Wednesday was actually a very light collation and not a full second meal.          [25] See Appendix II.

[26] For an illustration of this point, see WAM 33317, fos. 8–8ᵛ.

## (ii) Meals and the service of food

In the later Middle Ages, Benedictine monks found many occasions suitable for light, and not so light, refreshments: a party for family and friends after a First Mass, an obedientiary's party for his assistants, the sociable drink in the evening after Compline that had so stubbornly resisted attempts by the reformers two centuries earlier to dislodge it—the list was endless.[27] But an account of monastic diet properly focuses on dinner and supper, the formal meals.

On most days in the year in this period, dinner was probably served at 11 or 11.30 a.m. Most of the monks had been up and about for four to five hours, and some may have breakfasted on bread and ale; but they had not tasted cooked food since supper, a meal served in the late afternoon, on the previous day. This was a period of seventeen to eighteen hours, and on a considerable number of days in the year the interval was longer.[28]

The first dish at dinner in the refectory was pottage, made with oatmeal and containing vegetables or pieces of meat or fish, according to the day and season.[29] However, on most days in the year the meal in this room was constructed around three main dishes, to which the pottage was merely the preliminary. Two of these descended from the daily dishes mentioned in the Rule. Formerly these were known as 'generals', but now, if a name was used, as 'services'. The third, known as the Oakham pittance because it was paid for out of the monastery's income from the church of Oakham, represented a later addition to this basic fare.[30] The contents of these dishes were the same for every monk eating in the refectory. In the misericord, by 1500, a daily dish of beef seems to have edged pottage off the menu, and the beef was followed, every day, by two or three further dishes of boiled or roast meat. These, too, were the same for every monk. But, in each room, dinner often included extra pittances, and, in the case of these, neighbours at the same table might find that they were eating different foods. The number and quality of the pittances varied according to the liturgical status of the day. On a major feast day or anniversary, of which there were sixty

---

[27] For some of the occasions at Westminster, see *Monks*, 21–5; for an obedientiary's recreation for his assistants here, WAM 19700 ff.; and for the resilient drink after Compline, *RO* i. 283.

[28] For the monastic timetable, see below, pp. 154–9.

[29] The following account of dinner and supper at Westminster *c.*1500 has been pieced together mainly from the kitchener's accounts, for which see n. 8 above, the pittancer's (WAM 33336–51), and the treasurer's (WAM 19987–99, 23001–29), but the accounts of some other obedientiaries providing occasional pittances have also been used. For food served in the abbot's household at this date see WAM 33320, 33324, and for that served in the prior's household, WAM 33325. Though compiled much earlier, *Customary*, ii is still useful; see especially ibid. 98–135.

[30] WD 596; *Customary*, ii. 75–6. Oakham church was appropriated in 1231. The pittance, however, was probably a much older addition to refectory fare. It was not served on a small number of days in the year when other pittances were numerous.

or seventy in the course of the year, the pittances cost far more than the basic dishes and included foods that an ordinary monk would rarely see at other times, unless invited to dine with the abbot or the prior in his private apartments: small birds, expensive freshwater fish, especially pike, and game. On such a day, the average monk may scarcely have done more than peck at his 'services'. The meal ended with cheese. In the course of it, a monk would probably have dispatched a considerable part of his daily loaf, as also of his allowance of drink: the beverage of the day was normally ale, but wine was served on about a hundred feast days and anniversaries each year.

Supper was a light meal, at which the monks probably made do with a single cooked dish or at most two, followed on occasion by cheese and washed down by the remaining part of the ample daily allowance of ale. We can assume, too, that some of the daily loaf was still saved, as in St Benedict's day, for this meal.

Food was brought to the table in portions called messes.[31] A large mess contained food for four monks; a small mess, food for one or, less frequently, two. Large messes were characteristic of meat days, when both the misericord and the refectory were open. Small messes, considered suitable for many dishes of fish, were characteristic of fasts, when the misericord was closed, and quite frequently the entire number of these was served in the refectory. And even when fish were not brought to the table in individual messes, it often suited the cook to reckon quantities in this way in the kitchen. But how many messes of each kind were needed at any one meal? On this crucial point the evidence is sometimes circumstantial, sometimes explicit, but always, when explicit, less abundant than we could wish. Nevertheless, in sum the evidence suggests quite clearly that the kitchener worked to norms which scarcely varied from year to year. At dinner, he normally provided thirteen large messes—eight in the misericord and five in the refectory—or fifty-two individual ones. If, however, these numbers were in normal use, the actual number of messes served at dinner was often a little larger or smaller; and for major festivals the norm itself was probably different from that considered appropriate for ordinary days.

At supper, the actual number of messes may have fluctuated more than at dinner. But on an average day the kitchener probably provided ten large messes or forty individual ones at this meal.

These figures may seem small, given a community which in principle numbered forty-eight monks. At most times of the year, however, there were absentees—monks studying at Oxford, travelling on business for the community, or engaged on one or other of the employments that were so often considered legitimate reasons for absence from a Benedictine house in

---

[31] The subject-matter of this paragraph and the next two is discussed in detail in Appendix II.

the late Middle Ages; and on most days in the year some monks could be relied upon to absent themselves from the common meals. In fact, the kitchener probably intended five of the eight large messes and about forty of the fifty-two individual messes at dinner for the monks themselves and the rest for seculars—for such officials, servants, and guests as were entitled to eat what the monks ate. And if this allowance for seculars itself seems small, we must remember that few of the people in question, if any, would have been entitled to quite as much food as was set before a monk: the twelve extra messes for seculars were enough to feed more than twelve people. Very few seculars were entitled to supper, and this explains why the number of messes provided at this meal was smaller than at dinner.

In a large secular household of the period, and almost certainly in the secularized household of the abbot of Westminster, the dishes at a meal, however numerous, would probably have been put together to form two or three so-called courses. At the conventual meals, they may have been served one or two at a time, as probably happened in an earlier period—an arrangement enabling a small number of servers to keep all the tables supplied with food and yet avoid very ragged timing.[32] In addition to cups for the ale or wine, three different kinds of vessel, commonly described as plate, dish, and saucer, were used by each monk.[33] The saucer was for custards and runny dishes, and the dish for pottage. The plate may have been used as a receptacle for the leftovers at each stage of the meal. But it is also possible that it was used as we use a plate, as a receptacle for food to be consumed at the meal, and on the whole the evidence points to this conclusion. Certainly there are few or no references in our sources to bread trenchers. Plate, dish, and saucer were made of pewter. Meals began and ended with a Grace, the timing of which was determined at the top table. Both in the refectory and in the misericord, a reading took place while they were in progress. This practice may seem to imply that the pace was leisurely. Yet, as with most formal meals where considerable numbers eat together, the system was hard on slow eaters sitting at the bottom tables where the service was apt to be slow.

Every meal should have proceeded in a silence broken only by the voice of the reader, and perhaps this often happened. But the silence could not avert, though it might delay, critical comment when this seemed necessary.

[32] *Customary*, ii. 107, 116, 126, etc., but the evidence is not entirely clear. In Abbot Nicholas de Litlyngton's household in 1371–2, the meal was arranged in two courses, except on Fridays, when only one was served (PRO SC6/1261/6).

[33] For plates, potagers, and saucers, see e.g. WAM 6597; for dishes and saucers, WAM 6647; for plates, dishes, and saucers, WAM 9480. However, the several terms are not used in consistent senses. For the purchase of 50 sets of plates, dishes, and saucers for Abbot Wenlok's household in 1287, see WAM 24490. The so-called 'garnish' of vessels purchased from time to time by the convent of Westminster is to be understood as a dozen sets of plates, dishes, and saucers, with possibly a charger and salt-cellar or two added (WAM 19985, 23003, 23005, etc.).

'Rebukyd therfor', wrote the kitchener in his account on a day in 1521, against an entry recording a 'service' of sprats.[34] Brother Thomas Gardyner, the kitchener in question, had studied at Cambridge as well as Oxford and was a man of some little distinction, as distinction was measured in the monastery at this time. But nothing could save a kitchener if something was wrong with the sprats at dinner. In fact, every detail of a monastic meal was, and always had been, a topic of absorbing interest to the participants. Should the mess contain four herrings or five? Was it right to divide the haddock into two or into three? How long should the pike be from tip to tail? To St Benedict's later disciples, questions like these were the stuff of chapter decisions, no less.[35] What kind of diet was it that provoked such interest? The main components were fish or meat, depending on the day, and cereal foods, and these will now be considered in detail.

## (iii) The diet

### (a) Fish[36]

In the monastery, fish was considered to be a food for dinner rather than supper. Indeed, of all the varieties, only cockles and mussels, which are molluscs, were served at the latter meal—mussels, typically, at the suppers which the monks now consumed on Sundays in Advent and Lent; cockles, in the late spring, when the Lenten fast was over, and then infrequently.[37] At dinner, however, a monk normally ate fish on c.215 days in the year. On Fridays, there were in fact only two main dishes; on other fish days at least three. In an average year, c.570 dishes of this food had to be found for the convent's dinners, and in nearly every case portions for about fifty persons were needed. The total quantity involved was very large: on a rough estimate, c.210 cwt. (10,800 kg.) of edible fish found its way on to the tables, and the dead-weight involved—the weight of the fish on the slab or in the barrel, before preparation for the table—was considerably greater. Moreover, these figures relate to the main dishes provided by the kitchener and exclude the extra pittances which were occasionally provided by other obedientiaries: the quantities are the bare minimum involved.

Of the 570 dishes of fish served by the kitchener in the course of a normal

---

[34] WAM 33330, fo. 4ᵛ. For Thomas Gardyner, the kitchener, see *Monks*, 175, and *BRUO* ii. 743. His offence may have been to disregard a convention that sprats were served as pittances but not as main dishes.

[35] *Customary*, ii. 76, where, almost certainly, the detailed and formal directions about the allowances per mess of fish represent decisions in Chapter. For the pike 22 inches long prescribed for the feast of Relics at the Abbey of Bury St Edmunds in the early 13th cent., *de iure antiquo*, see *Customary of Bury St Edmunds*, 54–5.

[36] Dr Helen Clarke, Dr C. K. Currie, Miss Jane Hands, and Dr Alwyne Wheeler have been kind enough to answer questions which I addressed to them on fish, fishing, and fish remains. I am extremely grateful to them for doing so, but emphasize that none is to be identified with any suggestions or conclusions in the following account.

[37] In some years, mussels were also served at supper on Wednesday in Oct. and Nov.

year, *c.*50 per cent consisted of preserved fish—that is, of fish that had been salted, smoked, dried, or pickled in brine—and *c.*50 per cent of the fresh varieties. Only a small proportion of the fresh fish came from stew-pond or river: nearly the whole was sea-fish. By the end of the Middle Ages, this pattern of consumption seems to have been typical of great households.[38] Yet at Westminster it also reflects the monastery's proximity to the highly developed fish market of London: the Abbey's kitchener, ferried by the boatman whom he employed, probably went shopping here two or three times a week—if not daily, as, to our knowledge, had been expected of his predecessors in office in the thirteenth and fourteenth centuries.[39] A reference in 1491–2 to the purchase of fish 'of a Skerborowe man in the schype' shows that the kitchener or his assistants sometimes pursued their search for the best sea-fish as far as the quayside.[40] Nevertheless, dace and small roach, which are freshwater fish, were served frequently in the monastic refectory in winter, and pike, an expensive kind of freshwater fish, was a festal dish: with its cinnamon and ginger sauce, pike was as much a part of a major feast day at the Abbey as the ringing of bells and the wearing of copes at the High Mass.[41] Moreover, the fresh salmon eaten on feast days probably came from the River Thames, where the monks had a claim to a tithe of all such fish caught between Staines and Gravesend.[42]

In the diet of a large household, crustacea—as, for example, shrimps and crab—and molluscs could never be more than makeweights. The kitchener at Westminster served shrimps at dinner on about fifteen days in the year, and he never served molluscs at this meal. For the main dishes day by day at dinner, the choice lay between white fish and fatty fish, and more depended on it than can have been realized at the time, for the latter are richer in Vitamin A and Vitamin D than the former. Far more often than not, the kitchener chose white fish. In an average year, the latter probably provided *c.*85 per cent of the total weight of fish served in main dishes at dinner and supper (see Table II.2) and *c.*75 per cent of the total served in all dishes. The difference between these two estimates is explained by the fact that salmon

---

[38] C. Dyer, 'The consumption of fresh-water fish in medieval England', in M. Aston (ed.), *Medieval Fish, Fisheries and Fishponds in England* (BAR British Series, 182 (1988) ), i. 27–35; C. K. Currie, 'Medieval fishponds in Hampshire', ibid. ii. 275. The latest reference to Westminster Abbey's fishpond, which was in the infirmary garden, occurs in 1397–8 (WAM 19386). However, the pond may have continued in use until the end of the Middle Ages. The minor role of fresh-water fish in the monastic economy, even in houses with a considerable extent of ponds, is well illustrated in J. Bond, 'The fishponds of Eynsham Abbey', *The Eynsham Record*, 9 (1992), 3–17.

[39] For the kitchener's boat and boatman in 1491–2, see WAM 33317, fos. 11, 11ᵛ; for daily shopping expeditions on the part of the kitchener or the master cook at the beginning of the 14th cent., WD 94, and for a hint of a similar practice *c.*1270, *Customary*, ii. 76.

[40] WAM 33317, fo. 3.

[41] For pike on feast days, see WAM 33318, fo. 2ᵛ, WAM 33323, fo. 3ᵛ, WAM 33340, 33351.

[42] *Flete*, 64–8; and for fresh salmon on solemn days, see WAM 33323, fos. 44, 54. But the actual consumption of salmon is recorded only if the fish was purchased.

TABLE II.2. Estimated Weight Per Annum of Fish served in the Refectory at West-minster Abbey, *c.*1495–*c.*1525[a]

| Fish | Weight | | Weight as % of total |
| --- | --- | --- | --- |
| | lb. | g. | |
| A. White fish | | | |
| Cod family | | | |
|    cod[b] | 228 | 103,512 | 1.0 |
|    green fish[c] | 1,156 | 524,824 | 5.0 |
|    haburdens & ling | 7,382 | 3,351,428 | 31.0 |
|    stockfish | 2,809 | 1,275,286 | 12.0 |
| *Total, cod family* | *11,575* | *5,255,050* | *49.0* |
| Dace & rochet/roach | 1,602 | 727,308 | 7.0 |
| Pike | 144 | 65,376 | 0.5 |
| Plaice | 1,005 | 456,270 | 4.0 |
| Whiting | 5,548 | 2,518,792 | 23.0 |
| Other varieties | 205 | 93,070 | 1.0 |
| *Total, white fish* | *20,079* | *9,115,866* | *84.5* |
| B. Fatty fish | | | |
| Eel | 1,082 | 491,228 | 4.5 |
| Herring | 1,867 | 847,618 | 8.0 |
| Mackerel | 243 | 110,322 | 1.0 |
| Other varieties | 466 | 211,564 | 2.0 |
| *Total, fatty fish* | *3,658* | *1,660,732* | *15.5* |
| C. Total, all fish | 23,737 | 10,776,598 | 100.0 |

*Notes*: [a] The estimates are of the weight of edible fish in main dishes, but excluding crustacea and molluscs. The former were served in such dishes on *c.*15 occasions in an average year; the latter were served at supper on *c.*25 occasions and were the only fish served at that meal. In an average year, *c.*570 main dishes of fish were served at dinner, and this number was made up as follows: *white fish* cod 6, green fish 28.5, haburdens and ling 182, stockfish 74, dace and rochet, or roach, 40, pike 6, plaice 46, whiting 97, other varieties 5; *fatty fish* eel 40, herring 28.5, mackerel 6, other varieties (mainly salmon and sprats) 11. It is assumed that the kitchener normally provided 52 messes of each dish and that mess-weights were as given in Appendix II, where further information about fish dishes will also be found.

[b] The kitchener seems to have reserved the actual name 'cod' for fresh cod.

[c] 'green fish' were fish pickled in brine.

and conger eel, both fatty fish, were favourite choices for the pittances which special funds provided on special days. At this date, the cod family dominated much of the market in white fish, and, accordingly, in the mo-nastic refectory cod was king: in various forms, but principally as so-called ling and haburdens, it made up nearly half the total quantity of fish served in the course of a year. After cod, whiting, which was served frequently, especially in winter, and in messes which were large even by refectory standards, was the most important fish in the monks' diet. Plaice, however, was quite a frequent dish from April to October.

In all these respects, the kitchener was not giving the monks what he considered to be good for them, or even what it was easiest for him to provide. He was responding to their likes and dislikes, and especially to their low regard for the herring—the commonest form of fatty fish, and, for its cheapness and the ease with which it could be stored salted in barrels, a natural favourite with all kitcheners. Two centuries earlier, herring had probably been eaten much more frequently in the refectory at Westminster. At the end of the Middle Ages, it was a frequent dish only in Lent, and again in the autumn, when fresh herring were easily obtained in the London markets.[43] Salt eels were found tolerable in Lent but not often at other times. Conger eel, however, was a delicacy, and, with a vinegar dressing, as likely as pike or salmon to appear on the table on major feast days.[44]

If the monks of Westminster had minds of their own about fish, the variety which they now enjoyed was not extravagant by contemporary standards. Their consumption *c.*1500 can be compared with that of the monks of St Swithun's Priory, Winchester, in the same period. The monks of Westminster had the more varied diet on fish days, but their advantage in this respect was small in comparison to the great disparity of wealth between the two houses, the Abbey having an income almost twice that possessed by the Priory.[45] A comparison of the dishes served in the refectory at Westminster on fish days with those served at the abbot of Westminster's table confirms the impression that the monks were not extravagant. Turbot, gurnard, thornback ray, and sole were all served quite frequently at the abbot's table.[46] If, however, the monks ate these fish at their own table, it was normally as pittances, not as items in the kitchener's repertoire of ordinary dishes. Conger eel, a treat at the monks' table, was quite a common dish at his; and at his table the salmon was normally fresh and the dishes containing it frequent; but at theirs fresh salmon was, like conger eel, a treat.

[43] Cf. the implied welcome for fresh herring at Bury St Edmunds in the 13th cent. (*Customary of Bury St Edmunds*, 39). For herring at Westminster Abbey earlier, see WAM 33333, the kitchener's day-account for 21–9 Jan. 1335, recording the service of herring on 3 of 4 fasts occurring in that period: *c.*1500, herring were rarely eaten by the monks of Westminster in Jan. See also A. Saul, 'The herring industry at Great Yarmouth, *c.*1280–*c.*1400', *Norfolk Archaeology*, xxxviii (1981–3), 33–43, at 36–7.

[44] For salt eels two or three times a week in Lent 1502, see WAM 33318, fos. 60–4. For conger eel on feast days and vigils, see WAM 33318, fo. 114, WAM 33323, fo. 22ᵛ, WAM 33340, 33347. The relatively cheap 'conger eels' served at dinner on some ordinary days in the early summer were probably river, not marine, species.

Stewed eel was served occasionally on feasts and on solemn vigils such as Christmas Eve.

[45] C. J. Bond, 'Monastic fisheries', in Aston (ed.), *Medieval Fish, Fisheries and Fishponds in England*, i. 69–112, at 74–5. The net income of St Swithun's in 1535 was £1,507 p.a.; the comparable figure for Westminster Abbey is £2,827 p.a. (*RO* iii. 473; Harvey, *Estates*, 63).

[46] WAM 33320, 33324 (the day-accounts of Abbot John Islip's household for, respectively, 27 Oct. 1500–19 May 1502 and 29 Sept. 1509–28 Sept. 1510).

Some varieties of fish were served in individual messes, some in messes for two or four. Whatever the arrangement, the exact quantity per mess is rarely recorded. Yet in the case of the main varieties of fish, we can make an informed guess at the portions that were normally in the cook's mind when he dished up.[47] Thus one-sixth of a ling or cod made an individual portion in a main dish, and so did one roach, or one to three whiting—depending, presumably, on size—or four to five herring. If pike was served as a pittance, each monk could normally expect to receive a quarter of a fish. Moreover, the evidence suggests that fishmongers were able to supply the monastery with some varieties of fish in standardized sizes, for this is probably how we should interpret the kitchener's references to 'large cod' and 'small cod', and 'large plaice' and 'small plaice'. Large plaice, it appears, were used for pittances; if so, we can probably assume that 'small plaice' were used for the ordinary courses, the services.[48]

What was the average weight of the fish in question at the time? Medieval fishing, being less intensive than modern forms of the art, may have allowed fish to attain a larger average size before they were taken than is the case today.[49] The analysis of fish-bone evidence from medieval sites which have been excavated is beginning to provide historians interested in diet with some norms, and, wherever possible, I have used this evidence. In some other cases, an estimate has been based on equivalents which seem to have been in the kitchener's own mind. For example, it seems clear that he equated one average ling with one and a half average stockfish. Much of the so-called 'ling' of this period was probably a superior kind of preserved cod, and for cod, fish-bone evidence suggests a norm. Thus the equation enables us to estimate the weight of one of the kitchener's average stockfish.[50] In these and other ways it has been possible to estimate, however imperfectly, the average weight of the varieties of fish most commonly eaten in the refectory at Westminster, and so to arrive at an estimate of the weight of the messes served there on fish days. In the case of the common eel, the kitchener

---

[47] For details relating to mess weights of fish, see Appendix II.

[48] For large cod in 1521–2, see WAM 33330, fo. 5ᵛ; and for small cod, ibid., fo. 14ᵛ. Both large and small cod were used for pittances. For large plaice for pittances in 1508–9, see WAM 33323, fos. 22ᵛ, 23ᵛ, 58ᵛ, 59ᵛ; and for small gurnard in a service course and large gurnard in pittances, WAM 33322, fos. 8–8ᵛ. Cf. a perceived tendency in the weight of fish represented by fish skeletons from late medieval sites to cluster about certain sizes (A. Wheeler and A. Jones, 'Fish remains', in A. Rogerson, 'Excavations on Fuller's Hill, Great Yarmouth', *East Anglian Archaeology, Report no. 2: Norfolk* (Norfolk Archaeological Unit, 1976), 208–26, at 216–17; A. Wheeler, 'Fish bone', in H. Clarke and A. Carter, *Excavations in King's Lynn, 1963–1970* (Soc. for Medieval Archaeology, Monograph Ser., no. vii, 1977), 407–8). Were Havelok's 'playces brode' (*Havelok*, line 897) a random sample or sorted fish?

[49] For useful short accounts, see Wheeler and Jones, 'Fish remains', 220–2, and R. Nicholson, 'The fish remains', in C. O'Brien *et al.*, *The Origins of the Newcastle Quayside* (Soc. Antiquaries of Newcastle-upon-Tyne, Monographs Ser. iii, 1988), 138–49, at 141–2.

[50] Stockfish itself was normally dried cod, but the name was also applied to a variety of cheap, preserved fish (Bond, 'Monastic fisheries', 73).

himself provides a very useful clue to the weight of a mess, for his accounts show that he required 40 to 48 lbs. of fish for a dish of stewed eel, and 20 to 24 lbs. for a dish of baked eel.[51] He probably obtained his norm of fifty-two messes, and sometimes more, from these quantities.

Mess weights varied with the fish: a mess of plaice or eel for one monk probably contained *c*.0.5 lb. (227 g.) of edible fish; a mess of cod in its various forms, *c*.0.75 lb. (341 g.); and a mess of herring or whiting, 1 to 1.25 lbs. (454 to 568 g.). At dinner when three main dishes of fish were served, the total per capita allowance was probably *c*.2 lbs. (908 g.); when only two were served, it was in the range 1.25 to 1.5 lbs., depending on the varieties of fish—say 1.33 lbs. (604 g.).

## (b) Meat

Following the common practice of monks, the community at Westminster consumed meat under two forms and in two rooms: flesh-meat in the misericord, the room specially built for this irregular purpose, and meaty dishes in the refectory. Meaty dishes were served in the refectory on *c*.150 days in the year; flesh-meat in the misericord on about the same number. Birds were served in each room, but more often in the misericord than the refectory. I shall describe mainly the diet of flesh-meat enjoyed by monks who were on the rota for the misericord, this being more comparable than the other to the diet enjoyed on meat days at the top table in a large secular household of the period. In principle, the rota in use permitted the individual monk to eat in the misericord on one day in every two when it was in use. Thus he could expect to eat flesh-meat on *c*.75 days in the course of the year; and since meat, unlike fish, was normally served at supper as well as dinner, he could expect to eat it twice on most of these days.

At least four dishes of flesh-meat were served at dinner, with another to follow at supper, and, invariably, one of the four consisted of beef; as we have seen, for those on the rota for the misericord, a dish of beef replaced the pottage served at the beginning of every dinner in the refectory. The meat may have been stewed—a method of cooking which, in this period, sometimes involved part-roasting first[52]—but the sources shed no light on this point. One of the dishes that followed consisted of boiled meat, the other two of roast—as, for example, veal and mutton, or pork and goose. In the winter, the boiled meat was either pork or mutton. But the monks never tasted boiled pork in summer: that is to say, they never tasted it between Easter, when the consumption of other meats was resumed after

---

[51] Stub eel for stewing and shaft eel for baking (e.g. WAM 33323, fos. 7ᵛ, 8ᵛ, 14, WAM 33328, fos. 9, 9ᵛ). Baked eel was served frequently in Lent.

[52] *Two Fifteenth-Century Cookery Books*, ed. T. Austin (EETS Original Ser. xlii, 1888), 72. Much of the beef used in the abbot's household was 'powdered' (i.e. cooked with spices) (WAM 33320, 33324).

the Lenten fast, and mid-September, when the winter regime began again in the refectory and misericord. In this season, therefore, it was boiled mutton every day. Some other seasonal changes can also be identified. Lamb was mainly a dish for the late spring and early summer; veal was eaten on occasion throughout the year, outside the fast seasons, but frequently from April to August. Over the year as a whole, a dozen different meats, including poultry, were served in the main dishes at dinner and supper, and the special pittances served on feast days brought in more, including venison, game birds such as teal and snipe, and swan or cygnet.[53] Yet there was always a strong probability that a monk eating in the misericord would be given mutton once, if not twice, at dinner, and be asked to eat this meat again at supper.

In the course of a year, the kitchener provided *c.*600 dishes of flesh-meat at dinner and a further 150 at supper, and he needed 136 cwt. (6,924 kg.) of edible meat for these dishes. On a rough estimate, *c.*1500, mutton accounted for 46 per cent of the total weight of flesh-meat served in the main dishes each year, beef for 24 per cent, pork for 14 per cent, and veal for 11.5 per cent. (See Table II.3.) It will be clear that no other meat reached double figures.

If any proof is needed that Benedictine monks belonged to upper-class society, it is found in these proportions. Lower down the social scale, the quantity of beef consumed at this date would almost certainly have exceeded the quantity of mutton.[54] It is scarcely necessary to add that only an upper-class household could have afforded the sheer quantity of meat placed before the monks.

Some of this meat came from the Abbey's own pig farm. This was situated near the monastery, and the pigs reared there were fed partly on bran from the Abbey's mill.[55] Some of the meat may have been supplied, by agreement, by the lessees who now farmed the monastery's demesnes in the Home Counties: to our knowledge, the abbot of Westminster obtained livestock in this way.[56] But the absence of a slaughterman from the monastery's pay-roll at this time, and the lack, as it appears, of any regular facilities for slaughtering beasts, suggest that the monastery now obtained most of its meat as dead-stock. It came, in fact, from local butchers, of whom a great many existed in the late medieval town of Westminster.[57] The butchers

[53] WAM 33297, fos. 4ᵛ, 7ᵛ, WAM 33336, 33341, 33343–4. References to the expenses of taking cygnets in the Thames occur from the 1440s (WAM 18594, 23077 ff.). On occasion, however, cygnets were purchased and fattened on oats.

[54] Cf. Dyer, *Standards of Living*, 59–60 (where a greater importance in aristocratic diet in general is suggested for beef), and ibid. 156.

[55] For the sale of surplus bran by John Clerk, the Abbey's pig-keeper, 1529–35, see WAM 30274. The location of the pig-farm is not known.

[56] For a late example, in 1536, see WAM 30970.

[57] Rosser, *Medieval Westminster*, 138–41, 241–3.

TABLE II.3. Estimated Weight Per Annum of Meats Served in the Misericord at Westminster Abbey, *c.*1495–*c.*1525[a]

| Meat | Weight | | Weight as % of total |
|------|--------|--------|----------------------|
| | lb. | g. | |
| Beef | 3,600 | 1,634,400 | 24.0 |
| Veal | 1,748 | 793,592 | 11.5 |
| Mutton | 7,005 | 3,180,270 | 46.0 |
| Lamb | 172 | 78,088 | 1.0 |
| Pork[b] | 2,117 | 961,118 | 14.0 |
| Poultry | | | |
| chicken & hen[c] | 115 | 52,210 | |
| duck | 42 | 19,068 | |
| goose | 88 | 39,952 | |
| pigeon[d] | 5 | 2,270 | |
| *Total poultry* | *250* | *113,500* | *1.5* |
| Game | | | |
| cony | 329 | 149,366 | 2.0 |
| Total, all meats | 15,221 | 6,910,334 | 100.0 |

*Notes*: [a] The estimates are of the edible flesh-meat served in main dishes at dinner and supper. In an average year *c.*600 main dishes were served at dinner and *c.*150 at supper, and the numbers were made up as follows: *at dinner* beef 150, veal 88, mutton 229, lamb 13, pork 84 (25 boiled and 59 roast), hen or duck 1, goose 10, cony 25; *at supper* veal 8, mutton 104 (91 alone, 13 with chicken or pigeon), lamb 10, pork 8 (roast), chicken (with mutton) 12, hen 4, duck 3, pigeon (with mutton) 1, cony 13. However, the average conceals considerable variation from year to year in the choice of meats at supper, within the range shown in the table.

It is assumed that the kitchener provided eight large messes of each dish, each for four monks, at dinner, and five such messes of the sole dish at supper, and that mess weights were as given in Appendix II.

[b] Excluding bacon: this meat was normally served in the refectory.

[c] The kitchener's accounts always distinguish between these two. Chicken was rarely, if ever, served at dinner, and at supper it was served with mutton as an accompaniment. Hen was served on its own at both meals, but normally at supper.

[d] The kitchener could obtain pigeon from the Abbey dovecot without payment, and consequently the service of this meat may be under-recorded in his accounts. However, its poor showing among main dishes may be explained by the fact that it was typically a meat for pittances.

supplied joints as well as whole carcasses, thus making it possible for the entire company present at a meal to eat identical joints—as, for example, shoulders of mutton at supper.[58] Nearly all the meat was fresh. Bacon, it is true, had a place in the monastic diet, but probably in the refectory, not the misericord. In the former room, the service of bacon collops—better known to us as bacon and eggs—shortly before Ash Wednesday each year was evidently intended as a last treat before the beginning of the Lenten fast.[59]

Catering practice in the monastery betrays the existence of firmly established views on the suitability of particular joints for particular purposes. Chine of pork, for example, was for boiling, loin of mutton for roasting; and shoulder of mutton, though considered appropriate for supper, is never mentioned at dinner. On occasion in May and June, a monk could expect to eat green goose at dinner, and in October and November he would sometimes have fat goose.[60] Chicken and hen were typically dishes for supper, although the former was not served on its own at this meal, but always with mutton.[61] Methods of cooking, too, were sometimes varied according to the meal. Roast veal, for example, was considered appropriate for dinner, but the veal for many a dish at supper was 'boiled' or 'stewed'.[62]

In the case of meat, as in that of fish, the kitchener and cook made use, when catering, of standardized quantities.[63] Thus half a loin of mutton made a mess for four, and so did a quarter of a loin of pork, a quarter of a fat goose, a whole green goose, one small cony, or half a large one. Two mutton carcasses provided both the roast and the boiled dishes of that meat at dinner for the entire company of thirty-two catered for in the misericord. Moreover, some of the joints mentioned in our sources bore a notional ratio, which was constant from year to year, to the whole carcass of the animal in question, and equivalences existed between joints taken from animals slaughtered at different ages. Thus one loin of mutton was equated with one quarter of a dressed carcass, and one loin of pork—that is, a loin of the mature animal—was equated with one fat pig—that is, with one whole young pig. Of course, the kitchener must occasionally have used more or less of the carcass in question than these norms imply, and he sometimes entered different quantities in his account: we are simply to understand that, taking one day with another, these were the quantities he used.

How much meat did these conventions provide for the individual monk

---

[58] WAM 33323, fo. 42ᵛ, WAM 33327, fos. 8, 15ᵛ, WAM 33330, fos. 4, 12.

[59] WAM 33323, fos. 11, 49ᵛ, 50, WAM 33329, fo. 13, and WAM 33330, fos. 11ᵛ, 12. The dish was probably served at supper in the *cawagium*. If, however, as seems likely, the Abbey cured its own bacon, the consumption of this meat may be under-recorded in our sources.

[60] For green geese and, by implication, fat geese, see WAM 33318, fos. 50ᵛ, 51ᵛ, 71, 72ᵛ, etc., WAM 33330, fos. 1ᵛ, 3ᵛ, 21, 22ᵛ.

[61] e.g. WAM 33318, fos. 2, 2ᵛ, 3ᵛ, etc. Pigeon and mutton made another dish for supper.

[62] e.g. WAM 33322, fos. 20ᵛ, 20*, 20*ᵛ, WAM 33330, fos. 16, 16ᵛ, 17.

[63] For further details about the mess-weights considered in this and the next two paragraphs, see Appendix II.

of Westminster on an average day? At this point it is necessary to make highly questionable assumptions about the age at which animals were slaughtered, the weight of carcasses, the percentage of edible substance per carcass, and so on. Meat was normally served in messes for four monks. Very tentatively, I estimate that a mess of beef for four contained *c*.3 lbs. (1,362 g.) of edible meat, a mess of mutton about the same, and a mess of roast pork a little more. But a mess of boiled pork weighed only 2.5 lbs. (1,135 g.). To eat the flesh of young animals, the monks were prepared to sacrifice mere quantity, and in the case of lamb, for instance, a mess for four may have weighed only a little over 1 lb. (454 g.).

So much for messes for four. The daily per capita allowance at dinner in the misericord at Westminster was probably 2.25 lbs. to 3 lbs. of edible meat (1,022 g. to 1,362 g.), depending on the varieties served on the day in question. When flesh-meat was also served at supper—and this was the normal practice on such days—the range was probably 2.5 lbs. to 3.5 lbs. (1,135 g. to 1,589 g.)—say 3 lbs. (1,362 g.). However, it is necessary to take into account the rota, which made it impossible for the individual monk to enjoy flesh-meat on every meat day, but obliged him, every other such day, to resort to the refectory, there to eat dishes in which meat was merely one ingredient among several. Even in the refectory he could hope for an allowance that appears generous by present-day standards, for on a rough estimate the per capita allowance of meat and offal at dinner in this room was 0.75 lbs. (341 g.), and on some days a little extra followed at supper.[64] Yet this was little enough compared to the allowance in the misericord. With this circumstance taken into account, the average allowance on a meat day in a normal week drops to a little under 2 lbs. (908 g.)

The daily allowances of meat at Westminster Abbey were probably not unusual for the English aristocracy or gentry of the period—indeed, an average of not more than 2 lbs. may have been rather modest by late medieval and sixteenth-century standards.[65] Even so, they are impressive testimony to that love of meat for which Englishmen have been famous over so much of their history. In the household of the archbishop of Arles in the early fifteenth century, the average per capita allowance was *c*.215 g. (less than 0.5 lb.) of edible meat.[66] In such a household, the average would always have been much lower than the actual allowance at the high table, the only

---

[64] An estimate based mainly on the kitchener's outlay on meats for this room. The two meatiest dishes served here were froise, made with pork or veal, and mortress, made with pork. For the puddings, offal, and 'sauce' served at suppers in the *cawagium* in the winter of 1491–2 see WAM 33317, fos. 8–8ᵛ.

[65] See L. Stone, *The Crisis of the Aristocracy, 1558–1641* (Oxford, 1965), 558, where per capita meat consumption in a 16th-cent. aristocratic household is estimated at *c*.8.5 lbs. (3,859 g.) per week—*c*.6% higher than the weekly consumption implied for the monks of Westminster by the figures given in the text.

[66] i.e. *c*.310 g. including bones (Stouff, *Ravitaillement et alimentation en Provence*, 228). For a suggested deduction of 30% for bones, see ibid. 236.

figure that can usefully be compared to the allowances for monks. Yet it is unlikely that as much meat was set before the archbishop and those eating at his table as would be allowed to the monks of Westminster a century later. Moreover, the figures at Westminster at the end of the Middle Ages compare well—if that is the appropriate word—with the figures for Gregory King's Englishmen at the end of the seventeenth century. King estimated that the lucky half of the population which could afford to eat meat regularly in his day consumed on average 147.5 lbs. (67 kg.) per person per annum.[67] At the beginning of the sixteenth century, a monk of Westminster ate meat on fewer than half the total number of days in the year and had a full allowance on only half that number. Yet his total allowance of this food amounted, if I am right, to c.285 lbs. (129.5 kg.) per annum.[68] And this figure relates only to the basic dishes provided day by day: it excludes most of the extra dishes to be anticipated on feast days.

Moreover, animal fat had an important place of its own in the monastic diet. Centuries earlier, under the form of lard, this food had been the first product of four-footed beasts to be admitted to monastic tables, and, despite all the relaxations of diet introduced since that time, the monks of Westminster retained their fondness for it. Hence 'principal pudding', a festal dish named after the principal feasts on which it was consumed. This was normally made with 6 lbs. of currants, 270 to 300 eggs, a large quantity of breadcrumbs, and at least 18 lbs. (8,172 g.) of suet. When lifted from the pot, it must have been a rather damp mass of fat, spotted here and there with currants.[69]

On an average day outside the fast seasons, meat and fish together, excluding the animal fats used as ingredients of other dishes, accounted for c.23 per cent of the energy value of a monk's diet. (See Figure II.1.) Yet these items accounted for as much as 47 per cent of the convent's total outlay on food, and for a slightly higher percentage if we include the cost of the spices that were added to many of the dishes of meat and fish served in this period. (See Table II.1.)

*(c) Bread and alcoholic beverages*

To the two major items of diet which have been described, we must add a generous daily allowance of bread and ale.

---

[67] J. Thirsk and J. P. Cooper (edd.), *Seventeenth-Century Economic Documents* (Oxford, 1972), 783–4, cited, with other telling figures, in K. V. Thomas, *Man and the Natural World* (London, 1984), 26. King's estimate excludes imported Dutch beef and Westphalian bacon. Cf. C. S. L. Davies, 'Les rations alimentaires de l'armée et de la marine anglaise au xvi$^e$ siècle', *Annales, ESC* xviii (1963), 139–41.

King does not distinguish male from female rates of consumption. I am grateful to Mrs Dorothy McCarthy for pointing out to me that the per capita rate for males would have been nearer than the undifferentiated rate to the monastic figure.

[68] Assuming 150 meat days @ 1.9 lbs. (863 g.).

[69] e.g. WAM 33318, fos. 9$^v$, 21$^v$, 29, WAM 33327, fos. 10, 19. Veal and spices were also ingredients.

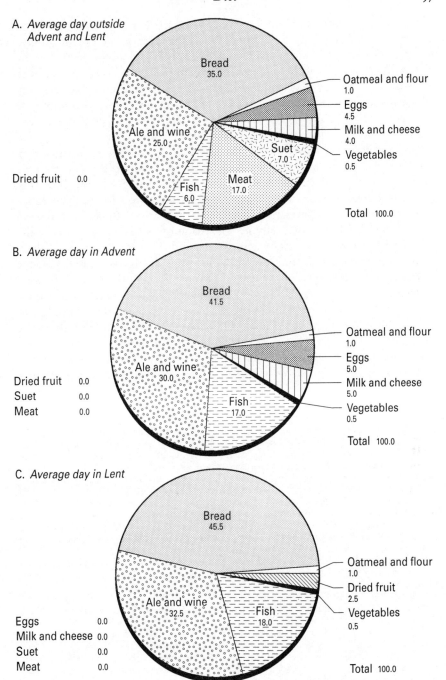

FIG. II.1. Percentage Contribution of Different Foods to the Energy Value of the Diet of the Monks of Westminster, *c.*1495–*c.*1525

Naturally, the monks drank the first, or best, ale drawn off from every quantity of malt entering their brewery. In this period, the brewer rarely, if ever, used any but barley malt, and he probably obtained forty-five to fifty gallons of best ale from every quarter.[70] If so, the convent's ale was probably as good as that obtainable anywhere at this time. The price at which the ale in question was now valued, $1\frac{1}{4}$ d. per gallon, also points to its high quality.[71] Even so, consumption habits suggest that it must have been weak by modern standards. Every monk received an allowance of a gallon per day, and this was but the basic ration. On most occasions of drinking outside the normal pattern of meals, he could expect an extra pint or two, and if his duties were of an unusually thirst-producing kind, his daily allowance was increased: hence the special ration for the precentor when he sang the long office of a feast day.[72] Moreover, ale was much used in cooking. 'Umbles', for example, was made by cooking sheep's entrails, mixed with breadcrumbs and spices, in ale, and this was a common dish in winter.[73] Nor was ale the only alcoholic beverage of a monk of Westminster at this time: on solemn vigils and feast days, and on all the other occasions of conviviality which have already been mentioned, he drank wine, sometimes in generous measure: on a well-endowed anniversary, for example, the individual ration might be a quart.[74] On an average day, alcohol in the strict sense—the ethanol in the ale and wine—probably supplied 19 per cent of the whole energy value of a monk's diet—a figure contrasting in a remarkable way with the probable contribution of alcohol to the average diet today: this is 5 per cent[75] (Table II.4).

[70] WAM 18941, 31916, and 33315 (the baker's and brewer's accounts for, respectively, 1526–7, 1528–9, and 1520–1). However, these accounts are hard to interpret. The following measures are used: barrel (probable capacity: 30 galls.), kilderkin (15 galls.), firkin (10 galls.), tub or tin (7 galls.), 'olla' or pail (5 galls.). Only best ale is accounted for in 1520–1. In 1526–7 and 1528–9, two inferior kinds of ale are also mentioned: 'forinsic' or 'servants' ale', and 'god's blessing'. WAM 31914, an inventory of the brewhouse made in 1529–30, mentions 3 measures for 'god's blessing', and these held, respectively, 30 galls., 10 galls., and 7 galls.

[71] WAM 5919*. This list of corrodies, compiled 1503 × 25, values conventual ale @ $1\frac{1}{4}$ d. per gall. and the conventual loaf @ $\frac{3}{4}$ d. A monk's corrody of bread and ale for a year was thus valued @ c.£3 (= 365 × 2d.). The same value is recorded in 1395–6 (WAM 19880) and had probably been used at Westminster throughout the intervening period. For fluctuations in the actual price of ale, see Dyer, Standards of Living, 58.

[72] The special allowance also included bread and is sometimes entered as capa, signifying a feast in copes (WAM 18941, fos. 3, 4, 5ᵛ, etc., WAM 31916, fos. 3, 4ᵛ, 9, etc.; and for an earlier period, WAM 18887).

[73] WAM 18887, where mortress, jussell, and charlet—all dishes served in the refectory on meat days—are also mentioned as dishes requiring ale. For ale as an ingredient of gruel, see WAM 18941, fos. 10ᵛ, 13ᵛ, 15, etc.

[74] WAM 5403, 18526 ff.; and see above, pp. 39, 44. Most of the wine consumed was Gascon wine @ 8d. per gall., rising to 1s. per gall. in the early 16th cent.

[75] DH 41, p. xx. It has been assumed that the ale consumed by the monks of Westminster was equivalent in strength to present-day pale ale. Alcoholic beverages, which ensured an intake of protein and carbohydrates as well as ethanol, probably contributed as much as 25% to the energy value of the monastic diet on a normal day (Fig. II.1).

The daily loaf of a monk of this period was made from wheaten flour, and it probably weighed 2.5 lbs. (1,135 g.) or a little more before baking and c.2 lbs. (908 g.) after.[76] It was valued at ¾d., a figure unchanged since the late fourteenth century and high both for that period and for the early sixteenth century.[77] Clearly, the conventual loaf, as it was called, was a relatively fine product of the bakery. Yet it was by no means the finest bread eaten in the monastery. The abbot of Westminster, though entitled to draw bread from the monastic bakery, nevertheless purchased a different bread, described as 'white', quite regularly, and on important feast days and anniversaries the monks themselves were given so-called 'wastel bread'. This was a biscuity loaf, made from flour which had been refined with the aid of a bolting cloth, and baked in an exceptionally hot oven.[78] Occasionally, as on the anniversary of Abbot William Colchester, in October, the monks had enriched bread—the so-called buns of the period.[79] At the end of the Middle Ages, extras such as anniversary buns and the breadcrumbs used in cooked dishes must have added at least 0.25 lb. (114 g.) to the daily allowance of bread. If so, on an average day bread contributed c.35 per cent of the total energy value of a monk's allowances of food and drink, and bread, ale, and wine together contributed 60 per cent of the total. Yet these items accounted for only 40 per cent of the convent's total outlay on food, and bread on its own for no more than 13 per cent. (See Table II.1, and Figure II.1.)

## (d) Fruit and vegetables

How often were fruit and vegetables, or dairy produce, added to the basic fare of fish, meat, bread, and ale? This is a difficult question, because it was perfectly possible for the produce of a home dairy or garden to reach the

---

[76] Inferences from WAM 18941, 31916, and 33315, and from the concurrent cellarer's accounts (WAM 18903–45, 30274). These sources show that from each qu. wheat, the Abbey miller produced 1 qu. fine flour, 0.3 qu. bran, and an unspecified but evidently smaller quantity of so-called 'middling flour' (*media farina*): say 0.4 qu. offal in all. From each qu. fine flour, the baker produced, on average, 106 conventual loaves, or the equivalent in the form of 'large' loaves and half-sized loaves, when these were needed. If each qu. flour weighed c.276 lbs., each conventual loaf contained, on average, 2.6 lbs. flour. Fifty faggots were used per 500 loaves. For the assumed weight of 276 lbs. per qu. flour, see M. Prestwich, 'Victualling estimates for English garrisons in Scotland during the early fourteenth century', *EHR* lxxxii (1967), 536–43, at 537. In recognition of the relative fineness of the bread, I have allowed for 20–5% loss of weight in cooking. For a smaller loss in monastic baking of an earlier period, see H. Hall and F. J. Nicholas (edd.), *Select Tracts and Table Books relating to English Weights and Measures (1100–1742)*, in *Camden Miscellany*, xv (Camden 3rd ser. xli 1929), 31. The weight of the conventual loaf at the beginning of the 15th cent. was probably much the same as c.1500, but in the mid-14th cent. considerably less (WAM 18830, 18887). [77] See n. 71 above.

[78] WAM 18941, fos. 4, 5ᵛ, 9ᵛ, etc. These loaves were called *placente*, and c.100 were made per qu. flour; 30 faggots were used per 100 loaves. For the white bread used in the abbot's household, see WAM 33320 and 33324, and in that of the monk-bailiff, WAM 23025*. For a glimpse of a more complicated past in the history of the monastery's bread, see *Customary*, ii. 98. [79] WAM 19982, 19984 ff.

tables in a great household without attracting notice at any stage of the accounting procedure in that institution. The vagaries of accounting practice in this respect are clearly reflected in the kitchener's accounts at Westminster. The onions, for example, that were served with salt eels are accounted for in 1507–9, but not in 1502–3 or 1518. In each year the vegetables in question came, almost certainly, from the monastery's kitchen garden, but some kitcheners considered it appropriate to account for such produce, and others did not.[80]

Nevertheless, fresh fruit and leafy vegetables, which are among the best sources of Vitamin C, were probably rare items of diet in the monastery in this period. Indeed, the evidence, in part direct, in part circumstantial, points to the conclusion that these items were rarer now than in the early Middle Ages. In that earlier period, the monks of Westminster may have been well supplied from their vast garden, which we know as Covent Garden, and from their vineyard nearer home. The employment of a vine-dresser until the end of the fourteenth century tells us that vines were still cultivated until that time.[81] At this relatively late date, it is more likely that the grapes were consumed at table than made into wine. At the end of the Middle Ages, however, the vineyard is not mentioned, and Covent Garden was on lease or under arable crops.[82] The kitchen garden which continued in use in the vicinity of the monastery—we do not know exactly where it was situated—can scarcely have supplied produce on the scale implicit in the earlier arrangements. Yet there is no evidence of the regular purchase of fruit and vegetables on a scale sufficient for about fifty monks. Onions with the salt eels, 'green peas' at dinner two or three times a week in Lent, fresh peascods and beans two or three times a week at supper in a short summer season—the list could be lengthened, but, even when a very frequent consumption of herbs is included, it probably does not indicate a saving intake of the vital nutrient over the year as a whole.[83] At the end of the Middle

[80] WAM 33322, fos. 16ᵛ, 18, 18ᵛ, etc., WAM 33323, fos. 12ᵛ, 13ᵛ, 51, etc. Cf. WAM 33318, fo. 17ᵛ, WAM 33328, fos. 19, 19ᵛ, 20, etc. An inventory of the kitchen in 1491 lists 100 ropes of onions, ½ bus. beans, and 6 beds of leeks among that department's store (WAM 6647).

[81] The vine-dresser drops out of the cellarer's pay-roll between 1407 and 1416, but part of the vineyard was already on lease in the 12th cent. (WAM 18888–9; *Gilbert Crispin*, 41). For the ideal of fruit at table in season in the 13th cent., see *Customary*, ii. 90–1, and for pear trees in the royal garden at Westminster in the very period of the Customary, *Close Rolls, 1261–64*, 29. (I am indebted to Dr John Maddicott for the last reference.)

[82] Rosser, *Medieval Westminster*, 136 and n. Note, however, that the gardener employed by the Abbey kitchener in this period may have been an entrepreneur who engaged and paid subordinate staff (below, pp. 165–6).

[83] For 'green' (i.e. good) peas—but sometimes just 'peas'—on most Mondays, Wednesdays, and Fridays in Lent, or leeks in lieu, see WAM 33323, fos. 12ᵛ–16ᵛ, 51–4, WAM 33329, fos. 14ᵛ– 17ᵛ. For fresh peascods and beans, WAM 33318, fos. 30–35ᵛ, 76–82, WAM 33322, fos. 32ᵛ–34. Note also the regular use of beans and peas in pottage, a daily dish in the refectory. Most of these, however, must have been dried.

Ages, fresh fruit was evidently regarded as a treat in the monastery and this explains why it was served more frequently at the abbot's table than at that of his monks. Yet not even at the abbot's table was this a frequent food: in 1510 Abbot John Islip had quinces, apples, and warden pears at the beginning of the year, oranges three or four times from January to April, and strawberries in June and July.[84]

## (e) *Dairy produce*

Dairy produce, however, was a prominent part of the monastic diet. Historians of diet use this term in two different ways: to denote milk products and eggs, and to denote milk products alone. Even a small acquaintance with the sources of the period seems to show that eggs were normally well represented in genteel diet, whether inside or outside the cloister: the monks of Westminster were probably not unusual in consuming, as they did, about five per person per day under various forms outside Lent.[85] They derived a considerable percentage of their intake of Vitamins A and D from this source. The question mark is over the consumption of milk and milk products, and principally cheese. Here, too, our sources convey a clear message: the monks consumed these foods regularly, and they loved them.

Formerly, indeed, the monks of Westminster had consumed milk products to the point of becoming ill. 'Digestive syrup for the convent in May', reads the apothecary's account in 1351, and a very elaborate syrup it was.[86] The month of May normally includes the Rogation days, and did so in 1351. On these days, however, the monks of Westminster ate an exceptionally rich kind of cheese flan, and we seem to learn from this entry that they had not always known where to stop. At the end of the Middle Ages, they found a place for milky foods in the routine of ordinary days and enshrined them in the celebrations on feast days. Now, on some feast days of the highest status, cheese flans by day were considered no bar to dowcet—a custardy dish containing milk, cream, and eggs, beside sugar and currants— in the evening.[87] On many ordinary days in summer, the monks of this

---

[84] For quinces, apples, and warden pears in Jan. and Feb., see WAM 33324, fos. 17ᵛ, 23, 46–7; and for the oranges, ibid. 22ᵛ, 24–25ᵛ, 33ᵛ. In Mar. 1510 the vicar of Feering gave the abbot a present of apples, together with a small dog (ibid. 29ᵛ).

[85] WAM 33317, recording the purchase of *c.*82,000 eggs over a period of 32 weeks in 1491–2, broken by Lent in the latter year. (In these entries, 'C' = 120 and 'cast' = 6.) I have assumed that the kitchener was catering for 52 and that he actually used the eggs over a slightly longer period than 32 weeks. Liveries of eggs to corrodians on meat days, in lieu of meat, probably accounted for 200 to 240 per week.

[86] *Sirrippus digestevus pro conventu in Maio* (WAM 19331). Cf. a similar entry in 1352, where the context of Rogationtide is explicit (WAM 19332). For the flans, sometimes referred to in general terms as 'pittances', *c.*1350, see WAM 19845*, 19848–9, 19852–4, and *c.*1500, WAM 33318, fos. 26–26ᵛ, 69–69ᵛ, 111ᵛ.

[87] e.g. WAM 33329, fos. 26, 26ᵛ. Occasionally, butter is mentioned as an ingredient.

period had milky dishes like charlet—itself made with chopped meat, eggs and milk[88]—if eating in the refectory. Except during Lent, all monks probably had cheese at dinner, and on many days those eating in the refectory had this food again at supper. In one way or another, the per capita allowance of food from Easter to mid-September included, on average, 0.5 pints of milk per day; throughout the year, excepting only Fridays and the six weeks of Lent, it probably included at least 2.5 oz. (71 g.) of cheese a day.[89] Another milk product, butter, was used in cooking. In fact, it is impossible to read the records of this period without realizing that special care was taken to include milk products in the monastic diet. Yet dairy produce in this sense accounted for only 3 per cent of the monastery's outlay on foodstuffs. (See Table II.1.)

### (f) The nutrient content and energy value of the diet

Such were the allowances of food at the common meals in one of the richest Benedictine houses in England towards the end of the Middle Ages. Of course, in the monasteries of the period, the common meals and the meals actually consumed were no longer one and the same. This was the very point of Thomas Cromwell's Injunction that in each monastery the monks should eat together in the same room; he knew that monks absented themselves from the common meals and he wished to end the practice.[90] Quite frequently, at Westminster, office-holders, for example, ate in private; and occasionally more widespread forms of absenteeism can be detected— as at Christmas 1500, when the entire convent deserted the refectory, and the meals without flesh-meat that would have been their lot there, to eat with the abbot in his house at La Neyte.[91] No doubt, from time to time monks of this house used their very ample wages to buy something better than, or at least different from, the common diet—an extra pint or two of wine, perhaps, or fine white bread in place of the coarser conventual loaf.

---

[88] For charlet, see WAM 33329, fos. 28, 28[v], 29, etc., WAM 33330, fos. 16, 17, 17[v], etc. However, meat, an essential ingredient of the dish, is never mentioned in these entries: we must assume that the kitchener used pork or bacon from the Abbey's home-grown pigs. For charlet made with cut up veal or pork, see *Two Fifteenth-Century Cookery Books*, ed. Austin, 17, 117, and for the large cooking pot said to be for charlet, which is mentioned at the Abbey in 1353–4, WAM 19849.

[89] Actually 16 oz. per week = 2.67 oz. (76 g.) per cheese day. This estimate is based on expenditure on this item in relation to current prices. The refectorer paid for cheese at dinner, the kitchener for that eaten at supper. For the refectorer's accounts, see WAM 19585–616, and for the understanding reached in the early 13th cent. that monks eating irregular food outside the refectory should, like those eating regular food in that room, have cheese at dinner and supper, see WD 632.

[90] Wilkins, *Concilia*, iii. 790. The rota, consigning some, on meat days, to the refectory, where they could not eat flesh meat, was now abandoned.

[91] WAM 33320, fo. 8. La Neyte was situated in present-day Pimlico. For Benedict XII's decree prohibiting the use of rooms for eating other than the refectory during the Christmas period, see Wilkins, *Concilia*, ii. 609.

Yet if the common meals do not tell us the whole story of monastic eating and drinking, they do tell us what most of the community ate on most days in the year, and what the appropriate allowances were considered to be.

What, then, did this diet amount to? Outside the fast seasons of Advent and Lent, an average week in the monastery comprised four meat days and three fish days, and in principle every monk ate flesh-meat on two of the meat days and meaty dishes on the other two. In principle, he ate seven dinners per week and five or six suppers. We know enough about the dishes served on each kind of day to estimate, very roughly, the nutrient content of a monk's allowances of food and drink in the normal months of the dietary year, and their calorific value, and so to arrive at an estimate for an average day. Estimates can also be made for the fast seasons. These estimates are shown in Table II.4.[92] As a bench-mark, the Dietary Reference Value (DRV) for each nutrient is also shown in this table. However, it is important to realize that DRV is not a recommended daily intake. The term covers more than one kind of value: in Table II.4 it indicates, in the case of some nutrients, the current average intake of the population, and, in the case of others, the Reference Nutrient Intake (RNI). RNI itself represents the estimated requirement of an individual with high needs.[93] The estimates relating to the monastic diet prompt some general conclusions. First, on the deficiencies of the diet.

It is widely agreed that if upper-class diet in general had deficiencies in this period, these related to the intake of vitamins, and especially Vitamins A, C, and D. The monks of Westminster consumed enough fatty fish and eggs to be assured of an adequate intake of Vitamin D. Indeed, their intake of this vitamin was probably excessive. However, their diet was certainly deficient in Vitamin C and perhaps deficient in Vitamin A. RNI for Vitamin C in the case of a male adult is 40 mg. per day, although 25 mg. or less may be sufficient. Yet, even on an optimistic view, the monastic diet provided, on average, only 5 to 7 mg. of this vitamin per day, according to season. RNI for Vitamin A in the case of a male adult is 700 micrograms per day. On an average day outside the fast seasons, the monastic diet provided *c*.610 micrograms. Given the fact that Vitamin A can be stored in the liver, intake at this level would probably have been sufficient to compensate for the fast seasons when the diet provided smaller amounts of the nutrient. But no monk consumed his entire allowance of food and drink, and it will be suggested below that a monk of Westminster may normally have consumed 60 per cent of his allowance.[94] If so, at *c*.370 micrograms per day outside the

---

[92] In the following discussion of the nutrient content and energy value of the diet of the monks of Westminster, and for the analysis of data underlying Table II.4, I am greatly indebted to Professor David Conning and Miss Anne Halliday, of the British Nutrition Foundation. It is hardly necessary for me to add that I am solely responsible for any errors.
[93] DH 41, pp. iii and *passim*.     [94] Below, p. 70.

*Diet*

TABLE II.4. Energy Value and Nutrient Content of the Diet of the Monks of Westminster, *c.*1495–*c.*1525[a]

|  | Energy value kcal. | Protein g. | Fat g. | Carbohydrate g. | Alcohol[b] g. | Dietary fibre g. |
|---|---|---|---|---|---|---|
| A. Allowances on average day outside Advent and Lent | 6,207 | 320 (20.5)[c] | 185 (27) | 558 (33.5) | 167 (19) | 90 |
| *DH Dietary Reference values*[d] |  | *15%* | *33%* | *47%* | *5%* | *18* |
| B. Allowances on average day in Advent | 5,291 | 316 (24) | 93 (16) | 539 (38) | 167 (22) | 90 |
| C. Allowances on average day in Lent | 4,870 | 273 (22) | 62 (12) | 547 (42) | 167 (24) | 92 |
| D. Consumption @ 60% on average day outside Advent and Lent | 3,723 | 192 (20.5) | 111 (27) | 335 (33.5) | 100 (19) | 54 |

*Notes*: [a] The following per capita allowances are assumed: *Daily throughout the year*: 2.25 lb./1,022 g. bread; 0.19 oz./5.40 g. oatmeal; 0.37 oz./10.50 g. flour; 1.23 oz./35 g. peas and beans; 1 gall. (= 10.11 lb./4,592 g.) ale; a cupful (5.81 oz./165 g.) claret. It has been assumed that the ale was equivalent to present-day pale ale. *Daily except on Fridays or in Lent*: 5 (= 7.92 oz./225 g.) eggs; 0.18 pint (= 3.52 oz./100 g.) milk; 2.67 oz./76 g. cheese; 2 oz./57 g. suet. (The last item, however, was not eaten in Advent.) *Daily on meat days*: either (for a monk eating in the misericord) 2.60 lb./1,180 g. meat at dinner and 0.40 lb./182 g. at supper, or (for a monk eating in the refectory) 12 oz./341 g. meat or offal served in meaty dishes at dinner and 4 oz./114 g. offal at one supper in every 3. *Daily on fish days*: 2 lb./908 g. fish (1.70 lb./772 g. white, 0.30 lb./136 g. fatty), but on Fridays only 66% of this allowance. *In Advent*: 4 oz./114 g. molluscs at 2 suppers per week. *In Lent*: 4 oz./114 g. molluscs, 4 oz./114 g. nuts, and 4 oz./114 g. raisins at 1 supper per week.

Some of these allowances—e.g. those for peas and beans, suet and wine—represent the daily average for items that actually reached the table at less regular intervals.

fast seasons, he may have experienced a deficiency over the year as a whole. Yet these are the only deficiencies that can now be identified.

If the diet had few deficiencies, it had two or three very striking positive features. The first of these is the prominence of alcoholic beverages, and especially ale. As I have pointed out, the alcohol in these accounted for 19 per cent of the whole energy value of the diet on a normal day.[95] This conclusion depends on the assumption that the strength of the best brew of ale in the monastery was equivalent to that of pale ale today. The basic allowance of ale at Westminster, one gallon per person per day, was probably

[95] Above, p. 58 and n. 73.

TABLE II.4. (*cont.*)

| Thiamin mg. | Riboflavin mg. | Nicotinic acid equiv. mg. | Vit. C mg. | Vit. A μg. | Vit. D μg. | Calcium mg. | Iron mg. |
|---|---|---|---|---|---|---|---|
| 3.6 | 5.3 | 159 | 7.2 | 611 | 14.9 | 1,162 | 53 |
| *1.0* | *1.3* | *17* | *40* | *700* | *10* | *700* | *8.7* |
| 3.6 | 3.6 | 141 | 6.5 | 532 | 32 | 1,277 | 40 |
| 3.4 | 2.9 | 129 | 5.3 | 78 | 28.5 | 898 | 35 |
| 2.2 | 3.2 | 95 | 4.3 | 367 | 9 | 697 | 32 |

*Note* [a] *cont.* Butter was used in cooking and is allowed for in the values used for the dishes in question.

Outside the fast seasons of Advent and Lent, the average day relates to an average week in which the individual monk was assigned to the misericord for 2 meat days and to the refectory for 2, and ate fish on the remaining 3. In Advent and Lent all days were fish days.

[b] i.e. the ethanol in the alcoholic beverages in the diet.

[c] Figures in parentheses are percentage contribution to energy content. Conversion factors: protein 4 kcal./g.; fat 9 kcal./g.; carbohydrate 3.75 kcal./g.; alcohol 7 kcal./g.

[d] i.e. in the case of Energy Value, Protein, Fat, Carbohydrate, and Alcohol, the current Population Average for the United Kingdom; and in other cases the Reference Nutrient Intake (RNI). See DH 41, pp. xx–xxiv; and for the definition of RNI as 'an amount of the nutrient that is enough, or more than enough, for about 97% in a group', see ibid., p. v.

a common ration for high and middle ranking personnel in great households of the period, whether ecclesiastical or secular. Nor is it difficult to believe that many workers in late medieval England—as, for example, agricultural workers in the harvest season—could actually dispatch this quantity of ale day by day. It is as an allowance for religious occupied, as a rule, in light work, that a gallon per day attracts attention: the allowance seems to indicate a level of consumption several times higher than that of the vast majority of male adults in England and Wales today.[96] In fact, a Benedictine monk now had several opportunities for drinking in the course of the day,

[96] *General Household Survey*, 1988 (Office of Population Censuses and Surveys: Social Survey Division, HMSO, London, 1990), table 6.1.

and he would probably have found that time passed rather slowly without these. Moreover, it is unlikely that the upper classes drank much water in this period: if they slaked their thirst at all, it was on alcoholic beverages. The average monk of Westminster may often have consumed the greater part, if not the whole, of his allowance of ale. How often he exceeded the intake of 50 g. alcohol at which adverse effects on the body may be anticipated, is, of course, uncertain. However, it is safe to conclude that his daily intake was normally far above this level.

Another striking feature of the diet is the high protein content. Today, protein contributes 15 per cent to the average energy intake of the adult population of the United Kingdom; fats contribute 33 per cent, and carbohydrates 47 per cent. Outside the fast seasons, a monk of Westminster's allowances of food and drink derived 27 per cent of their energy value from fats, 33.5 per cent from carbohydrates, but as much as 20.5 per cent from protein. The actual allowance of fats and carbohydrates was much larger than in the average diet of the present day, but in relative terms it was less important. Protein, on the other hand, was much more important. This pattern reflects the upper-class character of monastic diet: lower down the social scale in late medieval England, the intake of protein would have been smaller and that of carbohydrates, if not of fats, larger.[97] But the pattern belongs to a region as well as a class: it was a North European, and perhaps distinctively English, pattern. In the diet of the archbishop of Arles' household, analysed by Stouff, carbohydrates, supplying *c.*70 per cent of the energy value of the whole, were relatively more important than in the monastic diet, and protein, supplying *c.*16 per cent, was less so.[98] The large protein content in the diet of the monks of Westminster is explained by the quantities of meat and fish consumed in the monastery in an average week. It suggests the possibility of renal disorders. Excessive protein is not itself the cause of renal malfunctioning, but it exacerbates an existing problem of this kind. A monk with such a tendency would have found it hard to cope with this feature of his diet.[99]

The energy value of the allowances which I have described was very large indeed. Outside the fast seasons of Advent and Lent, the per capita daily allowance probably had an average value of *c.*6,210 kcals—nearly twice the average requirement of a moderately active man today—and the actual value was often considerably larger than this: on a day when flesh-meat was eaten

[97] As implied by the data in Dyer, 'Changes in diet in the late Middle Ages', 26 (table 2), and 36–7, and id., *Standards of Living*, 158 (fig. 4). See also S. Mennell, *All Manners of Food* (Oxford, 1985), 45–6. For some of the cultural issues involved, see Goody, *Cooking, Cuisine and Class*, ch. 4.

[98] Stouff, *Ravitaillement et alimentation en Provence*, 237 (table 29), 245–6 (tables 33 and 33 *bis*).

[99] I am indebted to Dr A. B. Loach for help on this point. See also below, p. 109.

at dinner and supper, it was c.7,375 kcals. Even in Lent, the severer of the two fasts, the average value did not fall below c.4,870 kcals. per day.

## (g) *How much was consumed?*

So much for the allowances. But how much of these did the monks of Westminster actually consume? How much, indeed, did they have the opportunity of consuming, and how much was quietly appropriated to other uses by interested parties before it reached the tables in the refectory or misericord?

Peculation was part of the economy of waste pervading the life of a great household, and some loss was only to be expected as the day's roast mutton or fried whiting was passed along the chain of servants responsible for its production. After all, some servants lived quite legitimately on the leftovers of the monastic meals: to take a little before the meal would be merely to anticipate.[100] But in a monastic household, where the proper contents of a mess were so carefully prescribed and the topic of such keen interest to the consumer for whom they were intended, the difference between the theoretical contents and the actual was probably not large. In such a household, the wise thief raided the larder or the leftovers themselves but did not touch the messes intended for the table. If, however, the daily allowances which have been described were somewhat reduced by theft, they were also augmented by extra dishes, imperfectly recorded in the sources and for that reason largely omitted from the foregoing account. It can probably be assumed that the net allowances at the common meals at Westminster, after appropriate additions and losses have been taken into account, were of the order of magnitude which has been described.

The question, how much was actually consumed, is, of course, as little susceptible to a precise answer in a monastic setting as anywhere else. I wish only to suggest that a monk of this period, for all his sedentary way of life, consumed considerably more, day by day, than we do: more, that is, than the moderately active man mentioned above. This conclusion the sources will, I believe, sustain.

The first vital clue to actual levels of consumption in the late medieval monastery occurs at the beginning of the fifteenth century—nearly a hundred years before the period on which this investigation of the monks' diet has focused, but at a time when catering arrangements were essentially the same.

At the beginning of the fifteenth century, and probably in 1417, the Abbey's lay brethren petitioned the abbot and convent for an improvement in their lot.[101] There were six brethren at this time, and they were the

---

[100] Below, p. 174; and for anxiety on the part of the General Chapter, possibly about such a practice in an earlier period, see *Chapters of English Black Monks*, i. 10, 36–7, 79.

[101] LNQ 85–85ᵛ; and for the emoluments of the lay brethren, see also WAM 19004 ff.

Abbey's resident almsmen, receiving small allowances in kind and cash, but depending to a large extent at meal-times on the leftovers of the refectory: there they occupied a special table, known as 'the table for the poor'.[102] It will already be clear that they were not the only people dependent on the leftovers in question, and that a number of low-ranking servants were in the same position. Moreover, the servants may have been able to move about the room with greater freedom while the meal was actually in progress—an advantage for anyone scraping a living together in this way. But the lay brethren had a corporate identity which made it easy for them to articulate complaints. They were already entitled to a special allowance of ale on Fridays and other solemn fasts, and the reason for this is rehearsed in their petition: on these days, many monks ate in the refectory.[103] Now, in 1417, they asked for an additional cash allowance of 2*d*. on Fridays, to supplement their cooked food on that difficult day, and this was conceded.

This episode lifts a corner of the curtain on some important conventions of monastic life at the time. In the second decade of the fifteenth century, the community at Westminster numbered about fifty monks, as it was to do a century later. On most days of the week, it is clear, a considerable number absented themselves from the common meals, and we can assume that these were mainly the office-holders and senior monks living in private chambers. However, on Fridays and other solemn fasts, the absentees tended to turn up: one fasted on such days by eating the common meal, and nothing better or more private. And perhaps the good attendance at dinner on fasts owed something to the fact that there was no supper, no second meal, to follow on that day. But evidently, when absenteeism fell, the whole economy of the refectory was affected. Normally, the needs of the lay brethren and others having claims on the leftovers could be satisfied by using the portions of the absentees as well as the broken meats of the monks who had actually participated in the meal. If, however, absenteeism fell significantly, the lay brethren felt the pinch, and it was for this reason that they asked for an additional allowance of 2*d*. on Fridays. The telling point is the modesty of their request, for they did not, it appears, ask for 2*d*. each, but for 2*d*. to be shared among the six. In the early fifteenth century, 2*d*. purchased perhaps fifteen to twenty herring or about half as many salt eels: say four to five

---

[102] This is the *tabula pro pauperibus* mentioned, with its plain table-cloths, in WAM 19558. The children of the song school and grammar school had first call on the leftovers of the misericord.

[103] . . . *et in feriis sextis et aliis jeiuniis solempnibus quum multi fratres prandent in refectorio, tunc percipere solent tanqardum suum plenum servisie, videlicet pro maiore parte j galonem et j potellum*. Nevertheless, in 1417 the lay brethren seized the opportunity of asking for an extra gall. of ale per day, and this request was granted. For the tankard of ale as a customary allowance for the poor, see A. Lascombes, 'Fortunes de l'*ale*: à propos de Coventry, 1420–1555', in *Pratiques et Discours alimentaires à la Renaissance* (Actes du Colloque de Tours, 1979), ed. J.-C. Margolin and R. Sauzet (Paris, 1982), 126–36, at 129.

pounds of edible fish of the commonest varieties.[104] The lay brethren said in effect that when the refectory was full, it was quite uncertain whether that amount of cooked food would be left for them at the end of the meal.

A century later, the situation was essentially the same, but the tell-tale circumstance was now the provision for guests. At this date, few guests, and none of any consequence, ate with the monks in the refectory: most were entertained by the abbot, prior, or monk-bailiff in their separate establishments, or, if of very humble status, fed by the cellarer in his commodious apartment in the Abbey precinct. For those who did eat with the monks, there were enough bread and ale to spare from the monk's own allowances, and enough cooked food too—except, in the case of cooked food, on Fridays and on some other fasts, when it was quite usual to provide fish especially for guests.[105] Evidently, the conventions were much what they had been at the beginning of the fifteenth century: normally there was, from the administrative point of view, a useful level of absenteeism from meals, and guests were fed, as were servants and the lay brethren, by recourse to the portions put out for absentees. However, on Fridays and the other fasts in question, attendance was much better; and devout visitors to the Abbey may have preferred these days to others. In these circumstances, it was necessary to provide something especially for the guests: unless this was done, there would not be enough to go round. But, again, very little extra food was needed to put things right: a stockfish or two, and sometimes less, was sufficient. In this period, as a century earlier, when the refectory was full there was, it appears, little or no slack in the system.

It must, I think, be concluded that a monk of this period consumed most of his allowance of food on Fridays and other comparable fast days—not the whole of it, because the servants could not be left to starve, but a large proportion, and certainly a very large proportion of the cooked food. In fact, a monk's allowance was smaller on such days than at other times, for on Fridays there was no supper, and at dinner the monks abstained from all forms of dairy produce and had only two main dishes of fish beside the dish of pottage with which the meal began: say 4,470 kcals. for the energy value of the meal as a whole. If a monk consumed a very large proportion of his total allowance on this day of the week, it does not follow that he did so

[104] For some pointers, see J. E. T. Rogers, *A History of Agriculture and Prices in England*, ii (*1259–1400*) (Oxford, 1866), 557.

[105] WAM 33322, fos. 3, 4, 4ᵛ, 6, etc., WAM 33323, fos. 4, 4ᵛ, 5ᵛ, 7, etc., WAM 33329, fos. 2ᵛ, 10, 14ᵛ, etc., WAM 33330, fos. 2ᵛ, 3, 4, etc. The references are from the years 1506–9 and 1520–2. The absence of an explicit provision of this kind for guests in some years, but not in all, suggests that some kitcheners were more meticulous than others in accounting for small items of expenditure. c.1400, 3 loaves and 3 galls. of ale were provided daily throughout the year for guests dining in the refectory (WAM 18887): perhaps 6 to 8 guests daily were then envisaged as the norm. Explicit provision of bread and ale for guests was rare by 1500, though not unknown. For an example see WAM 31916, fo. 24ᵛ.

on other days: Friday's food was, so to speak, a survival kit, enabling him
to make landfall safely on Saturday, when there would be a normal dinner,
and in the evening light refreshments, if not a full supper. Yet, even on a
Friday, the total allowance of food, including bread and ale, had an energy
value considerably in excess of that deemed necessary for a moderately
active man today. If, however, the monk left 25 per cent of his allowance
on this day untouched—a reasonable assumption—his energy intake would
have been *c*.3,350 kcals. This is a little above, though still very near, the
average requirement today of *c*.3,160 kcals. on the part of a rather heavy,
moderately active, man.[106] On an average day, when the food and drink
placed before him had an energy value of *c*.6,210 kcals., he would have needed
to consume only 55 per cent, or a little less, of his average allowance to
achieve this intake, and could have left as much as 45 per cent for the
servants and the poor. But the average monk probably felt freer to indulge
himself on days of the week other than Friday: say 60 per cent consumption
on an average day. If so, at *c*.3,730 kcals., his energy intake was large but by
no means spectacular.

## 5. Conclusions

I began with three questions relating to the diet of the upper classes in
England in the later Middle Ages, and these I have tried to illumine with the
help of a monastic sample. However, a final question claims attention. How
typical *was* monastic diet of that to be found at comparable levels of secular
society outside the cloister? Were the excess of protein and the high energy
value to be found there, too? Is it possible that the gentry outside the
cloister also loved dairy produce and consumed it to an extent which has
left little or no trace in the records?

Diet tends to be a conservative feature of human existence, and institutional diet is more conservative than most other forms. Milky foods, which
were important sources of vitamins, owed their secure place in monastic
diet at the end of the Middle Ages to this conservatism. The Benedictines
had taken to such foods in the early Middle Ages, when they consumed
much less meat than they were to do later. But when, later, they lost their
inhibitions about meat, they did not abandon the cheese and the custards.
These foods may or may not have been prominent in the diet of secular
households, where meat had never been forbidden food. I suggest only that
we cannot determine this point by reference to the amounts spent on these
items, for the latter were cheap.

Equally, special factors may help to explain the large amounts actually
consumed on most days in the year, if I am right, by monks. By the end
of the Middle Ages, some of the public rooms in a Benedictine monastery

---

[106] Above, p. 35.

would have had fires in winter, but the complex of monastic buildings as a whole must still have been exceedingly cold. In winter, monks needed a great deal of extra energy to keep warm, and having adopted the level of consumption that was necessary in winter, they continued at or near this level in summer. Secular households, knowing better how to make themselves comfortable, may not have shivered so much in winter, with consequences for the proportions actually consumed of food allowances that were probably quite as large as the monastic allowances.

In other major respects, however, the diet which I have described, and especially the generous allowances of bread and ale, of meat and fish, will surely seem very familiar to anyone acquainted with arrangements in secular households of the period. Even the modest consumption of spices has parallels.[107] A monastic sample helps us to fill in and to some extent correct the detail of a structure that is already sufficiently clear in outline. And knowing more of the detail, we can perhaps the better identify the hazards to health of the upper-class diets of this period. Historians have devoted a good deal of attention to the possibility that these diets were deficient in vitamins, and rightly so. The dangers of the undoubted excesses have been, on the whole, less well considered. The example of the monks of Westminster, who were surely on average rather obese, seems to direct us along this other line of enquiry.

[107] Dyer, *Standards of Living*, 63.

# ⊰ III ⊱

# *Sickness and its Treatment*

## 1. The Empirical Approach

THE historians of sickness and its treatment in the Middle Ages must envy the recent achievements of the historians of population change in the same period. If, even now, less is known about population change in the Middle Ages than in the early modern period, medievalists are much better informed about the subject than were their predecessors a generation or two ago. This advance has been made possible by a drastic narrowing of the field of enquiry, from the vaguely drawn 'country' that was so often written about earlier to specific villages and manors: the historical demographers have learnt how to exploit small-scale observations to brilliant effect.[1]

There has been no comparable advance in the study of sickness or its treatment. The view, itself quite widely held, that one was probably better off in this period without professional medical care than with it, owes more to the study of academic medicine than to acquaintance with actual practitioners at work or to knowledge of the vital statistics of identifiable groups of patients.[2] As for the study of morbidity—the rate of illness—a medievalist finds it hard to point to a single systematic study on the subject with an English reference.[3]

These gaps in our knowledge are not in the least surprising. Hospital records of the right kind are scarce, and in any case sickness in the Middle Ages normally ran its course at home, where it altogether eludes our analytical probes. Monastic sickness, however, was of necessity institutionalized, since monks lived together in communities, most of which possessed an infirmary;

---

[1] For distinguished examples of the particularity referred to in the text, see *Land, Kinship and Life-Cycle*; and for some of the pitfalls in village and manor case-studies, L. R. Poos and R. M. Smith, '"Legal windows onto historical populations?" Recent research on demography and the manor court in medieval England', *Law and History Review*, ii (1984), 128–52. But the literature is now very large.

[2] Cf. C. Rawcliffe, 'The hospitals of late medieval London', *Medical History*, xxviii (1984), 1–21, at 9, where this view is expressed in the context of actual practice. For an important account of academic and not-so-academic medicine after 1500, full of implications for an earlier period, see [R.] G. Lewis, 'The faculty of medicine', in J. McConica (ed.), *History of the University of Oxford*, iii (Oxford, 1986), 213–56.

[3] Cf., for a later period, M. Pelling, 'Illness among the poor in an early modern English town: the Norwich census of 1570', *Continuity and Change*, iii (1988), 273–90. For the pioneering work of Lord Amulree on sickness at Westminster Abbey, see below, p. 100 n.

and these communities can provide the identifiable group that is needed for exact observation in this field. I shall consider mainly sickness and its treatment at Westminster Abbey in the later Middle Ages. To some extent my study will cover the period from the end of the thirteenth century to the Dissolution of the monastery in 1540. But much of it will relate to a shorter period, 1375–1529, which has left unusually good sources, lending themselves to systematic analysis. First, however, I shall describe the size of the community at Westminster, its social and geographical origins, way of life, and urban environment—all essential items of information if we are to understand the record of sickness there.

## 2. The Monastic Community at Westminster Abbey

### (i) Numbers and recruitment

For most of the period 1375–1529, the community at Westminster was, in principle, a community of forty-eight monks, not counting the abbot or prior, although a larger number—fifty-seven or fifty-eight at the peak—is recorded in the years around 1400. In the second half of the fourteenth century, a period of general reappraisal of the monastic life at Westminster, the abbot and convent identified this as the optimum number for their community. Abbot Litlyngton's gift to the refectory in 1378 of a set of forty-eight trenchers and twenty-four salt-cellars, each marked with his initials and the coronet of the Despenser family, to which he belonged, shows that the decision had been taken by that date.[4] A century later obedientiaries distributing wages to the monks regarded forty-eight, not counting the abbot and prior, as the normal number; and it is of interest too that they expected forty of these to be priests and eight to be 'novices'—a term which in the context distinguishes a monk who was professed but not yet ordained.[5] In fact, from the late fourteenth century onwards, recruitment was normally conducted with the number forty-eight in mind and deliberately adjusted to the peaks and troughs of mortality in the community which might otherwise endanger it. In consequence, novices entered, not in a steady trickle, but at a conspicuously uneven rate: six, eight, or an even larger number might be recruited in one year, but none at all in the two or three years following. The eight professions, for example, which occurred in 1479–80 nicely compensated for the seven deaths of the previous year. But there had been no professions in the latter year or the year before, and there would be none again until 1482–3.[6] Of course, the pattern

---

[4] *Flete*, 135–6; *Monks*, 86. Litlyngton's gift included 24 trenchers and 12 salt-cellars for the misericord, the room where, according to Benedict XII's ruling, half the community but not more might eat on meat days (above, p. 40).      [5] WAM 24068*.

[6] *Monks*, 166–9. Forty-eight was briefly set aside as the optimum number *c*.1400, when additional income accruing from the foundation of Richard II encouraged more ambitious ideas.

was not always as neat as this, and the convenience of instructing novices in batches of a certain size was another influence on the chronology of recruitment. Yet only policy could have produced the remarkable stability of numbers that characterized the late medieval community at Westminster. Over the whole period 1375–1529, the number of professed monks at or about Michaelmas (29 September) each year was, on average, forty-six.[7]

Such a system of recruitment implies the existence of a feeder mechanism, for it is not to be thought that even the wealthiest and best-known monasteries in late medieval England could lay hands on six or eight new novices at a moment's notice. For much of this period, the Abbey's novices were normally in the age-range 18 to 21 at profession; but towards the end of it they were rather younger and in some cases as young as 15. Without doubt, at Westminster, as at Durham Cathedral Priory, many potential recruits to the monastic life were housed and educated for a time in the school attached to the almonry, until vacancies should occur in the main establishment.[8] The time of probation was now effectively divided between a period spent in the almonry before the novice's formal clothing and profession, and a period spent in the monastery after those rites of passage. Thus even the country boys among the new recruits may have had some preliminary experience of the urban environment in which they would live subsequently, as monks. And what an experience it must have been! The almonry was situated outside the west gate of the monastery, and adjacent to a close-built and insanitary shopping area. The Abbey gatehouse housed, on its first floor, a prison. From time to time, moreover, the whole area was thronged by hundreds of beggars: these did not live in the neighbourhood but moved into it when a distribution of alms was announced, bringing with them whatever infections they had picked up on the way.[9] Not even the occasional carting away of muck from the sanctuary, which had become customary by the mid-fifteenth century—an operation financed in part by the Abbey and in part by its tenants—nor the special clean-up when royal visitors were expected, can have done much to remove the hazards to health,

---

[7] WAM 19867–999, 23001–25, 23702–960. The vital information relates to the distribution of instalments of monastic wages by the treasurers and the warden of Queen Eleanor's foundation at the end of each year of account. In the case of Queen Eleanor's foundation, the actual distribution was delayed until a few days after the anniversary on or about 28 Nov., early in the next year.

[8] R. B. Dobson, *Durham Priory, 1400–1450* (Cambridge, 1973), 60–1. On the almonry school at Westminster, which divided into a grammar school and a song school in the late 14th cent., see above, p. 25. When the grammar school moved to new quarters in 1461, the song school, and, almost certainly, the would-be novices, remained in the almonry. But the would-be novices may have joined the grammar-school boys for some lessons.

On age at profession, see below, pp. 118–21.

[9] For the almonry and its environs, see Map I, and Rosser, *Medieval Westminster*, 69–74, 155–8, 233–4; for an 18th-cent. plan of the gatehouse and prison, WAM 18411; and for the beggars, above, pp. 28–9.

from dirt and other causes, for those living in the area.[10] We may think that only the fittest among the recruits can have survived this baptism long enough to be clothed and professed as monks of Westminster.

Yet, even among those tested in this way before entry, social and geographical origins may have told subsequently. In his great biographical register of the monks of Westminster, E. H. Pearce suggested that most novices entering this community came from towns and villages on or near the Abbey's estates.[11] If so, the intake would indeed have been diverse, for the demesne estates of the Abbey extended into nearly a dozen counties and supported many different kinds of urban and rural settlement. In reaching this conclusion, Pearce relied heavily on the many place-name elements occurring in the surnames of the monks of Westminster: these, he believed, indicated actual place of origin. This interpretation is convincing for the early Middle Ages, but what of later periods?

The old-established practice of naming a novice after his local village or town can be traced very late at the Abbey: it had scarcely disappeared when the sixteenth-century fashion for pious names, such as Faith, Hope, and Charity, began to make itself felt. Indeed, the old custom was still strong enough, on occasion, to keep out the new. John Islip, who entered the monastery in 1479 and was to be the last but one in the long line of abbots of Westminster, was probably the son of Nicholas Barton, the miller of Islip, in Oxfordshire. As a monk he seems to have adopted the name 'Patience', but it never 'took' within the community, and he was normally known by the name of his native village.[12] John Wheathampstead, who entered in 1519–20 and survived to become a petty canon of the cathedral foundation in 1541, was actually John Horne of Wheathampstead.[13] In some other cases, however, the locative surname, which, on a superficial view, records the place of origin of the monk in question, was actually the settled name of the novice's family which he kept after profession: what evidently mattered was that he should have a name of the right kind, not that it should denote his place of origin. The practice of retaining a locative surname, if the novice already possessed one, can be traced in the later fourteenth century and may date from an earlier period. William Sudbury, professed in 1373 and one of the few really learned monks of Westminster

---

[10] WAM 19669, 19673, etc. The Abbey's tenants contributed 13s. 4d. p.a. to the expense of cleaning the sanctuary, and the Abbey itself sometimes as much, sometimes less. For the special effort in preparation for the king's return from France in 1432, see WAM 19672.

[11] *Monks*, 36–8; and see Harvey, *Estates*, Map II.

[12] For a reference to John Islip as John *de Pacientia*, see *Monks*, 168. For Nicholas Barton, see PRO C1/371/30, where he is described as a yeoman; for his identity as a miller, see WAM 14859. Abbot Islip acted as Barton's executor. For essential comment on locative surnames, see P. McClure, 'Patterns of migration in the late Middle Ages: the evidence of English place-name surnames', *Econ. Hist. Rev.*, 2nd ser. xxxii (1979), 167–82. In southern and midland England, outside the cloister, surnames, including locative names, tended to become hereditary c.1350. For a 15th-cent. example of the reversion of a monk of Westminster from the locative name 'London' to his family name, see *Monks*, 146.     [13] WAM 37044; *Monks*, 186–7.

known to us at this time, was not himself from Sudbury in Suffolk, although his father, Henry de Sudbury, a London skinner, may have been.[14]
Moreover, it had long been the practice for novices with well-known names
to keep them. Hence the occurrence of a name like le Gras in the Abbey
lists: Br. Richard le Gras, a monk of Westminster in the mid-thirteenth
century, may well have been a son of Henry III's servant, William le Gras.[15]

The evidence, although nearly always less specific than we could wish,
suggests that, in the later Middle Ages, the Abbey's precinct, the town of
Westminster, and the City of London may, together, have been as important
to the monastery as catchment areas for the recruitment of novices as its
country estates, if not more so. The Abbey's numerous servants and dependants lived here; so, too, the many ministerial and clerical families without whom the business of the Palace of Westminster and the lawcourts
could hardly have been carried on. Each of these groups probably supplied
the monastery with many recruits. Names such as Murimouth and Wynwyk,
Thornwerk and Tamworth, which occur in the monastic lists, were also
familiar names in royal administration or that of the monastery itself.[16]
Equally, a name like 'Karlill' reminds us of the metropolitan source of
recruits which had always been important to the community at Westminster: John Karlill, a monk of Westminster professed in 1397–8, bore the same
name as Adam Karlill, a prominent London grocer of the period, and a
connection is likely.[17] Occasionally, all these strands seem to come together,
as they must so often have done at the time. Walter Gedney, professed as
a monk of Westminster in 1394–5, and Thomas Gedney, professed some
twenty years later, bore the same name as John Gedney, a London draper
who supplied the monastery with cloth and ended his days as a corrodian,
housed in the Abbey's precinct.[18] A connection between the draper and one
or other of the monks, if not both, seems likely. But a John Gedney was
Richard II's clerk of works in the 1390s, and a connection between this
Gedney and the two monks is also a distinct possibility.[19]

---

[14] *Cal. of Wills enrolled in the Court of Hustings, London*, ed. Sharpe, ii. 225; *Monks*, 113.

[15] *Monks*, 48–9; Harvey, *Estates*, 389 and n. Cf., for an earlier period, *Lanfranc's Constitutions*, 112 and n.

[16] For monks so-named, see *Monks*, 95, 110, 149, and 188. Robert Wynewyke was a Gilbertine
canon before his profession at Westminster in 1367. For Richard Murimouth, clerk of the
wardrobe *temp*. Edward III, see Tout, *Chapters*, iv. 110; for John Winwick, keeper of the privy
seal *temp*. Edward III, and his family, *Cal. Papal Reg., Petitions*, i (1342–1419), 355–6; for
William Thornwerk (d. c.1460), the Abbey's mason, rent-collector, and tenant in the town of
Westminster, and corrodian, Appendix V, no. 63; for Thomas Tamworth, alias Tonworth, who
held the office of auditor at the Abbey 1517–32 and was auditor of the royal Exchequer, WAM
23015–25, 23027–8, and *L & P Henry VIII*, i(2), 2349, 2575, etc.

[17] *Monks*, 127; and for Adam Karlill, a prominent London grocer of the period, see Beaven,
*Aldermen*, i. 10, 34, 71, etc. See also *Westminster Chronicle*, 494; B. Wilkinson, 'The Peasants'
Revolt of 1381', *Speculum*, xv (1940), 12–35, at 33–5; and S. L. Thrupp, *The Merchant Class
of Medieval London [1300–1500]* (Chicago, 1948), 329.

[18] *Monks*, 125, 132–3. For John Gedney, see Appendix V, no. 56.

[19] Colvin (ed.), *History of the King's Works*, i. 192, 194.

Some novices, however, came from towns at a greater distance from the Abbey. John Cambridge, professed in 1418–19, was actually the son of a Cambridge man and probably himself from that town.[20] Nicholas Salisbury, professed a few years later, was, almost certainly, from Salisbury: his alias, 'Thomer', was evidently his family name, and, if so, we can assume that 'Salisbury' signified his place of origin.[21] In fact, many of the novices who entered Westminster Abbey in the later Middle Ages had been born and bred in an urban environment of one kind or another and belonged to the broadly based middle class of late medieval England. Even before they entered the almonry school—if they did—they were familiar with the hazards of an urban environment.

## (ii) Way of life and environment

In common with other Benedictine communities of the period, the community at Westminster fell into two groups. On the one hand were those who observed the common life, as it was then understood, in something approaching its entirety; on the other, those who were, in varying degrees, exempt from its demands. The former, the so-called cloister-monks (*claustrales*), kept the round of services going in the abbey church, ate their meals in common, and slept in the common dormitory. But office-holders like the cellarer and the sacrist were not expected to fulfil all these obligations, or even the greater part of them, and some monks, though not burdened with administrative cares, were deemed too distinguished, or merely too old, to be held to the humdrum routine. At any one time, moreover, two or three monks would probably be studying at Oxford, and towards the end of the Middle Ages this number rose to five or six. Most of the privileged group, though by no means all, occupied private apartments in the monastery and could take some of their meals there; others slept in the common dormitory, ate in public, but absented themselves from a number of the daily offices in the church. In a normal year, the privileged group probably accounted for *c*.66 per cent of the entire number of monks in the community, the cloister-monks for only *c*.33 per cent.[22] Of the entire number of monks in the community, *c*.45 per cent probably occupied private chambers.

---

[20] WAM 25364.    [21] *Monks*, 140.

[22] Novices, professed but not yet ordained, have been counted as cloister-monks. The probable break-down of the privileged group *c*.1500 is: office-holders, 12 major (including the abbot and prior) and 8 minor; university students, 4; permanent invalid, 1; other monks living privately in the infirmary, 7; recluse, 1. Total: 33. *c*.1400 there were more office-holders but only 2 students. For the students, see B. F. Harvey, 'The monks of Westminster and the University of Oxford', in F. R. H. Du Boulay and C. M. Barron (edd.), *The Reign of Richard II* (London, 1971), 108–30, at 112–13. Cf. the testimony of the prior of Peterborough Abbey in 1437 that, of the community of 44 monks in that house, only 10 or 12 (23 per cent or 27 per cent) normally participated in choir duties. However, he seems to have included monks undergoing the seyney—as many as 7 per week—among the absentees (*Visitations of Religious Houses*, iii. 273; and see below, p. 98).

The age-range of the community considered as a whole was very wide: it
stretched at times from the mid-teens to the eighties. However, for much
of the fifteenth century, the majority of monks were probably under the
age of 40, and about one-third under the age of 30. (See Figure IV.4.) Since
nearly all monks spent some years after profession as cloister-monks, this
group was probably, on average, the younger of the two which have been
identified.

Whichever group he belonged to, a monk of this period enjoyed in many
respects the material standard of living of the substantial gentry, and he
lived in buildings of a splendour and proportions fit for the nobility. Sanitary arrangements in the monastery were perhaps neither better nor worse
than those normally found in the residences of the gentry and nobility—a
surprising suggestion, it may appear, for the superiority of monastic water
systems and sewerage arrangements has become a commonplace of the social
history of the period. Certainly, the monastic plant was often impressive,
and it was so at the Abbey, which possessed a system taking piped water
to every major department in the monastery, and the inclusion of a filter
mechanism in the Abbey's system shows that the importance of pure water
was recognized.[23] Maintenance systems, however, were not always quite
as good, and where these arrangements were defective, great was the fall.
Normally, the weak point was not the main water system but the disposal
of effluent from the latrines, and here too the Abbey shared in the common
experience.

The use of latrines in the monastery was socially segregated: there were
latrines for, respectively, the monks, their officials, and the lay brethren
of the monastery, as well as some latrines for common use. Every major
department in the monastery had a public latrine, and one existed in the
infirmary itself.[24] The reredorter, the monks' principal latrine, was drained
by a so-called vault, a subterranean passage running across the entire

---

[23] For references to piped water in e.g. the treasurers' office, see WAM 19936, 19948; in the
sacrist's WAM 19678, 19692; and in the infirmary, WAM 19382, 19458, 19465; and see also
Map II. For the filter mechanism, see J. T. Micklethwaite, 'On a filtering cistern of the fourteenth century at Westminster Abbey', *Archaeologia*, liii (1892), 1–10, and G. Coppack, *Abbeys
and Priories* (English Heritage, London, 1990), 91–2; and for the better-known water-system
at Christ Church, Canterbury, R. Willis, *The Architectural History of the Conventual Buildings of the Monastery of Christ Church, in Canterbury* (London, 1869), 158–72, and Coppack,
op. cit., 81–3.

[24] For the public, or 'common', latrines in e.g. the sanctuary, see WAM 19672; in the almonry,
WAM 18991, 19053; and in the infirmary, WAM 19421. The latrine opening off the infirmary
cloister, which was kept under lock and key, was evidently for the monks, and possibly for
those living in private chambers in this department (WAM 19374, 19441); see also J. T.
Micklethwaite, 'Notes on the Abbey buildings of Westminster', *Archaeological Journal*, xxxiii
(1876), 15–48, at 34. A latrine by the oxhouse in the cellarer's office was for officials and is
described as 'new' in 1385–6 (WAM 18867). A latrine in the auditors' office is mentioned in
1518–19, when the operation of cleaning it cost the large sum of 5s. (WAM 23018). For the lay-
brethren's latrine in the almonry, see WAM 19019.

monastic site, from the water-course known as Long Ditch, on the west boundary, to debouch its contents into the River Thames on the east side by way of the fishpond of the Palace of Westminster. Such drainage systems were apt to develop faults: the brick or stone lining of the subterranean parts might cave in, the adjacent soil move into the available space, and the effluent seep into the soil inside and outside the ruined stretch of drain. In 1531 repairs to this vault necessitated 175½ man-days' labour of varying degrees of skill, and a small amount of night work as well, at a cost to the Abbey of £7 12s. 0½d.—a considerable outlay for the period.[25] Some other latrines in the monastery drained into cess-pits, and the condition of these was at times obnoxious. When the cess-pit serving the monks' latrine in the infirmary was reconstructed in 1369–70, tiles and mortar were used for a covering to contain the stench. The fact that the infirmarer noted the purpose of the outlay in his account suggests that the coverings of the monastery's cess-pits at this time were normally less substantial and less effective.[26]

Responsibility for cleaning the latrines was shared between the obedientiaries. It fell to the almoner to look after the reredorter itself, but the operation we glimpse in his accounts more resembles an episodic cleaning up than a routine keeping clean of the sensitive area. In 1440–1 two labourers who performed this task earned 1s. for the job, a sum suggesting that it occupied them for a whole day. The work must have been unpleasant.[27] Nor were other latrines better kept. In 1462–3, the sum of 3s. 4d.—the equivalent, in this period, of five days' wages for a skilled worker—was spent on cleaning the lay brethren's latrine in the almonry.[28]

As for the impression conveyed by our sources that the monks were not exactly houseproud, this no doubt has many parallels elsewhere. Yet it deserves notice. In the early fifteenth century, the refectorer appears to have had all his table-linen laundered for an outlay of 4s. per annum. The sum was perhaps double, but not much more than double, the amount which a monk living in a private chamber might expect to spend on laundry for a year. Thus, in 1396 the laundress who saw to the needs of Br. Richard Exeter in his private chamber received 2s. for six months' ordinary service and extra work during his last illness.[29] The monks, we may suspect, often

---

[25] WAM 24859. For the course of the drain in the Abbey's precinct, see Maps I and II. (I am particularly indebted to John and Sarah Blair for help on this point.) For remarkably similar repairs to the successor of this drain, the Abbey's so-called 'great sewer', in 1715, see WAM 24846.

[26] WAM 19347. The cess-pit was lined with urnel (Kentish ragstone), on which see L. F. Salzman, *Building in England down to 1540* (Oxford, 1952), 129. For the stench of the public latrine in the almonry in the 1360s, see Rosser, *Medieval Westminster*, p. 69.

[27] WAM 19048. Work on one of the almonry latrines, by 3 men for 2 days, is also mentioned in this account. [28] WAM 19069.

[29] WAM 6603, and for the refectorer's outlay, WAM 19509–37. At his death in 1400, Br. John de Canterbury, who had occupied a chamber in the infirmary, owed his laundress 3 years' arrears of pay, and his executors gave her 6s. 8d. (WAM 18883A).

ate off sordid table linen. 'Twice this year', wrote the refectorer in the early sixteenth century, of the operation of cleaning the salt-cellars used at meals in the refectory, as though to explain the expense of it all.[30]

Outside the monastery was the town of Westminster—a town with a core population of c.2,000 at the beginning of the fifteenth century, perhaps as many as 3,000 a century later, and, additionally, a considerable number who came and went according to need.[31] Here, a marshy site made for an unhealthy environment; so too did the unusually large number of resident victuallers, and especially butchers, whose trade was with the Abbey and the Palace of Westminster; in this period, where there were butchers there were also slaughter-houses and a great deal of noisome refuse to be disposed of somehow or other.[32] And if to be the haunt of prostitutes was to be urbanized, then late medieval Westminster was urbanized. In 1523 a dozen people were presented in the manor court for keeping brothels or being themselves prostitutes, and the problem was not new: a brothel called the 'Maydenshed' is mentioned in 1447 and said to be then frequented by Benedictine monks.[33]

The monks moved in and around the monastery, and beyond it, with a freedom that will surprise those unfamiliar with the open nature of Benedictine life in the Middle Ages. On occasion the whole community processed through the streets of the town. At a time of national emergency Abbot Colchester (1386–1420) urged his monks to process in this way every Friday.[34] Individually or in small groups the monks took holidays away from the monastery.[35] In the monastery they were visited by their families from near and far—a purpose for which the cellarer set aside 200 loaves and 200 gallons of ale per annum in the early fifteenth century.[36] When the parliamentary Commons met in the monastery, every monk must have rubbed shoulders with the knights and burgesses, since the rooms which they used—first the chapter house, but later the refectory—opened off the main cloister. Towards the end of the Middle Ages, monks made the pilgrimage to Walsingham, to the Rood of Grace at Boxley, and to the older

---

[30] WAM 19607–8. Cf. the banning of ornaments, as likely to collect germs, in the cottages provided for tuberculosis patients in Papworth Village Settlement in the early 20th cent. (L. Bryder, *Below the Magic Mountain: A Social History of Tuberculosis in Twentieth-Century Britain* (Oxford, 1988), 161).     [31] Rosser, *Medieval Westminster*, 168, 176.

[32] Ibid. 138–41, 241–2; id., 'The essence of medieval urban communities: the vill of Westminster 1200–1540', *TRHS* 5th ser. xxxiv (1984), 91–112, at 99–100.

[33] WAM 50778; Rosser, *Medieval Westminster*, 143–4; and for the 'Maydenshed', PRO KB 9/997, m. 61. I am indebted to Dr Isobel Harvey for the last reference.

[34] WAM 6221. The occasion of this exhortation was probably the rebellion of Owen Glendower and Henry and Thomas Percy in 1403. For an explicit reference to the distribution of alms in the town by monks in person in 1460–1, see WAM 19067.

[35] Below, p. 99; and for the general practice, *RO* i. 284–5, and ii. 246.

[36] WAM 18887, where the allowance is said to be for parents and sisters. For bread for parents in later bakers' accounts, see WAM 31916, fos. 4 and 24ᵛ; WAM 33315, fo. 6ᵛ.

shrine of St. Thomas at Canterbury.[37] Servants were in daily attendance, bringing into the monastery whatever infections they had picked up in the town of Westminster, where many of them lived. In fact, the monks were no whit protected by their mode of life from the infections that afflicted their neighbours in the town of Westminster and the City of London or from those of a more distant provenance. Who, then, looked after the monks when they were ill?

## 3. The Treatment of Sickness at the Abbey

### (i) The infirmarer and his assistants

The key person in a monastic infirmary was always the infirmarer himself, and he was a monk. Once, this official would probably have been regarded, inside and outside the cloister, as a *medicus*, for in a very general sense he was a medical practitioner, and down to the twelfth century this is the only meaning that the title necessarily conveyed in England. In the later Middle Ages, the growing professionalism of the art of medicine denied him the title and much of his former importance at the actual bedside and in the dispensary. Moreover, it was now unlawful for a priest—and virtually all monks of Westminster were priests in this period—to practise surgery, as perhaps infirmarers had done formerly.[38] Yet even now infirmarers at Westminster were evidently chosen with special care, and some remained in post for a very long time. John de Mordon, in the mid-fourteenth century, and John Ramsey, in the late fifteenth, each held the office for more than twenty years—a very unusual episode in the annals of office-holding at the Abbey, and a sure indication that each possessed skills which could not easily be replaced.[39] In the case of an infirmarer, academic qualifications were mistrusted. Accordingly, although the Abbey sent more than seventy

[37] For Richard Charing's pilgrimage to the shrine of St Thomas of Canterbury in Aug. 1484 and Thomas Clifford's to Walsingham at the end of Sept. that year, see WAM 33289, fo. 17ᵛ; for Prior Mane's pilgrimage to the Rood of Grace in May 1511 and May 1512, WAM 33325, fos. 13ᵛ, 48ᵛ; and for the pilgrimage of Thomas Ledgold and Christopher Goodhaps to Walsingham in Aug. 1529, WAM 31916, fos. 25, 25ᵛ.

[38] *Decretals of Gregory IX*, Bk. III, tit. 50, cap. 9, cited in Rawcliffe, 'The hospitals of late medieval London', 8 and n. By this decretal, based on a decree of the Fourth Lateran Council (1215), surgery involving burning and cutting was forbidden to priests, deacons, and subdeacons. The indispensable work on medical practitioners in late medieval England is still *MPME*, now supplemented by F. Getz, 'Medical practitioners in medieval England', *Social History of Medicine*, iii (1990), 245–83; and see C. Rawcliffe, 'The profits of practice: the wealth and status of medical men in later medieval England', ibid. i (1988), 61–78. R. S. Gottfried, *Doctors and Medicine in Medieval England, 1340–1530* (Princeton, NJ, 1986) is to be used cautiously. For the meaning of 'medicus' in an earlier period, see E. J. Kealey, *Medieval Medicus: A Social History of Anglo-Norman Medicine* (Baltimore, 1981), 34–5, and, earlier still, V. J. Flint, 'The early medieval "medicus", the saint—and the enchanter', *Social History of Medicine*, ii (1989), 127–45.

[39] *Monks*, 88, 150, and for the list of known infirmarers, ibid. 201.

monks to the university during the period under consideration, not one of these, as far as we know, held the office of infirmarer at a later stage in his career. Yet infirmarers were expected to be bookish men, and for this reason a number who had formerly been precentor were appointed to the office: in a Benedictine house the precentor normally looked after the library. John de Mordon, who became infirmarer in 1357, had been precentor; so, too, Robert Davers, who became infirmarer in 1525 and was one of the last to hold the office.[40] Evidently, the passage of nearly two centuries had not undermined the view that the one office might fit a monk for the other.

The infirmarer's principal adviser was a professional physician, a *medicus* in the contemporary sense of the word. Once, this official enjoyed a corrody which included wine and flans—a corrody, in fact, of a superior kind.[41] In the later Middle Ages, however, he served the Abbey in return for a fee and livery. The convent's physician, as he was called, belonged to what was now, in the metropolitan area, a graded profession, and arrangements at Westminster reflect some of the nice distinctions characterizing it. Mr Geoffrey—his full name is not known—who served as the convent's physician from 1395 to 1409, received a fee of £2 13s. 4d. per annum and, as livery, a robe with furs of lambskin. By the Abbey's standards, the fee was a substantial one and comparable in amount to those offered by the monks of this period to important royal clerks whose good will they valued. However, the robe signifies that Mr Geoffrey ranked as a mere valet in the conventual household. Some of his predecessors had received considerably larger fees and robes with furs of budge—a very superior lambskin— robes with three furs instead of two or robes described simply as 'large robes', any of which ensured that they would be given a place above the valets on formal occasions.[42] Similar distinctions occur among the physicians who were not retained by the Abbey but consulted on occasion. Even in the later fourteenth century, some charged as little as 3s. 4d. for a consultation.[43] But when Mr Robert de Renham, a London physician, was summoned to

[40] *Monks*, 173. William Litlyngton (infirmarer 1391) and John Kympton (1450–9) had, to our knowledge, also been precentors (ibid. 108–9, 137).

[41] *Customary*, ii. 79, where the reference to wine and flans is evidence that the *medicus* of this period enjoyed a comprehensive corrody. There is no evidence of such an arrangement later, and some evidence that it had lapsed: see Appendix V, no. 67, and for 'wine and flans', below, p. 172. For the physicians mentioned in the following account, see Appendix III, nos. 17–43.

[42] For the much larger rewards of medical practice in royal and aristocratic households, and the possibility that these were not given solely in respect of medical practice, see Rawcliffe, 'The profits of practice', 66–72.

[43] WAM 19380. The physician was John Emme. c.1460 a fee of 3s. 4d. was given to an unnamed priest-physician (WAM 33288, fo. 26ᵛ). In 1440–1 a physician who was probably the convent's physician, and therefore in receipt of an annual fee, received 2s. 4d. for inspecting the urine of a number of sick monks (WAM 19419).

Abbot Walter de Wenlok's bedside much earlier, in December 1307, he received £1, in a silk purse, for one consultation and the sum of £5 for another. Mr John le Gros, who also attended on the second occasion, received as much as £2. Wenlok's case, however, was desperate, and he was dead within the month.[44]

However high he stood in his profession, the convent's physician was expected to visit his patients in the monastery and may have entered into a contract specifying this duty. For these visits, he might receive small, additional, payments, but would not necessarily do so. If out of town, and therefore unavailable, he forfeited his fee for the period in question: indeed, in 1361–2, the physician forfeited his robe as well as a quarter's fee because he had been away for that period.[45]

Although some of the physicians who attended the late medieval community at Westminster engaged in tasks that would have been considered surgeon's or apothecaries' work in Italy or France, where distinctions were more sharply drawn, their role in general seems to have been quite well defined. By the mid-fourteenth century, their characteristic work was diagnosis and the prescribing of the appropriate treatment; the treatment itself they often delegated to others. In 1354–5, for example, it was the physician who prescribed treatment for Br. John Bampton's *tibia*—a term which, in the context, probably denotes varicose ulcers in the region of the shin-bone—but the surgeon who carried it out; and two years later it was the physician who prescribed a clyster for a sickly monk named R. Solers, but the apothecary who dispensed it.[46] When, as frequently happened, a physician supplied medicines to the infirmary, it does not follow that he actually dispensed them: he may have had an apothecary working under his direction or in partnership with him. Such arrangements are clearly indicated in the mid-fourteenth century, when the convent's physician, accompanied by an apothecary, met the infirmarer once a year, to go through their bill for medicines and agree on a timetable for payment.[47] Yet the line must not be drawn too clearly: some physicians did dispense the medicines which they prescribed for the monks: in 1386–7, for example, it is implied that a woman physician did so.[48]

[44] *Walter de Wenlok*, 208, 212. The two physicians incurred the expense of riding from London to Pyrford (Surr.), where Wenlok died.

[45] WAM 19341. The physician was William de Pyl. On contracts, see Rawcliffe, 'The profits of practice', 62–3.

[46] WAM 19334, 19336. J. Bosevill', mentioned on the latter occasion, also dispensed some medicines for a case of *tibia*. On this condition see below, p. 109.

[47] WAM 19332–3. On these two occasions the physicians were Henry de Wygneston and William Walleram.

[48] 'Et mulieri phisiciane pro labore et medicinis factis fratribus J. Farnyngho . . . [9 other names follow] xls.' (WAM 19370).

The infirmarer did not give his custom exclusively to one apothecary, and in some years did business with several: as many as five are mentioned in his account for 1305–6.[49] Nevertheless, the fact that many of the physicians of this period had close working relationships with particular apothecaries ensured that at any given time one was more important than any other in the economy of the infirmary. In the middle decades of the fourteenth century, this position was occupied by Thomas Walden, a London apothecary whose son, another Thomas, was in practice with him. The elder Walden began to serve the monks of Westminster in 1339 and was their principal apothecary during the Black Death of 1348–9, a catastrophe in which about half the community died. The plague Walden survived, but he could not escape the occupational hazard of his profession—waiting for the client to pay the bill. The old debts which the infirmarer finally settled in March 1350 amounted to as much as £30, a sum which would probably have kept three or four monks of this period in food and clothing for a year.[50] Yet assisted, perhaps, by the prestige of his connection with the Abbey, Walden prospered. Some of his wealth found its way into the monks' hands, for he founded a chantry in the Abbey with a lump sum of £100—a substantial endowment for a private chantry at this time.[51]

Some of the basic ingredients of the medicines which the physician prescribed were prepared by the infirmarer himself and his assistant, who was a secular clerk or layman, and these two were capable of dispensing some whole recipes. The apothecary was needed for complex recipes and for those which were too time-consuming for a busy infirmarer to attempt. He might come into the infirmary for this purpose—and would need to do so if using herbs from the infirmarer's garden—or dispense the medicines in question on his own premises or those of the physician with whom he was associated. Thomas de Ely, one of the apothecaries named in 1305–6, dispensed some of the medicines which he supplied for the monks in the monastery and some, it is implied, elsewhere.[52] Much later, in 1496, during the protracted illness of Abbot John Estney that year, medicinal waters needed by the patient were distilled in the abbot's house at La Neyte from betony, centaury, honeysuckles, and other plants. The apothecary, for his part, supplied made-up cordials, lozenges, and pills, including the so-called

[49] Mr Guy, J. de Cantuaria, J. de Sudwerk, John de Notegarshale, and Thomas de Ely. For these and other apothecaries employed by the Abbey, see Appendix III, nos. 1–16. Briefly, in 1340, the infirmarer employed an apothecary-surgeon, who received a stipend of 10s. per quarter and messed with the other servants in the infirmary (WAM 19326, 19329).

[50] WAM 19331. Of the sum of £30, £10 may actually have been received a little before Mar. 1350. Cf. Rawcliffe, 'The profits of practice', 74–5.

[51] Harvey, *Estates*, 395. Cf. Gottfried, *Doctors and Medicine in Medieval England, 1340–1530*, 79–81.

[52] WAM 19319. It is implied in WAM 19345 that the normal duties of the infirmarer's clerk included the fetching of medicines and other necessities for sick monks from London.

golden pills that were quite frequently administered to well-to-do patients in this period: golden pills he supplied by the boxful.[53]

The surgeons who attended the monks of Westminster often worked under the physician's supervision. Each, however, was more of a craftsman and less of a diagnostician than he. Very occasionally an abdominal operation—as, for example, the correction of a rupture—is mentioned, and this kind of work may have been commoner than the very few explicit references in our sources may seem to suggest.[54] But the bread-and-butter work of the surgeon was the treatment of fractures and wounds, including ulcers, the application of plasters, and purging if effected by means of clysters. (Purging by means of medicines taken through the mouth was a task for the physician and apothecary.) In fact, anything applied externally was within his province, and it was the surgeon who normally made up the plasters and other remedies required in such cases. The surgeon probably dispensed many of these in the infirmary, and occasionally the cost of the raw materials is recorded in the infirmarer's accounts.[55] For much of his work, but especially when performing internal operations or setting broken bones, he needed, in addition to his other skills, the art of keeping the patient still, for this was, of course, a period when anaesthetics were non-existent or of a rudimentary kind.

No surgeon employed at the Abbey in the later Middle Ages attained to the status of a feed retainer. Yet if the surgeon's social status was low or equivocal, as this fact implies, he was nevertheless well paid for the operations and courses of treatment that he carried out: indeed, in his case good pay may be regarded as a form of compensation for low status. In 1393–4 the total cost to the infirmarer of the surgery required by three monks was £2 16s. 8d.[56] If the same surgeon was in charge of the three cases, his earnings amounted to more than half the fee currently received by the convent's physician as a retainer for a year. Even women surgeons, whose rates of pay may have been in general lower than those offered to the men, received some quite large fees. The woman who treated another case of *tibia*, that of

---

[53] WAM 33291, fos. 2, 5ᵛ, 8ᵛ, 9, etc., and for the golden pills, ibid., fo 20ᵛ. Absinth, horehound, pimpernel, and 'pelesot' are also mentioned among the items distilled. For 'pelesot' ('pilosella,' mouse-ear hawkweed), see T. Hunt, *Popular Medicine in Thirteenth-Century England* (Cambridge, 1990), 409. The distillery was in the garden of the abbot's house, which was near the Abbey, in present-day Pimlico.

[54] WAM 19318 (a case of rupture in 1297–8, for which the surgeon received 4s.). For a case of surgery on genitals, see n. 57 below.

[55] e.g. in 1347–8: 'in albo coreo pro emplastris empto viij d.' (WAM 19330). The white wine and olive oil mentioned here, if not the honey and vinegar, were probably for use by the surgeon.

[56] The cost per monk was respectively 10s., £1, and £1 6s. 8d. (WAM 19380); and for the fee of £5 p.a. received by Mr John, the convent's physician, for the year June 1394–June 1395, see Appendix III, no. 24. The ambiguities of the surgeon's status in 14th-cent. France are discussed in M.-C. Pouchelle, *The Body and Surgery in the Middle Ages* (Oxford, 1990), *passim*.

John de Mordon in 1374-5, received £1 10s. 6d. This was less than the sum
of £2 which had already been spent on surgery for this case before she was
called in, but by contemporary standards it was certainly more than pin-
money.[57]

Because surgeons were not retained but paid by piece-rates, they are
seldom identified in our sources. In fact only four are named there: William
de Otewyk and William de Wodestret in the early fourteenth century; John
Bradmore and William Wadesworth at the end of the century.[58] John
Bradmore had been admitted to practice by the authorities of the City of
London—a pointer to the current, though only partially successful, moves
towards the establishment of a licensed profession.[59] It will already be
apparent that the infirmarer occasionally employed women in a surgical
capacity. If to be called in second, on the failure of another practitioner to
cure the patient, is to be highly regarded, the woman who treated Br. John
de Mordon in 1374-5 stood well in her profession.[60]

In a monastic infirmary routine care of the sick always presented the
authorities with a difficult problem, because needs fluctuated from week to
week, and quite frequently the infirmary had no in-patients at all. Moreover, even when beds were occupied, needs varied: sometimes day and night
attendance was needed, sometimes a much less intensive form of care. Some
of these problems could be solved by seconding labour from other departments in the monastery as need arose, and in the early fourteenth century
this practice is recorded at Christ Church, Canterbury. Here, two servants
were provided for every chamber in the infirmary that was actually occupied. One of the two also worked in the priory kitchen: he was probably
a permanent member of the kitchen staff, released for part-time work in the
infirmary when need arose there.[61] Roland Hyde, who received 12d. at
Westminster Abbey in 1536-7, for watching for four nights at the bedside
of a sick novice, was probably one of the monastery's regular servants.[62] But
it was also possible to hire sick attendants *ad hoc*, by the day or week, and
this practice is recorded at Westminster in the first two decades of the
fifteenth century. Wages of 2d. and 4d. are variously recorded for what

[57] WAM 19351. In the same year, surgeons treating, respectively, John de Somerton's hand
and Roger de Denham's genitals received, in each case, £1.

[58] Appendix III, nos. 44-7.

[59] H. T. Riley (ed.), *Memorials of London and London Life in the xiiith, xivth and xvth
centuries* (London, 1868), 519-20; and below, Appendix III, no. 44. For the background see
R. S. Roberts, 'The personnel and practice of medicine in Tudor and Stuart England', pt. ii,
*Medical History*, viii (1964), 217-34, at 218-20.

[60] WAM 19351. For women physicians employed by the Abbey in the late 14th and early
15th cents., see Appendix III, no. 22.

[61] *Pro qualibet camera actualiter occupata per infirmum duo garciones, quorum alter
permutatur in coquina cum cocis Conventus* (J. Brigstocke Sheppard (ed.), *Literae Cantuarienses*
(3 vols., RS 1887-9), ii. 94). In practice the arrangement would probably have worked out as
suggested in the text.                                                    [62] WAM 19502.

is in each case described as a day and a night's attendance.[63] The infirmarer probably offered a cash wage of 2*d*. for day and night duty, together with full board, or an additional 2*d*. in lieu. The board wages were relatively high for this period at the Abbey—higher in fact than those currently received by the infirmarer's cook and butler. But we must remember that the sick attendant's wages were his entire emoluments: many others working in and around the Abbey in this period belonged to the monastery's permanent establishment and in consequence were entitled to a stipend or livery, if not both, as well.[64] The sick attendant's pay was in fact rather low.

## (ii) The infirmary buildings

The Abbey's infirmary, where physician, apothecary, surgeon, and others all attended when needed, was no isolation hospital. In common with every other kind of hospital in the Middle Ages, a monastic infirmary was used for other purposes beside the care of the sick, and the infirmary at Westminster was no exception to the rule. Indeed, at times the sick had to struggle to retain an adequate foothold here. In the later Middle Ages, their chief rivals were senior monks who had grown weary of the common life and wished to live privately. Possession of a chamber in the infirmary, or even half a chamber—for a chamber was a commodious apartment—would enable them to do this. Some of the monks competing for the desirable accommodation were themselves invalids, who wished to live permanently in the infirmary; rather more were probably still capable of following the routine prescribed for healthy monks but lacking in the will to do so. The chambers in the infirmary were so much sought after by monks of this disposition that the prior, who allocated them, was able to demand payments that we recognize as key-money. In 1484, when several chambers changed hands, Prior Essex received payments of £2, £3, and £3 10*s*. respectively from the new occupants of three chambers.[65] It seems probable, too, that corrodians—that is, seculars who had purchased life annuities from the Abbey—were occasionally housed in the infirmary.[66] Of the six or seven chambers which existed in the late medieval infirmary, only two were actually reserved for the use of the transient sick.

If senior monks were always there, other intruders into the infirmary

---

[63] WAM 19392–407. Towards the end of Br. Richard Tedyngton's life, in 1487, a woman assisted in his chamber, and her work may have included some actual nursing (WAM 33289, fo. 51ᵛ).

[64] Below, pp. 168–76.

[65] WAM 33289, fo. 17ᵛ. The sums mentioned in the text were paid for chambers shared, in each case, by two monks. For a fourth chamber, apparently in sole occupancy, the payment was £1 6*s*. 8*d*. For an earlier reference to a payment that was probably key-money, see WAM 23503; and for a vivid glimpse of the kind of pressure exerted by senior monks and permanent invalids on the chambers in the late 15th cent., WAM 6213.

[66] Appendix V, nos. 9, 16; see also the hint of secular occupation in WAM 6213.

were birds of passage, here today and gone tomorrow, but not easily ignored while present. A society wedding is recorded in 1405–6, and several
visits by the prince of Wales and other magnates in the same year.[67] For a
time in 1430–1, Humphrey, duke of Gloucester, may have used the chapel
in the infirmary as his private chapel.[68] And there were always the royal
clerks, scurrying from the king's palace on the east side of the monastery to
the main cloister area of the monastery and finding the short cut through
the monks' infirmary very convenient for the purpose.[69] It was, it appears,
simply asking too much to try and reserve amenities so conveniently situated in the legal and administrative capital of late medieval England for the
sick for whom they had been primarily created. Even so, the infirmary was
probably the quietest part of the monastery, and this explains why it was
chosen as the site for both the studies for which the community felt a need
towards the end of the Middle Ages. The earlier of these, built in 1391–2,
was apparently a free-standing structure in the garden.[70] The other, built a
century later, was at first-floor level, in the infirmary itself but with an
external flight of steps giving independent access.[71]

   The actual buildings in use at the beginning of the fourteenth century
were nearly 150 years old and rather out of date. The belief, which has
enjoyed some support, that these buildings were arranged, very precociously,
around a cloister rests on a misunderstanding of a passage in the legate
Ottobuono's Constitutions for the Abbey in 1268: Ottobuono here refers
to the monastery's main cloister and to the passage leading from this to the
infirmary, but not to an infirmary cloister.[72] In the old infirmary, and following the common practice of the early Middle Ages, the sick were accommodated in a hall forming a westward extension of the chapel; and the
beds were arranged in two aisles, separated by a space in which the infirmarer
and his servants could move.[73] In 1298 this infirmary was damaged by fire,
but perhaps not quite as badly damaged as the monks liked to pretend in

---

[67] WAM 19397. The marriage was between William, lord Botreaux and Elizabeth, daughter
of John, lord Beaumont. The bridegroom may have had a house in the precinct: see the later
reference to 'domus Botreux' in WAM 23081. On the use of the chapel, see also Westlake,
*Westminster Abbey*, ii. 331.                                              [68] WAM 19416.

   [69] For their rough treatment of obstacles encountered *en route*, see WAM 19334, 19336. These
references, however, are to the old infirmary. For Ottobuono's attempt, in 1268, to keep the
intruders out, see WD 28ᵛ.

   [70] WAM 19376. The *nova domus* referred to here is probably the study mentioned in the
Dissolution inventories; see *Abbot's House at Westminster*, 47.

   [71] WAM 19474. For this room, which had a window requiring 14 ft. of glass, see also Westlake,
*Westminster Abbey*, ii. 326–7.                      [72] WD 28–28ᵛ; BL Cotton Faustina A III, 210.

   [73] Westlake, *Westminster Abbey*, ii. 319–20, where the suggested plan is consistent with the
reference to the servants in attendance on, respectively, the north side and the south side of the
old infirmary in *Customary*, ii. 244. On monastic infirmaries in general, see R. Liddesdale
Palmer, *English Monasteries in the Middle Ages* (London, 1930), 154–9; R. Gilyard-Beer,
*Abbeys: An Illustrated Guide to the Abbeys of England and Wales* (HMSO 1976), 40–3; and
Coppack, *Abbeys and Priories*, 76–8.

the fund-raising efforts which followed.[74] At any rate, it is hard to believe that a fire could have disturbed the infirmarer's existing arrangements as little as this one did, or that the old buildings would have served, as they did with only modest repairs, for sixty or seventy more years had the damage been half as serious as reported at the time.

The new infirmary, which did indeed follow the cloister plan, was begun in 1364 or 1365, early in Nicholas de Litlyngton's abbacy, but probably not finished until three or four years after his death in 1386.[75] Of the former complex of buildings, only the chapel of St Katherine survived: hall, kitchen, chambers and parlours, storehouse—itself a huge room, taking three or four years to complete—and the other offices were all new. There were probably five chambers in the new complex. A sixth had evidently been added by 1430–1, when it is referred to as 'the new chamber', and another was built by William de Chertsey (d. 1487) at his own expense.[76] Both these additions were probably built for the transient sick. Both, however, were quickly appropriated by permanent residents. In the new infirmary, as in the old, some accommodation must have been provided at ground-floor level. However, at least two of the chambers, and possibly more, were at first-floor level. If so, nearly all the ground-floor level was available for the hall, parlours, and offices. The rooms on the ground floor served the needs of day-patients as well as those of walking cases among the in-patients, and the hall was needed also for guests. Separate accommodation was provided for the cook, but quite possibly for no other servants. Some of the lower servants in the infirmary probably slept in the kitchen, or where they could, and servants attending sick monks slept in the chambers of the latter.[77] The new infirmary was served by piped water, as indeed the old may have been; it may be fortuitous that the only rooms in which this amenity is mentioned are the kitchen and buttery.[78]

In the infirmary parlours, there were hangings of red and green worsted,

---

[74] For references see Harvey, *Estates*, 51, and for arrangements in the infirmary immediately after the fire, WAM 19318.

[75] For the details underpinning the following account, see WAM 19344–74, 19419*, and Westlake, *Westminster Abbey*, ii. 324–6. There is also much useful detail in Micklethwaite, 'Notes on the Abbey buildings of Westminster', 31–6. The infirmary cloister was roofed and the garth turfed in 1389–90. For the ample accommodation in a chamber in the new infirmary, see WAM 18883A.

[76] For the first of the new chambers, see WAM 23503 (a reference suggesting that it was already, in 1431–2, in private occupation), and for Chertsey's chamber, WAM 6213. These, with two others, made up the four said to be in private occupation in 1484 (WAM 33289, fo. 17ᵛ). The infirmarer's own chamber and the two reserved for the transient sick made up the seven. One of the original six is said to be 'by the chapel' and may have been a little apart from the rest (WAM 19375). The Dissolution inventories, which mention only six chambers, probably omit the infirmarer's own (*Abbot's House at Westminster*, 46–8).

[77] The latter practice is implied in WAM 6213. For the cook's chamber, see WAM 19441.

[78] WAM 19382, 19414, 19458, 19465–6.

and blue cushions patterned with tree foliage and birds in flight.[79] At the beginning of the fifteenth century, a curtain with a *historia*, a pictorial representation of some kind, is mentioned in one of the two chambers set aside for the sick.[80] In these chambers, the infirmarer provided the beds, pallets, or mattresses, and the straw which the latter covered. Indeed, his purchase of a second-hand feather-bed in 1400 suggests that he sometimes provided more comfortable furnishings than a pallet.[81] The sick monk brought his own bedclothes: hence the use of the phrase *cum pannis*—'with bed-clothes'—to denote a monk who was an in-patient in the infirmary.[82] By custom the rushes covering the floor of the chambers were renewed on the vigils of principal feasts, of which there were about twelve in the course of a year, and whenever a monk was buried.[83] The chambers had fires, so also the infirmary hall, and at least one of the parlours.[84]

Outside the cloister area, walking cases and convalescents could take the air in the garden on the south side of the infirmary and in the orchard there, admire the vines, and watch the occupants for the time being of the infirmarer's fish-pond.[85] From the 1460s onwards, they could applaud the skill of healthy monks practising at the archery butts placed at that time in the infirmarer's garden.[86] If, however, they went in the opposite direction, they could perambulate the tombs in the monks' cemetery: this was very near the infirmary, but on the north side. Yet, wherever one was, it must often have been difficult to forget the plumbing. One of the infirmary latrines opened off the cloister and another was by the entry to the garden.[87] Moreover, the main drain of the monastery, which gave such trouble in 1531, ran under the infirmary garden for part of its course.[88]

---

[79] For the cushions, see WAM 19404; for the purchase of green worsted, WAM 19452, 19458; and for the red and green hangings, *Abbot's House at Westminster*, 46.

[80] WAM 19404; cf. the 'peynted clothes' hanging in both chambers at the Dissolution (*Abbot's House at Westminster*, 47).

[81] WAM 18883A. The purchase was made from the goods of the deceased John de Canterbury. For the pallets and straw, see WAM 19325, 19339, 19395; and for the infirmarer's obligation to provide straw for the beds, *Customary*, ii. 245.

[82] A common usage: for another example, see *Customary of Bury St Edmunds*, 14, 59. However, in the early 16th cent., the phrase *cum pannis* is used at Westminster to denote monks who lived privately in chambers in the infirmary, and in this monastery it may now have been reserved for this group (WAM 18941, fo. 3; WAM 33315, *passim*).

[83] *Customary*, ii. 245. The vigil of the Ascension ranked as a principal feast for this purpose.

[84] For the talwood and faggots used in the hall and chambers, see WAM 19394 ff.; and for andirons and bellows, signifying fires, in the parlour, *Abbot's House at Westminster*, 46.

[85] For the garden, see Map I. In 1440–1 it was said to measure 90 ft. (29.5 m.) from the entrance 'towards the west' to the stone wall of the king's garden (WAM 19419). For the fish-pond, mentioned in 1305–6 and 1310–11, see WAM 19319, 19321; for the apple crop, signifying the existence of an orchard, WAM 19343; and for the vines (down to c.1400), WAM 19386, 19390. See also, for the infirmarer's garden, J. Harvey, *Medieval Gardens* (London, 1981), 84, 110, 112, 140.

[86] In 1462–3, 5 labourers spent 18 days clearing the ground for the butts, and 35 cartloads of turves were purchased for the latter (WAM 19443).

[87] WAM 19374, 19389.       [88] Above, p. 79.

## (iii) The regimes for sick monks

Although the infirmary at Westminster was used so freely for purposes other than the care of the sick, gaining access if one was actually ill was never easy. There might, of course, be an emergency, when it would be necessary to waive formalities: the Abbey's Customary, compiled in the thirteenth century, instances an attack of gout, making it suddenly impossible to climb the stairs to the dormitory where monks normally slept.[89] In principle, however, a monk wishing to enter the infirmary sought the permission of the prior and convent at the daily chapter meeting.[90] Everything that we know about the conduct of affairs in the infirmary makes it easy to believe that access was in practice carefully regulated, and there were sound reasons why this should be so. In the Middle Ages, sickness, like mortality, was variable. It was a wise infirmarer who husbanded his resources, particularly his beds, for the emergency that might come at any time. Moreover, despite every relaxation of the common life in the later Middle Ages, an earlier convention that a monk did not surrender lightly to illness may still have made itself felt from time to time.[91]

In principle, there were two regimes for the sick, and it is convenient to refer to them as the regimes of, respectively, a day-patient and an in-patient. However, these terms were not in contemporary use: at the time, a day-patient was described as a monk 'outside the choir'[92]—a reference to the fact that he did not participate fully, if at all, in the office—and, for the reason mentioned above, an in-patient was said to be in the infirmary 'with bed-clothes'.[93] It is hardly necessary to say that an in-patient spent his nights as well as his days in the infirmary. A day-patient took his meals there and could, if necessary, spend the rest of the day in one of the infirmary parlours. He might or might not take medicine or undergo other forms of treatment, of which the commonest was a special diet, and, after diet, a seyney or blood-letting. Day-treatment was regarded as essentially short-term treatment, and in only one of the years—1305–6—for which we have evidence did the average number of days per patient per annum exceed fourteen.[94] Moreover, in most years, the common individual period of attendance for such treatment was two days. For a seyney, only three or four

---

[89] *Customary*, ii. 234. We are reminded by this passage that in the old infirmary all the sick were nursed at ground-floor level.

[90] Ibid. ii. 23, 234; and for other restrictions on the infirmarer's freedom of action, which lend credibility to these rules, below, p. 93.

[91] On some earlier attitudes, see P. Hordern, 'The death of ascetics: sickness and monasticism in the early Byzantine Middle East', in W. J. Shiels (ed.), *Monks, Hermits and the Ascetic Tradition* (SCH xxii, 1985), 41–52.

[92] *extra chorum*. For many examples, see WAM 19318–19.          [93] Above, p. 90.

[94] WAM 19318–30. These accounts cover in whole or in part 11 years in the period 1297–1348. In 1305–6 the average per patient p.a. was 16.8 days. It is of interest that a monk with a fever was treated, in Aug. 1352, as a day-patient, not as an in-patient (WAM 19332).

days, counting both the first and the last, were normally allowed.[95] In practice, however, in-patient treatment was often as short as the periods which have been mentioned, for, if the infirmarer was reluctant to fill his beds, he was naturally eager to empty them again as soon as possible. This is one reason—there were, of course, others—why stays, or periods of residence, of eight nights or less were very common: in the period 1375–1464 more than 60 per cent of all known stays in the infirmary were as short as this. (See Table III.2.)

## (iv) Diet

For both day-patients and in-patients, the principal form of treatment was the infirmary diet. Formerly, one of the distinctive features of this diet was the inclusion of flesh-meat: in the infirmary, but nowhere else in the monastery, with the sole exception of the abbot's table, flesh-meat might be served quite regularly. However, by the fourteenth century, the rules on diet were so far relaxed at Westminster that even healthy monks normally consumed meat several times a week, and a room, the misericord, was set aside for the purpose.[96] Even at the beginning of this century, the rhythm of meat days and fish days in the infirmary differed in only one or two respects from that observed by healthy monks elsewhere in the monastery. The most important of these related to the diet during Advent, the four weeks preceding Christmas: during Advent in this period, there were meat days for sick monks, but not for others.[97] Remarkably, in the 1330s—between 1334 and 1339—the Advent fast was reintroduced in the infirmary, and from that time onwards the routine was virtually the same for the sick and the healthy.[98] Both groups now abstained altogether from meat during Advent and Lent; but in most other weeks of the year, both consumed meat on four days and fish on three.

In the later Middle Ages, the distinctive feature of infirmary diet was its sensitivity to individual need. In the rooms where healthy monks took their meals, the menu was common to everyone present, and to depart from this practice was to commit the offence of singularity. In the infirmary, a degree of singularity was permissible and, indeed, to be anticipated. To achieve the appropriate diet, it was necessary to consider the properties of foods in relation to the patient's specific symptoms and humoral make-up. In practice,

---

[95] *Customary*, ii. 239; *Walter de Wenlok*, 237. For actual seyneys lasting three days in the late 14th cent. see WAM 19356.          [96] Above, pp. 41–2.

[97] A practice mentioned explicitly in 1297 (WAM 19318). See also WAM 19319, 19321–4, where the larger cash pittances on Sun., Mon., Tues., and Thurs., compared to those paid on Wed., Fri., and Sat., signify meat-eating on the former days. However, the Advent fast was generally observed in the infirmary in 1309 (WAM 19320). In the infirmary, the Lenten fast began on Mon. before Ash Wednesday; for healthy monks eating in the refectory, a modified fast was kept from Septuagesima, two weeks earlier. Cf. Wilkins, *Concilia*, ii. 609.

[98] WAM 19325–6.

of course, a compromise was achieved between individual need and the routine always favoured by institutions.

We can assume that, in common with other monks, those who were sick had a daily allowance of bread and ale. At dinner each day they probably had pottage, and—if they were capable of consuming it—a dish of meat or fish identical with one of the main courses served to healthy monks in the refectory or misericord. The large mess allowed to a sick monk at this stage of the meal may be explained by the expectation that he would have an attendant to feed.[99] Other dishes of cooked food, apparently of a normal size, were chosen according to individual need, and the sick monk paid for what he ate. To cover the cost, the infirmarer gave him a daily allowance, known as a pittance. Changing the rates for pittances was a solemn affair, necessitating discussion and resolution in chapter. The rates introduced in 1386 persisted until the monastery was dissolved in 1540: throughout this period, the normal rates were 3*d*. per meat day, and 2*d*. per fish day, but on a feast day, which was observed with or without meat according to the day of the week on which it fell, the rate was double the normal rate for the kind of day in question.[100] The total outlay on cooked food involved in these arrangements was not actually larger than the kitchener's daily outlay on this item for a healthy monk: the system was remarkable, not for its extravagance, but for its flexibility. Arrangements of this kind were common in Benedictine houses. In practice, a sick monk probably made his choice each day from a range of dishes decided upon in advance by the infirmarer. It was considered irregular for the patient to go into the kitchen. However, evidence from St Albans Abbey suggests that he sometimes did so.[101]

In reaching decisions about food and drink for his patients, the infirmarer at Westminster had to contend with a surprising amount of—as it may now appear—red tape. It was not enough to agree with the physician or apothecary on a dietary regime for the patient in question: the abbot's approval or the prior's was needed for apparently quite trivial decisions. In 1334–5, for example, it was necessary for the infirmarer to consult both the abbot and the prior of the monastery before Walter Twyning, who was unable to drink ale, could be given wine instead.[102] In the same year, it was the abbot who decided that Br. Nicholas de Harleston, a patient in the infirmary, should forgo his pittances from 2 October.[103]

---

[99] For pottage, in which oatmeal, salt, pepper, and saffron were ingredients, see WAM 19328, 19386 ff.; and for the large dish of meat or fish, *Customary*, ii. 235. Cf. *Customary of Bury St Edmunds*, 15–16.

[100] WAM 19370 ff. The previous rates were: 2*d*. per meat day, 1*d*. per fish day, and for a feast, 4*d*. or 2*d*., according to the principle mentioned in the text. However, in recent years, only the Abbey's principal feasts had been marked in this way.

[101] *Gesta Abbatum*, ii. 103–4.      [102] WAM 19325.      [103] Ibid. No reason is given.

It is rarely possible to identify the actual dishes, other than pottage, which resulted from this closely controlled system. The purchase of tench for Adam de Laleham when he was ill, in 1305–6, suggests that the dish may have been prescribed by the physician or apothecary; similarly, the chine of pork purchased for William Torsey in 1354–5 may have been on prescription.[104] John de Canterbury, who died in his chamber in the infirmary in August 1400, was given roach, barbel, chicken, and pigeon on the very last days of his life.[105] The existence of a dovecot in the infirmary garden suggests that pigeon was in fact served quite frequently to the sick.[106] From the fact that milk occurs on prescription in our sources, we may perhaps conclude that it was not a normal item of infirmary diet; and the infirmarer's practice of selling part of his apple and pear crops from time to time suggests that fresh fruit may have been as undervalued in the infirmary as it was in the rooms where healthy monks ate.[107]

## (v) Medicine

In the vocabulary of the infirmary at Westminster, 'medicine' normally describes a remedy to be taken internally, but the word is also used in a wider sense: so-called medicines prescribed for cases of *tibia*, for example, were probably solutions in which the affected limb was bathed.[108] The term normally excluded plasters, ointments, and clysters—the remedies that were typically administered, and quite possibly manufactured, not by physician or apothecary but by the surgeon. Yet there were exceptions to this rule, too, and sometimes the word is merely a catch-all describing any remedy, whether administered internally or externally, which the infirmarer did not choose to categorize more precisely. In 1305–6, the 'medicines' required in the course of the year included a powder and plaster, depilatory water, syrup, liquorice, and so-called *calogogi* which were probably intestinal remedies.[109]

By no means all the infirmarer's patients needed 'medicine' which had been dispensed professionally. In 1297–8, a year in which we happen to have precise information, nineteen of forty-six monks (41 per cent) who spent

---

[104] WAM 19319 (where the tench is recorded with the year's medicines); WAM 19334.

[105] WAM 18883B. Mutton and beef were also served, but these items may have been for those in attendance. Cf. the funeral feast on Wed. 18 Aug., at which pike, salmon, plaice, tench, and 'flounders' were served; but salt fish and stockfish for the servants (ibid.).

[106] WAM 19390, 19394, 19470. In 1446–7, however, the dovecot was in the hands of a tenant (WAM 19424).

[107] For the apples see e.g. WAM 19341–2, 19350 ff., and above, p. 60. For milk on the physician's prescription for Richard de Abyndon in 1355–6, see WAM 19335.

[108] WAM 19334, 19336, etc.; and for *tibia* cases, see below, p. 109.

[109] WAM 19319. However, a distinction seems to be drawn here between electuaries and 'potions' on the one hand, and 'medicines' on the other. For a 14th-cent. understanding of some of the items in the list, see Hunt, *Popular Medicine in Thirteenth-Century England*, 45–52.

time in the infirmary as in-patients or day-patients were given medicine of this kind.[110] In 1305–6, numbers were similar: twenty-one of forty-five monks (46 per cent) spending time in the infirmary in either capacity were treated in this way.[111]

On occasion, monks requiring medicine were sent to London for the purpose. Thus in 1398–9, Richard Wyke, accompanied by two servants, went to London for a course which lasted four weeks. The three were given a maintenance allowance of 3s. 4d. per week and, in addition, enough money to buy fifty faggots. But the fact that Br. Richard died within the year suggests that his case was perceived as desperate and treatment in London as a last resort.[112] Nearly all patients requiring medicine seem to have been dealt with in the infirmary. For three years in the 1350s, our sources record the precise recipes for medicines to be taken internally which were made up by Thomas Walden, senior, the monastery's principal apothecary, for use here.[113]

Most of the simple and compound ingredients used by Walden were in common use at the time and are to be found in one or other of two twelfth-century works that were well known and widely used in the later Middle Ages: the treatise on simples sometimes attributed to Matthew Platearius, and known from its opening words as *Circa instans*,[114] and the *Antidotarium* attributed to Nicholas of Salerno.[115] Yet Walden may have shown some originality in combining compounds that appeared as separate recipes in the authoritative works. With the exception of the purgatives, most of his recipes would probably have had no action at all on the patient. They were in a sense analogous to placebos—inert substances which are administered to the patient but can have no action on him other than the psychological effect deriving from his expectation of an effect. Some of the purgatives used by Walden—as, for example, aloes and rhubarb—are still in use today. Others, like turpeth, are irritants and no longer used for the same purpose: some of these may have had a severe and debilitating effect on the monks

---

[110] WAM 19318. For the formalities which in principle preceded the taking of medicine, see *Customary*, ii. 235.

[111] WAM 19319.     [112] WAM 19387.

[113] WAM 19331–3. I am greatly indebted to Dr John Walker for help in interpreting these lists and assessing the probable effects on the patient of the medicines mentioned in them.

[114] *Liber de simplici medicina dictus 'Circa instans'*, in *Practica vel Breviarium Johannis Serapionis* (Lyons, 1525), fos. ccxxiii–lii; trans. P. Dorveaux as *Le Livre des Simples Medecines* (Paris, 1913). I have not seen the Venice 1497 edition. For comment, see Hunt, *Popular Medicine in Thirteenth-Century England*, 14–15, with references to earlier critical literature.

[115] For the text of the *editio princeps* (Venice, 1471) of the *Antidotarium*, see D. Goltz, *Mittelalterliche Pharmazie und Medizin dargestellt an Geschichte und Inhalt des Antidotarium Nicolai, mit einem Nachdruck der Druckfassung von 1471* (Stuttgart, 1976), appendix; for a 14th-cent., abbreviated translation, see P. Dorveaux (trans.), *L'Antidotaire Nicolas* (Paris, 1896), 1–37; and for comment, Hunt, loc. cit. The number of recipes in the *Antidotarium* varied with the edition.

for whom they were prescribed. Nevertheless, some patients treated in this way were to have energetic lives for many years to come. A young monk named John Bokenhull, for example, who was given turpeth in the course of a long illness in 1352, after milder purgatives had been tried and evidently found wanting, survived to hold major office and travel to the papal curia on business for the monastery.[116]

Whatever their effect on the patients, Walden's medicines were on the whole expensive. A preparation made up for the prior of Westminster in 1350–1 cost 5s. 7d.—a sum equivalent to very nearly half the stipend (12s.) of the infirmarer's cook for a year.[117] The cost of the medicines provided by Walden for the monks in 1351–2 ranged from 4d. to 10s. 10d. in the individual case, and most cost more than a labourer could easily have earned in a week, despite the current rising trend in wages.[118] Medicines for the shrunken community of twenty-five to thirty-five monks that existed at Westminster in this decade cost on average £5 per annum.[119] If the sum sounds small enough for a monastery with a net income of c.£1,500 per annum, it was in fact more than the infirmarer could easily find from the rather slender income on which he was expected to manage, and, as we have seen, some bills dragged on from year to year.[120]

## (vi) The seyney

The seyney—the operation of blood-letting—is rarely mentioned at Westminster in this period as a form of treatment for sick monks. In this respect, however, the sources are probably misleading. Blood-letting had been recommended by Galen as a means of correcting imbalances of the humours. In the later Middle Ages, it was specifically recommended for several kinds of sickness, including plague, and it is most unlikely that the infirmarer and his advisers neglected to employ it. Indeed, we can probably assume that the barber to whom the infirmarer paid a small annual stipend earned his money by letting blood.[121] The actual operation, a very messy one, normally took place outside the infirmary, in a place assigned for the purpose in the chamberlain's department.[122] Only monks too ill to be moved would have

---

[116] WAM 19332, where the prescription including turpeth is the last of 8 listed under Br. John's name. He entered the infirmary on 9 June; for his discharge on 25 Nov., see WAM 19333. See also *Monks*, 97; and for turpeth, Hunt, *Popular Medicine in Thirteenth-Century England*, 238 [40] and 242 [54].

[117] WAM 19331.        [118] WAM 19332.        [119] WAM 19331–8.        [120] Above, p. 84.

[121] For this part-time servant, see infirmarer's accounts, *passim*; cf. *Customary*, ii. 74. On the necessity of blood-letting within a few hours of the onset of *pestis*, see e.g. Bodleian Library, Oxford, MS Ashmole 1391, pp. 41–2; BL Add. MS 27329, fos. 236ᵛ–237. For the underlying Galenic principles, see R. E. Siegel, 'Galen's concept of bloodletting in relation to his ideas on pulmonary and peripheral blood flow and blood formation', in A. G. Debus (ed.), *Science, Medicine and Society in the Renaissance* (2 vols., London, 1972), ii. 243–75; and for a new approach to the study of the treatment, *Sharp Practice*, i (1987). (*Sharp* is the publication of the S[outra] H[ospital] A[rchaeo-ethno-pharmacological] R[esearch] P[roject]).

[122] An inference from *Customary*, ii. 238, where the sub-chamberlain makes the arrangements. A room in the bath-house in this department is the probable location.

had it in the infirmary. It fell to the infirmarer to provide beds for the sick for whom this treatment was specified, and some of the fortifying diet which they needed. The treatment was sometimes applied intensively. In 1379 Robert Denham actually had two seyneys in the space of six days.[123] However, it is possible that in such cases the patient was treated by cupping, or scarification, and not by the more drastic method of venesection.[124]

The seyney was also highly esteemed as a form of therapy for healthy monks. In these cases the preferred method was probably venesection, and the preferred vein one in the arm.[125] For healthy monks a rota existed, and in the mid-thirteenth century this could probably accommodate ten monks per week. Given a community numbering fifty to sixty monks and the inevitable interruption of the rota from time to time by the demands of the liturgical calendar, it is probable that a monk's turn came round seven or eight times in a normal year.[126] Arrangements *c*.1400 appear similar: then, the rota probably accommodated no more than eight monks per week, but the community was smaller than in the thirteenth century, and individual turns may have come round as frequently as in that period.[127] In the early sixteenth century, however, the seyney seems to have been a less frequent event in the life of the average monk than formerly. Arrangements at the monastic dinner now provide the essential clue. In this period, seyneys normally began on Monday afternoon, when the actual letting of blood occurred, and ended, after two days of convalescence, on Wednesday. We can be sure that patients undergoing this operation had a diet which included meat, for a fortifying diet was, by tradition, an essential concomitant of a seyney. However, their diet was not wholly a charge on the kitchener. At dinner, therefore, on Tuesdays which were also days for the seyney, the kitchener served fewer messes of meat than usual. His accounts, recording these economies, suggest that seyneys now occurred every two or three

---

[123] WAM 19356.

[124] For a reference to cupping in 1347–8, see WAM 19330; and for cupping at St Augustine's Abbey, Canterbury, as characteristic of a 'private' seyney—i.e. one taking place outside the rota—see *Customary*, i. 305.

[125] Ibid. ii. 190, referring to the arm, but implying that this was not the only method in use. At this point, however, this source follows *Lanfranc's Constitutions*, 94–5.

[126] See *Customary*, ii. 237–8, where a maximum of 10 monks is permitted at one of the weekly seyneys occurring on Sat. in Lent. At other times of the year, this number was probably divided between 2 seyneys, on, respectively, Wed. and Sat. The maximum size of the community, including the abbot and prior, at this date is indicated by the provision of 62 stalls in the choir of Henry III's church (P. Binski, 'Abbot Berkyng's tapestries and Matthew Paris's Life of St Edward the Confessor', *Archaeologia*, cix (1991), 85–100, at 85). *c*.1300, it numbered 55 (*Walter de Wenlok*, 198, 203).
Cf., in an earlier period, Peter the Venerable's seyneys 6 times a year (*Letters of Peter the Venerable*, ed. Constable, ii. 248–9; and see *MO* 455–6).

[127] In 1402–3 the cellarer allowed 2 loaves and 2 galls. ale per week for breakfasts (*jantacula*) for monks taking the seyney (WAM 18887). These quantities probably provided for a rota of 8 monks, each taking 2 breakfasts, per week. In 1402–3 the community numbered 51 monks, excluding the abbot and prior.

weeks and that the monks participated in batches of four or eight. The turn of the individual monk can hardly have come round more than four or five times in the course of a year. If the rota still catered in principle for the whole community, three times a year is more probable.[128]

The decline in the frequency of blood-letting may have a domestic explanation in the acceptance of meat-eating as a normal part of monastic life: this made it less necessary than previously to incorporate special occasions for meat-eating—of which a seyney was one—into the year's calendar. Nevertheless, it suggests the possibility that the sixteenth-century debate about the frequency of blood-letting, which continued long after the monasteries had passed into oblivion, had been anticipated in some late medieval cloisters.[129]

Yet the rota was one thing, the actual frequency of treatment another, for a monk might choose to have additional, so-called private seyneys, or to have fewer than the rota provided for, and in earlier periods these options were, to our knowledge, used. By convention, the prior of Westminster received small cash presents from other office-holders on the occasion of a seyney. From the presents which Prior Hadham received in 1305–6, we know that he had the treatment nine times in the course of that year.[130] In 1334–5, however, Prior Warwick had four well-spaced seyneys, in October, January, April, and July.[131]

Frequent or infrequent, seyneys at Westminster retained to the end the character of qualified, incomplete, relaxation that had always characterized them in Benedictine houses. By custom, monks taking the seyney as a routine matter slept in their usual places—in the dormitory or a private apartment—but were dispensed from a considerable part of their duties in choir.[132] Moreover, the special diet associated with seyneys made it necessary that monks undergoing them should eat apart, and an earlier generation of reformers in the Order laid down norms of behaviour for these occasions. Conversation was permitted, but only when the president gave the sign, and there was to be a reading first.[133] At Westminster, references at the end of the fifteenth century to two 'seyney books' seem to show that this formality

---

[128] WAM 33323, recording a reduction of 1 or 2 in the number of messes of beef, in most cases with an explanatory note that a seyney took place, on 12 Tuesdays, 2 Thursdays, and, exceptionally, 1 Monday, in 1508, and on 10 Tuesdays and 7 Thursdays in 1509 down to 13 Oct. There is some evidence that the reduction applied to boiled meat as well, and, occasionally, to roast meat. A mess was for 4 persons, and the community, excluding the abbot and prior, now numbered *c*.46 monks. For further examples of reduced catering in the misericord on account of seyneys, see WAM 33322. The estimate of the frequency of the seyney given above allows for the unrecorded seyneys of the fast periods in each year. Cf. *RO* ii. 245.

[129] P. Slack, *The Impact of Plague in Tudor and Stuart England* (London, 1985), 30.

[130] WAM 19319. See also WAM 18717, the chamberlain's account for 1291–2, recording 8 presents to a different prior for seyneys that year.          [131] WAM 19325.

[132] *Customary*, ii. 23–5, 237, 239; *Chapters of English Black Monks*, ii. 112, 128.

[133] *Chapters of English Black Monks*, i. 100.

was still practised, for we can probably assume that these books, which were handsomely bound, and chained, were made for use at meal-times.[134]

## (vii) Convalescence

After the illness came, in appropriate cases, the convalescent holiday, and holidays were sometimes prescribed for those who were merely threatened with illness. Who should pay for them was a matter for some haggling on the part of the obedientiaries. The infirmarer's note, in 1340, that John Wallingford was at Hendon without a pittance signifies that he had persuaded somebody else to pay for the invalid's food while he was away.[135] The therapeutic value of the holiday, however, was not in doubt. It consisted chiefly in the possibility of 'taking the air', it being already agreed in the fourteenth century that the air of the town of Westminster itself left much to be desired. Among the Abbey's manors, Hendon, Hampstead, and Wandsworth were all highly regarded on this account; so too Belsize— better known to us as Belsize Park—where the prior had a house.[136] We hear also of convalescents staying with the abbot at Denham in Buckinghamshire, going with friends to Paddington, dispatched to Hurley in Surrey, where the priory, a cell of the Abbey, could be expected to take them in, 'leaving town', or 'going into the country'.[137] Since the infirmarer contrived, as a rule, to avoid giving such monks the daily pittances they enjoyed while in the infirmary, his accounts rarely show how long the holiday lasted, and other sources do not supply this information. If, however, the infirmarer did not pay for his own holidays, nobody else would, and to this circumstance we owe the information that the convalescence he himself needed in 1320 or 1321, and took at Wandsworth, lasted three weeks.[138]

## 4. Morbidity in the Monastic Community at Westminster Abbey

Year by year,[139] how many monks needed the facilities which have been described? What, in fact, can be said about morbidity, the rate of sickness,

---

[134] J. Armitage Robinson and M. R. James, *The Manuscripts of Westminster Abbey* (Cambridge, 1909), 9–11. It is uncertain where the readings and the meals took place at this late date.

[135] WAM 19326.

[136] For convalescence or ordinary holidays at these places, see WAM 19322, 19325–6. In WAM 23179, Combe (Kent) is also mentioned as a venue. All these references are from the period 1298–1357. For Prior Mane's stay at Belsize in Aug. 1512 for a seyney, see WAM 33325, fo. 58.

[137] WAM 19322, 19325, 19331–3, 23179. For a probable case of convalescence at Stoke Priory in 1356–7, see WAM 19336.          [138] WAM 19322.

[139] In the following discussion of morbidity, the year of account is normally in use: 1375–1529 = 29 Sept. 1375–28 Sept. 1530.

in the community at Westminster? I shall discuss principally two aspects of this problem: the number of monks per annum who entered the infirmary as in-patients in the period 1375–1529, and the periods for which they were hospitalized.

The infirmarer of this period did not keep a day-by-day record of admissions and discharges, as some of his predecessors had done—or, if he kept such a record, no example has survived—but he did keep a careful account of his outlay on pittances—that is, on the daily cash payments which were given to sick monks in lieu of a dish of cooked food. With very few exceptions, every in-patient received pittances for the duration of his stay in the infirmary, and this arrangement made it necessary for the infirmarer to enter the names of in-patients in his accounts, together with the number of occasions on which they were admitted to the infirmary, and the total number of days for which they were, on each occasion, hospitalized. Our data on morbidity derive from these entries, and they are available for 96 complete years in the period 1375–1529: 62 per cent of years in this period are covered.[140]

To convert the infirmarer's days into the nights now more commonly used in the reckoning of stays in hospital is simple enough, but some other problems presented by his accounts are more difficult to resolve. These relate to the composition of the sample of monks who were exposed to in-patient treatment each year—the sample providing the indispensable basis for estimates of morbidity. The difficulty arises from the fact that the several groups of monks making up the sample—the cloister-monks, office-holders, and university students, to mention only three—made unequal use of the infirmary.

Cloister-monks, who had no other place to go when sick, entered the infirmary whenever they were sufficiently ill to make this appropriate, and the same is probably true of the minor obedientiaries—the deputies and assistants, who, though essential to the running of the departments in question, were nevertheless officials of the second rank. Our sources record many stays in the infirmary on the part of minor officials such as the granger (mentioned in 10 of the 96 years) and the assistant treasurer of Queen Eleanor of Castile's foundation (mentioned in 19).[141] However, of the dozen or so

---

[140] WAM 19352–492. Names of in-patients receiving pittances are recorded from 1378. The length of each stay is recorded from 1381. A few years, incompletely covered by the surviving accounts, have been excluded from consideration. Among these, 1460–1, with 21 in-patients between 1 Mar. and 29 Sept. and 43 monks in the sample, was evidently a year of high morbidity (WAM 33288, fo. 12).

For the pioneer study based on the infirmarer's accounts, but directed mainly towards the elucidation of case-histories, see Lord Amulree, 'Monastic infirmaries', in F. N. L. Poynter (ed.), *The Evolution of Hospitals in Britain* (London, 1964), 11–26. However, Lord Amulree was almost certainly mistaken in assuming that the infirmarer continued to pay pittances to day-patients after the mid-14th cent.

[141] The granger was one of the cellarer's assistants. The monk named second of the two who

major obedientiaries, only the almoner (15), the precentor (21), and the refectorer (34) seem to have resorted to the infirmary at all frequently: the rest are rarely, if ever, mentioned as in-patients. Indeed, only on three occasions is it now possible to identify the holder of any other major office among the year's in-patients: the chamberlain spent time in the infirmary in 1405–6, the warden of the Lady Chapel in 1471–2, and the chamberlain again in the same year.[142] To some extent, the failure of this group of monks to become in-patients has a natural explanation, for, in a large Benedictine house of the period, good health must have been almost a prerequisite of promotion to a major office. Yet it seems clear that another factor was at work: unlike their deputies and assistants, the Abbey's major obedientiaries had apartments of their own in the monastery and they preferred, if possible, to stay there when sick. Why, then, did the almoner, the precentor, and the refectorer behave differently? Quite simply, each of these had quarters that were not at all well suited to a sick person. The almoner's quarters were in an exposed position outside the monastic precinct; the precentor, despite his great importance in the conduct of services, probably made do with a corner in the vestry; and the refectorer's quarters were at first-floor level in the *cawagium*, the chamber built inside the refectory in the course of the fourteenth century.[143]

With the exception of these three, and the infirmarer himself, who, willy nilly, had his illnesses in the infirmary, the major obedientiaries have been excluded from the sample. So, too, a small number of permanent invalids whose inclusion could only obscure changes in morbidity from year to year.[144] It is also necessary to make appropriate adjustments for the student monks, who were present in the monastery for only part of the year, and for some others who are, for different reasons, special cases.[145] When all the

accounted annually for Queen Eleanor's foundation was actually second in importance to his colleague. For the names to look for, see *Monks*, 206–8. It is to be noted, however, that the holders of many minor offices cannot now be identified: the actual number of stays in the infirmary on the part of holders of these offices was probably larger than the number that can now be traced.

[142] WAM 19397, 19453. John Feryng, chamberlain in 1405–6, was also warden of the Lady Chapel. The stays in the infirmary of these three obedientiaries have been excluded from the data in Fig. III.1 and Tables III.1–3.

For the names of the almoners, precentors, and refectorers of this period, see *Monks*, 199–200, 202–4.

[143] For the almonry, see above, pp. 74–5; and for the *cawagium*, pp. 41–2. A bed is mentioned in the *cawagium* in 1391–2 (WAM 19508).

[144] The invalids of this period were: William Ledred (1378–81), Robert Athelard (1412–18), Peter Combe (1416–21), Richard Birlingham (1436–41), Reginald Shiplake (1443–5), Richard Illington (1466–70), William Barnell (1467–76), William Wycombe (1490–1), John Ramsey (1494–1500). Not all were continuously resident in the infirmary: Birlingham and Combe spent long periods at Hendon.

[145] Students have been counted as halves; so, too, novices in the year of their profession, and monks dying or departing in the year in question. For some periods of residence at Oxford by

due adjustments have been made, we are left with a sample which is always smaller than the total number of professed monks in the community, but, even so, statistically viable. Over the whole period 1375–1529, in the years covered by the infirmarer's surviving accounts, the average number of monks in the community per annum was 50.5,[146] and the sample exposed to in-patient treatment per annum was, on average, 35 (69 per cent). However, the actual number of monks in the community fluctuated from year to year, and so did the actual number in the sample. The smallest sample, comprising only 27 monks, occurs in 1378–9; the largest, comprising 46.5 monks, exactly twenty years later.

The age-structure of the community at Westminster changed in the course of the period under consideration. We have no evidence on this point before the fifteenth century. In the middle decades of that century, monks under the age of 30 probably accounted for c.30 per cent of the total, but by the end of the century their share was at times c.50 per cent. (See Figure IV.4.) We should allow for a corresponding change in the sample exposed to in-patient treatment in the infirmary. Nevertheless, throughout the entire period 1375–1529, we should allow for a specific bias in the sample towards youth. This arises from the fact that the major offices in the monastery were normally given to monks who had been professed for ten years or more, and, given what is known about age at profession, it seems probable that such monks were at least 30 years old, or not far short of that age, when first promoted.[147] Thus, the exclusion of most of the major obedientiaries from the sample has the effect of removing a class of middle-aged monks—in the broad sense of 'middle-aged'—whose inclusion would have raised the average age.

On average[148] over the whole period 1375–1529, 14 monks per annum (40 per cent of the sample) were admitted to the infirmary as in-patients, and the 14 needed 20 stays per annum (1.4 per in-patient). However, this long period may be divided into two shorter ones of unequal length and unequal morbidity: 1375–1464 (Period A), and 1465–1529 (Period B).[149] On average, in Period A the sample exposed to in-patient treatment comprised 36 monks per annum, and 15.5 monks per annum (43 per cent) actually became in-patients. On average, in Period B the sample comprised 33.5 monks per

---

monks in the 14th cent., see Harvey, 'The monks of Westminster and the University of Oxford', 121 n. For the short periods separating clothing and profession in Benedictine houses of this period, see Dobson, *Durham Priory, 1400–1450*, p. 62, and for a glimpse of a period of probation at Westminster in 1402–3 which may have lasted only 9 weeks, WAM 18887.

[146] The average relates to the number of professed monks, including the abbot and prior, in the community at the beginning of each year plus the number professed in the course of the next 12 months. This is also true of the actual samples for particular years that are mentioned in the following discussion. The average for the period 1390–1529, considered below, is 51.

[147] Below, pp. 119–21; and for the *cursus honorum* at Westminster, *Monks, passim.*

[148] In the following account, 'average' denotes the arithmetic mean.

[149] The infirmarer's account survives for 55 years in Period A and 41 in Period B.

annum, and 11.5 per annum (34 per cent) actually became in-patients. Unless the sources are deceptive, morbidity was lower in the community at Westminster in Period B than in Period A.

Yet morbidity was also more variable in the later period than in the earlier one. In the Middle Ages, morbidity, like mortality, went very often by peaks and troughs, and this was the case at Westminster Abbey. Fluctuations in morbidity here, in years for which the infirmarer's account survives, are shown in Figure III.1. It will be clear from this figure that most of the really conspicuous peaks occurred in Period A. On three occasions towards the end of this period—1447–8, 1457–8, and 1461–2—morbidity exceeded 60 per cent per annum of the sample, and on one—in 1462–3—it exceeded 70 per cent. In Period B, morbidity only once, in 1503–4, rose as high. However, the troughs occurring in Period A are much less conspicuous than those occurring in Period B. In Period A, morbidity in the sample only once—in 1396–7—fell below 20 per cent per annum; in Period B, it did so on six occasions,[150] and on two of these—1485–6, and 1489–90—it actually fell below 10 per cent. Together, the lower peaks and deeper troughs of Period B represent a more variable experience of morbidity than the higher peaks and shallower troughs of Period A. This difference between the two periods can be expressed statistically by means of the standard deviation and coefficient of variation of morbidity in each period. (See Table III.1.) The rise in both these measures in Period B compared to Period A indicates that levels of morbidity were more variable from year to year in Period B.

Moreover, as Table III.2 shows, the in-patients' length of stay changed significantly in Period B.[151] In Period A, in-patients needed, on average, 1.5 stays in the infirmary per annum, and in Period B, 1.4—an insignificant difference. However, the stays tended to be longer in the later period. In Period A, 63 per cent of the recorded stays lasted 8 nights or less, and only 18 per cent lasted more than 21 nights. In Period B, only 40.5 per cent of the recorded stays lasted 8 nights or less, and 25.5 per cent lasted more than 21 nights.[152] Further, the intermediate periods—9 to 14 nights and 15 to 21 nights—accounted for higher percentages of the total in Period B than in Period A. In the latter, the average number of nights per stay was 16; in the former, it was 19.

These changes suggest that the character of the illnesses afflicting the monks of Westminster changed in the course of the second half of the

---

[150] 1476–7, 1480–1, 1486–7, 1504–5, and the two years mentioned in the text.

[151] A stay in the infirmary which began before the end of the year of account on 29 Sept. and continued after that date is recorded in our sources as two, and the total number of nights involved is, of course, divided between the two. However, in 1381–1413, when stays are dated by month and a check on the seriousness of the problem is therefore possible, not more than 17 of a total 700 (2.42%) were misrecorded in this way, and possibly fewer. Given this tiny percentage, which lends support to the conclusion that the early autumn was a slack time in the infirmary, it has seemed safe to ignore the problem in the following discussion.

[152] However, stays over 21 nights averaged 55 nights in Period A but 49 nights in Period B.

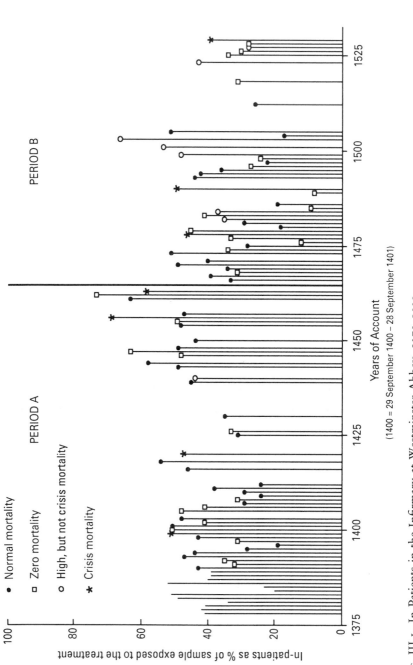

FIG. III.1. In-Patients in the Infirmary at Westminster Abbey, 1375–1529

Years of Account

(1400 = 29 September 1400 – 28 September 1401)

In-patients as % of sample exposed to the treatment

• Normal mortality

□ Zero mortality

○ High, but not crisis mortality

✷ Crisis mortality

PERIOD A

PERIOD B

Note: The blank years in this figure are those for which the infirmarer's account does not survive. For the mortality data, which are available only from 1390, see below, pp. 122–4, and Fig. IV.1a and b.

TABLE III.1. In-Patients Per Annum in the Infirmary at Westminster Abbey, 1375–1529

| Period A (1375–1464) | | Period B (1465–1529) | |
|---|---|---|---|
| Number of in-patients as mean annual percentage of the sample | 42.7 | Number of in-patients as mean annual percentage of the sample | 34.4 |
| Standard deviation | 11.5 | Standard deviation | 13.0 |
| Coefficient of variation | 26.9% | Coefficient of variation | 37.7% |

TABLE III.2. In-Patient Stays in the Infirmary at Westminster Abbey, 1375–1529

| | Number of nights | | | | | Total |
|---|---|---|---|---|---|---|
| | 1 or 2 | 3–8 | 9–14 | 15–21 | Over 21 | |
| *Period A (1375–1464)* | | | | | | |
| Number of stays | 190 | 602 | 150 | 98 | 222 | 1,262 |
| | 15% | 48% | 12% | 8% | 18% | 100% |
| Total number of nights | 377 | 3,853 | 1,772 | 1,826 | 12,191 | 20,019 |
| | 2% | 19% | 9% | 9% | 61% | 100% |
| *Period B (1465–1529)* | | | | | | |
| Number of stays | 65 | 197 | 123 | 96 | 165 | 646 |
| | 10% | 30.5% | 19% | 15% | 25.5% | 100% |
| Total number of nights | 115 | 1,168 | 1,412 | 1,648 | 8,048 | 12,391 |
| | 1% | 9.5% | 11.5% | 13% | 65% | 100% |
| *Period A + Period B (1375–1529)* | | | | | | |
| Number of stays | 255 | 799 | 273 | 194 | 387 | 1,908 |
| | 13.5% | 42% | 14.5% | 10% | 20% | 100% |
| Total number of nights | 492 | 5,021 | 3,184 | 3,474 | 20,239 | 32,410 |
| | 1.5% | 15.5% | 10% | 11% | 62% | 100% |

fifteenth century: it changed, that is, in the very period when morbidity itself actually declined. There were now, it appears, fewer acute illnesses, occasioning short stays in the infirmary, and more chronic illnesses, occasioning relatively long stays.

Of course, in patterns of institutionalized illness, we must always suspect the design of the administrator. Although our data suggest that acute illness declined in the monastery in the second half of the fifteenth century, it is possible that what actually declined was the sympathy of the infirmarer and his superiors towards this form of sickness. Or perhaps, as morbidity declined, the infirmarer worried less about the pressure on his beds and lost some of his former eagerness to discharge patients as soon as possible.[153] If so, periods spent in the infirmary would have lengthened, but actual forms of sickness need not have changed. And anyone familiar with accounts of any kind in the later Middle Ages will be aware of the possibility that the accounts of the infirmarer of Westminster Abbey are less reliable by 1500 than a century earlier. A change of this kind in our sources could create an entirely misleading impression of change in actual morbidity.

A common sign that late medieval accounts are becoming unreliable is the creeping in of stereotyped entries recording expenditure that does not change from year to year. But the later the accounts of the infirmarer of Westminster, the more variable the morbidity they seem to record. And it seems unlikely that infirmarers who were short of funds, as the Abbey's infirmarers are known to have been in the later Middle Ages, would have become more tolerant of malingerers in the same period. We have no independent means of verifying our data. But it is more likely than not that they reflect actual changes in sickness in the monastery and not merely the whims or inefficiency of successive infirmarers.

This study of morbidity at Westminster Abbey in the period 1375–1529 has focused exclusively on monks who entered the infirmary as in-patients. Yet, as we have seen, a second regime, that of the day-patient, was also in use.[154] In some earlier periods the number of day-patients whom the infirmarer treated per annum normally exceeded the number of his in-patients, and many sick monks experienced both forms of treatment in the course of a single illness.[155] By 1375, however, the infirmarer had ceased to give pittances to day-patients, and, that being so, he had no reason to enter their names in his accounts. The gap in our data resulting from this change is serious, and, in an oblique way, an entry in the infirmarer's account for 1402–3 brings this to our notice. This year, the auditors of the account felt the need to explain why they had acquiesced in the infirmarer's claim to have used 850 faggots in his fires, and they noted that there had been a large number of sick monks during the winter—they probably had in mind the long liturgical winter, extending from October to the beginning of Lent.[156] Yet the number of in-patients in the winter of 1402–3 was not large for the period, and none at all is recorded in the month of February: the entry must refer in part to day-patients, and to their need to be kept warm as they

---

[153] A possibility suggested to me by Richard Smith.

[154] Above, pp. 91–2.     [155] WAM 19318–330.

[156] WAM 19394. 700 faggots were used in 1400–1 and 800 in 1401–2 (WAM 19391–2). The quantity of talwood used in 1402–3 was slightly larger than in either of the previous two years. Lent in 1403 began on 28 Feb. In the period Oct. 1402 to Feb. 1403 inclusive, 13 monks spent time in the infirmary as in-patients. The corresponding figure in 1400–1 was 15, and in 1401–2, 20 (WAM 19391–2).

passed their time in the infirmary parlours or hall. The existence of a regime for day-patients helps us to see in-patient stays in perspective. It reminds us that we should not equate the short illnesses qualifying for in-patient treatment with illnesses perceived at the time as minor: on the contrary, the illnesses occasioning in-patient treatment were, or appeared to be, serious enough to claim beds in the infirmary and too serious to be dealt with under the other regime.

Since all we have are the data on in-patients, what conclusions do these suggest? At this point, it is necessary to anticipate the discussion of mortality in the community at Westminster in Chapter IV of this book. The relationship between morbidity and mortality in the late medieval monastery is, at first sight, surprising, even baffling. Mortality rates in the monastery rose dramatically in the second half of the fifteenth century: they rose in the very period when morbidity declined.[157] From year to year, morbidity and mortality sometimes moved in opposite directions, and, in particular, some years of high morbidity—as, for example, 1447–8 and 1462–3—were actually years of zero mortality. The mortality of monks of Westminster was in general even more variable from year to year than their morbidity, but it became less variable as it rose to these new levels: it became less variable as morbidity became more so. Again, we can express these changes statistically. In Table III.3, the measures of variability already applied to morbidity are applied to mortality as well. However, since the data on mortality begin only in 1390, 'Period A' in this table is shorter than in Tables III.1 and III.2: it runs from 1390 to 1464, and the data on morbidity have been recalculated accordingly. The coefficient of variation of mortality fell in Period B compared to Period A, and this points to a fall in the variability of mortality from year to year in the later period. But the coefficient of variation of morbidity rose in Period B: the variability of morbidity was rising. How, then, can we explain these contrasts?

To some extent the explanation lies in the use of two samples which are not identical: the pattern of mortality that I have described is that of the entire monastic community, but the pattern of morbidity that of a smaller sample, with a bias towards youth. Yet there is a large overlap between the two. Moreover, mortality in the late medieval monastery did not spare the young.[158] Professor James Riley has observed the tendency of morbidity to vary from period to period in an industrial sample in seventeenth-century Antwerp; and he has observed in the same sample the tendency of morbidity to decline as mortality rose.[159] Higher mortality rates, it appears, may leave survivors who are healthier than they would otherwise have been and

[157] Below, pp. 127–9.    [158] Below, pp. 138–41.
[159] James C. Riley, *Sickness, Recovery and Death: A History and Forecast of Ill Health* (London, 1989), 138–42. (I owe this reference to Dr Slack.)

TABLE III.3. The Variability of Morbidity and Mortality at Westminster Abbey, 1390–1529

| i. Morbidity | | | |
|---|---|---|---|
| *Period A (1390–1464)* | | *Period B (1465–1529)* | |
| Number of in-patients as mean annual percentage of sample | 43.7 | Number of in-patients as mean annual percentage of sample | 34.4 |
| Standard deviation | 12.2 | Standard deviation | 13.0 |
| Coefficient of variation | 28.0% | Coefficient of variation | 37.7% |
| ii. Mortality | | | |
| *Period A (1390–1464)* | | *Period B (1465–1529)* | |
| Mean annual rate | 33.0 per 1,000 | Mean annual rate | 36.0 per 1,000 |
| Standard deviation | 34.8 | Standard deviation | 34.0 |
| Coefficient of variation | 105.4% | Coefficient of variation | 94.0% |

who enjoy, in consequence, lower morbidity. A general truth of this kind may underlie the divergent trends in morbidity and mortality at Westminster Abbey in the period 1465–1529.

But we must also take into account the nature of the illnesses which were nursed in the infirmary. Like many medical institutions in existence today, the infirmary at Westminster in the Middle Ages served mainly the needs of those suffering from illnesses that do not actually kill the patient. Its characteristic work was directed towards acute but transient illness, on the one hand, and, on the other, towards the kinds of chronic complaint that permitted the sufferer to live more or less normally for much of the time, but occasionally made this impossible. In the course of the fifteenth century, the chronic complaints evidently gained at the expense of the acute ones. Even so, among those who entered the infirmary, life-threatening illness probably remained the exception rather than the rule.

## 5. The Diseases

What were these complaints that restricted a monk's activity from time to time but did not kill him, or, if they were fatal, did not have that effect for a considerable time? For an all too short period of about forty years (1381–1417), the infirmarer recorded the month or months in which in-patients were hospitalized.[160] It appears that in this period summer (June to August) was in some years the quietest season in the infirmary. Spring (March to May) was in some years a busier season than summer, and in some the

---

[160] WAM 19361–408. I hope to consider this evidence in greater detail on another occasion.

busiest in the entire year. The infirmarer was, it appears, more likely to have empty beds in the autumn (September to November) or winter (December to February) than in spring. Yet it is very hard to detect a clear seasonal pattern in this evidence. In fact our sources are never more reticent than in their references to disease, and only a few attempts at diagnosis can be made.

A place must be found for the early stages of diseases encouraged by the excesses of diet which have been described.[161] A lifetime spent in seisin of a gallon of ale per day may eventually issue in advanced sclerosis of the liver, but also bring about lesser forms of 'liver' on the way. The excessive intake of protein which seems to have characterized the monks' diet would have exacerbated any existing tendency to renal malfunctioning in the individual monk.[162] Dr Tony Waldron, using skeletal evidence, has identified hyperostosis (excessive growth of bone tissue) as a disease of a number of canons of Merton Priory—a number disproportionately large in relation to the size of the sample and given the rate at which the disease occurs today. He suggests that the disease, associated with the late onset of diabetes, may have been an occupational hazard for obese monks.[163] Here, then, is another possibility for the probably obese monks of Westminster.

The lesser illnesses treated in the infirmary include a complaint, or bundle of complaints, to which our sources give the name *morbus in tibia*—disease in the shin-bone. This was treated on occasion by applying white wine, and in some cases treatment continued for years rather than weeks or months. In the 1370s William Litlyngton was treated for this complaint over a two-year period, and at the relatively high cost of £4; he had been treated for the same complaint a few years earlier.[164] Sufferers included novices as well as the middle-aged and elderly. In cases of *tibia*, the infirmarer was probably treating varicose ulcers. Some of these may have been caused by a circulatory condition, perhaps exacerbated by much standing to sing the office; others, by the serious deficiency of Vitamin C which seems to have been as characteristic of the monastic diet as its surfeit of protein.[165]

Finally, we should note the effects on the individual monk of community life itself, and especially the consequences for health of an unrelenting

---

[161] Above, pp. 65–7.

[162] I am indebted to Dr Alan Loach for help on this point. See also DH 41, p. 82.

[163] T. Waldron, 'DISH at Merton Priory: evidence for a "new" occupational disease?', *British Medical Journal*, ccxci (1985), 1762–3. (DISH = disseminated idiopathic skeletal hyperostosis.) Merton Priory was an Augustinian house.

[164] WAM 19345, 19351; and for Litlyngton, who was professed in 1363–4, see *Monks*, 108–9. For the name *morbus in tibia*, normally abbreviated to *tibia*, see WAM 19334, and for treatment with white wine, WAM 19320, 19334.

[165] Above, p. 63. For a 12th-cent. reference to varicose veins, exacerbated by standing in choir, see A. Wilmart, 'Une riposte de l'ancien monachisme au manifeste de Saint Bernard', *Revue Bénédictine*, xlvi (1934), 296–344, at 334. I am indebted to Dr Henry Mayr-Harting for this reference.

institutional round. The Abbey's Customary, compiled in the thirteenth century, contains a telling, if idealized, description of a cloister-monk who needs a little time off: he has studied too hard, or overdone the chanting, or perhaps consumed too much or consumed the wrong things.[166] *Mutatis mutandis*, who that has ever lived in even the most agreeable of communities can fail to recognize the symptoms of a real, if ill-defined, malaise?

Yet in the end the diseases that did not kill the monks of Westminster are as elusive as those that did:[167] evidently, they changed in character to a significant extent in the second half of the fifteenth century, but we do not know why.

Were the monks of Westminster in the later Middle Ages a healthy or unhealthy group of people? A bench-mark will be useful as we try to answer this question, and, despite the great differences of period and social context that are involved, we may perhaps find it in the present-day experience of sickness. In 1988, 25 per cent of males in the age-group 16–44 who were interviewed on the subject of their own health reported long-standing illness, and 9 per cent reported restricted activity on account of illness in the fourteen days before the interview. The corresponding figures in the age-group 45–64 were 44 per cent and 11 per cent.[168] Moreover, 5 per cent of the age-group 16–44 and 8 per cent of the age-group 45–64 had in-patient experience in the twelve-month period before the interview.[169] For several reasons, the figures relating to the monks of Westminster are not directly comparable with these. The former relate, for example, to the use of a certain kind of medical service, namely in-patient treatment in a monastic infirmary, but the modern figures relate to self-reported illness, and the very use of two different measures is calculated to produce unequal results. Yet the modern figures do provide a useful point of reference.

During the period under consideration, all but a small percentage of the community at Westminster probably belonged to one or other of the two age-groups which have been mentioned, and for most of the period the younger age-group was probably the preponderant one. (See Figure IV.4.) Of most of the monks in this sample, it is probably true to say that they could have a day in bed only if they entered the infirmary as in-patients. Over the whole period, 1375–1529, 40 per cent per annum were in fact admitted as in-patients; most of this number were admitted only once in the course of the year; and most of their stays were for a period not exceeding eight nights. Yet if we could add the infirmary's day-patients to its in-patients, the incidence of sickness of a sufficiently serious kind to restrict activity would almost certainly rise well above that implied in today's figures.

[166] *Customary*, ii. 23.        [167] For the latter, see below, pp. 141–2.
[168] *General Household Survey*, 1988, table 4.1.
[169] Ibid., table 4.16.

Even so, knowing what we do know about the monastic environment, we can perhaps conclude that the community was remarkably resilient in the face of the hazards to health which it experienced day by day. To say this is not to say that the monastic expectation of life was good: on the contrary, it was low, and it fell in the course of the fifteenth century.[170] But until the last enemy actually struck, the monastic constitution, assessed on the basis of its need of in-patient treatment in the infirmary, performed well. Given its environment, the community at Westminster did well, we may think, if even half the monks who belonged to it managed to see the year through without needing such treatment. Or did many of the other monks of this period share the belief of the major obedientiaries that they were better off outside the infirmarer's chambers for sick monks than inside—and match his reluctance to admit them with an equal reluctance to be admitted? Here, unfortunately, the evidence fails us.

[170] Below, pp. 127–9.

# ⊰ IV ⊱

# *Mortality*

## 1. The Problems

THE data on mortality in late medieval England have been characterized as 'sparse and intractable', 'hard to win and treacherous to interpret', and who will disagree?[1] Recognizing that every piece of evidence counts, I shall begin with the death, in 1467, of a single monk, Br. Thomas Lambyrherst, of Christ Church, Canterbury. Thomas Lambyrherst had been a member of the community at Christ Church for twenty years and now held the office of shrine-keeper. In the monastery possessing the most popular shrine in England, that of St Thomas Becket, this was an extremely important office, and it placed its holder in an exposed position, for the shrine-keeper had a great deal to do with pilgrims. He died, we are told, on Good Friday (27 March) at about 7 o'clock in the evening. A death on a solemn day was always awkward for a community of monks, since the requiem Mass could not be allowed to encroach on the liturgy of the day. Yet not all the peculiar arrangements in the present case can be explained in this way. Br. Thomas died, not in the infirmary or in any part of the main claustral area, but in a chamber near one of the gates of the court, the open area separating the main monastic buildings from the edge of the precinct. The very fact that the place of death was noted suggests that it was unusual: it suggests, in fact, that when Br. Thomas became ill it had been considered appropriate to isolate him on the perimeter of the site.[2]

Normally, the body of a deceased monk, dressed for burial but with the

In this chapter, I am greatly indebted to Mr Jim Oeppen, of the Cambridge Group for the History of Population and Social Structure, and to Miss Ros Walley. Miss Walley's analysis of the data, completed under Mr Oeppen's supervision, formed her project for the diploma course in the Statistical Laboratory at Cambridge University in 1988. Mr Oeppen has provided the figures in the present chapter and advised on many points as the chapter took shape; for his comments on the statistical problems involved in the calculation of the life-expectancy of the monks of Westminster, see Appendix IV. For any errors in the chapter, I am solely responsible.

[1] J. Hatcher, 'Mortality in the fifteenth century: some new evidence', *Econ. Hist. Rev.*, 2nd ser. xxxix (1986), 19–38, at 22.

[2] For a plan of Christ Church, Canterbury, see Palmer, *English Monasteries in the Middle Ages* (1930), facing p. 114, and for the death of Thomas Lambyrherst *in quadam camera iuxta portam curie*, *The Chronicle of John Stone, Monk of Christ Church [Canterbury], 1415–1471*, ed. W. G. Searle (Cambridge Antiquarian Society publications, octavo ser. xxxiv (1902)), 98. For the procedure to be followed in the case of those dying on a solemnity, see ibid. 94–5.

face exposed, was laid on a special stone in the infirmary chapel for the commendation that preceded the requiem and subsequent burial; and if a monk died outside the infirmary, his body was nevertheless carried there for the purpose. The stone was also used for the anointing of the terminally ill—this, indeed, was its main function. Burial might take place on the day of the death itself, or on the next day: it was appropriate to act expeditiously but without undue haste, and everything probably depended on the number of hours of daylight that were available. Br. Thomas, however, as we are told by the chronicler of the house, was buried immediately, and in the night:[3] the grave must have been already prepared. Not until five days had passed did the monks gather in the infirmary chapel to commend his soul to God; and then, of course, there was no body on the stone.

Lanfranc, could he have seen all this, would have found the use of a stone for the commendation and anointing strange. In his *Constitutions* he seems to have envisaged that a dying monk would be anointed on his bed.[4] At the moment of death he was to be placed on the ground, on sackcloth and ashes, and there the body was to remain for the commendation. These, however, are mere details. In essentials the rites normally accorded to a Benedictine monk on his decease in the later Middle Ages were probably unchanged since the eleventh century. It is the maimed rites accorded, exceptionally, to Br. Thomas Lambyrherst, and the rush to dispose of his body, that speak of the later period rather than the earlier. They were considered necessary because Br. Thomas had died of plague, and whatever the afflictions of Lanfranc's monks, plague was not among them.

Of all diseases known in the Middle Ages, this was the most dreaded, and dull must the historian be who does not sense the fear that it occasioned. But to acknowledge plague's awesome character is one thing and easily done; to discover how it compared in importance with other forms of epidemic disease quite another, and much more difficult. The contemporary labelling of diseases is notoriously uncertain—or perhaps merely different from our own—and a so-called 'pestis' may or may not have been an outbreak of plague. In identifying diseases in this period we depend largely on circumstantial evidence—the season of the outbreak, the level of mortality, and so on—and as the tests have become more sophisticated, the task has become harder. For example, medievalists now have to take into their system Dr Slack's perception of the discrepant effects of plague on the one hand and fevers on the other on patterns of mortality in the early modern period, and make use of it, if they can, in the identification of

---

[3] *incontinente eadem nocte.*

[4] For anointing and commendation, see *Lanfranc's Constitutions*, 120–4. For anointing on the stone, described as 'customary' at St Albans Abbey at the beginning of the thirteenth century, see *Gesta Abbatum*, i. 246: the dying abbot was brought into the infirmary for the purpose. For the pound tapers lit at the anointing of monks of Westminster in 1523 and 1524, see WAM 19836.

outbreaks.[5] Moreover, the place of epidemic disease in general in the population history of the period, though long discussed, is still unclear. It is widely agreed that fluctuations in mortality, caused by epidemics, could determine the entire demographic character of the short run of years—the quinquennium, or even the decade—in which they occurred, but entirely uncertain how often they had this effect towards the end of the Middle Ages. And underlying every other question of this kind is a fundamental one about the importance of mortality itself among all the variables influencing population change. If we wish to understand why population has grown in some periods but stagnated or fallen in others, do we look mainly to births and to the social and economic conditions influencing the rates at which they occur, or to deaths and to the social and economic conditions influencing them? The last ten to fifteen years have been the day of fertility, the period when historians have emphasized the influence of this factor as never before. It had, we are told in respect of the early modern period, 'the pivotal role . . . in determining overall population growth'; and medievalists have embraced this view with equal enthusiasm.[6]

These problems cannot be solved by the study of mortality on its own. However, a better knowledge of mortality than we possess at present would certainly assist the enquiry, and monastic communities can provide some of the quantitative evidence that is needed. Dr John Hatcher's study of mortality at Christ Church, Canterbury in the fifteenth century has opened up new possibilities and must influence the debate for many years to come.[7] I shall attempt a comparable study of mortality at Westminster Abbey over a rather longer period, 1390 to 1529. But in the first place it will be useful to summarize Hatcher's conclusions.

## 2. Mortality at Christ Church, Canterbury, 1395–1505

At any one time in the later Middle Ages, the community at Christ Church numbered between seventy-five and ninety-five monks: by English standards it was large. Between 1395 and 1505, the exact period covered by Hatcher's study, a total of 414 monks was professed, and conclusions relate to this sample. In the 110 years in question, crude annual death rates in the sample reached crisis level, defined as a rate equivalent to 40 deaths per 1,000

---

[5] Slack, *Impact of Plague in Tudor and Stuart England*, 60–4.

[6] Poos and Smith, ' "Legal windows onto historical populations" ?', 142. For the variables in the Middle Ages and later, and the village or manorial focus now customary in studies of the former period, see also Smith, 'Some issues concerning families and their property in rural England 1250–1800', 1–86; id., 'Marriage processes in the English past: some continuities', in L. Bonfield, R. M. Smith, and K. Wrightson (edd.), *The World We Have Gained: Histories of Population and Social Structure* (Oxford, 1986), 43–99. For a more broadly based, county survey, see L. R. Poos, *A Rural Society after the Black Death: Essex 1350–1525* (Cambridge, 1991), ch. 6; and for the variables in a later period, M. W. Flinn, 'The Population History of England, 1541–1871', *Econ. Hist. Rev.*, 2nd ser. xxxv (1982), 443–57.

[7] 'Mortality in the fifteenth century.'

persons per annum, on no fewer than twenty-seven occasions: one year in four was a crisis year. The peaks actually occurred less frequently in the second half of the period (1451 to 1505) than in the first, but they were steeper when they did occur, and on eight occasions in the later period mortality exceeded 60 per 1,000 per annum. The trend or background level of mortality, which was already high in the first half of the period, nevertheless rose in the second half. If all these facts are striking enough, Hatcher's analysis of life-expectancy in the community at Canterbury is of unique interest and value: nothing like it, with a medieval reference, existed previously. Between the early fifteenth century and the late, the expectation of life of a monk at age 20 fell by eight years, and at age 25 by more than six. Over the whole period, the pattern of mortality at Christ Church was consistent, it is suggested, with an expectation of life at birth for the sample of 21 to 23 years. We can compare this figure with life-expectancy in the nineteenth century. In Wrigley and Schofield's analysis of English population between 1541 and 1871—which includes an analysis of life-expectancy in five-year periods—the quinquennial mean expectation fell below 30 on only three occasions.[8]

If life-expectancy falls, mortality is rising: indeed, life-expectancy is the purest measure we have of mortality. The rise in mortality at Christ Church in the course of the fifteenth century, revealed by this evidence, was more dramatic than any demographic change known to us in the early modern period: if it reflects a general trend, only the fall in mortality occurring in the nineteenth century, and associated with improvements in public health, is comparable in scale.[9] But was the experience of the monks of Christ Church typical of that of society as a whole? Much depends on the provenance of the new entrants to the monastery. If country boys, they may have fallen ready victims to the urban pool of disease they encountered when they came to Canterbury; if town boys, they may have been sufficiently inured to such infections. A lot depends, too, on the way of life of the monks in the long years after profession, and in particular on the degree of seclusion which they enjoyed from the health hazards facing ordinary men and women in their daily life. On all these points, Hatcher reserved judgement.

## 3. Mortality at Westminster Abbey, 1390–1529[10]

### (i) The population under observation

Although as rich as Christ Church, Westminster Abbey housed a smaller community: as we have seen, in the period under consideration, there were

---

[8] Ibid. 32; E. A. Wrigley and R. S. Schofield, *The Population History of England, 1541–1871: A Reconstruction* (Cambridge, 1981, reprinted with a new introduction 1989), 528–9.

[9] I owe this point to Mr Oeppen.

[10] In this part of the chapter the year of account is normally in use: 1390–1529 = 29 Sept. 1390–28 Sept. 1530.

normally forty-eight monks, including the abbot and prior, at Westminster at Michaelmas each year—a date at which it is easy to make a count—but sometimes more and sometimes fewer.[11] Hatcher's work on Christ Church was based principally on the priory's profession and obituary lists—sources of a kind which do not survive at the Abbey. It would be idle to pretend that the absence of these records is a trivial matter. Nevertheless, other sources, described below, provide biographical information which makes a study of mortality in the late medieval monastery feasible. Moreover, new professions occurring in the period 1390–1529 can be dated by year with a fair degree of accuracy. Thus, with new entrants added, and deceased or departed monks subtracted, the size of the population exposed each year to mortality can be established. At the beginning of the period, the actual number of monks in the community was forty-nine, and by the end, 279 new entrants had been professed.[12] The total population under observation is therefore 328. Of this number, thirty-eight (11.5 per cent) were still alive at the end of the period;[13] 245 (74.5 per cent) died as members of the community and thirty-six (11 per cent) departed from the monastery in the course of it; and, finally, the fate of nine (3 per cent) is uncertain—we do not know whether their careers as monks were terminated by death or departure. Most of the departures were legitimate and followed promotion to a benefice or to the priorship of one of the Abbey's dependent houses.

Although the precise event which terminated a monastic career is sometimes in doubt, the year in which it occurred is in many cases explicitly recorded and in others can be inferred from circumstantial evidence. The study of mortality rates at Westminster Abbey will relate to the entire

[11] Above, p. 74, where the period under consideration is 1375–1529 and the number given, 46, excludes the abbot and prior. The average for 1390–1529, excluding the abbot and prior, is identical.

[12] For names, see *Monks*, 124–88, but add, for the period 1390–1529, John Holbech, professed c.1430, ordained deacon 18 Dec. 1430, who died before 29 Sept. 1431 (WAM 18747, 19416, 23787; Reg. Wm. Gray (GL MS 9531/5), 13ᵛ). This John Holbech is to be distinguished from a namesake who was professed 1386–7 and died 1410–11 (WAM 19404; cf. *Monks*, 122). Add also Wm. Walden, professed c.1517, made deacon 7 Mar. 1516, and priest 28 Mar. 1517, who left or died soon after (Reg. Ric. Fitz James (GL MS 9531/9), 2nd ser. 173, 173ᵛ).
The identity of Richard Seyncler/Syncler, made deacon 28 Feb. 1428 and priest in Sept. 1428 and described as a monk of Westminster, is baffling. A mason named R. Sencler was employed by the Abbey in the 1390s, but no monk of this name is ever mentioned at Westminster, and no monk named 'Richard' is mentioned there in the period in question. See Reg. Wm. Gray (GL MS 9531/5), 5ᵛ, 8, and WAM 23463–7. Wm. Westminster, made acolyte 21 Sept. 1527, was probably identical with Wm. Hope, made deacon 18 Sept. 1529 and ordained priest 1530–1 (Reg. Cuthbert Tunstall (GL MS 9531/10), 2nd ser. 9, 12ᵛ; *Monks*, 188). Hugh Smallwood, who was anointed in Oct. 1523, was probably identical with Hugh Martin (WAM 19836; *Monks*, 186).
For an enumeration of 48 professed monks in the community on or about 29 Sept. 1390, see WAM 23717; this list, however, excludes the abbot.

[13] WAM 23960. This list, again, excludes the abbot; and the last 5 monks named were in fact dead by 29 Sept. 1530.

sample of 328 monks, excluding only the nine whose fate is uncertain. The study of life-expectancy in the community at Westminster will relate to the smaller number of monks, 279, who were professed in the period 1390–1529.[14] These dates are dictated by our sources. For the calculation of life-expectancy, the entire monastic career from profession onwards must come under observation. Before 1390, however, the record of new professions at Westminster is imprecise, and in consequence we do not know, or at best know very imperfectly, the years when the forty-nine monks already professed by that date actually entered. It follows that the forty-nine must be excluded from the calculation.

## (ii) The sources

What, then, are the sources supplying the essential information that profession lists and obituary lists would have supplied, had they only survived?

In the first place, on profession, a monk of Westminster became entitled to draw wages—a highly irregular institution, yet a persistent feature of the life of black monks from the thirteenth century onwards. At Westminster, wages came mainly from the surplus revenues of the foundations supporting royal anniversaries and chantries, especially those of Eleanor of Castile, Richard II and Anne of Bohemia, and Henry V, and each monk drawing wages is normally named in these accounts in the year in question.[15] Secondly, although, in accordance with ancient custom, the initial cost of a novice's first habit was borne by his family or patron, from the moment of profession he could turn to the chamberlain, the official responsible for clothing the community, for replacements; and the chamberlain, in common with the obedientiaries in charge of the royal foundations, kept detailed accounts in which each member of the community is named year by year.[16] In this period, therefore, a monk of Westminster normally comes into view in the year of his profession, and, unless he subsequently left the monastery, he remains in view until death. In most cases, though not in all, that event was marked by the infirmarer, who gave alms for the soul of the deceased; and, implicitly, the death was marked by the chamberlain, who entered the deceased's name last in his nominal list for the year.[17]

The sources which have been described contain many idiosyncrasies and some demonstrable errors, and they are in general less reliable towards the end of our period than previously. In 1516 Br. John Randall was made deacon

---

[14] However, of the 279, the two who were professed in the years 1390–4 have been excluded from consideration; for the reason, see below, p. 127 n. 47.

[15] For references, see below, p. 136 n. 79. The obedientiary in charge of Henry VII's foundation did not name the monks receiving wages at Henry's anniversary in his accounts.

[16] WAM 18732–822. Unfortunately this series now has many gaps.

[17] For the infirmarer's alms, see WAM 19375–492; and for the practice of obedientiaries administering wage funds in the year of a monk's decease, which also provides indispensable evidence for this study, below, pp. 136–7.

and in 1517 ordained priest by the bishop of London and identified on both occasions as a monk of Westminster. Yet he appears in no monastic list until 1521–2: he escapes notice in our sources for four or five years.[18] Pieced together, however, the evidence can normally be trusted to provide outline biographies of the monks in the population that we are to observe. Only on one point, the age of monks at profession, is it virtually silent. How, then, can we come by this vital piece of information?

## (iii) Age of profession at the Abbey

In the Benedictine life of this period, profession was the second of two rites of initiation experienced by every monk: the first was clothing—the putting on of the monastic habit. Clothing marked the beginning of the period of formal probation; profession, the commitment for life that, fortuitously, brings the new monk into our purview. Never more than a year separated the two events, and in the later Middle Ages perhaps only a few months or even weeks.[19] The rule of the Black Monk Order that a novice should be at least 19 years old at profession—unless it was useful or necessary to make an exception—meant, therefore, that he should be at least 18 at his clothing.[20] Knowles suggested that in the later Middle Ages novices were normally clothed at 18 and that the vast majority were clothed between that age and 20. Yet in the fifteenth century, he added, clothing at the age of 15 was common.[21] Hatcher, following Knowles but ignoring the distinction between clothing and profession, assumed that age at profession at Christ Church, Canterbury was 18 or thereabouts throughout the fifteenth century.[22]

If, at Westminster, we look beyond clothing and profession to ordination, the event which in principle marked the novice's final emergence from tutelage, it becomes clear that for much of the period under consideration novices here were normally older than 18 when they were clothed, and *a fortiori* older at profession. The priesting of a monk of Westminster is a well-recorded event, since the First Mass that followed within a few days was marked by gifts from the obedientiaries: they gave bread and wine to the new priest, who no doubt entertained his friends at a refection after the ceremony. References to these gifts in the obedientiary accounts of the period enable us to date the First Mass of 83 per cent of the monks who were professed 1390–1529.[23]

---

[18] Reg. Ric. Fitz James (GL MS 9531/9), 2nd ser. 173, 173ᵛ; cf. *Monks*, 187.

[19] For William Breynt, who was clothed at Westminster on 10 Nov. 1493 and professed in the course of the current year of account, i.e. before 29 Sept. 1494, see WAM 33290, fo. 18, and *Monks*, 175. But much shorter periods than this are a possibility (above, p. 101 n. 145). For the presumption of a year's probation at Westminster in the later 13th cent., see *Customary*, ii. 224.

[20] *Chapters of English Black Monks*, i. 10, 99.　　　[21] *RO* ii. 230–1 and n.

[22] Hatcher, 'Mortality in the fifteenth century', 27.

[23] i.e. for 231 of the 279 monks in question. Circumstantial evidence suggests that of the 48 monks for whom no First Mass is recorded, 15 were nevertheless ordained after profession, 20

The minimum canonical age for the priesthood at this date was 25,[24] but we should probably understand by this rule that the candidate was to have attained his twenty-fifth year: he was actually to be 24. In medieval conditions, such a rule can never have been strictly enforced—the most that can have been expected was that the candidate would be at least 24 years old or thereabouts. Even so, practice at Westminster is hard to reconcile with this requirement if novices were indeed normally professed at 18. In the period 1390–1469, the mean interval between profession and ordination at Westminster was about three years, the actual interval often only one or two. If, therefore, the novices of this period were normally professed at 18 or thereabouts, it would follow that many were priested well below the canonical age, and a significant number when they were only 19 or 20. The initiative at this juncture lay with the abbot or his chosen deputy who, in presenting novices to the bishop, testified that they were qualified for the orders that they sought; and the abbot knew that on the point of age the bishop or his deputy could apply no other test than physical appearance.[25] Yet it is unlikely that the abbot persistently misrepresented the true state of affairs. It is perhaps more likely that an understanding existed which exempted monks, who did not have cure of souls, from the canonical rule. If so, we should have to interpret the many papal dispensations of this period for the ordination of monks under age, including that obtained by Westminster Abbey itself in 1477, as enactments that merely legitimized the existing state of affairs.[26]

However, another feature of arrangements at Westminster points to a different explanation of the apparent anomalies. This is the practice of ordaining at different times and seasons monks who had been clothed and professed together, as a single batch. In 1435–6, for example, eight novices were professed, and seven of the eight, if not the entire number, had probably

probably died young, one left the monastery young, before ordination, one other died or left young, and 9 were already priests on entry. In 2 cases, the monk in question died soon after entry, but it is impossible to estimate age or status. For the dates of the First Masses derived from the evidence described in the text, see *Monks, passim,* and for the system, ibid. 22–3.

Fewer than 90 ordinations of monks of Westminster have so far been identified in bishops' registers 1390–1529. My search has not been exhaustive, but this low figure may also reflect a failure to register ordinations by suffragan bishops in the monastery itself.

[24] *Decretum,* D. 78, c. 5. See also R. N. Swanson, *Church and Society in Late Medieval England* (Oxford, 1989), 41–3, where, in a valuable account of ordination patterns among the secular clergy, 24 is seen as the 'governing age'.

[25] On the test of appearance in a later period, see K. V. Thomas, 'Age and authority in early modern England', *PBA* lxii (1976), 205–48, at 206–7.

[26] For examples, see *Cal. Papal Reg., Letters,* xiii, pp. 610, 708, etc.; and for the Abbey's privilege, below, p. 120. Such privileges were also common in the later 14th cent., when the shortage of priests was, for a time, acute. Cf. Pius II's decree of 1461, suspending those promoted to orders before the lawful age (*Magnum Bullarium Romanum Augustae Taurinorum Editum,* ed. L. Cherubini et al. (10 vols., Luxemburg, 1727–30), v. 165–6); and for hints of the efficacy of this ruling, see *Cal. Papal Reg., Letters,* xiii, pp. 488, 508.

formed a single batch at entry.[27] Of these seven, three said their First Mass three years later, another three said theirs four years later, and one waited five years. A natural explanation of this, to us surprising, way of ordering the novitiate would be the existence of differences of educational attainment on entry. But arrangements in the case of monks sent to the university, who were presumably the élite in respect of education, were as disordered as that of the entire sample. Thus, at the end of the fifteenth century, William Fenne said his First Mass five years after profession, but Thomas Gardyner his after seven years. Yet these two monks were professed in the same year and proceeded together to Gloucester College at Oxford.[28]

We must, it seems, conclude that the Abbey, being always rather short of priests to say the many Masses for the laity to which it was committed, now presented its novices for ordination on attainment of the minimum canonical age or soon afterwards, with scant regard for the time elapsing since profession. Nor did it remain content with the canonical age of 24. In 1477 Abbot John Estney obtained a papal dispensation for the ordination of four monks at the age of 21.[29] This dispensation, addressed to the present abbot and to the abbot for the time being, and containing no provision for voidance when four monks should have been ordained, was interpreted at Westminster as perpetual warrant for the ordination of four monks per annum under the canonical age:[30] it probably inaugurated a period when such ordinations were normal. To our knowledge, John Islip, born in June 1464, was only 21 at his ordination in December 1485.[31] But a very small number of other case-histories which happen to be recorded in detail suggests that the new age of ordination was, or came to be, more often 22 than 21. Robert Downes, William Eles, and John Marshall were professed late in 1501, and we are told that their ages were, respectively, 17, 19, and 21. Downes said his First Mass five years later, Eles his three years later, and Marshall his the year after profession. Each was probably 22 when ordained.[32] Moreover, if novices were

---

[27] *Monks*, 145–6. The possible exception is John Witney, who may have entered a little ahead of the others. Witney, described as a deacon in 1435–6 but a priest in 1436–7, is an example of a monk whose First Mass, though celebrated after profession, passed without notice in our sources (WAM 24013, 24015; cf. WAM 23794–5).

[28] Fenne was priested on 24 May 1499; Gardyner, on 27 Mar. 1501. Both had been made acolyte on 23 Dec. 1497 and subdeacon, when students at Oxford, on 31 Mar. 1498. Reg. Thos. Savage (GL MS 9531/8), 3rd ser. 4ᵛ, 9, 15ᵛ; *Monks*, 174–5; *BRUO* ii. 676–7, 743.

[29] *Cal. Papal Reg., Letters*, xiii, p. 581. The monks were to have attained their 22nd year.

[30] LNQ 151ᵛ. For the commemoration, in execrable verse, of John Estney as the abbot who persuaded the pope to lop three years off the lawful age of ordination, see Widmore, *Enquiry*, 204; and for the wider background, *RO* ii. 232–3.                                    [31] *Monks*, 167.

[32] WAM 12890ᵛ. A fourth novice, whose first name, *Jo[hannes]*, and age, apparently 15 (*xv*), can be read, was professed with Downes, Eles, and Marshall, but his surname is now lost through damage to the MS. He was probably John Fulwell, who is known to have died in 1502, the year of his profession. If, however, this identification is correct, the given age must be incorrect, since Fulwell was a priest. For these four monks, see *Monks*, 178–9, and for John Marshall's ordination on 1 Apr. 1503, Reg. Wm. Warham (GL MS 9531/8), 4th ser. 10.

now ordained as young as 21, we should have to conclude that they were quite commonly clothed, if not professed, in this house as young as 14. This, however, is unlikely. In the following account it is assumed that the age at ordination for a monk of Westminster from 1470 was 22.

If monks of Westminster were now ordained at the minimum permissible age or thereabouts, their age at profession can be inferred from the interval elapsing between these two events. In the period 1390–1469, the mean age at profession of those for whom a First Mass is recorded was, it appears, 21—three years above that assumed by Hatcher at Canterbury for the entire period covered by his study. However, at the end of this period, the age at which novices were admitted to clothing fell, and, with it, age at profession. From 1470, the actual age at profession at the Abbey was quite frequently as low as 15, and in one or two cases, though not more, it may have been even lower. In the period 1470–1529, the mean age at profession of those for whom a First Mass is recorded was 18—the identical age proposed for Canterbury. Thus Westminster Abbey exemplifies the fall in age at profession noticed more generally by Knowles in this period.[33] In this house it seems to have occurred c.1470, a few years before the fall in age at ordination: the latter was to some extent a response to the former.

It will already be clear that the age suggested as the norm at profession for monks of Westminster—21, falling to 18—is only approximate, but we may note here an additional reason for regarding it in this light. In the end, everything turned on a novice's own testimony about his age when he entered, and, as a matter of fact, it is always assumed in monastic sources that he knew his age. Nevertheless, we do well to allow for some little inaccuracy in this respect from time to time.[34]

The purpose of lowering the age at entry into the monastery was, almost certainly, to achieve a longer and better-ordered novitiate. If so, much of the benefit was in fact quickly lost by the decision to advance the age at ordination. No one familiar with the decision-making processes of a corporate body today will be in the least surprised at the speed with which the authorities at Westminster forgot the purpose of what had been in fact a policy decision about age at entry. The net consequences for the preliminary stage of a postulant's entry into the monastery may, even so, have been serious and lasting, for it is possible, indeed likely, that, as age at profession fell, so the antecedent period in the almonry was shortened.[35] If so, novices entering the monastery from the 1470s onwards—that is, over very nearly the whole of the second half of the period with which we are concerned—

---

[33] Above, p. 118.

[34] Cf. fallible testimony about age given on occasion in medieval courts (R. F. Hunnisett, 'The reliability of inquisitions as historical evidence', in D. A. Bullough and R. L. Storey (edd.), *The Study of Medieval Records: Essays in Honour of Kathleen Major* (Oxford, 1971), 206–35, at 206.    [35] For this period see above, p. 74.

were, on average, less well acquainted than their predecessors with the unhealthy urban environment in which they would live as monks and correspondingly less resistant to its pool of diseases.

## (iv) Crude death rates

To a remarkable extent, the Abbey's experience of mortality resembled that of Christ Church, Canterbury. I shall discuss, first, crude death rates—the number of deaths per annum, and the trend in deaths per annum over the whole period under consideration, in relation to the number at risk—and, secondly, the life-expectancy of the community. For the time being, the years that will be mentioned are years of account, beginning at one Michaelmas and ending at the next: thus, a reference to the year 1390–1 is to that which began on 29 September 1390 and ended on 28 September 1391.[36] The period 1390–1529 began on 29 September 1390 and ended on 28 September 1530; the period 1390–1459 ended on 28 September 1460.

The criteria for identifying a crisis year in mortality must vary according to the population under observation. The small size of the monastic population exposed each year at Westminster Abbey—an average of fifty-one over the entire period 1390–1529[37]—means that the critical minimum must be placed higher than is appropriate in the case of Christ Church, Canterbury. By setting the sights too low, we should sweep into the net some years when only two or three monks died, and fortuitous circumstances may explain two or even three deaths per annum in a population of about fifty. It will be assumed that the mortality rate in a crisis year in this house was at least three times the trend for the period; alternatively, that it was equivalent to a rate of 100 in a population of 1,000. The trend has been calculated as a moving average of 13 years. Since our data begin in 1390–1, the moving average of necessity begins six years later, in 1396–7.

In the period 1390–1529, these definitions throw up nine crisis years: 1399–1400, 1419–20, 1420–1, 1433–4, 1457–8, 1463–4, 1478–9, 1490–1, and 1529–30 (Figure IV.1(*a*) and (*b*)). Four of the nine—1419–20, 1433–4, 1463–4, and 1478–9—satisfy both criteria. Two years—1419–20 and 1478–9—are outstanding: in each of these, the mortality rate was at least 150 per 1,000, and the ratio to the trend nearer four than three.

In addition to the crisis years, we should also notice thirteen years when mortality, though falling short of crisis levels, was nevertheless well above

---

[36] 29 Sept. to 28 Sept. is the actual period intended when, as frequently happens, the account formally opens on 29 Sept. in one year and closes on 29 Sept. in the next. For an explicit statement to this effect see WAM 18674.

[37] In this case the average relates to the number of professed monks in existence at Michaelmas each year plus the number newly professed in the course of the next 12-month period. Cf. above, p. 102 n. 146 where the number given relates only to the years in the period 1390–1529 for which the infirmarer's accounts survive but is in fact identical to that given in the text above.

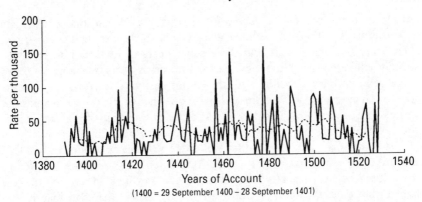

FIG. IV.1*a*. Mortality at Westminster Abbey, 1390–1529: Annual Rate and 13-year Moving Average

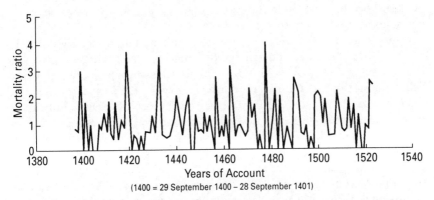

FIG. IV.1*b*. Mortality at Westminster Abbey, 1390–1529: Mortality Ratio

the trend for the period. These years, also shown in Figure IV.1(*a*) and (*b*), were: 1414–15, 1440–1, 1445–6, 1482–3, 1484–5, 1491–2, 1499–1500, 1500–1, 1501–2, 1503–4, 1508–9, 1523–4, and 1527–8. With scarcely an exception, these thirteen years satisfy both criteria: both the mortality rate and the ratio were noticeably higher than usual in the year in question. It is of interest that no fewer than five of the thirteen occur in a single decade, 1499–1508.

Even when the years of high mortality of the second order are taken into account, the beginning of the period under consideration appears relatively good, with only one bad year before 1414–15, and several years of zero mortality. Moreover, despite the occurrence of two consecutive crisis years, 1419–20 and 1420–1, the first half of the period, considered as a whole, had a better experience of mortality than the second half, and the difference consisted in the relative frequency of mortality of the second order. The period divides at the end of the year 1459–60. In the first half, 1390–1459, there were five crisis years and three other years of high mortality; in the second half, 1460–1529, there were only four crisis years but as many as ten other years of high mortality.[38] In the earlier period, one year in every nine was, on average, a bad year; in the later, one in five. In the earlier period, 38 per cent of deaths occurred in one or other of the years of high mortality; the corresponding figure in the later period is 50 per cent.[39]

The trend, or average mortality, was low in the years around 1400. This may, of course, be a misleading conclusion, which we should need to modify if our data began before 1390–1: if mortality was high in any recent year before that date, the actual trend in the 1390s was higher than that shown in Figure IV.1(*a*). But demographic data of necessity have a beginning and an end, and ours, beginning in 1390–1, point to low mortality a decade later. However, in the long period 1410–1509, the trend was normally above 30 per 1,000 per annum, and in the period 1460–1509 it was above 40 per 1,000 per annum in no fewer than twenty years.

In population studies relating to small numbers, finding the right benchmark is always difficult. For all the differences in scale that are involved, it is instructive to look at the national trend, estimated by Wrigley and Schofield, in the mid and late sixteenth century. In the period 1541–99, the crude annual death rate (CDR) reached 30 per 1,000 per annum only seven times, and in 1564–86 it was never higher than 26.3 per 1,000 per annum: in the entire period, it was well below the trend in the monastic community 1460–1509.[40] Yet Wrigley and Schofield's figures are for the whole population, including infants, the most vulnerable age-group, but the figures for the monastic community are for a population aged *c*.18 or above. Other things being equal, if the monastic data were for a population under observation from infancy, CDR here would be much higher than it is.[41] The trend in the monastery in the first half of the fifteenth century is particularly noteworthy, for peaks of mortality appear then to have been too infrequent to provide the necessary momentum for the high trend. The rise after 1460, however, does reflect in part the greater frequency of years of high mortality.

So far, as I have already pointed out, the years referred to in the discussion of mortality at Westminster Abbey have been years of account, beginning

[38] Cf. numbers for the two slightly different periods used above (pp. 107–8) in the study of morbidity: in Period A (1390–1464) there were 6 crisis years and 3 other years of high mortality; in Period B (1465–1529), there were 3 crisis years and 10 other years of high mortality. See further below, p. 144.

[39] 1390–1459: 43 of 114 deaths; 1460–1529: 66 of 131 deaths. The comparable figures for 1390–1464 are 51 of 129 deaths (39.5%), and for 1465–1529, 58 of 116 deaths (50%).

[40] Wrigley and Schofield, *Population History of England, 1541–1871*, 234 n., 531. It is scarcely necessary to point out that Wrigley and Schofield use calendar years.

[41] Another point that I owe to Mr Oeppen.

on 29 September and ending on 28 September in the next calendar year.[42] This usage has been necessary in order to survey the entire period 1390–1529. However, it has disadvantages, and these include the difficulty of comparing patterns of mortality in the monastery with patterns in other places: there, as likely as not, the calendar year, running from 1 January to 31 December, will be in use. Down to 1515, the evidence at our disposal is sufficiently precise for us to be able to assign each death in the monastery to a calendar year, despite the fact that this is not how it is normally recorded in our sources.[43] Figure IV.2(*a*) and (*b*) shows the data for the period 1390–1515 according to calendar years.

It will be noticed, first, that not every bad year by the one mode of reckoning has a matching bad year by the other. For example, 1471 claims a place in the list of crisis years, although neither of the related years of account, 1470–1 and 1471–2, ranks as a year of high mortality. Conversely, neither of the calendar years 1414 and 1415 is in the new list, although the year of account 1414–15 qualifies as a year of high mortality. Nine calendar years—1400, 1420, 1434, 1458, 1464, 1471, 1479, 1491, and 1500—were in fact crisis years in the Abbey; and in seven other calendar years—1441, 1445, 1483, 1485, 1502, 1503, and 1508—mortality was well above the trend for the period. Secondly, however, it will be noticed that mortality rates in two calendar years attained levels not attained in any year of account. In 1420 the rate was 284 per 1,000 and the ratio six times the trend; and in 1464 the rate was 232 per 1,000 and the ratio 4.9—nearly five times the trend. It follows that the mortality rate and ratio in each of these years were higher than in the related years of account: these were, for 1420, 1419–20 and 1420–1, and for 1464, 1463–4 and 1464–5.

These differences between mortality analysed by calendar years, on the one hand, and by years of account, on the other, direct attention to the seasonal incidence of deaths in this period at Westminster. In some years of high mortality, deaths occurred mainly in the late summer and autumn. If, when this happened, the total number of deaths is split between two years beginning or ending on or about 29 September, what was in fact one exceptional peak will appear as two lesser peaks. This happens when we divide the wholly exceptional mortality of the summer and autumn of 1420 into that occurring before 29 September and that occurring after this date. On the other hand, even in years when mortality peaked in these seasons, deaths might also occur at other times. In some of these cases, the calendar year throws up the more dramatic results; in others, the year of account does so.[44]

---

[42] Above, p. 122.

[43] For the evidence, see below, pp. 135–8. The transition from years of account to calendar years brings into consideration for the first time the periods 1 Jan.–28 Sept. 1390 and 29 Sept.–31 Dec. 1515. However, it is virtually certain that no deaths occurred in either.

[44] On the seasonal incidence of mortality see further below, p. 138.

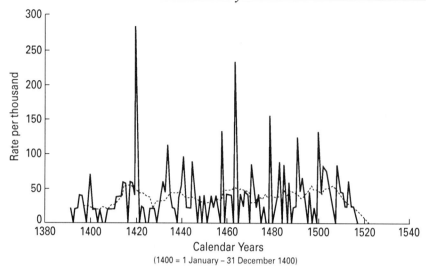

FIG. IV.2*a*. Mortality at Westminster Abbey, 1390–1515: Annual Rate and 13-year Moving Average

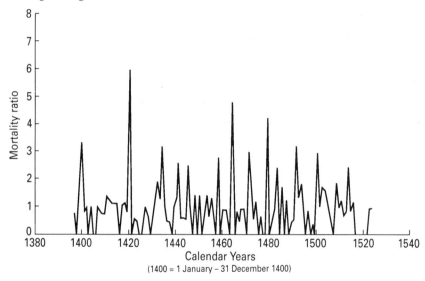

FIG. IV.2*b*. Mortality at Westminster Abbey, 1390–1515: Mortality Ratio

The list of calendar years of high mortality has one other remarkable feature: few of the years in question—only six of the total of sixteen occurring in the period 1390–1515—coincide with years when epidemics attracted notice in London, or indeed elsewhere. In 1420, the most destructive year of all at Westminster, an epidemic of plague is mentioned in Norfolk and another at Canterbury, but none in London.[45] Conversely, major epidemics are mentioned in London in some years—as, for example, 1407—when the monks of Westminster apparently escaped unscathed.[46]

## (v) Life-expectancy

In the middle decades of the fifteenth century, life-expectancy in the community at Westminster declined by a dramatic margin, and this is the clearest indication we have that mortality rates in the monastery rose dramatically at this time. At this point, in order to achieve full comparability with developments at Canterbury, the monks of Westminster have been ordered in 25-year, overlapping, cohorts, beginning in 1395–6, this being Hatcher's way of ordering the monks of Christ Church, Canterbury.[47] Thus the first cohort consists of monks professed 1395–1419, the second, of those professed 1405–29, and so on. In Figure IV.3, expectation of life at age 20 (e20) is shown at the average year of death for the cohort in question, and reckoned from the mid-point of their 25-year period. The appropriate adjustment has been made for the fact that novices were not in fact 20 when they entered, but at first 21 and later 18, by moving the mid-point back one year in the case of the cohorts entering down to 1475 and forward two years in the case of those entering subsequently. These conventions mean, for example, that e20 for the first cohort appears in 1437, and for the second, in 1447. Again, these conventions are also followed in the presentation of the Canterbury data.

Each cohort includes monks who were absent from the monastery from time to time for short periods and who, during that time, experienced mortality environments differing from that of the monastery.[48] These monks may have been quite numerous. A small number were absent for longer periods. But the great majority of monks making up the cohorts were based in the monastery for by far the greater part of each year. Thus, down to the early sixteenth century, when, as I shall explain, a new situation began to take effect, this evidence relates to individuals whose mortality environment was indeed normally that of the monastery.

[45] J. M. W. Bean, 'Plague, population and economic decline in the later Middle Ages', *Econ. Hist. Rev.*, 2nd ser. xv (1963), 423–37, at 428, 430; Hatcher, 'Mortality in the fifteenth century', fig. 2; and for the uneven geographical incidence of epidemics later in the 15th cent., R. S. Gottfried, *Epidemic Disease in Fifteenth Century England: The Medical Response and the Demographic Consequences* (New Brunswick, NJ, 1978), 96–107.

[46] Bean, 'Plague, population and economic decline', 428.

[47] Hatcher, 'Mortality in the fifteenth century', table 2. Hatcher uses calendar years (1 Jan.–31 Dec.). This, however, does not affect the comparison of the Canterbury and Westminster data in 25-year overlapping periods.

The use of cohorts beginning in 1395 for the Westminster data has made it necessary to exclude from consideration monks professed 1390–4. There were only two: Benedict Middleton and Edmund Whaddon; see *Monks*, 124–5. [48] See also on this point Appendix IV.

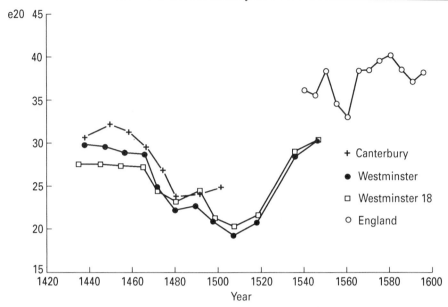

FIG. IV.3. Life-Expectancy at Age 20

*Key*        +   Canterbury: the estimates for Christ Church, Canterbury (Hatcher, 'Mortality in the fifteenth century', table 2).
             ●   Westminster: the estimates for Westminster Abbey, assuming 21 as the age at profession 1395–1469 and 18 as the age 1470–1529.
             □   Westminster 18: the estimates for Westminster Abbey, assuming 18 as the age at profession 1395–1529.
             ○   England: period estimates by back-projection from 1871, communicated by the Cambridge Group for the History of Population and Social Structure.

The cohorts of 1395–1419 and 1405–29 and the next two to enter had a life-expectancy at age 20 of 29 to 30 years. For the cohort of 1435–59 and that of 1445–69, e20 was progressively lower. The next cohort, 1455–79, held its own and actually had a slightly better experience than its predecessor. Then, however, e20 fell again. For the cohort entering 1475–99, it was less than 20 years, and 10 to 11 years lower than that for the cohort of 1395–1419.

Such was the fall in life-expectancy of the monks of Westminster. These estimates assume, for reasons explained earlier, that monks of Westminster were professed at the age of 21 or thereabouts down to the 1470s and at 18 thereafter. If, however, following Hatcher, we assume that age at profession in a Benedictine house was 18 throughout the period under consideration, life-expectancy for the earlier cohorts is somewhat reduced, and the ensuing fall is of about eight years. Whichever assumption we make about age at profession, there is a striking similarity between the trend at Westminster and that at Canterbury: at Canterbury, e20 fell by eight years between *c*.1440 and *c*.1480. (See Figure IV.3.) In each house, life-expectancy declined in the space of a few decades by a spectacular margin.

At Canterbury, records relating to mortality cease to be comprehensive in 1505. At Westminster, as we have seen, they continue to be useful until 1529—long enough for us to form an impression of life-expectancy in the community in the early sixteenth century. The dates of the last two cohorts in the population under observation are, respectively, 1495–1519 and 1505–29. Their life-expectancy shows a dramatic upturn from the nadir represented by that of the cohort professed 1475–99. However, the quality of the Westminster data declines in the early sixteenth century. The decline occurs for two reasons. First, the obedientiary accounts of the monastery, our principal source, lose some of their former accuracy as sources for the careers of individual monks. Secondly, many of the monks who were professed in this period were still alive at the Dissolution of the monastery in 1540, when they passed into ordinary clerical or secular life. There, it becomes much harder to discover when they died. Consequently, we do not know the year of death of half the number of monks in the last two cohorts.[49] In sum, the evidence is good enough to sustain the conclusion that the life-expectancy of the population under observation rose in the early sixteenth century—that it moved, so to speak, in a Wrigley and Schofield direction—but not to provide an exact measure of the change that occurred. Yet, despite the rising trend in the last decades at Westminster, it is very likely that a considerable gap existed between the monastic expectation of life over most of this period and life-expectancy nationally in the early years of the period analysed by Wrigley and Schofield. (See Figure IV.3.)

## 4. The Fatal Diseases

### (i) Implications of the monastic way of life

What were the diseases that killed the monks of Westminster, and killed them, on average, at an earlier age in the second half of the fifteenth century than in the first half? Towards the end of this century, the sources at Canterbury identify the symptoms and diseases which had been observed in the monks of this house who died at this time: sweating sickness, plague, and tuberculosis head the list for frequency of cases in the short period in question, and at the bottom are so-called frenzy, fever, and hernia.[50] At

---

[49] Twenty-five of 54 deaths are unknown in the case of the cohort professed 1495–1519; and 23 of 41 deaths in the case of the cohort professed 1505–29.

[50] Hatcher, 'Mortality in the fifteenth century', table 3.

Westminster, we are entirely dependent on circumstantial evidence in identifying the killer diseases—and, indeed, in identifying most other kinds of disease there too. The most telling circumstance of all is the way of life of the monks: what they ate and how this was prepared and served; sleeping arrangements; personal hygiene or the lack of it; and sanitary arrangements. The list of sensitive areas is long, and most items in it are, in general, neglected areas of study. Some have already been considered earlier.[51] Here, I shall discuss two others: sleeping arrangements in the monastery, and personal hygiene. Did these features of community life at Westminster change in the period under consideration in ways that could help to explain changes in the pattern of mortality?

### (a) Sleeping arrangements

The monks' dormitory at Westminster was a vast room, 173 ft. × 34.5 ft. (52.7 m. × 10.5 m.),[52] and if it had not actually been built to overawe the young novice on his first few nights in the monastery, this was, no doubt, its effect on him. In the later Middle Ages, 50–60 per cent of the community probably slept here, and the rest in private quarters, and these proportions did not change in the course of the fifteenth or early sixteenth centuries.[53] The dormitory was twice rebuilt or restored on a large scale—for the second time in 1449–50, after a conflagration caused by an incautious act on the part of Br. George Norwich, a future abbot of Westminster, but at the time only a novice.[54] But the basic size had been determined once for all time in the late eleventh century, when the community probably numbered eighty or thereabouts.[55] Even for eighty it was spacious—and of set purpose, for it was always considered important that monks should avoid bodily contact with each other, and especially in the dormitory. The space proved useful when cubicles were introduced. This amenity is not mentioned at Westminster until the 1340s but was almost certainly introduced earlier. From the late thirteenth century onwards, the General Chapter of the English Black Monks found it necessary to condemn the introduction of any kind of partition into dormitories—a sure sign that the innovation was already becoming popular.[56] Following a common practice, the partitions at Westminster consisted of curtains: blue muslin is mentioned as the material in the 1360s, buckram at the end of the fifteenth century.[57] References to iron

---

[51] For diet, see above, pp. 62–7, and for sanitation, pp. 78–9.

[52] *Royal Commission on Historical Monuments: Westminster Abbey*, 82b.

[53] Above, p. 77, where the occupants of private chambers are estimated at 45% of the whole.

[54] *Monks*, 141; and for the rebuilding in 1449–50, below, pp. 206–7. For an account, probably exaggerated, of the first fire, in 1298, see *Flete*, 117.      [55] Harvey, *Estates*, 85.

[56] *Chapters of English Black Monks*, i. 80, ii. 47, etc.

[57] WAM 18727, 18729, 18785, etc., and for an earlier reference to muslin, WAM 18723. At the end of the 15th cent., curtains of blue buckram for a window or windows in the novices' part of the dormitory are mentioned (WAM 18789).

bars and rings in this room fill in a little more of the detail.[58] We are to envisage curtains of a certain height, hanging from supports which projected from the wall—an arrangement ensuring a new privacy for monks when dressing or undressing, but doing little or nothing to impede the spread of infections when these were present.

Beds in this dormitory were lined with straw, and provided with a canvas mattress or pallet, which rested on the straw and probably itself contained straw. In the thirteenth century, custom decreed that the straw should be changed at least once a year and the dormitory itself cleaned on this occasion.[59] It is, of course, possible that these prescriptions are a poor guide to the actual frequency of the operations in question. Yet the pointers we have to actual practice are not encouraging. In the late fifteenth century, the novices' chambers in the dormitory were cleaned, and new straw placed on the beds, at the arrival of every new batch of novices, but not, it appears, more frequently.[60] No similar expenditure is recorded in respect of the cubicles of professed monks: quite possibly, these monks were expected to pay for such tasks out of their wages. And even in this late period, when, both inside and outside the cloister, the dangers of dirt were in general much better appreciated than had been the case earlier, the monastic dormitory was still treated somewhat casually. When, following their usual practice, the parliamentary Commons met in the Abbey refectory in 1489–90, the monks removed the mats which normally covered the stone cloister walks and placed them—no doubt with a good deal of dust, too—in the dormitory: there, they evidently calculated, mats would be safe from the boots of heavy-footed knights and burgesses.[61] To save the mats, the dormitory, it appears, could be treated as a box-room.

Yet in one respect sleeping arrangements did improve in the course of the later Middle Ages, for special night-clothes now came into use. Previously, in conformity with Benedictine practice in general, the monks of Westminster slept in their daytime undergarments. The purpose of this uncomfortable practice was to avoid the necessity of undressing in public. We are not told how often, in this earlier period, undergarments were actually changed, but the expectation that hands would need a special wash after the event suggests that the intervals may have been infrequent.[62] The division of the dormitory into cubicles removed the need, we may think, for such scruples. But the monks of Westminster probably continued to wear their daytime shirt, drawers, and stockings in bed for a considerable time to come. Indeed,

[58] WAM 18754, 18784.    [59] *Customary*, ii. 148–9.

[60] The almoner was responsible for these tasks (WAM 19097, 19104, 19110). The novitiates of this period may have been short; the intervals between the arrival of new batches were sometimes very long: see above, pp. 73, 118.

[61] WAM 19098; and for a glimpse of wear and tear on the mats in the cloister and refectory during parliaments before the monks learnt to put the mats away, WAM 19025.

[62] *Customary*, ii. 145.

this practice was confirmed as the norm for the Order as late as 1421: what the General Chapter disputed on this occasion was only Henry V's desire to add the outer habit to the requirements.[63]

By the end of the fifteenth century, a novice's initial set of clothes at Westminster included a so-called night-coat—a clear indication that the community as a whole was now using garments of this kind. The amount of cloth apparently required to make a novice's night-coat at this time— only $2\frac{1}{4}$ yards of the outer cloth and $4\frac{1}{4}$ yards of the lining—suggests that it was rather short: it was probably thigh length.[64] If so, it is likely that the daytime drawers and the stockings were still worn in bed. Yet if the monks of this period shed only their daytime shirts on getting into bed, they did better than most of their predecessors.

### (b) Personal hygiene

Monastic legislators tended to regard washing and shaving, though not, of course, bathing, as acts which monks would perform in common and at regular times and seasons; and some of the acts in question—as, for example, foot-washing on Saturdays and Maundy Thursday—were solemn rituals.[65] At Westminster Abbey, this view of the operations was by no means superseded in the fourteenth century. Thus, in 1344–5 the chamberlain's purchases of two bowls for the foot-washing of senior monks tells us that the Saturday rite, described in the Abbey's Customary, at which novices and junior monks acted as servers for the seniors, had survived the lapse of eighty years.[66] Yet the decline of the common life, itself so well marked by this date, inevitably eroded older conventions. According to an earlier convention, monks of Westminster shaved each other, working in pairs, once a fortnight and did so in a cloister that was open to the elements.[67] By the 1290s, however, this system was evidently superseded, for the monks now employed a barber on a regular basis, and may long have done so.[68] By the mid-fourteenth century, the status of razors as possessions which monks

---

[63] *Chapters of English Black Monks*, ii. 121, 124; cf. ibid. 115. See also Harvey, *Monastic Dress*, 27–8. Neither of two inventories, made c.1400, of the goods of monks living in private chambers at Westminster refers to night-clothes (WAM 6603, 18883A).

[64] Harvey, *Monastic Dress*, 27–8.

[65] *Lanfranc's Constitutions*, 8–10, 26, 92–4; *Customary*, ii. 169–70, 173–5; *Chapters of English Black Monks*, i. 261, 262. Although the Customary at times follows Lanfranc's Constitutions verbatim, it also diverges from this source. To some extent it records actual practice at Westminster c.1270.

[66] WAM 18723; *Customary*, ii. 173–5. Respect for seniority at the Maundy tended to nullify its moral significance but is implied in our source.

[67] *Customary*, ii. 171–3. Cf. *Chapters of English Black Monks*, i. 54. At a shaving, head as well as beard were shaved: see *Lanfranc's Constitutions*, 92 n.

[68] WAM 18717. The 'domus rasture' opening off the cloister, which is mentioned much later, may date from the rebuilding of the latter after the fire of 1298; the provision of this room marks the end of the heroic practice of open-air shaving. Charcoal was used here in the 15th cent., presumably in a brazier (WAM 18771).

gave to each other as presents points to a flight from the barber's services into private shaving. In 1351–2 the infirmarer gave seven razors—presumably one per person—to the monks who had taken his place on the rota for reading in the refectory at meals.[69]

As the norms were bent, so a new scope was allowed to private judgement, and not only in the matter of shaving. Br. Richard Exeter and Br. John de Canterbury died within four years of each other, the one in 1396, the other in 1400, and each had occupied a large private chamber for many years. Yet Br. John's household effects included four sets of basins and ewers, but Br. Richard's only two.[70] The difference in the scale of provision of the essential amenity for the washing of face and hands, in apartments comprising, as each chamber did, several rooms, suggests the operation of different judgements about the importance of the act and pleasure to be derived from its consequences.

Like washing and shaving, the laundering of clothes was to some extent privatized in the late medieval monastery, and no doubt with similar consequences. Formerly, the chamberlain was responsible for laundry. By *c.*1270, however, when the Abbey's Customary was compiled, the service which he provided was evidently found by some to be inadequate, for it is implied in this source that monks occasionally, though quite irregularly, had their clothes laundered in the town of Westminster.[71] Two centuries later, shirts and drawers seem to have been the only items of monastic attire still laundered at the chamberlain's expense: we are to conclude that other garments—as, for example, stockings and, in due course, night-clothes—were laundered at the expense of the wearer.[72] The existence of private arrangements for laundry explains how it was that the chamberlain provided utensils for laundresses whom he did not himself employ.[73] Laundry bills were now in fact paid by the monk himself, out of his wages. Were his clothes cleaner or more sordid on this account? At this point the evidence fails us. Yet we do know that at the beginning of the sixteenth century, the laundry bill for four novices over a six-month period amounted to 4*s.*[74] The outlay sounds

---

[69] WAM 19332.

[70] WAM 6603, 18883A; and see *Monks*, 101–2, 107–8. Exeter's death probably occurred late in 1396. Both his basins and ewers were in the hall (*aula*) of his chamber. A basin and ewer from John de Canterbury's effects were sent to the manor house at Steventon, the country retreat of monks of Westminster when studying at Oxford.

[71] *Customary*, ii. 147. See also ibid. 103, 153, and for Westminster laundresses, Rosser, *Medieval Westminster*, 198.

[72] WAM 18748, 18752, 18755. Strails, the upper and lower bed-coverings, were also laundered by the chamberlain. *c.*1425–*c.*1485, the quantities of soap purchased for this purpose varied in the range 75 lbs. to 150 lbs. p.a.; later, however, they are measured in firkins, kilderkins, or barrels (WAM 18743 ff.). [73] e.g. WAM 18789.

[74] WAM 18793, fo. 12. Both bills were paid by the chamberlain, Br. Thomas Brown, in his capacity as 'tutor', or patron, to the novices in question during their period of probation. It was now a common practice for senior monks to undertake this role. For another example see WAM 33290, fo. 18.

little enough, but it was as much as the refectorer spent in a six-month period on the laundering of the considerable amount of table linen for which he was responsible:[75] it suggests perhaps that novices were expected to wear clothes that were—by the rather low standards of the period—presentable.

How clean were the bodies underneath? The monks of Westminster rarely took baths. This, of course, does not distinguish their way of life from that of their social peers outside the cloister, for in the Middle Ages baths seem always to have been rather rare events in upper-class society. However, it is of interest that baths may have been less common in the monastery in the later Middle Ages than in some earlier periods. Once, they had been taken as often as four times a year: at Christmas, Easter, at the end of June, and at the end of September. At these seasons, the entire community had participated. The attendants in the bath-house dealt with four monks a day, and their working day lasted from Prime at daybreak to Compline in the evening—a bath, in fact, was a lengthy business. But in the late twelfth century or the early thirteenth, a reforming party brought this arrangement to an end and restored the primitive Benedictine principle, enshrined in the Rule, that baths were especially for the sick, and not to be taken by others on a regular basis.[76] We do not know how often they were taken by healthy monks of Westminster in the later Middle Ages, but that some were taken is shown by the employment of a well-rewarded bath attendant. In the fifteenth century, this official received two *hogeman* loaves daily, and a stipend of 18s., rising to £1, per annum, together with a valet's livery of clothing valued at 10s. per annum; and he was probably entitled to board on days when his services were actually required.[77] The combination of *hogeman* loaves, an inferior variety, with the livery of a valet, who normally received superior, conventual, loaves, reflects some of the equivocal status of bathing itself in the monastery at this time. Yet these emoluments represent a high level of material reward for what was, after all, only part-time work: they point to the unpleasant and arduous nature of the bath-attendant's duties.

## (c) *What did the changes amount to?*

In the course of the later Middle Ages considered as a whole, we can detect changes in the way of life at Westminster Abbey that must have affected the

[75] WAM 19595–612, recording annual payments of 8s. p.a. to a laundress. Additional payments were sometimes made for mending. Outlay c.1400 was lower (above, p. 79).

[76] *Customary*, ii. 155–6. The influence of *Lanfranc's Constitutions*, 8–10 is apparent. See also *Rule*, cap. xxxvi.

[77] WAM 18734–89. The stipend was £1 p.a. from the late 1440s. For the loaves, see WAM 18887. The double ration may mean that this servant was expected to employ an assistant. For the full corrody of bread, ale, and cooked food enjoyed by two bath-attendants on working days in the mid-13th cent., see *Customary*, ii. 155–6; and for the general level of valet's emoluments in this period, below, p. 175. It is possible that baths existed near the infirmary, on the east side (Micklethwaite, 'Notes on the Abbey buildings of Westminster', 36).

health of the monks, and in some cases the effects were beneficial. Had it not been for the constraints of the common life, the beneficial changes might have been more numerous or occurred earlier: left to their own devices, the monks of Westminster would perhaps have been earlier into night-clothes and more frequently into the bath. Yet it would be hard to argue on the basis of our evidence that the monks of this period possessed an innate preference for cleanliness that needed only a freer environment to triumph, and impossible to argue that all the changes facilitated by the decline of the common life were, in the present context, benign. Benign or harmful, the changes do not cluster in the mid-fifteenth century, the period when mortality itself changed so dramatically; and even the benign changes left the general level of hygiene so low that they must be deemed makeweights, not major influences.

For every feature of monastic life, matching health-hazards can be identified. Thus, inadequate personal hygiene encouraged lice and opened the way to typhus; fragile sanitary arrangements encouraged enteric fevers; excessive allowances of food and drink, continued over an entire monastic career, carried the threat of heart disease and exacerbated the risk of renal failure. As for plague, rats—carriers of this disease—were certainly to be found in and around the monastery. 'Item a Redd sumpter cloth moche eaten wyth Rattis' reads the Dissolution inventory of the goods in the abbot of Westminster's well-appointed residence.[78] The entry tells us that rats had been at the goods stored in Abbot Benson's wardrobe.

## (ii) Patterns of mortality

How far does the detailed pattern of mortality in the monastery enable us to match possible diseases to actual victims? With this question in mind, I shall discuss the period 1390–1515, when our sources enable us to assign deaths to calendar years, and, in particular, mortality in the bad years occurring in this period. As we have seen, there were sixteen such years: in nine of these mortality reached crisis level; in the remainder, it was high, but even so of the second order. Between 1 January 1390 and 31 December 1515, 224 monks of Westminster died, and, of this number, 93 (41.5 per cent) died in the sixteen bad years. Of the 93, 63 (representing 28 per cent of the entire number) died in the crisis years, and 30 (13.5 per cent) in the other years of high mortality. It will be useful to consider the seasonal incidence of mortality in these years, its age-incidence then, and, finally, the length of the antecedent illnesses.

### (a) Seasonal incidence

Although our sources rarely date a monk's death by day or month, they do betray a broad seasonal pattern of mortality, and in some years something

---

[78] *Abbot's House at Westminster*, 39–40. The entry was later deleted, perhaps because the cloth was not a disposable chattel.

more detailed than this. The vital evidence is contained in the accounts of the obedientiaries who administered monastic wages. As we have seen, the greater part of the sums needed came from the surplus income of the funds supporting royal anniversaries. In principle, wages were distributed soon after the anniversary with which they were associated. Accordingly, wages from Eleanor of Castile's fund—the oldest, richest, and, in the present context, always the most useful of the three—were distributed soon after 28 November, the date of the queen's death and normally that of her anniversary.[79] However, the distribution related to the previous year of account which had closed on 28 or 29 September: thus, when the wardens of this fund made their distribution, they were looking back on a year which had ended two months previously. Much of the value which their accounts have in the present context is explained by this time-lag.

At the beginning of the period under consideration, the wardens of Queen Eleanor's foundation confined their distribution of wages to monks who had survived the entire year of account which had recently ended, and ignored the claims of those who had died in the course of it: indeed, they excluded even those who had survived to the end of that year, at Michaelmas, but died before 28 November. In 1417, however, they introduced the practice, never subsequently abandoned, of making posthumous payments in the case of the deceased. These payments consisted of a proportion of the sums that would have been due had the monks in question survived for the entire year, and the money was given to the friends who had undertaken the general administration of their goods.[80] At first, no attempt was made to adjust such payments to the number of weeks or months elapsing before death. Soon, however, refinements were introduced. Thus, Br. John Bury, who, as we happen to know, died on 11 March 1453, received posthumously a quarter of his previous annual share as a priest when wages for the year 1452–3 were distributed at the end of the following November; but Br. John Wilton, who died on 8 May in the same year, received posthumously half his normal share at the same distribution.[81] On first consideration, these

[79] Exceptionally, the actual date of the distribution is recorded in 1482 (2 Dec.), 1511 (5 Dec.), and 1512 (7 Dec.) (WAM 33289, fo. 15; WAM 33325, fos. 31ᵛ, 69). The account for the previous year was audited on the same occasion. For the main accounts of this foundation, see WAM 23717–960; for those of Richard II's foundation, WAM 23970–4121, and Henry V's, WAM 24122–235. The anniversary of Richard II and Anne of Bohemia was observed at the end of Feb., Henry V's on 30 Aug.

E. H. Pearce used the wage data in these accounts to date deaths at Westminster Abbey (*Monks*, 28–30, and *passim*). I have reworked the evidence, with more particular questions in mind than Pearce's, but rarely disagreed with his broad interpretation.

[80] For an example identifying the actual recipient of the money, see WAM 33288, fos. 20–1, where payments to Prior Mane in respect of anniversary wages owing posthumously to Br. Humphrey Litlyngton are recorded. Litlyngton died on 17 Apr. 1502. For the first posthumous payments, in 1417, in respect of Br. Robert Barton and Br. William Broughton, see WAM 23762.                    [81] WAM 23826; *Monks*, 128, 151.

shares may appear puzzling, for Wilton survived only two months longer than Bury but received twice as much. Very probably, however, the wardens of the fund had now adopted the practice, long followed by some other obedientiaries, of regarding Easter as the mid-point of the year for the calculation of wages. They now gave half shares in the case of those who survived until Easter, but a smaller share, determined *ad hoc*, in the case of those dying before that all-important date in the monastic calendar: Easter in 1453 was on 1 April.

If the introduction of posthumous shares helps to elucidate the seasonal pattern of mortality, so too does the wardens' practice of entering the names of all monks who died before the anniversary on 28 November in a special place in the list of recipients of wages: the deceased always came at the end, and they did so even if they had survived throughout the previous year of account ending at Michaelmas. Consequently, the accounts for this fund contain precious information about deaths in October and November—a sensitive period in the chronicle of mortality.

In due course, the other royal foundations developed similar conventions in the matter of wages, and the accounts of all three foundations survive in excellent series.[82] This kind of evidence is, of course, no substitute for the monastery's missing obituary list, for the latter no doubt contained the exact day and month of each monk's death. Pieced together, however, the evidence does enable us to assign a great many of the deaths occurring in the fifteenth or early sixteenth centuries to one or other of two unequal portions of the year: the end of November—the date of Queen Eleanor's anniversary—to Easter, on the one hand, and Easter to the end of November, on the other. Since the earliest date on which Easter can fall is 22 March and the latest 25 April, this means that we can assign the deaths in question either to a period of four or five months, comprising, in a loose sense of the terms, winter and early spring, or to one of seven or eight months, comprising late spring, summer, and autumn. Although broader than we could wish, this periodization is useful, because a number of diseases, including bubonic plague, are much more likely to occur in the second of these divisions of the year than in the first. In some years, the evidence is sufficiently detailed for us to distinguish an early autumn, ending on or about 29 September, from a late autumn, extending from that date until the end of November. Moreover, it is normally possible to assign winter deaths, on the balance of probabilities, to one or other of the two possible calendar years. As for the period down to 1417, when the wage data are unhelpful in the present context, this happens also to be the period when the infirmarer not only recorded the exact length of his patients' stays in the infirmary but also dated these by month.[83]

[82] For references see n. 79 above.
[83] WAM 19375–409. Major obedientiaries are a special case, since they rarely entered the infirmary when ill. However, their date of death tends to be recorded in other sources.

In this period, therefore, we can often assign a monk's last illness, and so his death, to a particular month.

What, according to this evidence, was the seasonal pattern of mortality in the sixteen bad years of the period 1390–1515?

Of the 93 deaths in these years, 26 (28 per cent) probably occurred in the winter or early spring; 64 (69 per cent) in the late spring, summer, or autumn; and 3 (3 per cent) cannot now be assigned to either portion of the year. However, late spring, summer, and autumn claimed more victims in the crisis years than in the years of high mortality of the second order. Thirty deaths occurred in the latter years, and of these a minimum of 15 and maximum of 18 (50 per cent to 60 per cent) occurred in the three seasons in question. But 63 deaths occurred in the crisis years, and, of these, a minimum of 49 and maximum of 52 (78 per cent to 83 per cent) probably occurred in these seasons.

Moreover, it appears that in some of the crisis years the summer and autumn were actually the dangerous seasons—and dangerous by any standards. In 1420, 6 or 7 of the year's 13 deaths occurred in the summer or early autumn, and a further 5 in the late autumn.[84] In 1479, 5 of the year's 7 deaths probably occurred in the late summer or early autumn, and the remaining 2 in late autumn.[85] These were two of the three worst years for mortality at the Abbey in the whole period under consideration. In the third, 1464, when 11 monks died, the deaths were more widely spaced over the year. Yet it is a striking fact that 6, all of young monks, probably occurred in the summer or early autumn.[86]

## (b) Age-incidence

From c.1430, and for a century, we can reconstruct, very roughly, the age-structure of the community at Westminster. At any one time in this period monks under the age of 30 probably made up 30 per cent to 50 per cent of the whole[87] (Figure IV.4). At first sight, variability within such a wide range

[84] Wm. Amundesham's death on 14 July 1420 is explicitly recorded, and circumstantial evidence suggests that T. Bodenham died at about this time. J. Botkesham, B. Middleton, T. Preston, and R. Tonworth evidently died later but before 29 Sept. R. Selby's death on 29 Sept. is explicitly recorded. W. Belden, W. Petham, and T. Tonley died between that date and the end of Nov. Abbot Colchester died in Oct., and probably on 18 Oct., the day later observed as his anniversary. WAM 19412, 23768, 23996, 33289, fo. 15; *Monks*, 122, 129.

[85] T. Barker, R. Purcell, J. Selly, J. Ware, and T. Westow died before 29 Sept. but evidently, from the wage data, not long before; T. Prymer and R. Huntingdon evidently died between 29 Sept. and the end of Nov. WAM 19460, 23872, 23874, 24043–4, 24157, 24159.

[86] The wage data suggest that, of the 11, J. Kingston survived into the summer, and J. Ashby, N. Harvey, W. Pavor, R. Stokeley—who said his First Mass in June or July—and N. Whaplode until the late summer or early autumn; but the infirmarer had distributed alms for their souls by 29 Sept. The year's remaining victims were W. West (died before Easter, i.e. before 1 Apr.), T. Pomeray (not long after Easter), and W. Milton and H. Tudbery (in each case at the end of the year). WAM 19445, 23844, 23846, 24148–9; *Monks*, 157, 159.

[87] At Michaelmas 1430, 48 monks in a community then numbering 53 (91%) had been professed since 29 Sept. 1390, the date at which it becomes possible to estimate the age of

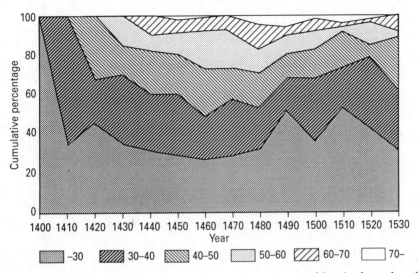

Fig. IV.4. Age-Structure of the Community at Westminster Abbey in the 15th and early 16th Centuries

*Note*: The figure relates to monks professed after 29 Sept. 1390, and the age of such monks has been estimated from the date at which they said their First Mass. At the beginning of the 15th century, these monks represented the smaller part of the community. By 29 Sept. 1430, however, *c*.90 per cent of the community had in fact been professed since 1390, and by 29 Sept. 1441 the community included only monks professed since that date. For the importance, and limitations, of the First Mass as an indicator of age, see above, pp. 118–21.

may seem remarkable. Certainly, any marked variability in age-structure must have affected many facets of monastic life, including the ease or difficulty of maintaining discipline. The range reflects the changing interaction of a number of factors, but principally the age of monks at profession and the life-expectancy of the community. The lower end of the range (30 per cent) is characteristic of the years *c*.1440 to *c*.1470. New professions, which normally added to the number of young monks, were actually quite frequent in these decades, and a decline in life-expectancy under way; but the decline had not yet affected the entire age-structure of the community. The higher end of the range (*c*.50 per cent) occurs in the years 1485 to 1515, though not consistently in that period. In these years, the effects of the decline in life-expectancy were more pervasive, and the novices recruited to fill gaps, when they occurred, were, on average, two or three years younger than their predecessors in the mid-fifteenth century.

monks at profession; from Michaelmas 1441 the community included only monks professed since 29 Sept. 1390.

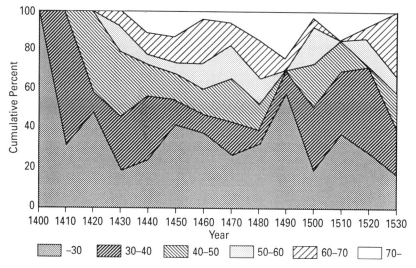

Fig. IV.5. Age at Death of the Monks of Westminster in the 15th and early 16th Centuries

*Note*: The figure relates to monks professed after 29 Sept. 1390, and at first, therefore, to only a small proportion of the total number of deaths. By 29 Sept. 1430, however, *c*.90 per cent of the community had been professed since 1390, and from 29 Sept. 1441 the community included only monks professed since that date.

With these proportions in mind, we can appreciate how severely young monks suffered in some of the years of high mortality in the mid and late fifteenth century. The harsh experience of the under-thirties over the century considered as a whole is well illustrated by their percentage share of deaths in this period (Figure IV.5). However, they suffered more severely in the actual crisis years than in the other years of relatively high mortality. In 1458, 1464, and 1471, a total of 22 monks died, and as many as 12 of this number (55 per cent) were probably under 30 years old at the time. Yet these crisis years occurred in the period when the age-group in question made up only 30 per cent of the monastic community. In the six crisis years occurring in the mid and late fifteenth century considered as a whole—1458, 1464, 1471, 1479, 1491, and 1500—a total of 41 monks died, of whom 20 (49 per cent) were probably under 30 years old at the time. These crises take us into the period, beginning *c*.1485, when the under-thirties became relatively more numerous in the community considered as a whole than they had been in the middle decades of the century. Yet when all these changes are taken into account, we can say that young monks suffered severely in the crisis years under consideration.

The years when mortality was above the trend, or average, but did not reach crisis level were rarely, if ever, as dangerous to young monks. In those which occurred in the mid or late fifteenth century—1441, 1445, 1483, and 1485—a total of 18 monks died, of whom 4 or 5 (22 per cent or 28 per cent), but not more, were probably under 30 years old at the time. Moreover, after 1500 this age-group did even better. No crisis year occurred between 1500 and 1515, the end of the period under consideration. However, in 1502, 1503, and 1508—all years of second-order mortality—a total of 12 monks died, of whom only one (8 per cent) was probably under 30 years old.

### (c) Length of illness

Finally, length of illness. Given the nature of our sources, this can be measured only in terms of hospitalization—that is, by the number of nights that the monk in question spent in the infirmary in the course of his last illness. The infirmarer's accounts at Westminster survive for approximately two years of high mortality in every three. As we have seen, not every monk of this period was eligible for in-patient treatment at the infirmarer's expense, when ill, and not every one who was eligible for such treatment chose to receive it.[88] The evidence is in fact patchy. Nevertheless, it does show that there was no common pattern to hospitalization in the years of high mortality. For example, in 1458, a crisis year, most of those who died spent four to seven nights in the infirmary; in 1464 most spent twelve to sixteen nights there.[89] In 1471 three of the year's four deaths, which occurred, it appears, in the autumn, were probably preceded by periods in the infirmary of, respectively, twenty-five, eighty-six, and as many as 107 nights.[90]

## (iii) The difficulty of identifying the diseases

The lesson, if obvious, is important: one part of the evidence, considered in isolation from the rest, can be highly misleading. In particular, the seasonal incidence of deaths in years of high mortality, so often regarded by medievalists as the vital clue to the identity of epidemic diseases, may well mislead

---

[88] Above, pp. 100–2.

[89] 1458: 7 monks died, all in the late spring, summer, or autumn. One did not enter the infirmary. The other 6 spent, respectively, 7, 29, 5, 4, 4, and 4 nights there. R. Chesterfield's 29 nights were broken into 4 stays of, respectively, 5, 11, 8, and 5 nights. WAM 19432–3; and for the wage data suggesting when death occurred, see WAM 23835–6, 24142, 24031.

1464: For 3 of the 11 who died we have no evidence. The remaining 8 spent, respectively, 6, 6, *12*, *14*, 15, *16*, *16*, and 109 nights there. (In this list, the italicized figures relate to the 6 monks who probably died in the summer or early autumn.) R. Stokeley's 6 nights were divided between 2 stays (4 and 2 nights), and J. Ashby's 16 nights between 3 stays (14/1/1). W. West, who spent 109 nights in the infirmary, was probably *c*.65 years old. WAM 19445, 19460. For the seasonal incidence of mortality this year, see above, p. 138.

[90] R. Westminster's 25 nights formed a single stay. E. Bridgewater's 86 nights, though probably continuous, were divided (57/29) between two years of account. J. Martin's 107 nights were divided between 3 stays (48, 21, and 38), which may have begun in the latter part of 1470. No stay is recorded for R. Breynt, the year's 4th victim. He probably died in the summer or early autumn; the others in the late autumn. WAM 19452–3, 23857, 24035.

us if considered on its own. If 1458, with its short, sharp illnesses, was a plague year at Westminster—and this seems likely—it can scarcely have been plague, although it may have been enteric disease, that took so much longer to kill some of its victims in 1471. And in 1464 the diagnosis of plague is, again, questionable. Yet Bean, in an important study of plague outbreaks in the later Middle Ages, which awards the badge sparingly, identifies 1464 as a plague year in London and perhaps nationally.[91]

In general, it is very difficult to translate our knowledge of patterns of mortality in the community at Westminster into confident, or even not-so-confident, identifications of the diseases that actually killed the monks in particular years. Certainly, as the example of 1464 shows, we should hesitate to conclude that when London had an epidemic of plague—or of any other disease—the monastic community at Westminster suffered too. And the lack of correlation between years of high mortality in the monastery in the fifteenth and early sixteenth centuries and the years known to have been epidemic years in London in that period points to the same conclusion.[92] Yet even the conclusion that the pattern of mortality in the monastery diverged from that of London has an interest extending beyond the monastery: it may mean that the town of Westminster also had an experience of mortality that differed from London's.

## 5. The Population Trend in Late Medieval England

### (i) Inferences from a monastic case-study

If the identity of the killer diseases at Westminster normally eludes us, the mortality itself in this house was real enough. Was the monastic experience of mortality in the later Middle Ages—so severe, as it now appears, not only at Canterbury but also at Westminster—typical of the experience of society in general? Or was it perhaps better or worse? We have no reason to think that it was in general better, and certainly none to think that the monks of Westminster benefited from a secluded way of life. In the later Middle Ages, Benedictine life was remarkably unsecluded, and, as we have seen, life at Westminster was no exception to this rule.[93] It was, we may think, a case of a roughly equal vulnerability to disease, shared between those inside the cloister and those outside. In common with the monks, the townsmen of Westminster experienced a high trend in mortality in the late fifteenth century. The urban trend was particularly high in the years 1490 to 1510—the very period when monastic life-expectancy fell to its lowest point for a century.[94]

---

[91] Bean, 'Plague, population and economic decline', 429.
[92] Above, pp. 126–7.    [93] Above, pp. 80–1.
[94] Rosser, *Medieval Westminster*, 177–80, and esp. fig. 9, showing burials in St Margaret's church from 1464. A year-by-year comparison of monastic and urban mortality is difficult, since the urban data relate to a year beginning on or about 1 June and the monastic data to a

Yet special risks to health were, and indeed are, implicit in any form of community life. If infections are present, every characteristic feature of that life—as, for example, the habitual preparation and service of food for large numbers, and the need to keep large numbers of utensils clean—becomes a flash-point, needing only a single spark to set disaster in train. In these conditions, one case of infectious or contagious disease can have a knock-on effect not necessarily experienced when the same disease appears elsewhere. It is quite possible, even probable, that mortality rates in the late medieval cloister were somewhat higher than those normally encountered elsewhere.

However, in a monastic community of this period not all were equally at risk. At this point, the distinction between the so-called cloister-monks, who followed the common life, and the office-holders and senior monks who were in varying degrees exempt from it, is important. It was the cloister-monks who kept the office going, slept, invariably, in the common dormitory, ate the common meals, and entered the chambers for sick monks in the infirmary when they were ill. It was the cloister-monks who were especially at risk when disease struck. In the late Middle Ages, this group normally accounted for c.33 per cent of the entire community, and it had a bias towards youth, for most monks began as cloister-monks.[95] It was in fact young monks—those under the age of 30—who were most thoroughly exposed to the dangers arising from community life, and they were quite possibly exposed to a degree of risk which did not threaten their age-group elsewhere. Moreover, as the normal age at profession dropped in the late fifteenth century, new entrants, the youngest group of all, may have become more vulnerable to the diseases of the town of Westminster, because, as we have seen, they were probably less well prepared than formerly by a period of waiting in the almonry.[96]

Even so, it is possible—to make no higher claim—that the evidence from Westminster Abbey does reflect the direction and scale of wider changes in the late Middle Ages. It is not only the general level of mortality at Westminster that we have to explain, but also a particular sequence of changes there: a dramatic decline in expectation of life in the mid-fifteenth century, followed by an up-turn in the early sixteenth. The former exactly matches the contemporary trend at Canterbury; the latter, taking us into a period not covered by the Canterbury evidence, accords with the demographic picture of mid-Tudor England as drawn by Wrigley and Schofield.[97] Environmental conditions do not help us much with these changes, for they

year beginning on 29 Sept. or 1 Jan. For an example of a year (1527–8) when mortality was relatively high in the monastic community but evidently much higher among its servants, see below, p. 168 and n. 84.

[95] Above, pp. 77–8. But some who were in other respects privileged also slept in the dormitory.                                                    [96] Above, pp. 121–2.

[97] Wrigley and Schofield, *Population History of England, 1541–1871*, 160 ff.

did not themselves change in ways that can possibly explain either the fall in expectation of life in the community in the mid-fifteenth century or the reversal of that trend after 1510. If, moreover, the vulnerability of new entrants contributed to the former change, it can hardly have done so to the latter. The monastic experience seems to reflect a sequence of profound changes in mortality which the monastic life on its own cannot explain.

## (ii) The role of mortality

I began with some general questions about the influence of epidemic disease in general and plague in particular on population change in late medieval England, and the importance of mortality itself as one of the variables in the demographic situation of that period.[98] Plague, it seems, must still abide our question. At Canterbury, there were at least thirteen outbreaks of plague in the fifteenth century, and the disease accounted for c.20 per cent of all deaths in the community at Christ Church then.[99] At Westminster, plague outbreaks are difficult to identify—as, indeed, they are in every situation where sources of the exceptionally informative kinds found at Christ Church, Canterbury are lacking. As for epidemic disease in general, the monastic experience seems a little to detract from its importance. The years of high mortality at Westminster—and we must look for the epidemic years among these—begin a little too late to explain the high average rate of mortality which is already in evidence in the second decade of the fifteenth century; and their continuance in the early sixteenth century did not prevent a fall in average mortality and a rise in life-expectancy then. Arguably, the years of high mortality do not quite explain the scale of the decline in life-expectancy occurring after c.1435: there are not quite enough of them. In fact, the experience of mortality at Westminster directs our attention quite as much to endemic as to epidemic disease, and to the chronic complaints as much as to the acute. But we must, of course, remember that plague may itself have been endemic in the town of Westminster in the late Middle Ages, as perhaps it was in London.[100]

The available evidence—and there is all too little of it—suggests that aggregate population figures in England declined by a perceptible margin in the early decades of the fifteenth century, but that there then ensued several decades of gentle 'sag': indeed, most decades until 1500 were of this kind. At the beginning of the sixteenth century, aggregate figures were lower than they had been in the late fourteenth century and considerably below the 2.8 millions suggested by Wrigley and Schofield for 1541.[101]

---

[98] Above, pp. 113–14.    [99] Hatcher, 'Mortality in the fifteenth century', 29.

[100] For a cautious view in respect of London, see Slack, *Impact of Plague in Tudor and Stuart England*, 13, 68, 133. But epidemics of one kind or another were almost yearly events in London (ibid. 60).

[101] Hatcher, *Plague, Population and the English Economy*, 63–5, 69.

How is a dramatic decline in life-expectancy in the mid-fifteenth century—if it occurred generally—to be fitted into this picture? Or, to put the question another way: how was it that overall population figures merely sagged and did not themselves fall dramatically? The only possible explanation is surely that fertility itself was at a high level: the sag resulted from a challenge by high mortality to high fertility. If so, England in the mid-fifteenth century experienced what Poos and Smith have characterized as 'a high pressure' situation: both fertility and mortality were high.[102]

If this was the situation down to *c.*1500, we have to ask how, by 1541, population could possibly reach the figure of 2.8 millions suggested by Wrigley and Schofield for that date, or, indeed, come near it. Such a rise was perhaps possible, given two conditions: first, a fall in mortality on the scale hinted at by the figures—the patchy figures—for the community at Westminster in these decades, but general and not localized; and, secondly, the continuance of fertility at a high level. Such a rise was possible if mortality declined but did not take fertility with it. And in the two situations which have been sketched in—that of the mid and late fifteenth century on the one hand and the early sixteenth on the other—it is surely hard to deny pride of place to mortality among the variables tending to produce such dramatic changes.

---

[102] Poos and Smith, '"Legal windows onto historical populations"?', 142; cf. Poos, *A Rural Society after the Black Death: Essex 1350–1525*, 129.

# V

# *Servants*

## 1. Perspectives

IT has often been assumed that the number of servants employed by monasteries in the Middle Ages was very large and could have been smaller with advantages to the monks themselves, if not to those whom they employed. Thus, in a famous work, G. M. Trevelyan characterized the life of monks in Chaucer's England as one of 'sauntering comfort'; and Trevelyan's references to the monks' abandonment of manual labour and their employment of 'armies of servants' point to some of the ways in which, in his view, this state of affairs had come about.[1]

Given a belief in the moral significance of numbers in such households, it is not surprising that Cardinal Gasquet's treatment of the subject achieved a notoriety that has still not quite faded 100 years after he wrote. Gasquet's interests centred on the Dissolution and its consequences for those who had formerly lived in the monasteries or been supported by them. He estimated that for every member of the religious orders on the eve of the Dissolution, there were ten servants or dependants of various kinds, and the number of religious he put at 8,000.[2] Such an estimate made it easy to believe in the idleness of the 'abbey-lubbers', the lazy hangers-on delineated by Thomas Starkey—indeed, in institutions where, if Gasquet was right, so many people were at hand for the various jobs, it was quite essential to find some who did virtually nothing. 'How thynke you', says Cardinal Pole to Thomas Lupset, after touching on the wastefulness of the temporal peers in England— 'How thynke you by the maner usyd wyth our byschoppys, abbottys and pryorys, towchyng the nuryschyng also of a grete sorte of idul abbey lubburys, wych are apte to no thyng but, as the byschoppys and abbottys be, only to ete and drynke? Thynke you thys a laudabul custume, and

---

[1] G. M. Trevelyan, *English Social History: A Survey of Six Centuries, Chaucer to Queen Victoria* (3rd edn., London, 1946), 48. But about numbers Trevelyan said only that the servants were more numerous than the monks (ibid. 10). Cf. the classic account in *RO* iii. 260–4, evidently written with the need to correct exaggerated accounts much in the author's mind.

[2] F. A. Gasquet, *Henry VIII and the English Monasteries* (8th edn., London, 1925), 359–60. Cf. G. Baskerville, *English Monks and the Suppression of the Monasteries* (London, 1937), 286.

to be admyttyd in any gud pollycy?'[3] Starkey's shaft was aimed at the households of monastic prelates, and not at the monastic establishment as a whole, but the damage has proved difficult to contain.

Large or small, the size of monastic establishments at the end of the Middle Ages does indeed illumine one of the social problems of the mid-sixteenth century, that of finding employment for the servants of the religious after the Dissolution, and many beside Gasquet have been interested in the topic for this reason.

Yet monastic servants, it may be suggested, deserve our attention, not because they enable us to take the moral temperature of the institutions they served, and not only as a footnote to the rise of poverty in sixteenth-century England—although here there are still some details to be filled in—but for their intrinsic interest. It seems likely that, in the late medieval and early modern periods, the great majority of youths from poor families, and some from the not-so-poor, spent part of their adolescence and early manhood in service of one kind or another. Professor Phythian-Adams has suggested that normally, in the late Middle Ages, the sons of poor households were not at home after the age of 12.[4] It was the fate of many of the youths in question to serve in large households, and sometimes in monastic households. At present, we know far too little about the conditions of employment which faced them on entry, and little enough about those of the servants already in post above them in the hierarchy. Accounting practice, departmental organization, retaining at fee and livery—all these features of household life in the later Middle Ages have been intensively studied over many years; but the conditions of employment of those who actually did the work have on the whole been neglected.[5]

I shall discuss three aspects of servant life in monastic households: the actual number of servants in existence at the end of the Middle Ages; their working day and year over a rather longer period; and, finally, their earnings —generally, over that longer period, and more particularly in the years around 1500. In the discussion of earnings, arrangements at Westminster Abbey will provide a case-study.

---

[3] Thomas Starkey, *A Dialogue between Pole and Lupset*, ed. T. F. Mayer (Camden 4th ser. xxxvii, 1989), 87. (I have modernized the punctuation of this passage.) Cf. Hugh Latimer's strictures on the number of bishops' and abbots' servants, as reported in *Three Chapters of Letters relating to the Suppression of Monasteries*, ed. T. Wright (Camden Soc. xxvi, 1843), 38.

[4] C. Phythian-Adams, *Desolation of a City: Coventry and the Urban Crisis of the Late Middle Ages* (Cambridge, 1979), 82–3. The seminal study is A. Kussmaul, *Servants in Husbandry in Early Modern England* (Cambridge, 1981); see ibid. 97, 168–9, etc. For the urban bias of service, see P. J. P. Goldberg, 'Urban identity and the poll taxes of 1377, 1379 and 1381', *Econ. Hist. Rev.*, 2nd ser. xliii (1990), 194–216, at 201–8; and for perceptive comment in a regional context, M. Spufford, *Contrasting Communities: English Villagers in the Sixteenth and Seventeenth Centuries* (Cambridge, 1974), 31–3.

[5] For an exception, see K. Mertes, *The English Noble Household, 1250–1600: Good Governance and Politic Rule* (Oxford, 1988), 61–74.

## 2. Monastic Households

### (i) Definitions

In a field where so much turns on the meaning of words, the terms in use should be defined without delay. A monastery's servants constituted its permanent establishment. In monasteries of any size this group included a relatively large superstructure of lay and clerical administrators who looked after the ceremonial life of the household, saw to the accounts and all the other paper-work, and supplied legal and other forms of professional advice. We should recognize many of these superior servants as consultants. In the household hierarchy, which, in the later Middle Ages, was commonly graded, the laymen among them normally ranked as squires or gentlemen. Below this superstructure were the departmental staff, and these fall into two categories. Many were workers of the kinds needed by great households in every period: these performed the essential routine tasks, some skilled and some not so skilled, of cooking, serving, fetching and carrying, and so on, that enabled the whole complex organization to lumber on from day to day. Others, however—and these were a minority—were craftsmen providing services that in a more highly developed economy would have been entrusted to outside contractors or to wholesale or retail suppliers: there were, for example, brewers, tailors, and chandlers on monastic pay-rolls in this period. Whatever their sphere of duty, the general workers and the craftsmen normally ranked as valets or yeomen—two terms that became interchangeable—or as grooms or pages.[6] The persistence of this grading system into the sixteenth century—and not only in monastic households—explains why the authors of the early Tudor sumptuary laws found it necessary to regulate the dress of servants who were also yeomen.[7]

Although only one grade separated the yeomen from the grooms, the difference in importance was often great. In monastic households of this period, obedientiaries tended to depute the day-to-day management of their departments or of major concerns within the latter, to lay officials, and most of these probably ranked as yeomen. Whoever was head in this sense might well enjoy the right of appointing the subordinate staff. This right is referred to, or implied, in the appointment to such offices at Bolton Priory, for

[6] For a glimpse of grading in a medium-sized monastic establishment towards the end of the Middle Ages, see *Monastery and Society in the Late Middle Ages: Selected Account Rolls from Selby Abbey, Yorkshire, 1398–1537*, ed. J. H. Tillotson (Woodbridge, 1988), 57, 73, 134, etc., and in a large monastic establishment, *Rites of Durham*, 144–7. For an earlier period see *Visitations of Religious Houses*, iii. 339.

[7] 24 Henry VIII, c. 13 (*SR* iii. 431); and for a sceptical view, see J. C. K. Cornwall, *Wealth and Society in Early Sixteenth-Century England* (Cambridge, 1988), 13–14. For yeomen in a secular household in the late 16th cent., see *Household Papers of Henry Percy, Ninth Earl of Northumberland (1564–1632)*, ed. G. R. Batho (Camden 3rd ser. xciii, 1962), xxiii; and see also Stone, *Crisis of the Aristocracy, 1558–1641*, 213.

example, in 1528, and at Fountains Abbey four years later.[8] It is implied, too, in every contract with the head of a household department which gave him control of the so-called corrodies, or wages, of lower-ranking servants. Such an arrangement resembled the serjeanties once used to fill the principal offices in noble households, including that of the king himself.[9] Unlike the earlier serjeants, however, the yeomen managers of the later Middle Ages held for life or a term of years, and not in perpetuity. Yet even these terms distinguished the yeomen from servants of lower rank, who rarely had this degree of security.

In a typical monastery, most of these servants were distributed between two households; that of the abbot or prior, who lived separately from his monks, and that of the convent.[10] Normally, the high-ranking servants frequented the prelate's household—a circumstance tending to ensure that this was in general large and expensive to run, for if there were squires and gentlemen to be entertained, there could be no stinting of yeomen and grooms to serve them. Most of the craftsmen probably belonged to the conventual household, although prelate and convent alike made use of their services. Domestic servants were, of course, to be found in each household. This distribution means that the one establishment cannot usefully be studied in isolation from the other. Although the prelate's household maintained greater ceremony than the convent's, and may have experienced behavioural problems that were unknown or less common in the latter, the two establishments were in fact complementary institutions. The one existed mainly to represent the monastery in the world outside the cloister and impress the visitors; the other, to house, feed, and clothe the monks who kept the corporate religious life of the monastery going from day to day.

## (ii) Numbers

Seventy years after Gasquet, Dom David Knowles examined the problem of numbers and arrived at conclusions very different from Gasquet's—as, indeed, others had done in the meantime. The Commissioners appointed in 1536 to survey the smaller monasteries were instructed to enquire in each such house how many 'servants or hinds' were commonly kept there. Using the original returns for between fifty and sixty houses of men, and excluding

---

[8] R. W. Hoyle, 'Monastic leasing before the Dissolution: the evidence of Bolton Priory and Fountains Abbey', *Yorks. Arch. Jnl.* lxi (1989), 111–37, at 129–30; *Fountains Abbey Lease Book*, ed. D. J. H. Michelmore (Yorks. Arch. Soc., Record Ser. cxl, 1981), nos. 232, 235. See also below, p. 152.

[9] E. G. Kimball, *Serjeanty Tenure in Medieval England* (Yale, 1936), ch. 2; and for examples in a monastic household, E. King, *Peterborough Abbey, 1086–1310* (Cambridge, 1973), 58–61.

[10] A simplification, since in some Benedictine abbeys the claustral prior, the all-important disciplinary figure, was scarcely less detached from the common life than the abbot himself. Yet his household was small in comparison to the abbot's. On priors, see *Visitations of Religious Houses*, i. 244–5.

hinds, the agricultural servants, from consideration, Knowles estimated that in these houses, in the years immediately preceding the Dissolution, there was, on average, one servant to every religious; and he inclined to the view that the ratio in the greater houses, which survived for a few years longer, was probably the same.[11] From these houses, however, we lack the same extent of systematic evidence and depend a great deal on what ordinary monastic sources care to reveal about the number of servants.

Given the presence of craftsmen as well as domestic servants in household establishments, a ratio of 1 : 1 for servants to monks may be regarded as modest. If correct, it means that, on the eve of the Dissolution, *c.*10,000 servants were employed in religious establishments of all kinds, and that, of this number, 3,000 to 4,000 were employed in monasteries. Even the larger of these figures represents a tiny percentage—perhaps as little as 0.4 per cent —of the population of England at the time. Wrigley and Schofield's estimate of population in 1541 is 2.8 millions.[12] And Knowles pointed to a remarkable circumstance tending to corroborate the conclusion that monastic establishments were of relatively modest size. This was the absence from the Dissolution lists, and from other sources of the period, of references to servants charged with the duty of personal attendance on the monks. Taken at face value, this evidence suggests that, except when ill, the monks of this late period received 'no routine personal service'; and Knowles instanced sweeping the cloister, making beds, and making up the fires.[13]

These conclusions have been generally accepted. Yet there is room for misgivings, and these are in fact prompted by the very lists that seem to offer the best data. One of the best known of all the lists is that surviving from the Augustinian priory at Butley, in Suffolk, a house of middling size which was dissolved in 1538; this has been in print since 1951 and was discussed by Knowles.[14] The thirteen canons who were still in the priory in 1538 employed, it appears, about thirty-five men and women, excluding agricultural servants, and to such a number one hesitates to suggest additions. But had the yeoman granger actually managed to receive and dispense all the grain coming to the priory's barns for the canons, as is implied, without assistance? This seems unlikely. Had William Sympson, the only porter mentioned, actually kept Butley's noble gatehouse single-handed by day

---

[11] *RO* iii. 262–3. The average conceals marked regional differences. For the articles of the enquiry, see *L & P Henry VIII*, x, no. 721, and Youings, *Dissolution of the Monasteries*, 160–1; and for some interesting figures relating to an earlier period, J. R. H. Moorman, *Church Life in England in the Thirteenth Century* (Cambridge, 1946), 265–7.

[12] Knowles and Hadcock, 494; Wrigley and Schofield, *Population History of England*, 1541–1871, table 7.8.  [13] *RO* iii. 263.

[14] *The Register or Chronicle of Butley Priory, Suffolk, 1510–1535*, ed. A. G. Dickens (Winchester, 1951), 71–3. My count of the household servants listed here differs from those in *RO* iii. 263 and A. G. Dickens, *The English Reformation* (2nd edn., London, 1989), 74–5. In the case of dairy workers who were also laundresses, I have allowed a half for each one enumerated.

and by night? Remarkable, if so, for he was now classified as 'impotent'—
a word signifying, in this context, 'impotent poor': in fact he was deemed
incapable of earning any kind of living for himself in the future. And had
the priory actually employed only yeomen waiters at table, as the list implies, and no lower-ranking servants to assist them? Not, at least, only a few
years previously, for in or about 1532, as we learn from a worried deponent
at the visitation of that year, a groom had been taken ill after gobbling up
some of the vegetables he was deputed to serve.[15] In each of these cases, we
may suspect that the servants of low rank have failed to win a place in the
list. As for the absence of references to personal service for the monks of
this period, it too is remarkable, for in some of the monasteries of early
Tudor England even the almsmen and lay brethren were supplied with a
servant or two.[16] In these circumstances, can we really believe that monks
normally made their own beds and themselves swept out the cloister?

In any count of monastic servants, the distinction between those who had
a corrody and those who did not is fundamentally important. A corrody
was a servant's keep, or the wages that might be given in lieu.[17] Thus, to have
a corrody was to be on the monastery's pay-roll; to be without one was to
have no direct claim on the monastery's resources. Whatever may have been
the convention followed in making up the Dissolution lists, the ordinary
monastic sources of the period are more likely to mention servants who
were a direct charge on official funds in this way than others, for most
of the relevant sources are financial records: they are the accounts of the
obedientiaries who paid the stipends and wages in question.

In the later Middle Ages, most who served in monastic households were
in fact a direct charge on official funds, but to this rule there were some
important exceptions. The first arose from the practice of entrusting some
departments in the household to entrepreneurs who not only engaged and
dismissed the subordinate staff—it has already been suggested that many of
the yeomen heading departments did this—but who were also responsible
for paying them. Once, this kind of arrangement had been quite common.
At Abingdon Abbey, for instance, it is illustrated in a late twelfth-century
source. A list compiled here in 1185, to facilitate the administration of the
monastery during the current vacancy—itself a very unusual kind of source
to survive—enumerates about eighty servants of one kind or another, and
most had corrodies. Of Martin, the master baker, however, we are told that
he had five servants at his own expense: these ate in the hall on four days
at Christmas, four at Easter, and one at Pentecost, but had no other claim
on the monks.[18]

---

[15] *Norwich Visitations*, 286–7, where *puer* signifies *garcio* (i.e. groom).
[16] WAM 19095–154 (where the servant of the lay brethren of Westminster Abbey is mentioned).                                                                          [17] Below, pp. 170–5.
[18] *Chron. Abingdon*, ii. 237–43, at 240. Note also the 2 servants in the brewery, 'Ærwardus'

Sooner or later, entrepreneurs like Martin the baker tended to shift the burden of paying subordinates in their department on to the broader shoulders of the monks whom they served: they became managers, responsible under the appropriate obedientiaries for running departments and subdepartments, but were no longer entrepreneurs in the strict sense of the word. Yet the former system never died out. This explains the existence in some late medieval houses of departments with, as it appears, a quite inadequate supply of labour. Such a department is mentioned at Fountains Abbey in 1536. In that year, the monks of Fountains made an agreement with one John Johnson and Margaret, his wife, which was to continue for the term of their lives. In return for the grant of a fee and a corrody of food, drink, and fuel, a dwelling-house and some land, John and Margaret were to keep the west gate of the Abbey when Ripon fair was in progress, and, at other times, at night, and wash and mend all the linen belonging to the abbey's buttery or guest-house, or to the abbot's chamber. Moreover, they were to have the entrails of cattle and sheep slaughtered in the Abbey's slaughterhouse—a clause betraying the fact that they intended to gain part of their livelihood by preparing the entrails in question for human consumption and selling the product—no doubt, on many occasions to the monks of Fountains themselves, for consumption in their refectory.[19] In a monastery of this period, sheets and table-cloths may not have been changed very often. Yet it is hard to believe that John and Margaret Johnson would perform all their tasks single-handed. We must conclude that they were to engage and pay the labour that they needed. But that labour would have left no trace in the accounts of the obedientiaries of Fountains, and it would be very surprising if the Dissolution Commissioners, making their rounds a few years later, took notice of it. Our knowledge of the arrangements involving John and Margaret Johnson is unusually detailed because the lease-book of Fountains Abbey, where they were recorded, happens to survive.

Secondly, some servants were retained by monks in an individual capacity and paid for out of private funds. For example, senior monks living in private chambers—of whom there were always a few in Benedictine houses in the later Middle Ages—employed servants of their own. It was, indeed, assumed by the General Chapter of the Black Monk Order, which tried in vain to eradicate the use of private chambers, that a monk possessed of this

and 'H', who ate in the hall on the same 9 days but had, it appears, no other claim on the monastery: normally, they must have been a charge on the master brewer.

[19] *Fountains Abbey Lease Book*, ed. Michelmore, no. 237. John and Margaret were also to wait at table if asked to do so, but in return for wages. They agreed to pay 5s. per score of cattle entrails and 1s. 4d. per score of sheeps' entrails. The entrails of cattle slaughtered before Christmas were excepted from the arrangement, perhaps because John and Margaret would not have been able to cope with such a quantity. See also ibid., no. 276.

amenity also had a servant of his own.[20] Some, to our knowledge, had more than one. At Westminster Abbey, Br. Richard Exeter, a former prior who died in 1396 after a very long retirement, employed a clerk and a cook and sent his washing to a laundress; and since cooks did not as a rule run a household unassisted, Br. Richard probably had one or two other menials as well.[21] Moreover, from the thirteenth century onwards, all monks normally had wages or pocket money, which could be used to bespeak service that might otherwise have been lacking, and eventually very considerable sums of money, comparable to the entire income of many secular households outside the cloister, were involved.[22] In general, the existence of private funds goes far towards explaining how it was that personal attendance is so rarely mentioned in our sources: monks were in a position to pay for this themselves, and were accountable to no one if they did so.

Finally, even among those who were a charge on official funds, there were some who received no cash emoluments, but only food and drink, and, if they were lucky, clothing, and these too may escape notice in our sources. At Durham Cathedral Priory, where the records are second to none, it was the visitation records and chapter ordinances, not the ordinary accounts of the obedientiaries, that alerted Professor Dobson to the presence in that monastery of what he aptly describes as 'a multitude of boys, providing a chaotic supply of unskilled labour and receiving neither regular wages nor livery'.[23]

If some of those who have been mentioned were not really servants at all, but boys and youths waiting to be allowed to engage fully in that occupation, others cannot be so easily dismissed: they were in a real sense part of the monastic establishment. The total number of those who belonged to such an establishment, and *a fortiori* the number of those who depended for their livelihood on the various kinds of service required from day to day by monks, is now, in the strict sense of the word, incalculable—incalculable, but larger than the number readily disclosed by our sources. At Westminster Abbey, in the early sixteenth century, a community of about fifty monks employed nearly twice that number of servants, and this figure relates only to those who were on the pay-roll and belonged to the official establishment; it excludes others.[24] Those most likely to escape notice were undoubtedly the servants of low rank or no rank at all and the new, young entrants struggling to get a foot on the ladder.

---

[20] *Chapters of English Black Monks*, i. 66; cf. ibid. 103, and ii. 36. The need of obedientiaries for private chambers was recognized by the Chapter.     [21] WAM 6603.

[22] *RO* i. 287-9; ii. 240-3. At Westminster Abbey *c.*1500, even a junior monk who was a priest received *c.*£8 per annum. A senior monk received considerably more—probably £11 or £12 p.a. Cf. Dyer, *Standards of Living*, 195-6.

[23] Dobson, *Durham Priory, 1400-1450*, 121.     [24] Below, p. 164.

## 3. Servant Life

### (i) The monastic day

The working day of monastic servants depended on the monks' own day, and to understand this we must understand how time was kept in the monastery.

In the Middle Ages, several different ways of reckoning time were in use, inside and outside the cloister, and on occasion they were simultaneously in use. One, based on the so-called artificial day running from sunrise to sunset, divided this period into twelve hours, and the artificial night—sunset to sunrise—similarly into twelve. It will be clear that these hours were unequal: they were long on days in summer and nights in winter, but short on winter days and summer nights. The use of this method is envisaged in the Rule of St Benedict, which, for example, prescribes that Matins, the night office, shall be at the eighth hour of the night, and Terce at the second hour of the day.[25] Its use is also assumed in the Gospel parable of the labourers in the vineyard, where the eleventh hour at which the final batch of labourers is hired is only one hour before sunset.[26] A Lollard sermon written in the late fourteenth century or the early fifteenth seems to show that a preacher of this period could expect his audience to understand the twelve-hour day of the parable without any word of explanation from him.[27] From this circumstance we should perhaps conclude that this method of time-keeping was still in common use in Richard II's England and that of Henry IV.

Another method used the canonical hours themselves as pivotal points for the day as a whole. The daylight hours began with Prime, which was said when daylight was full, and ended with Vespers or Compline in the evening, and since it was a poor parish church that did not ring the principal hours on its bell, this method was perfectly practicable even at a remove from monastery bells. This explains how it was that 'the hour of Prime' could be used in village by-laws regulating the times of access to the growing crops in the common fields.[28] But, given the close dependence of the canonical hours on the sequence of light and darkness, this method of reckoning time

[25] *Rule*, caps. viii, xlviii; and see Vogüé and Neufville, *La Règle de Saint Benoît*, vi. 1172.

[26] Matt. 20: 12.

[27] *English Wycliffite Sermons*, i, ed. A. Hudson (Oxford, 1983), 379. The outer dates for the composition of the sermon-cycle to which this sermon belongs are 1384–1414 (ibid. 199). On the artificial day, see also Lyndwood, *Provinciale*, Lib. I, tit. 3 (p. 24). For the hour as an indeterminate period of time, see R. Glasser, *Time in French Life and Thought*, trans. C. G. Pearson (Manchester, 1972), 56.

[28] W. O. Ault, *Open-Field Husbandry and the Village Community* (Transactions of the American Philosophical Soc., NS lv, pt. 7 (Philadelphia, 1965), nos. 8, 17, 33, etc. (translated in id., *Open-Field Farming in Medieval England: A Study of Village By-Laws* (London, 1972), nos. 8, 17, 33, etc.). For parish priests who disingenuously caused the bell to be rung for the canonical hours, though not intending to be present themselves, see *Councils and Synods*, II. i. 378; II. ii. 1019.

slid easily into reliance on the position of the sun in the sky: in the case just cited, the villager who did not hear the bell for Prime would have little excuse, even so, for breaking the by-law, because Prime was said when daylight was full.

Finally, there was clock-time in our sense of the term: the division of the natural day into twenty-four equal hours, the whole system being monitored by mechanical clocks. The natural day was the period during which the sun apparently executed an entire revolution about the earth. It was sometimes reckoned from sunrise to sunrise, sometimes from midnight to midnight, but by the end of the Middle Ages midnight to midnight prevailed. By the end of the fourteenth century, especially in towns, clock-time was supplanting the others as the public or official way of reckoning time, and a century later it was well enough known at all levels of society for those who drafted the Statute of Artificers in 1495 to think it appropriate to weave its set times and equal hours into some very particular prescriptions about the working day.[29] Even so, they were content to define the working day from mid-September to mid-March in old-fashioned terms as the period from sunrise to sunset.[30] Their resort to this older way of reckoning reminds us that even where clock-time was in principle in use, it must often have been overridden by the simple need of many workers for daylight. There was little point in keeping a hatmaker or weaver at his task if, working by candle-light, he would botch his job or cause a fire.[31]

By the fifteenth century, clock-time had become the official method of reckoning time in most Benedictine houses, and the mechanical clocks on which this system depended may have appeared in some houses at a much earlier date.[32] The adoption of clock-time ensured that the natural seasons lost some of their earlier, huge influence on the monastic day. Even so, the new system, with its bias towards fixed times for performing routine tasks, seems never to have become second nature to monks in the Middle Ages. Since the time determined by the clock was relayed to those who needed to

[29] 11 Henry VII, c. 22 (*SR* ii. 585–7). For comment, see G. Langenfelt, *The Historic Origin of the Eight Hours Day* (Stockholm, 1954), 44–8. On the natural day, see also L. C. Hector, 'The beginning of the "natural day" in the late fourteenth century', *Journal of the Society of Archivists*, ii (1960–4), 87–9; and on the 14th cent. as the critical period in the adoption of clock-time, J. Le Goff, 'Le temps du travail dans la "crise" du xiv$^e$ siècle: du temps médiéval au temps moderne', *Le Moyen Age*, lxix (1963), 597–613, trans. in Le Goff, *Time, Work, and Culture in the Middle Ages*, trans. A. Goldhammer (Chicago, 1980), 43–57.

[30] 'the springing of the day . . . till nyght of the same day.'

[31] For regulations forbidding night work in these and other trades, see Riley (ed.), *Memorials of London and London Life in the XIIIth, XIVth, and XVth Centuries*, 217, 239, 243, 278, 307; and for the dangers of taking a candle into the byre after dark, *Seneschaucy*, ch. 52, in *Walter of Henley and Other Treatises on Estate Management and Accounting*, ed. D. Oschinsky (Oxford, 1971), 282.

[32] C. F. C. Beeson, *English Church Clocks, 1280–1850: Their History and Classification* (rev. edn., Ashford, 1977), 4–25; J. Geddes, 'Iron', in J. Blair and N. Ramsay (edd.), *English Medieval Industries: Craftsmen, Techniques, Products* (London, 1991), 178–9.

be informed of it by means of a bell, plenty of scope existed for human error, or for a deliberate ignoring of the time according to the clock, if it happened to be inconvenient. This human factor is well exemplified in the subsacrist of Norwich Cathedral Priory who was delated at a visitation of the monastery in 1532 for ringing the bell for Matins—at this date, and for a long time past, normally a midnight office in large houses—at 2 or 3 a.m.[33] We may suspect that the subsacrist simply liked the old custom of saying Matins at the eighth hour of the night—roughly 2 a.m. And even when the official life of the community ran quite smoothly on clock-time, a private preference for the old system might surface occasionally. In the mid-fifteenth century, the prior of Westminster apparently used the old system of the twelve-hour night and twelve-hour day when recording the time of events in this house. Br. Reginald Shiplake, he wrote, died at the eighth hour of the night; Br. John Cambridge, at the eleventh hour of the day; and the dormitory was set on fire by Br. George Norwich at the ninth hour of the night.[34] Yet officially Westminster Abbey now used clock-time and may long have done so. The following description of the Benedictine day in the age of clock-time will inevitably make arrangements appear simpler and more coherent than they were.

Matins, as I have just pointed out, were now commonly recited at midnight. In Benedictine houses on ordinary days, this office probably lasted an hour to an hour and a half, but on feast days considerably longer. On its conclusion monks returned to bed.[35] Formerly, it had been the custom to rise before daybreak for Lauds, the office which preceded Prime and was said before full light. In the fifteenth and sixteenth centuries, however, a fixed hour for rising seems to have been in common though not universal use, and it was 7 a.m. or thereabouts. Rising at 7 a.m. is mentioned or implied as established practice at Durham and Westminster; and at his visitation of Ramsey Abbey in 1439, William Alnwick forbade the monks to leave the dormitory before 7 a.m.[36] Nor was the practice considered appropriate only in Benedictine houses: in 1529 John Longland, one of Alnwick's successors

---

[33] *Norwich Visitations*, 268; and see above, p. 154.

[34] WAM 33289, fos. 2ᵛ, 64ᵛ. John Cambridge died in 1446 and Reginald Shiplake in 1445. In 1386 a more pragmatic observer noted that Abbot Nicholas de Litlyngton died *hora prandendi* (LNQ 86).

[35] *RO* i. 280 and n.; and for the drastic shortening of the office authorized by the General Chapter in 1277–8, ibid. 22–4. For practice in some of the newer Orders, ibid. ii. 238.

[36] According to the best witness, the cloister at Durham was unlocked at 7 a.m. (*Rites of Durham*, 86). For Westminster see *Foedera*, xi. 90 and *Cal. Cl. R., Henry VII*, ii (*1500–1509*), no. 389; for Ramsey, *Visitations of Religious Houses*, iii. 307. However, in 1520 the monks of Norwich Cathedral Priory were told to rise at dawn (*Norwich Visitations*, 194). Cf. *Lanfranc's Constitutions*, pp. xxxv–xxxvii and nn.

Whatever the prescribed time for the community as a whole, individual monks might have to rise earlier; for an example at Westminster, see below, p. 158.

in the see of Lincoln, decreed that the canons of Dorchester Abbey, an Augustinian house, should recite Prime at 7 a.m.[37]

Once they were up, the monks of this period had a day that was divided, like the secular day outside the cloister, into a morning, an afternoon, and an evening. In the case of the cloister-monks—if they were observant—a sequence of liturgical duties, broken at one point by Chapter, occupied most of the time until dinner, but many others were differently employed. At Peterborough Abbey in 1437, it was said that only ten or twelve of a community numbering more than forty actually assisted at the monastic offices.[38] But many of those absent from choir would have been present at dinner. The normal time for this meal was probably 11 or 11.30 a.m., but a little later on fast days, since on fasts dinner might not be eaten before Vespers were recited.[39] Yet even on these days the meal was not long delayed, for it was now customary to advance the hour of Vespers precisely in order to avoid a long wait for dinner. At Westminster Abbey, towards the end of the Middle Ages, we are told that during Lent Vespers followed immediately on the day's High Mass.[40] In some houses, young monks were allowed a light breakfast between the High Mass of the day and dinner: if young monks are denied breakfast, it was said at Peterborough, they eat so much at dinner that they fall asleep in the afternoon when they should be studying.[41] Indeed, in some monasteries breakfast seems to have been regarded as a normal form of refreshment for all monks, whatever their age, and in these houses we must find a place for it in the day's arrangements.[42]

How the monks of this period spent their afternoons until supper, which was probably taken at 5 p.m. or thereabouts, is one of the still unsolved problems in monastic history. If junior monks were required to study in this part of the day, some seniors may have done so too by choice. At Durham a later source records that all senior monks went to their carrels in the north cloister after dinner for a period of study;[43] and yet it seems unlikely that the entire community of St Cuthbert was quite as bookish at this time as this custom would imply. The walks which were evidently valued in Benedictine circles for health's sake were probably taken after dinner.[44]

[37] *Lincoln Visitations, 1517–1531*, ii. 203.

[38] *Visitations of Religious Houses*, iii. 273. At any one time 10 to 15 were absent from the monastery. Cf. ibid. 304; see also above, p. 77, where it is estimated that the cloister-monks at Westminster Abbey represented 33% of the entire community.

[39] *Rule*, cap. xli.

[40] *Westminster Chronicle*, 315. For the view that to wait until after 12 noon for dinner was to wait a long time, see *Lincoln Visitations, 1517–1531*, iii. 82; and for Sir Thomas More's comment on corresponding developments outside the cloister, *Apology*, ed. Trapp, 106.

[41] *Lincoln Visitations, 1517–1531*, iii. 82.

[42] Ibid. ii. 169. But Humberstone had only 5 monks, including the abbot.

[43] *Rites of Durham*, 83, 87.

[44] Youings, *Dissolution of the Monasteries*, 153. Walks, whenever taken, were threatened by

Moreover, both at Durham and at Westminster sermons to the people, if it was a day for such an event, took place during this part of the day: at each house the prescribed hour was 1 p.m., and some monks participated.[45] At Durham it was later remembered that the sermons had lasted two hours.

Our sources make it clear that the evening which followed supper was a somewhat convivial affair and, in the eyes of many monks, not nearly long enough. The last office of the day was Compline. Monks who spent too long drinking in the refectory after Compline, monks who retired to the dormitory with the rest of the community, only to creep downstairs for a further bout of drinking—these are commonplace figures at visitations of the period.[46] The officially approved bedtime was probably 8 p.m. or thereabouts in winter and 9 p.m. in summer—the times decreed by William Gray of Lincoln at his visitation of Peterborough Abbey in 1432.[47] No doubt the same hours were in William Atwater's mind when he decreed, a century later, that the last drinks should be served at Peterborough not later than 7 p.m. in winter and 8 p.m. in summer.[48] But later hours are mentioned and evidently had a certain following. Drinking until 10 or 11 p.m. or even later is mentioned, though by a witness who may not be entirely reliable, at Ramsey Abbey in 1439.[49] Such hours, however, were always condemned by the authorities outside the cloister, who considered it unlikely that a monk going to bed at 10 or 11 p.m. would put in an appearance at midnight for Matins.

In general, we should envisage thirteen or fourteen hours' daytime activity for the average monk of this period, beginning at or about 7 a.m. Of course, there were exceptional days, when some rose earlier. On certain feast days, for example, the first Mass in Benedictine houses was said at dawn, and at the very least a celebrant, with a deacon to assist, was needed on the occasion. And a wealthy testator, endowing a chantry or anniversary, could insist on an early hour: Margaret Beaufort prescribed that the first Mass of her chantry in Westminster Abbey should be said soon after 6 a.m.[50] But we shall not go far wrong if we think of an average day which began c.7 a.m. and continued for thirteen or fourteen hours. In late medieval

the Injunctions of 1535–6, which forbade monks to leave the precinct of their monastery (Wilkins, *Concilia*, iii. 790; Youings, op. cit. 149).

[45] *Rites of Durham*, 39; *Cal. Cl. R., Henry VII*, ii *(1500–1509)*, no. 389 (p. 142).

[46] *Visitations of Religious Houses*, ii. 11, 20, 22–3; iii. 273, 297, etc.; *Norwich Visitations*, 162. Such irregularities were not confined to Benedictines or to male religious. See *Lincoln Visitations, 1517–1531*, ii. 84, 95, 193, etc.; ibid. iii. 100. For the drink after Compline, see *Chapters of English Black Monks*, ii. 33–4, 71, etc., and above, p. 43.

[47] *Visitations of Religious Houses*, i. 102; and see *RO* ii. 238–9.

[48] *Lincoln Visitations, 1517–1531*, iii. 78.

[49] *Visitations of Religious Houses*, iii. 304.

[50] *Cal. Cl. R., Henry VII*, ii *(1500–1509)*, no. 770 (p. 291). Her son was less demanding (ibid., no. 389 (p. 140)).

England, 7 a.m. may have been a common hour for the aristocracy and greater gentry to rise, but outside the cloister only the exceptionally devout went to bed as early as 8 p.m., the better to rise in time for the devotions that would follow in the morning. One of the exceptions was Cicely, Duchess of York, the mother of Edward IV and Richard III and a formidably devout woman, who rose at 7 a.m. and was in bed by 8 p.m.[51] Even in devout circles, however, there was no parallel for the midnight office: this added an hour to the active period of an observant monk and gave an eccentric twist to the overall shape of his day.

## (ii) The working day

How hard did servants work in such a household? In a seminal essay first published in 1967, E. P. Thompson drew the distinction between a task-oriented existence and a time-oriented one. In the former, the working day and week are highly irregular, and the worker himself is sometimes busy, sometimes idle, but never constrained by the clock. In a time-oriented existence, characteristic, it was suggested, of industrial capitalism, he learns to use time purposefully and is disciplined by the clock. Thus a farmer who tends his sheep in the lambing season is task-oriented, but a tailor working a ten- or twelve-hour day is time-oriented.[52] Yet a disciplined sense of time can exist in certain contexts independently of clocks and of the pressure of industrial capitalism. Where, then, should we place the much-criticized monastic servants in this scheme of things?

The artisans—the plumbers, for example, and the masons and brewers—on the pay-roll were the least affected by the monk's own timetable: they were constrained more by the hours of daylight than by the monastic day. The artisans' day, therefore, was longer than the latter in summer but shorter in winter. The conditions under which many artisans worked—indoors, and neither alone nor in a crowd—made some forms of idleness very congenial. If the lunch-break could be taken with half a dozen others in the mason's shed, out of the wind and rain, it was no doubt tempting to linger over it. Equally, the very dependence of artisans' labour on daylight encouraged employers paying by the day or week, as many did, to be vigilant. The rules which the dean and chapter of York made for their masons in the second half of the fourteenth century were time-oriented, although the time in question was not clock-time but a curious mixture of the artificial day with

---

[51] W. A. Pantin, 'Instructions for a devout and literate layman', in J. J. G. Alexander and M. T. Gibson (edd.), *Medieval Learning and Literature: Essays presented to Richard William Hunt* (Oxford, 1976), 412. Lady Margaret Beaufort, however, rose soon after 5 a.m. (ibid. 413). For a glimpse of the hour of rising among the aristocracy and gentry, see *Household of Edward IV: The Black Book and the Ordinance of 1478*, ed. A. R. Myers (Manchester, 1959), 201.

[52] E. P. Thompson, 'Time, work-discipline, and industrial capitalism', *P & P* xxxviii (Dec. 1967), 56–97, reprinted in Thompson, *Customs in Common* (London, 1991), 352–403.

the canonical hours and the meal-times of the chapter, and other, rough and ready, measures. In summer, for example, the masons were to begin work at sunrise, and begin breakfast when the bell for the office of St Mary the Virgin rang and continue for only so long as it took to walk half a mile. They were to end their rest after dinner when the vicars choral, who evidently had less than the full meal, left the canons' dinner table; and at the end of the day they were to work until the ringing of the bell of St. Mary's Abbey or until dusk.[53] These rules exemplify the shift noticed by Thompson, away from task-oriented work and towards timed labour, that tends to occur when the work in question is done, not by an independent worker, but by an employee for an employer.[54]

York Minster was a secular foundation, and its complex of buildings much larger than most that we have to envisage in monastic England. *Mutatis mutandis*, however, we can envisage similar attempts at a discipline based on time-oriented work for artisans in the larger monasteries of the period, if in no others. As for its success, in such a system this must have depended less on the attitude of the employer himself than on that of the master craftsmen to whom others worked—as at York Minster the afternoon's work would have begun promptly if the master mason knocked on the shed door when the vicars choral rose from table, but not otherwise.[55]

However, in a monastic establishment, the prime suspects for idleness are the domestic servants. If anyone's existence in this period was task-oriented, surely theirs was, and the task of each was, quite simply, to attend to the needs of the monks from the hour of rising until bedtime, in so far as these fell within the sphere of duty of his department. At one end of the day, the domestic servants made the fires needed to warm the hands of those who celebrated dawn Masses on the feasts of St Mary the Virgin in winter;[56] at the other, they served the last, lingering drink after Compline. Even the well-dressed but apparently idle squires in the abbot's household were task-oriented: their task was simply to be present and to be seen to be present, and they evidently gave themselves wholeheartedly to it.

[53] *The Fabric Rolls of York Minster*, ed. J. Raine, jun. (Surtees Soc. xxxv, 1859), 171–3, 181–2. For the ordinance of 1370, see also D. Knoop and G. P. Jones, *The Mediaeval Mason* (3rd edn., Manchester, 1967), 223–4; and for a translation of the ordinance of 1352, Salzman, *Building in England down to 1540*, 56–7. The details given above are from the ordinance of 1352. The provisions of both ordinances are considered in Langenfelt, *Historic Origin of the Eight Hours Day*, 38–41, and 44.

[54] Thompson, 'Time, work-discipline, and industrial capitalism', 61–3; id., *Customs in Common*, 358–61.

[55] Cf. the knock which he was to give to signify the end of the interval for breakfast (*Fabric Rolls of York Minster*, ed. Raine, 172).

[56] Such fires on feasts of the Virgin are implied in the following outlay by the warden of the Lady Chapel at Westminster Abbey in 1398–9: *Et in j quarterio carbonni empto hoc anno pro celebrantibus missam in yeme, viijd.* (WAM 23196). For the ensuing breakfasts, referred to variously as 'recreation', 'pittances', and *jantacula*, see WAM 23201–2, 23206, 23209, etc. See also *Monastery and Society in the Late Middle Ages*, ed. Tillotson, 221.

Yet there were also busy servants. Busiest of all were the servants, found in every monastery of any size, who looked after the monastic church itself: these watched the shrine and—no less important—the visitors, saw to it that the vestments, vessels, and candles were *comme il faut* for every service at every altar, swept the church and kept it clean, and locked it at night. At Westminster, and no doubt universally, they could be deployed from time to time on other work.[57] Even so, their duties made it necessary for this group actually to live in the church. At Westminster, their chamber, built in 1338, was at, and presumably over, the north door of the abbey church; at Durham, two slept in a room in the vestry, and two in a room in the north aisle.[58] And after the servants of the church, the busiest were the kitchen staff, who had to produce a complex meal for large numbers by 11 a.m. or thereabouts, and do the shopping first. For them a day beginning at sunrise is indicated, and on most days in the week the demands on them rose again to a pitch in the late afternoon, as supper-time approached.

Moreover, in the late Middle Ages, we can detect moves in the direction of a more disciplined use of time, and a hovering sense of a working day that was to be filled with activity of one kind or another. In this context, the very use of rotas is significant, for it implies the clear distinction between work and leisure without which work-discipline must always be fragile.[59] In some monasteries steps were taken to correct the inequalities in the work-load from department to department by employing servants across the departmental boundaries. At Durham, for example, members of the kitchen staff and the staff of the bakery, brewery, and malthouse helped to man the bell-ringing team (an important body in any monastery);[60] at Westminster the servants minding the church also had the far more dangerous tasks of cleaning gutters and chasing rooks.[61] We must allow, too, for the employment of domestic servants on the tasks that were never remitted to anyone in particular on a regular basis but arranged and rewarded *ad hoc*. There were, for example, messages to be carried, and bills to be paid at shops in the town. Moreover, many household chores that would later be regarded as regular tasks were, in this period, done *ad hoc*, when it seemed necessary, but not before. For George Norwich's installation day as abbot of Westminster in 1463, the small knives were cleaned, and 2*d.* paid for the task.[62] In 1523–4, those who cleaned the large candlesticks and two basins

---

[57] *Customary*, ii. 58 (a late 13th-cent. reference). One of the four mentioned here was the servant of the vestry. Later, there were four servants of the church in addition to this servant, and the four had a servant of their own (WAM 19756 ff.).

[58] WAM 19621; *Rites of Durham*, 22. For a reference at Westminster in 1476–7 to the table (*mensa*) of the servants of the church in the sacristy, see WAM 19724.

[59] K. V. Thomas, 'Work and leisure in pre-industrial society', *P & P* xxix (Dec. 1964), 50–62, at 51–4.       [60] *Rites of Durham*, 39.

[61] WAM 19756 ff. These tasks were actually performed by the servant of the servants of the church, who received 6*s.* 8*d.* p.a. for his pains.       [62] WAM 24548.

for lamps in the convent's household after Christmas—in preparation, perhaps, for Candlemas—received 2s.[63]

Nevertheless, there was a good deal of slack in the working day of the average servant, and the reasons for this are found in the very nature of the monastic household. In common with so many other large establishments, in more or less any period we may have in mind, a monastic household was overmanned for much of the year, the better to cover the special times and seasons. To be fully stretched, such a household needed the special services and special meals of a major feast day of the Church, distinguished visitors to entertain, or a bout of illness to fill the empty beds in the infirmary, and preferably all three simultaneously. Monastic communities were quick to notice inflated numbers in the household of their abbot or prior. But they had in common with him a general attitude to servants more like that of a master to his dependants in a system of clientage than that of an employer to his employees in a capitalist society. In such a household it was probably hard to be dismissed, whatever one's behaviour.

## (iii) The working year

If, however, the normal working day was undemanding, the working year was unusually full. It is a commonplace of studies on working conditions in pre-industrial societies that employment was normally discontinuous. Climatic hazards often interfered with work, and they also deflated demand on the part of all those who had to earn money before they could spend it. In any case, consumer demand was in general low. And however pressing the demand, the Church forbade the faithful to do work for gain on Sundays and a large number of other feast days in the year. Moreover, some feasts had vigils that were also to be observed. Every year some of the other feasts in the calendar coincided with Sundays and did not, for this reason, give rise to extra holidays. Even so, the Church's rules ensured that for most people there were only $4^1/_2$ to 5 legitimate days for gainful employment in an average week—say a maximum of 250 or 260 working days in the year.[64]

As an exception to the rule that employment was discontinuous, household service, and especially domestic service, deserves to be better known than it is. The need for meals, for fires and personal service, for security at

---

[63] WAM 33298, fo. 8.

[64] Thomas, 'Work and leisure in pre-industrial society', 52–5; B. F. Harvey, 'Work and *festa ferianda* in medieval England', *JEH* xxiii (1972), 289–308, at 295–303. For the differences from diocese to diocese in the feasts that were, ideally, to be observed, see C. R. Cheney, 'Rules for the observance of feast-days in medieval England', *BIHR* xxxiv (1961), 117–47. In some forms of employment, and notably those of building craftsmen, the convention whereby the worker received wages for one feast day in every two observed as a holiday tends to obscure the extent to which the working week was in fact interrupted. For an explanation of the system, see Salzman, *Building in England down to 1540*, 66.

the gatehouse—for everything, in fact, that enabled the great organization to function properly from day to day and show a brave face to the world—varied little from day to day; and in the case of a monastery we must remember also the constant need for assistance at services. The Church had never attempted to restrict the work of those who did these and other necessary tasks. The so-called 'servile work' which she forbade on holy days was the work that could as well be postponed to another day, and especially such work if done for gain.[65] Domestic servants, therefore, could work continuously throughout the year without committing any offence by doing so. Many, indeed, actually worked much harder on feast days than on other days, for the meals in great households were more elaborate on these days than on others, and the visitors to be cared for more numerous. The unique character of such employment consisted in the marriage between this unrelenting year and the day that was often so easy.

## 4. Earnings at Westminster Abbey

### (i) A bench-mark

The nature of the working year explains the unique rewards of household service, and these are my final topic.

In outline, the emoluments of household service are clear enough: they consisted normally of board, or wages in lieu, a stipend—that is, a periodic cash payment—and a livery of clothing. But what these added up to is much less clear; and in any case the sum would have worked out somewhat differently in different situations. Earnings at Westminster Abbey *c.*1500 will show what a servant could amass in one way or another in a large, wealthy Benedictine house, in an urban and, indeed near-metropolitan situation at the end of the Middle Ages. First, however, a bench-mark will be useful.

Time was, said the Doctor in the *Discourse of the Common Weal*, in the mid-sixteenth century, when 40*s.* per annum was a good wage—or, as we may prefer to say, stipend—for a yeoman, and 20*d.* per week sufficient in board wages; and he seems to have had household service in mind.[66] Once, he said in effect, it was possible to get a middle-ranking household servant for £6 6*s.* per annum, of which the greater part was given in lieu of board; and he valued board at just under 3*d.* per day. The whole point of his remark is that the level of earnings for this kind of work had once been, but no longer was, reasonable from the employer's point of view. Yet in the

[65] Harvey, 'Work and *festa ferianda* in medieval England', 290; ibid. 299–304.

[66] *A Discourse of the Common Weal of this Realm of England*, ed. E. Lamond (Cambridge, 1954), 82. For specific comment see Cornwall, *Wealth and Society in Early Sixteenth-Century England*, 10–14; and for further insight into a neglected topic, the actual earnings of in-servants in the early 16th cent., Spufford, *Contrasting Communities*, 31–3.

early sixteenth century the sum mentioned was itself no mean one. To earn £6 6s. per annum in the course of a year, a journeyman artisan qualifying for the highest wages prescribed in the Statute of Artificers of 1495 would nevertheless have needed to find employment on very nearly every lawful day for work, in winter and summer alike: working for these wages five days a week throughout the year, he would have earned c.£6 per annum.[67] Moreover, the board wages which were envisaged exceeded the 2d. per day allowed by the Statute for this purpose. Where, then, are earnings at Westminster Abbey to be put in relation to this bench-mark?

## (ii) The servants

At this date, the Abbey probably employed c.110 servants in one or other of its households, and this establishment served a community of about fifty monks. Large though the number may sound, it excludes the considerable force of masons and carpenters currently engaged on the fabric of the Abbey church or the new work in Henry VII's chapel there. It also excludes the elusive people who scraped a living in the Abbey's households but were not on the official pay-roll: the number relates, in fact, to those who had corrodies—that is, a guaranteed livelihood—at the Abbey's expense. Some were administrators. However, the number of these was not unduly large for a large establishment, and when we have deducted from the 110 the auditors, abbot's chaplains, and the like, we are still left with about ninety people who serviced the various household departments and kept the whole, vast organization going from day to day.[68] A minority of these were

---

[67] For the statutory rates, see 11 Henry VII, c.22 (*SR* ii. 586). Cf. Phythian-Adams, *Desolation of a City*, 132–3.

[68] A difficult figure to estimate, since we have to allow for pluralism. It seems likely that all the following servants had a separate identity. The order within each department is alphabetical. The actual designation 'servant' denotes one who, in the sources, is called—as not all were—*serviens*. A considerable number of 'servants' in this sense, though not all, ranked as valets and had managerial responsibilities.

*Abbot's household*: 10 to 15. *Prior's household*: butler, cook, keeper of Belsize (the prior's country house), 2 grooms, squire (an ornamental figure with no duties that can now be discerned). *Monk-bailiff's household*: butler, chamber groom, clerk (probably a general factotum), cook, keeper of horses, kitchen groom. *Convent's household*: (i) *almonry*: almoner's servant, lay brethren's servant, serjeant of almonry; (ii) *cellar*, including granary and hostelry: baker and 2 assistants, brewer and 2 assistants, carter, cellarer's servant, granary servant, hostelry servant, maltman, miller; (iii) *chamber*: barber, bath-attendant, clerk (who also acted as rent-collector), cobbler, skinner, tailor; (iv) *gatehouse* (including prison): gaoler, janitor; (v) *infirmary*: butler, cook, infirmarer's servant, gardener, kitchen groom; (vi) *kitchen*: boatman, clerk, cook, gardener, under-cook; (vii) *lady chapel*: bell-ringer, chandler, cleaner of ornaments etc., clerk (a general factotum); (viii) *misericord*: butler, under-butler; (ix) *parlour*: keeper; (x) *refectory*: 2 servants of the refectory; (xi) *sacristy*: butler, carpenter, chandler, cook, glazier, keeper of clock, keeper of sanctuary gate, plumber, sacrist's servant, 4 servants of the church and their servant, shrine-keeper's servant, tiler, vestry servant (responsible for repairing vestments). *Extra-departmental*: an uncertain number of laundresses.

The number given for the abbot's household is an estimate based on hints in the household day-accounts for 1500–2 and 1509–10: no actual list survives from this period. The 8 *famuli*

craftsmen, who, for example, baked the monastery's bread or mended its pipes when the need arose; but the majority were domestic servants in a more general sense. Nearly all the ninety ranked as valets or grooms in the household hierarchy, and these are the servants whose earnings are to be considered. First, however, we must take note of the important relationship which existed between valets and grooms in this monastery.

The managerial system described above, whereby servants ranking as valets ran the departments and sub-departments from day to day and appointed the necessary staff, was a feature of the household at Westminster in the later Middle Ages.[69] It had replaced an earlier system of hereditary serjeanties which previous generations of monks had been at pains to terminate. This they had achieved by the costly process of repurchasing the freehold of the offices in question from the current holders, when the latter could be persuaded to part with it.[70] By the sixteenth century, however, the new system was to some extent overlaid by another practice—that of entrusting entire departments to high-ranking administrators or consultants, who themselves appointed the working heads of department and could, if they wished, retain in their own hands all the patronage normally exercised by the latter. The position of such people closely resembled that of the earlier serjeants, but with one important exception: the former, unlike the latter, did not hold in perpetuity but for a life-term or a term of years. It became customary, for example, to entrust the Abbey's gatehouse and the office of janitor there to the chief steward of the prior and convent for the time being, the official responsible for holding the courts of their manors. It was in these circumstances that Thomas Cromwell was admitted to the office of janitor at the Abbey in September 1533—as it happened, between two of the sessions of the Reformation Parliament. Cromwell was to be steward, and his appointment as janitor followed naturally from this fact.[71]

It is tempting to conclude that personal observation by the new janitor in the gatehouse at Westminster underlay the belief, hinted at in the Injunctions of 1535–6, of which he was, in another capacity, the author, that monks were apt to venture beyond the precinct of their monastery without having good reason for doing so.[72] In fact, Cromwell was explicitly

---

mentioned in Abbot Norwich's household in 1463 must be regarded as a skeleton staff, Norwich being newly elected (WAM 24548).

[69] Above, pp. 148–9, 151–2.

[70] The serjeanty of the almonry survived until the Dissolution, when the current holder, Anthony Cotton, received an annuity of £6 p.a. from the Court of Augmentations (PRO LR 6/58/14, fo. 17ᵛ; ibid. 61/1, fo. 100, etc.).

[71] WAM Register Bk. ii, fos. 288–288ᵛ. In his capacity as steward, Cromwell received livery @ 20s. p.a. and evidently ranked as a gentleman (WAM 23029). For earlier instances of the association of the office of janitor with that of chief steward, see WAM Register Bk. i, fos. 92ᵛ–93; ibid. ii, fo. 67.

[72] Wilkins, *Concilia*, iii. 790; Youings, *Dissolution of the Monasteries*, 149.

permitted to perform his duties in the gatehouse at Westminster by deputy. With his new office he acquired the right to appoint the valet who would run the department from day to day: hence the clause in his grant, confer- ring on him all the corrodies pertaining to the gatehouse. But by no means all the key appointments had been devolved in this way. A more typical head of department than Thomas Cromwell at this date was Thomas Valentyne, who was in charge of the Abbey's brewery from 1514 to 1528 and ranked in the household as a valet. Valentyne also had his own brewery in the town of Westminster. He was a churchwarden of St Margaret's, and later warden of one of the gilds in that church.[73] Thomas Hogan, who had charge of the Abbey's bakery at a slightly earlier date, served as master of the Assumption gild in St Margaret's, and as chief constable of the town of Westminster.[74] Like Cromwell, Valentyne and Hogan had commitments elsewhere but in the monastery and we can assume that both worked only part-time for the Abbey. Both, however, were local men of middle rank, with none of Cromwell's prominence in national life. Each was profession- ally well qualified for his job in the monastery and this he was expected to perform in person.

However appointed, the household valet at Westminster was in a position of authority from day to day over the grooms in his department, and if he actually appointed the grooms and controlled their emoluments—as many a valet did—the relationship between the two was analogous to that between a master craftsman and a journeyman or apprentice working in his shop: indeed, in some cases this was the actual relationship between valet and groom. It was this relationship that provided much of the infrastructure in the monastic household. It was probably as effective a mechanism for main- taining order there—and as much needed—as the relationship between master and journeyman or apprentice proved to be in the workshops and house- holds of urban society outside the cloister.[75]

A minority of the Abbey's servants had jobs which made it necessary for them to live in, and we can assume that all the young servants of groom's rank or less were resident, whatever their duties. In the past, many resident menials may have slept on the floor. In the later Middle Ages, however, most departments probably possessed a chamber with one or more beds for their use, and in some cases a well-appointed bed. When Br. Richard Exeter, a former prior, died in 1396, his bed, which would have been of a superior kind, was given to the four servants of the church for their chamber over the north door.[76] At the Dissolution in 1540, the porter's lodgings in the

[73] For Valentyne, see Rosser, *Medieval Westminster*, 159–60, 403; and for the social rank of such a person in Westminster at this time, ibid. 367. For Valentyne's livery as a valet, valued at 10s. p.a. and continued until 1532, see WAM 23012–22, 23025, 23027.
[74] Rosser, *Medieval Westminster*, 381; and for his livery of a valet's robe, WAM 23007–12.
[75] Phythian-Adams, *Desolation of a City*, 134–5.
[76] WAM 6603. However, the servants did not get the tester, which was disposed of separately.

abbot's house in the precinct boasted a feather bed and a coverlet worked with flowers—the cast-offs, no doubt of some well-furnished monastic bed, but feathers and flowers for all that.[77] In this household, even the scullions had their chamber, and mattresses, bolsters, and coverlet for the bedstead in it.[78] But most servants probably lived in houses or cottages in the precinct, and some possessed substantial tenements there, if not more than one. Thomas Valentyne, the master brewer, leased from the Abbey several tenements in Long Ditch, just outside the sanctuary, and John James, who was valet of the convent's parlour, leased several from it within the sanctuary.[79]

Non-residence implies married status for many of the servants, and the probability of the working wife; and both the married servant and the working wife are well-attested features of servant life at Westminster in this period. Some of the work that women did in this monastery was generated not by the monks themselves but by the inmates of their song school and grammar school. In the early sixteenth century, as we learn from an account-book relating to the two schools, one woman, described as 'Roger's wife', sewed shirts for the boys; another, 'Peter's wife', made their hose; and a third, 'Grimshaw's wife', did their washing.[80] We can safely assume that Roger and Peter were Abbey servants of one kind or another, and to our knowledge Grimshaw was on the staff of the misericord.[81] In the late medieval monastery, women did the laundry, made mats for the cloister and other parts of the monastery, repaired vestments, and weeded the garden.[82] They may also have prepared the entrails of slaughtered animals for the table, as they did in some other houses in this period.[83] Among these tasks, however, only laundering and work on vestments earned a stipend at the Abbey: women worked on the other tasks in return for a day's or half-day's wage or a wage per task. Yet a poignant episode suggests that women may also have been employed on general duties as full members of the establishment. In 1528 thirteen so-called 'familiares' of the monastery died on a single day, 4 May, in what was evidently a violent epidemic in the precinct. They are listed simply by Christian name—John, Katherine, John, Joan,

---

[77] *Abbot's House at Westminster*, 39.

[78] Ibid. In draft Injunctions for the Abbey in 1536, it was decreed that the abbot's servants who had nowhere else to go should sleep in the monk-bailiff's office, itself to be deemed in future to be outside the precinct (WAM 12787). See Map I.

[79] Rosser, *Medieval Westminster*, 382–3, 403. The parlour (*locutorium*) was a place for monastic recreation and the receiving of visitors. John James also leased the manor of Hampstead from the Abbey.

[80] WAM 33301, fos. 2ᵛ, 7, 11, 18, 18ᵛ, 19ᵛ. Roger's wife also made table-cloths. The accountant was the sub-almoner, who was responsible for the schools.

[81] Ibid., fos. 2ᵛ–3, where his livery of a gown @ 10s. p.a. identifies him as a valet.

[82] Making mats: WAM 18966. Making and repairing vestments: WAM 19621, 19643, 19645, etc. Weeding (in the abbot's garden at La Neyte): WAM 33291, fo. 5. Outside the precinct, women were also employed to turn, stack, and carry hay (WAM 18844, 18980). Every major department in the monastery used the services of one or more laundresses.

[83] *Monastery and Society in the Late Middle Ages*, ed. Tillotson, 166; see also ibid. 158, and above, p. 152.

Thomas, Katherine, Thomas, Elizabeth, John, John, John, William, John—and, as this stark list shows, four of the thirteen were women.[84] The description, 'familiares', implies that they were regular members of the establishment.

## (iii) Livery

Most of the full-time servants on the Abbey's pay-roll, and many serving only part-time, received the three kinds of emolument that I have mentioned: board, stipend, and livery.[85] Of these, however, only the last actually expressed the rank of the servant in question. Each year, a squire or gentleman received a so-called robe trimmed with furs, and in these cases the robe was probably a whole suit of clothes. Each valet or groom received livery which is normally described as a robe, but occasionally as a gown. In these cases, the livery probably consisted of a single garment without furs.[86] In 1354–5, we are told that the sacrist gave his 'servant'—by which term we are to understand his principal valet—a *cote hardie*.[87] The *cote hardie*, a short super-tunic, tight-fitting and with long sleeves, was coming into fashion in secular society at this time. The sacrist had a particular reason for favouring it. When distinguished visitors attended a service in the Abbey church, as many did from time to time, it was his duty to entertain them afterwards to light refreshments in the vestry. His choice of a *cote hardie* for his servant tells us that such of his staff as would be in the public eye on these occasions were expected to look well. The same consideration must have weighed heavily with the abbot of Westminster, who so frequently

---

[84] WAM 23003ᵛ; *Monks*, 166. The prior, William Mane, died the same day. The year 1527–8 was one of high but not crisis mortality in the monastic community; see Fig. IV.1a and b. In an early 15th-cent. list of the Abbey's valets in 1438–9, which appears to be a livery list, 4 of the 47 names are those of wives of other valets named in the list (WAM 33288, fo. 31). However, not all the 47 were household valets: some were lessees of manors belonging to the prior and convent. The list also includes the names of 28 persons ranking as 'gentlemen', five of whom were women and one, the schoolmaster's wife, a corrodian.

[85] Above, p. 163. In this and the following paragraph, I have tried to make sense of evidence which is to some extent confused and inconsistent. Moreover, by the end of the 15th cent., it is affected by the common tendency of financial accounts of this period to use standardized entries. The main evidence is provided by the accounts of, respectively, the steward of the abbot's household (WAM 24511–17, 24537–8, etc.), the conventual treasurers (WAM 19849–50, 19852 ff.), and the cellarer (WAM 18896 ff.), and by memoranda relating to livery in 1438–9 and 1443–4 (WAM 33288, fos. 30–30ᵛ). For purchases of cloth in the fair at Westminster in the early 14th cent., mainly for the livery of the monastery's clerks and squires, see WAM 50684–90. The clerks' livery was of coloured cloth, the squires' also coloured, but part plain, part striped.

[86] For references to the livery of these servants as a single garment (*toga*), see e.g. WAM 18896–8. Items other than robes are rarely mentioned. The chamberlain's clerk owed his shoe allowance to the fact that he collected the chamberlain's rents in London and elsewhere (WAM 18732 ff.).

[87] WAM 19623; and on the *cote hardie*, see N. Bradfield, *Historical Costumes of England* (2nd edn., London, 1958), 38–9 and J. Laver, *Concise History of Costume* (London, 1977), 63.

entertained distinguished guests at dinner: he, too, may have dressed his principal servants in the latest fashion.

Even in departments of the conventual household less exposed than that of the sacrist to the public gaze, the style and cut of livery garments may have varied according to the function of the servant in question. The cloth for both a valet's livery and that of a groom was part ray, or striped, part plain. In the mid-fifteenth century, 2 to 2¹/₂ yards of plain cloth and 25 to 27 pieces of ray of unspecified length were used for the livery of some valets.[88] For the greater part of the fifteenth century, the standard livery for a valet cost *c*.12*s*. and for a groom 8*s*. or 8*s*. 4*d*., but sometimes more, sometimes less.[89] A change in the style of the garment, enabling the tailor to use less cloth, may explain the fall in the normal cost of a valet's livery to 10*s*. per annum in the 1480s.[90] The distribution of livery was probably made at Christmas.[91] Even a valet's livery was less expensive than the tunic worn by each well-dressed inmate of Henry VII's almshouses at Westminster: this tunic, made of russet three 'large' yards wide, lined with black friese, and carrying on one shoulder an escutcheon displaying the Tudor rose, normally cost 14*s*. 6*d*.[92] Yet perhaps few other wage-earners in the late medieval town of Westminster can have spent as much on new outer garments year by year as was spent on the livery of one of the Abbey's valets or grooms.

## (iv) Stipends

Stipends—the compulsory savings, as they have been called, of the living-in servant[93]—did not express rank in the same neat way. The normal range for both valets and grooms in the Abbey's service was 6*s*. to £1 6*s*. 8*d*. per annum, but even given these broad limits, many apparent anomalies can be identified. We must conclude that many of these payments were in origin *ad hominem*, and may suspect that some had been agreed after a good deal of haggling between obedientiaries and the servants in their departments;

---

[88] WAM 33288, fos. 30–30ᵛ.

[89] WAM 19917–79. The costs mentioned in this paragraph are those of the cloth, and in the early 15th-cent., the unshorn cloth. They apparently exclude the cost of making it up: this was done in the chamberlain's department but is never entered explicitly in that obedientiary's accounts. Yet it is more likely than not that the cloth was made up.

[90] For 10*s*. and 8*s*. to 8*s*. 4*d*. as the normative costs of, respectively, a valet's livery and a groom's *c*.1500, see WAM 18903, 18909–13, 18915–16; and for the acceptability of short gowns as well as long ones in the second half of the 15th cent., Bradfield, *Historical Costumes of England*, 59, 63.

[91] As stated explicitly in the case of the janitor's groom in 1378 and that of the kitchen staff in 1520–1 (WAM 17694, 33329, fo. 12). For Christmas as the season for the issue of a corrodian's livery, see Appendix V, no. 62.

[92] WAM 24236 ff.; and for Henry VII's prescriptions, which were precisely carried out, see *Cal. Cl. R., Henry VII*, ii *(1500–1509)*, no. 390 (p. 146). Of the sum of 14*s*. 6*d*., 10*d*. represented the cost of making the tunic.

[93] Kussmaul, *Servants in Husbandry in Early Modern England*, 38.

and, in cases where work-loads were shared by more than one department, haggling over servants' pay sometimes occurred between the obedientiaries themselves.[94] But the anomalies may also express the pleasant or unpleasant nature of the work in question, and the presence or absence of incidental opportunities for profit. It was probably the unpleasant nature of the work that secured the relatively high stipend of £1 per annum for the monastery's bath-attendant, and the opportunities for incidental profit in their position that persuaded the master baker and master brewer to accept stipends of, respectively, 6s. 8d. and 5s. per annum in the same period.[95] Simply to have access to the monastic bakehouse and brewery in addition to their own premises in the town of Westminster was to be in a gainful situation, and we can probably assume that they quite frequently used the former premises for work of their own.

In the course of the fifteenth century, stipends were abandoned in the case of some highly skilled workers, who now received either a wage for every day worked or an inclusive sum for the job. The plumber, for example, was employed on these new, and, for him, potentially more lucrative, terms from the first or second decade of the century. Formerly, he received a stipend of 60s. per annum. Now, he received wages of 4d. on every day when he worked: he had only to work on more than 180 days in the year to gain by the new arrangement. Moreover, the monastery now paid the wages of his assistant, though it had probably not done so formerly.[96] But the plumber, who looked after roofs, gutters, and pipes, was a part-time worker, as were most of the other craftsmen employed by the Abbey. For full-time servants, and for those working part-time if their duties were, in the broad meaning of the term, domestic, stipendiary service continued to be the norm. In the kitchen, sub-almonry, and chamberlain's department, stipends were paid in quarterly instalments, and this may have been the universal practice in the monastic household.[97]

## (v) Board

For servants entitled to it, board was far more valuable than either stipend or livery, and in most cases more valuable than both these together. However, it consisted of two quite distinct components, and a right to the one did not imply a right to the other as well.

[94] For a hint of such haggling in an earlier period over board for the plumber, see *Customary*, ii. 74.          [95] WAM 18904–13.

[96] Under the new arrangements, the plumber was also entitled to a corrody on working days, or 6d. per day in lieu. The corrody was almost certainly long established, but the payment in lieu may not previously have been so high. Soon after these changes, the normal value of his livery was raised from 6s. 8d. p.a. to 9s. 6d. or 10s. 6d. p.a.: in fact he was advanced from groom's to valet's livery. WAM 19659–75.

[97] For the kitchen, see WAM 33317, fo. 11ᵛ; WAM 33329, fos. 12, 12ᵛ, 23, 37, 50; WAM 33330, fos. 6, 15ᵛ, 24ᵛ; for the sub-almonry, which paid the stipends of servants in the misericord, WAM 33301, fos. 1ᵛ, 8, 11, etc.; and for the chamberlain's department, WAM 18793, fo. 27ᵛ.

The first component was an allowance of bread and ale, known as a 'corrody in the cellar', from the circumstance that the cellarer was the provider of bread and ale for the monastery, and the cellar his department.

In the fourteenth century, many of the monastery's servants, and among them probably all the grooms, were given bread which is described as 'black': it was perhaps very dark but not actually black. This was made from scurril, a mixture of inferior wheat and rye, in which the former preponderated. A few servants were given an even coarser kind of bread made from bran—that is, from the husks or refuse of the grain passing through the mill.[98] By the early sixteenth century, however, an important change had evidently taken place, for all servants entitled to bread were now given the so-called conventual loaf, which the monks themselves ate and which is described from time to time as 'white'. The change from black bread to white for the servants is hard to date but probably occurred in the 1470s.[99] In the early sixteenth century, a loaf of conventual bread probably weighed 2 lbs. or a little more after baking, and in the early sixteenth century it was valued by the monastery at $3/4\,d.$[100] It was, no doubt, relatively white, as the 'black' loaf of the earlier period was relatively black, but the high value placed on it shows that it was made of a superior kind of flour. Although some valets had contrived to get more, and some grooms—indeed, some valets—had to make do with less, the normal allowance for a full-time servant was probably, at all times, one loaf per day.[101] As for the ale, a valet could expect to receive a gallon per day of the monastery's best brew, valued for the purpose at $1^1/4 d.$, and a groom $1^1/2$ gallons of the second best.[102]

In the early sixteenth century, a valet's corrody in the cellar of the standard kind was worth $c.£3$ per annum, but a groom's, with its inferior ale, less:

[98] For the cellarer's liveries of *panes nigri*, made, in 1353–4, from scurril or bran, and in 1402–3 from a mixture of the two, see WAM 18830, 18887. For the scurril provided by the granger for the baker, see WAM 19155 ff. Occasionally barley was used instead of rye. The servant's loaf was known as a *hogeman* or *meynebred/meynelof* (WAM 5908, 31754, 31756). *Knytenlof* survived into the 14th cent. as the name of a kind of black loaf that was distinct from the *hogeman* (WAM 5908).

[99] An inference from the fact that the cellarer's sales of surplus bran and bread made from inferior flour (*media farina*) increased by a considerable amount in this period (WAM 18896–8, 18900–2). For servants' liveries of conventual loaves in the early 16th cent. see WAM 18941, 31916, 33315. However, many loaves intended for servants are subsumed in the number delivered twice weekly to the 'black stool', a name for part of the cellar, where the loaves were distributed. [100] WAM 5919*, and above, p. 59.

[101] For the norm and deviations from it, see WAM 18830, 18887. Some apparent deviations are explained by the part-time nature of the work in question. A few servants received weekly corn allowances, or cash in lieu, instead of bread: for these allowances in the 15th cent., see WAM 19210 ff. It may have been usual to convert liveries of 1 loaf per day into 8 or even 9 per week—a convention that would explain the liveries at this rate recorded for a number of servants in WAM 5919*.

[102] WAM 18887, 31754, 31756, where 1 *gazo* = $1^1/2$ galls. For the monastery's best ale, see above, p. 58. These allowances may have been relatively generous; see Thurgood, 'Introduction' in *Account of the Great Household of Humphrey, First Duke of Buckingham*, ed. Harris, 6.

say—reckoning 1*d.* per day for the ale—£2 13*s.* 3*d.* per annum. In secular society outside the cloister, the total wages earned by many artisans and labourers in the course of a year probably did not exceed or even equal the larger of these sums.[103] For many in the monastery, the principal reward of service was the assured supply of bread and ale whatever the price of these staple foods in the open market.

The second component of board was an allowance of cooked food, termed the *coquina* or *mensa*, from the circumstance that the food in question was prepared in the kitchen and, in principle, eaten at table in one or other of the rooms for eating in the monastery. The number of servants entitled to this was much smaller than the number entitled to bread and ale, and, even among those of identical rank, actual allowances varied in the individual case. The standard allowance, unchanged from the thirteenth century on-wards, consisted of one or two dishes of generals per day, as served to the monks themselves.[104] In the later Middle Ages, however, some received their food in the refectory, where meaty dishes were eaten, but never flesh-meat, and some in the misericord, where flesh-meat was the quintessential food. Those receiving their food in the refectory were entitled to the so-called Oakham pittance, a course which the monks eating there enjoyed every day in addition to generals.[105] And an élite band of servants entitled to wine and flans when the monks had these festal foods is mentioned as early as the twelfth century.[106]

In the later Middle Ages, a considerable number of those entitled to cooked food received board wages in lieu, and, quite probably, some had asked for this arrangement. From the 1380s, for example, the butler and cook in the infirmary received 1½*d.* each per day in lieu of the board to which they had previously been entitled.[107] It is hard to believe that the infirmarer himself suggested such an arrangement for two servants so intimately con-cerned with the preparation and service of food in his department, but easy to believe that the butler and cook, well placed as they were to enjoy the best leftovers of the meals which they prepared, found the cash option more attractive than a formal allowance of food. Yet some who made this choice—if they did—may have regretted it subsequently, for the Abbey's board

---

[103] Phythian-Adams, *Desolation of a City*, 132–3.

[104] *Customary*, ii. 73–4, and for generals, see above, p. 43. In this and the following para-graphs I have, again, tried to make sense of evidence which is often ambiguous. Among the sources, the accounts of the new work show the immediate and, from the recipients' point of view, deleterious, consequences of the Statute of Artificers (1495) for artisans' wages at the Abbey (WAM 23568 ff.).                                                                                    [105] Above, p. 43.

[106] *Flete*, 97. The servants in question probably had wine on *c.*60 days per annum and [cheese] flans on *c.*25. Those entitled to wine and flans also received the so-called Benfleet pittance at dinner, for which see *Customary*, ii. 75–6.

[107] WAM 19366 ff. These wages may have related to drink as well as cooked food; see earlier references to the expense of providing *potus* and *coquina* for these and other servants in the infirmary (WAM 19326).

wages were slow to respond to adverse changes in the cost of living. The four servants of the church, who were jointly on board wages of 8*d.* per week by the mid-fourteenth century, had to make do with this rate for several years after the Black Death of 1348–9, notwithstanding the rise in prices following swiftly on that event: 8*d.* per week became 1*s.* per week only at the end of 1354.[108]

Servants who received cooked food were subject to the monastic routine of four meat days and three fish days per week, and observed the long Lenten fast, though not that of Advent.[109] On meat days, few were in fact given flesh meat: most had to make do with the meaty dishes and dishes of offal that were served in the refectory on these occasions. Whatever the form of food provided, few actually consumed it in the rooms where the monks ate: most collected their messes from a serving-hatch in the refectory or misericord, as appropriate, and repaired elsewhere—to the place of work in the monastery, or home to a cottage or house in the precinct—for the actual meal. Hence the monastery's employment of two menials who were known, respectively, as 'keeper of the frater hole' and 'keeper of the cord hole': the two were in charge of distributions at the serving-hatches in the frater, or refectory, and the misericord.[110]

Estimates of the value of a servant's cooked food must be based mainly on the board wages given in lieu when this was the preferred option. Since board wages changed little, if at all, from year to year, by using this measure we shall lose sight of many short-term fluctuations in the actual value of these allowances when received in kind. This, however, is unavoidable. For some part-time artisans, such as the chandler, the value of cooked food, *c.*1500, was, it appears as high as 2*d.* per working day.[111] The highest rate mentioned for a full-time servant at this date is exemplified in the 1*s.* per week received by the sacrist's servant; nevertheless, for some full-time servants cooked food may have been worth as little as $\frac{1}{2}d.$ per day.[112]

How, then, did those servants manage who had no allowance of cooked food at all? Many ranking as grooms were in this situation, and an episode towards the end of the fourteenth century suggests how they were expected to manage. In 1378 one Robert Norton was appointed janitor of the Abbey

---

[108] WAM 19621–3.

[109] For the provision of meat for servants during Advent, see WAM 33327, fos. 8ᵛ–9ᵛ; 33329, fos. 5–7.

[110] For these descriptions—aliases of, respectively, the under-cook in the kitchen and the under-butler in the misericord—see WAM 33301, fos. 7, 11, etc.; see also WAM 33317, fos. 11ᵛ, 12.

[111] WAM 19751, 19754, 19762, 19765. The chandler was also entitled to bread and ale on working days.

[112] For the allowance to the sacrist's servant of 52*s.* per annum (= 1*s.* per week) in lieu of *mensa*, see WAM 19747 ff. The estimate of $\frac{1}{2}d.$ per day relates to the servants mentioned in the next paragraph, who were dependent for cooked food on the valets to whom they worked or on leftovers in the refectory.

and keeper of the gatehouse prison, with the rank of valet, and with the janitorship he received a corrody of bread and ale, together with two messes of cooked food daily, as served to a monk. For his groom, who was to look after the gatehouse prison, Norton received a further allowance of bread, but apparently no ale or cooked food.[113] Evidently, if the groom was not to beg for cooked food—and, indeed, for ale—he was to depend on his master for it; and if this was the intention of the abbot and convent, it is easy to understand why they undertook to give Norton himself the very ample messes which the monks themselves received. But did Robert Norton and other valets similarly placed actually share their food with their grooms— or did they dispatch the grooms to the refectory and misericord, to get what they could of the broken meats of the monks' own meals? The practice of feeding servants on the leftovers of the monastic meals, which should have gone to the poor at the monastery gate, was condemned from time to time by the authorities in the Black Monk Order—a clear indication that it actually occurred.[114] Moreover, the practice was accepted without question in the Injunctions of 1535–6, where it is referred to in a matter-of-fact way implying its widespread existence.[115] It seems very likely that the grooms at Westminster often obtained their cooked food in this way. Yet their access to leftovers was sufficiently easy and regular for us to count the food in question as part of their earnings.

At the beginning of the sixteenth century, board at Westminster Abbey, for a servant entitled to cooked food as well as bread and ale, can in no case have been worth less than $2\frac{1}{2}d.$ per day, and in some cases the value was probably twice this amount. The servants in question received this exceedingly valuable emolument, or wages in lieu, on every working day in the year. In the case of many of the part-time servants, the number of such days was uneven from year to year. The glazier, for example, who was on the sacrist's staff and was presumably employed mainly in repairing broken windows or glazing new ones, apparently worked on a total of $144\frac{1}{2}$ days in 1520–1 but on only 70 in 1526–7; and such variability was not new in the 1520s.[116] Full-time domestic servants, however, who were continuously employed, received board day in, day out, throughout the year.

---

[113] WAM 17694. The cooked food is described as *deux mes de sosyne come un moign' de mesme le lieu*. *Sosyne* is probably an attempt at *coquina* in French, in a document which appears to have been drafted outside the monastery. Norton is said to be of Hants and may have performed his duties by deputy. In 1416, when the janitorship and sub-janitorship—the latter being the former groom's post—were separated from each other, the sub-janitor took the groom's bread and ale, but the janitor kept all the cooked food (LNQ 84).

[114] *Chapters of English Black Monks*, i. 37, 79; ibid. ii. 47.

[115] Wilkins, *Concilia*, iii. 790; Youings, *Dissolution of the Monasteries*, 150. A grant of the portership of Bolton Priory in 1528 implies that the porter's servant will participate in leftovers in the refectory (Hoyle, 'Monastic leasing before the Dissolution', 130).

[116] See WAM 31916, 33315, where the loaves to which this servant was entitled on days when he worked are recorded.

TABLE V.1. Official Earnings Per Annum of Full-Time Valets and Grooms at Westminster Abbey *c.*1500

| | Valet | | | | Groom | | | |
|---|---|---|---|---|---|---|---|---|
| | Minimum | | Maximum | | Minimum | | Maximum | |
| | £sd | % | £sd | % | £sd | % | £sd | % |
| Bread & ale (value) | 3.0.10ᵃ | 57 | 3.5.10ᵇ | 41.5 | 2.13.3ᶜ | 65 | 3.0.10ᵈ | 48 |
| Cooked food (value) | 1.10.5ᵉ | 28 | 2.16.2ᶠ | 35.5 | 0.15.2½ᵍ | 18 | 1.10.5ʰ | 24 |
| Livery (value) | 0.10.0 | 9 | 0.10.0 | 6 | 0.8.0 | 10 | 0.8.4 | 7 |
| Stipend | 0.6.0 | 6 | 1.6.8 | 17 | 0.6.0 | 7 | 1.6.8 | 21 |
| Total | 5.7.3 | 100 | 7.18.8 | 100 | 4.2.5½ | 100 | 6.6.3 | 100 |
| Equivalent pence per day | 3.53 | | 5.22 | | 2.71 | | 4.15 | |

*Notes:* ᵃ 1 conventual loaf @ ³/₄*d.* and 1 gall. best ale @ 1¹/₄*d.* per day.
ᵇ 1 conventual loaf @ ³/₄*d.* and 1 gall. best ale @ 1¹/₄*d.* per day; and wine @ 1*d.* on 60 feast days.
ᶜ 1 conventual loaf @ ³/₄*d.* and 1¹/₂*d* galls. second best ale @ 1*d.* per day.
ᵈ See note a above.
ᵉ Cooked food @ 1*d.* per day.
ᶠ Cooked food @ 1*s.* per week; and flans @ 2*d.* on 25 days p.a.
ᵍ Cooked food @ ¹/₂*d.* per day.
ʰ See note e above.

## (vi) What did it all come to?

### (a) *Official earnings*

Put together, board, stipend, and livery make broad and overlapping bands of pay for the monastery's full-time servants at this time. These are illustrated in Table V.1, where the smallest and largest totals within the reach of, respectively, full-time valets and grooms are shown. The sums shown here are estimates, and in some cases only rough estimates. Yet they probably do express the range of official earnings of full-time servants with corrodies—that is, with a secure place and regular livelihood in the monastic household.

It will be seen that the band for a valet comprised earnings in the range £5 7*s.* 3*d.* to £7 18*s.* 8*d.* per annum, and that for a groom, earnings in the range £4 2*s.* 5¹/₂*d.* per annum to £6 6*s.* 3*d.* per annum. The figures for a valet are equivalent to a wage of 3¹/₂*d.* to 5¹/₄*d.* per day, those for a groom, to a wage of 2³/₄*d.* to 4*d.* per day. In each case, the figures express the cash value of emoluments that were in fact received mainly in kind. In principle, emoluments in kind accounted for *c.*80 per cent to *c.*95 per cent of a servant's earnings, and even when board wages were received in lieu of cooked food, cash payments were still the smaller part of the whole for all except the highest-paid valet. Most valets were probably in the higher part of their band; most grooms in the middle part of theirs. To earn as much as even the lowest-paid valet in the monastic household, a journeyman crafts-man would indeed have needed to work on nearly all the legitimate days for work in the year; so, too, a labourer, to equal the lowest earnings of a groom.[117]

### (b) Total earnings

In the case of pre-industrial societies, however, we have always to distin-guish a worker's formal income, the rate for the job, from his total earnings, and both these from the total income of his household. Some of the Abbey's servants were, like Thomas Valentyne, the brewer, actually self-employed craftsmen and entrepreneurs. For them, service in the monastery was merely a form of by-employment, providing a welcome supplement to an income gained principally in other ways.[118] Others, though mainly dependent on their formal earnings as valets or grooms on the Abbey's establishment, could, if I am right, supplement these by forms of by-employment available to some extent in the monastery itself; and the income of many households, particularly the cash component, was swollen by the wife's earnings.[119] It would be surprising if in these and other ways actual incomes were not raised by a considerable margin above the levels suggested above for each grade of servant.

As it is, the figures take no account of tipping, an important if unquantifiable source of income for menial servants in this period, though one that shaded off imperceptibly into by-employment itself. To our knowledge, the abbot of Westminster gave many so-called 'rewards' of this kind to other men's servants, and some to his own, for particular services rendered, at home or abroad, or on account of the day—it was, perhaps, Christmas or Twelfth Night.[120] Guests coming to the monastery no doubt observed the same conventions. A tip of 3*d.* or 4*d.* here and there—and these were apparently common rates—and *a fortiori* one of 1*s.* or 2*s.* made a noticeable addition to the income of low-ranking servants whose official earnings amounted to not more than 3*d.* or 4*d.* per day. Nor should we forget the presents that were received from time to time in every great household of this period, as part of the contemporary ritual of gift-giving. During the twelve days of Christmas 1509, Abbot Islip received as gifts a quarter of a beef carcass, 3 lambs, 4 conies, 5 does, 5 boars, 5 peacocks, 12 geese, 12 hens, and 32 capons, and some apples and cheeses as well.[121] This

---

[117] Above, p. 164. Artisan and labourer could have achieved the targets with 4½ to 5 days' work per week throughout the year.

[118] For Valentyne, see above, p. 166.          [119] Above, pp. 167–8.

[120] WAM 33320, fos. 4, 5, 9ᵛ, etc.; 33324, fos. 1, 6, 9ᵛ, 18ᵛ–19, etc.

[121] WAM 33324, fos. 14ᵛ, 16ᵛ, 18ᵛ–19. The abbot himself would have been expected to re-ciprocate with hospitality or other forms of gift. For the wider context, see Heal, *Hospitality in Early Modern England*, 19–22.

was not, in fact, a great deal, given the abbot of Westminster's range of contacts or the need of his kitchen for meat at Christmas; and some of the presents came from the prior of Westminster and the monk-bailiff. Yet some of this meat probably found its way to menial households in the precinct. Indeed, if practice in the royal household across the road was imitated here, some of the Abbey's valets were actually entitled to share in gifts received by the monastic household.[122]

## 5. Conclusions

I began with three problems relating to monastic servants in the later Middle Ages: their numbers, their pattern of work, and their earnings.

Monastic servants, I suggest, were probably more numerous towards the end of the Middle Ages than has seemed likely to most recent historians of the period; and their pattern of work, in common with that of servants in other large households, had unusual features.[123] These, moreover, had the effect of raising the emoluments of full-time household servants above the levels that workers of comparable or even superior skills were assured of earning week in, week out elsewhere.[124] The administrative structure which makes it so difficult to count monastic servants, and especially the intrusion into it of secular managers and entrepreneurs, also makes it difficult to estimate their earnings: we do not know what proportion of the emoluments controlled by the managers and entrepreneurs was actually passed on to the servants whom they engaged.[125] Yet a large discrepancy between what the monasteries paid and the servants actually received is unlikely, and informal earnings helped to narrow the discrepancy that existed.

At the beginning of the sixteenth century, it was, it appears, possible to get a servant and valet, or yeoman, in a great household at Westminster for the total outlay which the Doctor in the *Discourse of the Common Weal* would later consider reasonable—that is, for £6 6s. per annum[126]—but very possible also for a person of this status and occupation to earn more there, and to do so in a mode of life that was not in fact demanding on a normal day. No significant change occurred in these respects down to the Dissolution of the monastery in 1540. Something, of course, must be allowed for the situation of Westminster Abbey in the legal and administrative capital of England, where the demand for labour was stronger than in many other parts of the kingdom. Even so, it is unlikely that the rewards of service at the Abbey were of a different order from those to be enjoyed generally in the greater Benedictine houses of the period, or, for that matter, in large secular households at that time.

---

[122] *Household of Edward IV: The Black Book and the Ordinance of 1478*, ed. Myers, 167, 179; and for the unlucky grammar master, ibid. 138.

[123] Above, pp. 150–3.     [124] Above, pp. 175–6.

[125] Above, p. 166.     [126] Above, pp. 163–4.

On the whole, we may think, a youth did well who entered this kind of household in the later Middle Ages and managed to establish himself there: he did well because he belonged to a distinct category, itself somewhat neglected by historians—that of workers who received a large proportion of their emoluments in kind. Such workers were well placed to survive the sixteenth-century price-rise without suffering a commensurate fall in standards of living—as their predecessors in service had been well placed to survive the price-rise of the fourteenth century. In the event, however, monastic servants, who had survived the earlier crisis in good numbers, vanished from the scene before they could really be tested by the later one: in common with their masters, they were casualties of the great demobilization that emptied the monasteries in the 1530s and 1540s. Only service in another institution as large and wasteful as the monastic household which they were obliged to leave could restore to them the particular kind of economic security they once enjoyed. How many found that is probably a question that can never be answered.

# VI

# *Corrodies*

## 1. Perceptions Old and New

HUGH LATIMER, in one of his sermons, had this to say about the monasteries, which had been dissolved by the time he wrote: 'When the end is naught, all is naught. So were these monks' houses, these religious houses. There were many people, specially widows, which would give over housekeeping, and go to such houses, when they might have done much good in maintaining of servants, and relieving of poor people; but they went their ways.'[1] Latimer referred to the monastic lodger or, as they sometimes said, the monastic sojourner. He would have known that monasteries had been in the habit of granting benefits resembling those of a lodger—including, for example, food and drink—to people who did not actually live in the monastery or even very near it; but it was the arrangements involving resident lodgers that he wished to condemn. In the monastic vocabulary, a lodger's bundle of privileges was a corrody (*corrodium*), and the same word was used of the privileges granted to non-residents.[2] In both cases, moreover, the recipient was known as a corrodian (*corrodarius*). I shall discuss corrodians as well as their corrodies.

Historians have in general found the corrodian, whether resident or non-resident, to be an eccentric and puzzling figure. Quite simply, the problem has seemed to be: why was he there at all? And, indeed—for Latimer was right: the female of the species also existed—why was she there at all? The short answer to this question, favoured by nearly all who have written on the topic, is that the arrangement was advantageous to both parties—to the corrodians and to the monks who took them in, but especially to the former.[3]

---

[1] *Sermons and Remains*, ed. G. E. Corrie (2 vols., Parker Soc. xvi, xx, 1844–5), i. 392.

[2] For these and wider uses of the term, and a suggested derivation from *conrei* (Old Fr., 'equipment'), see Thompson, 'Corrody', 116–17, and A. H. Thompson, *The English Clergy and their Organization in the Later Middle Ages* (Oxford, 1947), 174–5. *Corrodium* was also widely used of artisans' and labourers' board wages.

[3] For the several views summarized in the following paragraph, see e.g. Thompson, 'Corrody', 117–19; Moorman, *Church Life in England in the Thirteenth Century*, 267–71; H. M. Colvin, *The White Canons in England* (Oxford, 1951), 312–14; and for an older account which is still useful, R. H. Snape, *English Monastic Finances in the Later Middle Ages* (Cambridge, 1926), 143–4. For judgements stressing the long-term advantage to the religious in corrody agreements involving real property, see G. M. Cooper, 'The Premonstratensian Abbey of Bayham', *Sussex Archaeological Collections*, ix (1857), 145–81, at 159; and *Bath Cartularies* [i], xxiv.

A corrody was a special form of pension or annuity. Some corrodians enjoyed their privileges as a gift from the monks, but many, as will appear, paid for them. Moreover, those who paid normally paid in advance, by making over to the monastery in question either a piece of real property or a lump sum of money, and in one or other of these ways many purchased the right to enjoy their privileges for life. The perceived advantage to the corrodians was a degree of security for the future that the world outside the cloister could not give, and this was particularly valued by the weak and vulnerable. The gain to the monks was an addition to their estates, or to their cash in hand, not easily come by in other ways. Yet for the monks, it is argued, the system had dangers as well as advantages, and especially when corrodies were exchanged for money, for even if they charged enough for the corrody in the first place—and this depended on their capacity to predict how long the corrodian would live—the very possibility of raising money in this way encouraged them along the slippery slope of living beyond their income. Nor has it escaped notice that corrodies disturbed the peace of the monastic enclosure in a quite unnecessary way. From the belief that corrodians were in search of security, it has been an easy step to the belief that they were characteristically rather old—the senior citizens of medieval society, permitted to pass their declining years in an agreeable form of sheltered accommodation—and this belief, too, can be detected in some studies on the subject.

The legate Ottobuono, legislating at the Council of London in 1268, made a different point from any so far mentioned: the sale of corrodies, he said, defrauded the sick and the poor; and later authorities made his words their own.[4] Earlier, Archbishop Hubert Walter, attempting to put the troubled affairs of Cirencester Abbey in order, had spoken even more severely: the sale of corrodies, he said, resembled simony.[5] We do not have to ask whether the archbishop of Canterbury knew the meaning of this word when he used it: simony is the sale or purchase of spiritual things. But how could the sale of anything as earthy as portions of food, the central feature of most corrodies, be regarded as the sale of something spiritual? And how, exactly, would these things have been made available to the sick and poor had the corrodian not pre-empted them? So far, no account of the subject has, I believe, explored these questions.

I shall suggest, first, that the corrody system probably did absorb food and drink that would otherwise have gone to the poor, and, secondly, that

---

[4] *Councils and Synods*, II. ii. 788. Later authorities interpreted Ottobuono's prohibition of the sale of corrodies in a qualified sense: religious were not to grant more corrodies than they could properly support. I am grateful to Professor Michael Winterbottom for advice on the actual sense of this passage. See also below, pp. 191–2.

[5] *EEA* iii, no. 410; and for the text see *Cartulary of Cirencester Abbey*, ed. C. D. Ross and M. Devine (3 vols., Oxford, 1964–77), i. 295.

the distinction between grants in return for real property and grants in return for cash is of fundamental importance. The former grants were rarely to the disadvantage of the monks, but sometimes greatly to the disadvantage of the corrodian and his family.[6] In the latter case, however, the balance of advantage lay sometimes with the monks, sometimes with the corrodian. Yet the point is now often hard to determine—as it may often have been at the time.[7] And, finally, I shall suggest that marital status was quite as important a consideration as age in the calculations of the corrodians themselves. In a sense Latimer was right: widows enter into the matter.[8]

As a preliminary to all these topics of enquiry, the system itself must be described in greater detail.

## 2. The Main Kinds of Corrody

In common with other kinds of annuity, a corrody might include a cash allowance, but its distinctive feature was an allowance in kind. Indeed, the cash component crept into some arrangements only as a payment in lieu of benefits in kind for which the corrodian had no use: it was not central to the arrangements in question, as the benefits in kind were.[9] If, among the latter, fuel, light, clothing, and free housing are all mentioned quite frequently—as they are—victuals were the quintessential item. Allowances of victuals varied a great deal in detail, but underlying all the variety were two basic forms, and the difference between them is important.

### (i) Standardized arrangements

First, we must take note of the standardized arrangement, often referred to as a 'monk's corrody' or a 'servant's corrody'. A so-called monk's corrody included a daily ration of bread and ale, as given to a monk, together with the two dishes of cooked food at dinner which are mentioned in the Rule of St Benedict and which even the best-fed monastery always regarded as the centre-piece of the meal. But, throughout the Middle Ages, most monks actually had more than these two dishes, and a corrodian might have more too—if the extras were specified at the time. Accordingly, scattered through the surviving grants is a whole repertoire of phrases—'with buns', 'with cheese', 'with wine and flans when the monks have them', and, best of all, the umbrella phrase 'with pittances'—which enabled the more fortunate corrodians, or the more demanding among them, to approach the greater glory of the full monastic diet.[10] However few or many the extras that

---

[6] Below, pp. 192–8.      [7] Below, pp. 198–9, 205–7.      [8] Below, pp. 207–8.
[9] See e.g. Appendix V, nos. 53, 55, 64(i). On the relative importance of benefits in kind and cash benefits in some actual corrodies, see below, pp. 201–4.
[10] See e.g. Appendix V, nos. 2, 11–12; *Reg. Malm.* ii. 325; *Bath Cartularies* [ii], 31; and, from an Augustinian house, A. Heales, *Records of Merton Priory* (London, 1898), Appendix,

accompanied it, a monk's corrody gave a man, and *a fortiori* a woman, a sufficient ration of food and drink for a day, and if the ample messes served to a monk himself were used for the cooked food, there was something to spare, for a monk's mess included a share for the poor.[11]

As for a 'servant's corrody'—it always included a daily allowance of bread and ale, although often of the inferior kinds commonly given to lower servants. How much cooked food it included depended on the rank of the servant whom the monks and their corrodians had in mind. In some cases this item was omitted altogether: evidently, in these cases, it was assumed that the corrodian would give a portion of his own cooked food to his servant, or that the latter, like many of the monastery's own servants, would be allowed to consume leftovers of the monks' own meals.[12] But the servant's corrody, like the monk's corrody, represented a standardized arrangement: it related to a package that would have been familiar to everyone who ever put his head inside the monastic kitchen or refectory.

It was necessary for a corrodian whose benefits took this form to be in the monastery or its vicinity every day, if he was to enjoy his full benefits; and weekly attendance, to collect accumulated bread and ale, and perhaps raw materials in lieu of cooked food, was the indispensable minimum. Some, indeed, anticipating sharp practice on the part of the monastery in question, insisted on being present or represented when the allowances were measured out. Ernulf of Seint Oweyn, a twelfth-century corrodian of Malmesbury Abbey, stipulated that he or a deputy should be admitted to the monastery's cellar, to oversee the drawing of his daily ration of ale from the cask: he wanted to be sure that he received the best brew, to which he was entitled.[13] Many corrodians enjoying the kind of benefits which have been described were housed in dwellings in the monastic precinct, and the spouse and offspring who would share the dwelling are often mentioned in the agreement. But a male corrodian without these encumbrances might be offered a chamber in the monastery itself, and, if so, he would probably live

p. lx. The different daily values set on the victuals of corrodians at Glastonbury Abbey during the vacancy of 1322–3 may illustrate the same process of adding to the basic provision at the wish of the individual corrodian. See H. C. Maxwell-Lyte, 'Glastonbury Abbey in 1322', *Collectanea*, i (Somerset Record Soc. xxxix, 1924), 1–34, at 22–6; and for comment, I. Keil, 'Corrodies of Glastonbury Abbey in the later Middle Ages', *Proceedings of the Somerset Archaeological and Natural History Soc.* cviii (1964), 113–31, at 114.

Cf. the stark definition of the 'monk's corrody' to which corrodians with valid grants were entitled at Crowland Abbey, during the vacancy of 1328, as one loaf, $1\frac{1}{2}$ galls. conventual ale, and two dishes of cooked food per day (*Mon. Ang.* ii. 121).

[11] Above, pp. 13, 68–9.

[12] For servants' corrodies excluding cooked food, see Appendix V, nos. 15, 22, and 29; cf. no. 12, where cooked food is included. For servants' access to leftovers, see above, p. 174.

[13] *Reg. Malm.* ii. 323–5. But Ernulf probably had reason to be wary of monks; see below, pp. 194–6.

in the infirmary. In 1535, in one of the latest grants that they were ever to make, the monks of Fountains Abbey granted a corrody including living quarters in their infirmary to a priest named Thomas Wells, who was to be permitted to celebrate Mass in the infirmary chapel, the monks providing the necessary bread, wine, and candles.[14] Much earlier, Robert Tiptoft, one of Edward I's servants in Wales and Gascony, but also a corrodian of Westminster Abbey, no doubt found his chamber in the infirmary there a useful *pied-à-terre* when his duties brought him to London.[15]

## (ii) Selective arrangements

Secondly, however, there was the *ad hoc* arrangement which gave the corrodian in question, not a comprehensive and standardized allowance of victuals, but a selection, and one that often excluded cooked food. Such a corrody might consist, for example, of bread and ale without cooked food, or grain or flour but with nothing cooked, baked, or brewed. The exclusion of cooked food from the arrangements was convenient for those living at a distance, and appropriate for those near at hand who preferred home cooking to institutional food.[16] In these arrangements, quantities, too, were often settled *ad hoc* and not on the basis of a daily ration. Both features, the selective range of benefits and the tailor-made quantities, are well illustrated in the corrodies of Peterborough Abbey which were discussed by A. H. Thompson in a classic essay. One of these will serve as an example. In 1447 the monks of Peterborough granted a corrody to a local inhabitant named Henry Hopkyns, and the victuals comprised in it were: 24 loaves per week, and 24 gallons of ale, and, yearly, a quarter of oats for making oatmeal, and four bushels of salt.[17] No monk's corrody or servant's corrody here, but a list of items, and quantities exactly adjusted to the needs of Henry's household. Far from needing to be in the vicinity of the monastery every day, a corrodian who entered into this kind of arrangement could as well send a servant to collect his benefits once or twice a week, if as frequently, and in some of the grants made by Peterborough Abbey in this period it is envisaged that this will happen.[18] As for the monastery in these cases, it was in effect offering a range of services from which corrodians could choose, like customers in a supermarket.

The differences which I have tried to convey by contrasting 'selective' with 'standardized' were, in many cases, smaller than may at first appear, for the selective corrody was sometimes arrived at by subtracting items from the monk's corrody, which exemplifies the standardized arrangement, and adding new ones to what was left when this was done; and, as we have

---

[14] *Fountains Abbey Lease Book*, no. 240.   [15] Appendix V, no. 16.
[16] See e.g. Heales, *Records of Merton Priory*, Appendix, p. lx, where two corrodians living in the precinct are given the option of raw ingredients instead of cooked food.
[17] Thompson, 'Corrody', 122.   [18] Ibid. 120–1.

seen, even the monk's corrody, though universally known by a single name, varied in the individual case. Nevertheless, there were actual differences between the two kinds of corrody. Both existed from an early date. However, I shall not distort the facts, although I shall certainly simplify them, if I say that the standardized arrangement was typical down to the thirteenth century, and perhaps always typical of the somewhat grudging grants which monasteries made from time to time to royal nominees. From the thirteenth century onwards, however, the selective arrangement gained ground in transactions where corrodies were bought and sold, and from the mid-fourteenth century it was certainly typical of these.

## 3. Grants in General

### (i) How obtained?

It was possible to acquire a monastic corrody without payment, at least in the normal sense of this word. If, for example, it became necessary to ease the abbot or prior of the house into early retirement, on account of age, misdemeanour, or general incompetence, as not infrequently happened in Benedictine houses—and, indeed, in those of the newer orders, too—the proffer of a generous corrody, enabling him to live comfortably during his enforced rest, was a precondition of success for the monks or visitors charged with the delicate negotiations.[19] Moreover, in the late twelfth century and subsequently, corrodies were granted quite frequently to poor and not-so-poor secular clerks—a fact suggesting that monks felt some twinges of conscience about their success in appropriating tithes that would otherwise have gone to the secular clergy, or perhaps merely that bishops demanded this form of reparation when they licensed appropriations. Spalding Priory succeeded in appropriating considerably less than the entire rectory of Spalding, but the perpetual vicarage ordained here by the bishop of Lincoln at the end of the twelfth century included a very desirable corrody for a corrodian whose work obliged him to be a good deal out and about: in addition to a 'monk's corrody' of bread, ale, and cooked food daily, the vicar was to have fodder for his palfrey.[20] Trusted servants of the monastery might hope for a corrody of a kind in retirement and, in some houses, lodging in quarters set aside for this purpose. Such was 'the olde mane howse' reserved at Fountains Abbey for retired servants and others dependent on the monastery.[21] And a major reason for the monks' dislike of the

---

[19] For two Cistercian examples, see *Chron. Melsa* iii. 86–7, 275.

[20] *EEA* iv, no. 180. The vicarage also included tithes in the vill of Spalding and offerings, among which cheeses at Pentecost are mentioned. For a similar grant mentioning fodder see *Bath Cartularies* [ii], 16. It is of interest that 5 of the 15 persons entitled to monks' corrodies for life at Crowland Abbey in 1328 were chaplains (*capellani*) (*Mon. Ang.* ii. 121).

[21] *Fountains Abbey Lease Book*, no. 236; and for earlier parallels at, respectively, Crowland Abbey and Thornton Abbey, see *Visitations of Religious Houses*, ii. 59; ibid. iii. 380.

royal servants and retired warriors whom the king wished on them as corrodians from time to time must surely have been the fact that a quid pro quo was never forthcoming when these were taken in.[22]

Yet many corrodians purchased their privileges, and, as we have seen, payment normally took one or other of two forms: some corrodians made over to the monastery a piece of real property; others paid cash down. Many a monk's corrody, the standardized package of benefits which is much in evidence down to the mid-fourteenth century, was to our knowledge purchased with real property. It is noticeable, too, that in many cases the property made over to the monastery in exchange for a corrody was the entire estate of the would-be corrodian, and in consequence his family was disinherited by the transaction—hence the provision for offspring which was sometimes included in the agreement. No other feature of the corrody system has done as much as this to foster the belief that corrodians exploited their chosen monasteries; yet the need to provide for children followed inescapably from the consequences of the transaction for their existing prospects. Simon Payne of Friston, in Sussex, was, it seems, Mr Quiverful himself. As part of his agreement with the Premonstratensian canons of Bayham in 1290, Simon persuaded the canons to allow one of his sons, who may have been rather delicate, to live off the alms which were given to the abbey, put two others to a trade in the abbey until they could support themselves, and promise a little cash to each of his four daughters by two marriages—all in return for the freehold of his small estate in Friston; but the latter was, it appears, his entire estate.[23]

The selective corrodies, characteristic of the later Middle Ages, were normally purchased with cash, and, moreover, with cash payable in advance. On occasion, some large sums are mentioned: £100 and more—and this in a period when, in landholding society, a clear income of £100 per annum served to distinguish the greater gentry from the lesser.[24] In some cases, it is true, appearances are deceptive, for the corrody agreement actually masks a loan from the corrodian to the monastery. An agreement of this kind may well exemplify financial relations between the parties that were, in A. H. Thompson's phrase, 'constant and complicated'.[25] In such a case, it would

---

[22] For royal nominees, see below, p. 189.

[23] Colvin, *White Canons in England*, 313; see also Cooper, in 'The Premonstratensian Abbey of Bayham', 158–9.

[24] An inference from tax thresholds in 1436, for which see H. L. Gray, 'Incomes from land in England in 1436', *EHR* xlix (1934), 607–39, at 623; and for a perceptive discussion of this subject, S. J. Payling, *Political Society in Lancastrian England* (Oxford, 1991), 1–18. For corrody transactions involving down-payments of £100 or more in the 15th cent. see Thompson, 'Corrody', 119 n., and below, Appendix V, nos. 52, 54, and 64(i).

[25] Thompson, 'Corrody', 125, where the reference is to the financial relations of John de la Bere, bishop of St David's 1447–60, with Peterborough Abbey. Note also among transactions at Peterborough, the sale, in or before 1437, of a corrody worth £20 p.a. to Thomas Mortymere, reputedly for £300 or £400. The debt of £40 owed by the abbot of Peterborough to Mortymere, at the latter's death a few years later, suggests that there was a continuing financial relationship

be misleading to consider the purchase-price of the corrody without some knowledge of the wider context, and naïve to wonder how the corrodian who purchased it laid hands on so much ready money: he was a capitalist who could probably have afforded the sum involved many times over. Quite frequently, however, the transaction can be taken at its face value, and it is in these cases that the payments mentioned are sometimes large in relation to the known resources of the corrodians who paid them. Some remind us of the wide gap that often existed in the later Middle Ages between formal and actual earnings—a gap sometimes exemplified in the earnings of the clergy as well as those of the laity. Richard Saxilby, who paid £20 for his corrody at Westminster Abbey in 1460–1, was curate of the parish church of St Margaret's, Westminster, and his income in that capacity was probably not much, if at all, in excess of £10 per annum.[26] The sum of £20, though quite modest in comparison to some other payments for corrodies received by the Abbey in the fifteenth century, represents perhaps twice Saxilby's annual income as curate and suggests that he had other sources of income in addition to the latter.

## (ii) Term and mode of grant

The great majority of grants known to us were for a life-term, and when spouses were involved it was usual, from the thirteenth century onwards, to specify that the surviving spouse should have a life-interest; nor, in the early Middle Ages, were perpetual grants unknown. But we should beware, at this point, of a bias in our sources, which are much more likely to record life-terms or perpetuities than anything less permanent. In fact, corrodies were granted for a variety of terms and some were held, as land was some-times held, for no term at all, but insecurely, from week to week or month to month. From time to time in the second half of the fourteenth century, Westminster Abbey sold the corrodies of bread, ale, and cooked food of monks who were in residence at Oxford, and it probably did so on a weekly basis.[27]

between the parties (ibid. 119 n.; *Visitations of Religious Houses*, iii. 274–5, 281, 289). For implied relationships of a similar kind between the abbot of Westminster and some of the Abbey's corrodians in the mid-15th cent. see Appendix V, nos. 56, 62, 64.

[26] Appendix V, no. 65. Richard Saxilby paid a rent of £10 13s. 4d. p.a. to the Abbey sacrist for his curacy. For the suggestion that the sacrist, whether paying the curate of St Margaret's a stipend or, as in Saxilby's case, requiring him to take a lease of the curacy in return for a rent, would have intended to leave the curate with an income of £10 'more or less', see Rosser, *Medieval Westminster*, 341 n. 1; and for a glimpse of one of Saxilby's other interests, a tene-ment and garden in Long Ditch, ibid. 337 n. 17.

[27] WAM 19854–9, 19864, 19866. The monks in question were William de Yepeswich, John Stowe, William Colchester, Peter Combe, and John Farnago. See also Appendix V, no. 45. Cf. the claim of the abbot of Whitby in 1366 that the sale of a monk's corrody at Whitby helped to finance a monk at the university (*Chapters of English Black Monks*, iii. 68). For terms of a quarter, half, or whole year in secular lodging houses in the City of London in the mid-13th cent., see *Councils and Synods*, II. i. 336 [18].

If, however, he wished to stay for any length of time, it was a wise corrodian who obtained a written grant under the common seal of the monastery in question. If the abbot were to die, Exchequer officials administering the goods of the house during the ensuing vacancy might refuse to recognize the existence of corrodians who could not show such a grant, and fail to make specific provision for them; and they were more likely to adopt this attitude after 1300 than previously. As far as we know, even before 1300, keepers—the Exchequer officials—failed to make formal provision for corrodians. Yet they may in practice have made some allowance for them in their total provision for the monastery in question. Early in the fourteenth century, however, keepers began to scrutinize claims with a new particularity. The principle that corrodies were secure during a vacancy only if confirmed in writing is implied in the inquest into claims for allowances at Crowland Abbey during the vacancy of 1328: in the end, but not without careful scrutiny of claims, the Exchequer agreed to make allowances for sixteen corrodians who, we are told, possessed written documents under the common seal of the house.[28]

A corrodian with a life-grant was in a strong position, not only *vis-à-vis* the Exchequer but also in relation to the monastery itself, for at law he was possessed of a free tenement, and, to the indignation of the monastic Order, the Statute of Westminster II, enacted in 1285, permitted him to use the assize of novel disseisin against the monastery if his benefits were withdrawn.[29] The introduction of this remedy suggests that monasteries not infrequently grew weary of their corrodians and attempted to speed the parting guest. But we should remember at this point that corrodies which had been granted in perpetuity or for a life-term might, as free tenements, change hands *inter vivos*. In consequence, monks were sometimes in the unenviable position of having lodgers and near neighbours whom they had not selected themselves.[30] Nor did they select the royal nominees who were thrust upon them from time to time and who normally held for life.

---

[28] *Mon. Ang.* ii. 121. At Crowland and elsewhere, the practice of specifying the number of corrodians for whom allowances were to be made *abbatia vacante* was probably an innovation of this period; so too the specification of a precise rate per person per day. For the consequences of this change for our capacity to count corrodians see below, p. 189. The new particularity extended to the allowances made for the monks themselves during vacancies; see PRO C260/35/14, for the arrangements made at Abingdon abbey in 1322 and Thorney Abbey in 1323.
(I am greatly indebted to Dr Margaret Howell for generous help with these points and for the PRO reference.) For the rate at Crowland in 1328, see above, n. 10.

[29] Statute of Westminster II, cap. 25 (*SR* i. 84); *Councils and Synods*, II. ii. 964 [3], 966 [3]; D. W. Sutherland, *The Assize of Novel Disseisin* (Oxford, 1973), 135–6.

[30] For an example of the application of the mayor's seal to a deed of sale in London in the mid-14th cent. see *Cal. Plea and Mem. R. 1323–1364*, 204; and for 13th-cent. examples of life-grants with the right of alienation, *Bath Cartularies* [ii], 27, and Heales, *Records of Merton Priory*, Appendix, p. lx.

### (iii) Chronology and frequency

A chronology for the curious institution which has been described can take into account only long-term grants, since only these have left persistent traces in the records, and it must be said frankly that this is a serious limitation, both on the immediate enquiry and on the history of lodgers and lodgings more widely conceived. At present, all too little is known about the demand for temporary accommodation and keep in medieval England, and the supply of these amenities. The short-term arrangements which monasteries made from time to time with corrodians would enlarge our knowledge, if we could but trace them. If, however, our viewpoint is that of the monasteries, there can be no questioning the overriding importance of the long-term grants, which could have protracted consequences for monastic finances and the peace of the cloister. For these, a very broad chronology is now generally accepted, and on a superficial view it suggests a degree of success for the authorities who for so long tried to outlaw them. Take-off, it is agreed, occurred in the twelfth century, and throughout the next century grants proceeded at a brisk pace, to reach their peak for the entire Middle Ages in the years around 1300. Later, however—but exactly when is unclear—they declined, and by the early sixteenth century they were running at the very modest rate which is reflected in the returns to the Dissolution inquiries of the 1530s. In the lesser houses for men which were dissolved in 1536 and for which exact figures exist, there was on average less than one corrodian for every ten religious, and there is no reason to think that the average in the greater houses at this time was significantly different.[31] How well does this chronology withstand closer scrutiny?

Some of the questions put by the royal commissioners in 1536 were evidently understood differently from county to county, and to this extent Henry VIII's inquiry recalls the greater inquest of 1086. It may be on account of misunderstandings of this kind that the lesser houses in Sussex now claimed to have no corrodians at all other than two ex-priors who had been granted pensions.[32] Indeed, in 1536 questions were to some extent understood differently from monastery to monastery. Yet it is extremely unlikely that the actual number of corrodians in the early sixteenth century was of a different order from that suggested by these returns, for it is in fact quite unusual to uncover a grant in monastic sources in the half century or so before the Dissolution. And we are unlikely to discover that the practice

---

[31] *RO* iii. 267; see also Savine, *English Monasteries on the Eve of the Dissolution*, 241–5.

[32] *L & P Henry VIII*, xi, Appendix 2, pp. 591–2. For the safeguarding of the interests of corrodians in 1536, see 27 Henry VIII, cap. 28 (iii) (*SR* iii. 576), and, for comment, Youings, *Dissolution of the Monasteries*, 43. Cf. the marks left by the circuit organization of the Domesday inquiries on the information in the Survey relating to ploughlands (S. J. P. Harvey, 'Taxation and the ploughland in Domesday Book', in P. Sawyer (ed.), *Domesday Book: A Reassessment* (London, 1985), 86–103, at 88.

of granting corrodies for a long term began on a significant scale in any other century but the twelfth. I shall suggest that take-off then was intimately connected with a monastic campaign for the recovery of alienated property which gained momentum in the course of this century.[33] We shall not go far wrong if we date the real beginning to the middle decades of this century.

The existence of a peak in grants in the decades around 1300 is much less certain. To be precise, it is uncertain what the monks themselves contributed to an apparent peak at this time; and, that being so, it is also uncertain how we should see the latter in relation to the landscape on either side.

From *c.*1290 to the end of Edward II's reign, the king tried to exploit monastic corrodies as never before, and at the beginning of this period the monasteries, for their part, had not yet perfected the art of frustrating royal claims, as they were soon to do, by pleading poverty, or the lack of a precedent for what was demanded—or, indeed, by deploying any other argument that seemed serviceable on the occasion in question. Eventually, monasteries would succeed in containing royal demands and restricting them normally to houses of the king's patronage. When, however, in 1315, the clergy formally protested to the king about the burden currently imposed on monasteries by his demands, there was probably substance in the complaint; and Edward III's undertaking, in the first parliament of his reign, to ask for corrodies only 'where he ought', shows that the topic was still a lively issue.[34]

In the same period, Exchequer officials, administering the goods of monasteries when abbacies were vacant, began to note the precise number of corrodians claiming subsistence during the vacancy in question. Understandably in these cases, they took account of all corrodians, including the royal nominees, and not only those who had entered by purchase and who therefore represent the monastery's self-inflicted wounds. Our most notorious figures come from these sources, and no comparable figures exist for any earlier period. When, however, we can put the matter to the test, the peak in grants at this time proves to be, to a considerable extent, a result of factors outside the monks' control. In 1322–3, as we learn from a vacancy account of that year, Glastonbury Abbey, which then housed a community of sixty monks, had as many as nineteen corrodians. But only eleven of the nineteen had entered by purchase: six were royal nominees, and two were

---

[33] Below, p. 193

[34] 9 Edward II, statute 1 (*Articuli Cleri*), cap. xi; 1 Edward III, statute 2, cap. x (*SR* i. 173, 256). For comment, see *Corrodies at Worcester in the 14th Century*, ed. J. M. Wilson and E. C. Jones (Worcestershire Historical Society, 1917), 6–7; S. M. Wood, *English Monasteries and their Patrons in the Thirteenth Century* (Oxford, 1955), 107–11; J. H. Tillotson, 'Pensions, corrodies and religious houses: an aspect of the relations of Crown and Church in early fourteenth-century England', *Journal of Religious History*, viii (1974–5), 127–43. For the kind of argument that proved successful against the king after 1327, see Wood, *English Monasteries*, 114–15.

officials of the monastery.[35] In the mid-fifteenth century, visitation records point to the same conclusion. William Alnwick's visitation of religious houses in the diocese of Lincoln seems to have uncovered few serious breaches of the rules relating to corrodies. The abbot of Bardney Abbey, it was alleged in 1437–8, had sold a corrody without asking the consent of the four junior monks in the community—a somewhat brazen accusation, since three of the four, though professed for seven years, had not yet signed a deed of profession and were probably suspended from participation in chapter acts.[36] In a house where all was far from well at this time and the abbot clearly unequal to his responsibilities, we can only be impressed by the lack of more serious charges.

In general, it may be suggested, both in the early Middle Ages and later, monks were normally restrained in making grants of this kind. Certainly, the only comprehensive figures which exist at present point to this conclusion. At Glastonbury Abbey, a maximum number of ninety-six grants has come to light between c.1280 and the dissolution of the monastery in 1539, a period of c.260 years. Royal nomination accounted for forty-nine (51 per cent) of the total; sales for between twenty-five and thirty (26–31 per cent).[37] At Westminster Abbey, a maximum of about sixty-five grants can be traced over a somewhat longer period, c.1250–1540, and this figure includes ten which the king requested for his servants but which he may never have obtained.[38] Some grants made by the monks of Westminster may have escaped notice, but the surviving archive of this house is probably good enough for us to be confident that the actual figure for long-term grants was not much above sixty-five. Surprisingly, in view of their situation so near the royal palace, the monks of Westminster were more successful than the monks of Glastonbury in fending off the royal nominee; or perhaps their situation was a positive advantage in giving them early warning of an impending attack. A maximum of sixteen (25 per cent) of the known grants in the period 1250–1540 went to such people,[39] and, given as many as ten cases which are now uncertain, the actual number may have been considerably smaller than this. At any one time the Abbey may have had four or five corrodians on its books of its own volition, but if ever it had more the period was exceptional.

---

[35] Maxwell-Lyte, 'Glastonbury Abbey in 1322', 22–6; and for analysis, Keil, 'Corrodies of Glastonbury Abbey', 114. For the 16 corrodians of Crowland Abbey in 1328, which then had 41 monks, see above, p. 187. In both cases, however, the reference is to corrodians with written titles.

[36] *Visitations of Religious Houses*, ii. 15, 23. The deponent, John Sallowe, was one of the four. For William Gray's injunction relating to corrodies at Bardney, see ibid. i. 4.

[37] Keil, 'Corrodies of Glastonbury Abbey', 119–31. Nearly all the sales were made before 1340.

[38] Appendix V, nos. 7–69, among which 62 and 64 record double grants. The doubtful cases are nos. 18, 24–7, 31, 34, 38–40.          [39] Appendix V, nos. 16, 18–21, 23–7, 31, 34, 38–41.

## (iv) Consequences for the sick and poor

What, then, is the evidence pointing to the conclusion that corrodies robbed the sick and poor? There is very little explicit evidence of this kind, but the circumstantial evidence is strong. The legate Ottobuono's opposition to the sale of corrodies on these grounds, anticipated in a sense by Hubert Walter's perception of the practice as simony, is itself evidence that such an abuse was taking place at the time. Ottobuono spelt out his meaning: because corrodies were sold, fewer of the poor and sick were cared for in monasteries—or, for that matter, in hospitals—and alms were deflected from their proper destination.[40] There was, of course, a general sense in which the poor were robbed whenever monks took on a needless commitment, for the more numerous the calls on their resources, the smaller the surplus available for the poor guests whom St Benedict especially commended to their care.[41] But Ottobuono probably had something more particular in mind. Monasteries gave to the poor in quite specific ways, and principally by making over to them the leftovers of food and drink in the refectory and the monks' cast-off clothing. As we have seen, by the thirteenth century, Ottobuono's century, much of this surplus was given, not casually to the utterly poor— the naked poor, as they were called—but systematically to poor who were institutionalized, and sometimes to poor who were resident in the almonry itself.[42] This turning away from the naked poor made it easier than it might otherwise have been to give to those who were not actually poor at all but capable of offering a *quid pro quo* for their corrodies. Almost certainly, Ottobuono's words mean that some of the corrodies which were now being sold consisted of food and drink that would otherwise have found their way from the refectory to the almonry for the use of the poor and sick there.

Much later, we have a little specific evidence of this abuse. A monk's corrody—that is, his daily allowance of food and drink—was in principle placed on the table whether or not he was present to consume it, and in principle, at the end of the meal, it went with the broken meats to the poor. Thus the practice, already noticed at Westminster Abbey in the fourteenth century, of selling the corrodies of monks who were in residence at Oxford deflected the food and drink in question from the poor.[43] Similarly, the sale of the corrody that was by custom put out in the refectory for a deceased monk during the year following his death robbed the poor, since this, too, was intended for them. Yet we are told that when Br. Richard Tedyngton died at Westminster in 1487, his corrody was sold to a physician named Thomas during the ensuing year: he was probably Thomas Huntyngdon, physician to the convent of Westminster at this time.[44] At Thornton Abbey, in Lincolnshire, an Augustinian house, the alms sold by the canons acquired

---

[40] *Councils and Synods*, II. ii. 788.    [41] *Rule*, cap. liii.
[42] Above, pp. 16–21.    [43] Above, p. 186.    [44] Appendix V, no. 67.

a special name: they were 'little corrodies'; and some deponents at the visitation of this house in 1440 evidently connected the practice of selling them with the disappearance of a number of poor clerks who had formerly lived in the almonry and served the canons' Masses.[45]

## 4. Grants in Exchange for Real Property

### (i) Economic and legal contexts

Next, I shall discuss corrody agreements involving the surrender of real property by the prospective corrodian. These, I have suggested, were normally to the advantage of the monastery in question but sometimes to the disadvantage of the corrodian. But what grounds are there for reaching this conclusion?

It is well known that many agreements of this kind involved estates belonging to the lesser gentry or free peasantry. Less well noticed, perhaps, is the fact that many of the corrodians who offered that kind of property in exchange for a corrody were free tenants of the monastery in question. In such cases, the corrodians surrendered into the hands of the monastery property which the latter had granted to them or their ancestors, or which they had nevertheless held of the monastery on terms generally regarded as secure and heritable. The monastery, for its part, now acquired the full rights of an owner, as distinct from the restricted rights of a lord in the property. To use more technical language: the monastery now took back into its demesne part of the subinfeudated portion of its estate; and this, to the monks, was the main purpose of the transaction. When, for example, in 1147, the abbot and convent of Peterborough granted Robert of Torpel a monk's corrody for himself, together with corrodies, described as knights' corrodies, for four of his servants, and received in exchange Robert's surrender of all his land in the manors of Cotterstock and Glapthorn, they took back into their demesne lands which had been granted by their predecessors to one of Robert's ancestors before 1086.[46] Moreover, the recovery of land in this way for the demesne estate of the monastery seems to have been a common feature of the transactions under consideration, as of monastic land transactions in general, not only in the twelfth century, but also for a long time to come. Professor King has written of a 'continuous' movement of property to Peterborough Abbey from its own knights and freeholders in the late twelfth century and the thirteenth, and of 'sustained campaigns' on the Abbey's part, from time to time, to bring this about.[47] In

---

[45] *Visitations of Religious Houses*, iii. 372, 374, 380. But elderly friends and servants of the canons may also have lost by the sale of the corrodies in question.

[46] King, *Peterborough Abbey, 1086–1310*, 27–8; and, for the sequel, below, pp. 197–8.

[47] King, *Peterborough Abbey, 1086–1310*, 53, 67.

the thirteenth century, the monks of Ramsey pursued a considered policy of recovering freeholds for their demesne estate.[48] In the same period, the monks of Battle Abbey repurchased a considerable number of properties from tenants in Battle itself and in rural Kent and Sussex, and the role of corrodies in these transactions seems to have been important.[49]

Why were monks now so anxious to recover possession of estates which their predecessors had been content to alienate? There were, of course, sound economic reasons for such a policy. Land held in demesne yielded a much higher return to its owner than land granted in fee to a tenant, and monks, who had to struggle hard from the mid-twelfth century onwards to maintain their income in an inflationary age, were no doubt fully aware of this reason for recovering fees whenever they could. And a monastery's acquisitions on its own fee could easily be absorbed into its existing endowment.[50] But in all their calculations and contrivances, they were not motivated solely by economic considerations. In two important essays, Mrs Mary Cheney has shown how strong the ideological arguments for the recovery of alienated property were for the Church in general from the mid-twelfth century onwards. The alienation, said the canonists, was in itself unlawful, and the land in question was to be recovered, though always with due recompense to the occupier.[51] The principle was ancient; the momentum required to enforce it, new in this period. However modest the properties which the monks acquired by the sale of corrodies, the transactions are to be seen in this larger context—the need to recover what should never have been lost.

## (ii) The circumstances of the corrodians

Given the general context, what particular circumstances inclined monks or any of their tenants to enter into a bargain of this kind? Historical demographers, and historians employing their models, help us to make sense of many episodes which would otherwise appear confusing and disparate. Typically, they argue, the life-cycle of the poor in medieval and early modern England went through phases, described as phases of high risk, when a yawning gap might open between income and expenditure. If it did, the

---

[48] J. A. Raftis, *The Estates of Ramsey Abbey* (Toronto, 1957), 103–12. For the repurchase of fees by the monks of Westminster in the 13th and 14th cents., see Harvey, *Estates*, 164–9.

[49] E. Searle, *Lordship and Community: Battle Abbey and its Banlieu, 1066–1538* (Toronto, 1974), 144–54.

[50] B. J. Thompson, 'The Church and the Aristocracy: Lay and Ecclesiastical Landowning Society in Fourteenth-Century Norfolk' (Ph.D. thesis, Cambridge, 1990), 205. Dr Thompson also points out that acquisitions on the fee could not be vetoed by mesne lords.

[51] M. Cheney, 'The litigation between John Marshal and Archbishop Thomas Becket in 1164: a pointer to the origin of novel disseisin', *Law and Social Change in British History*, ed. J. A. Guy and H. G. Beale (London, 1984), 9–26, at 19–21: id., 'Inalienability in mid-twelfth-century England: enforcement and consequences', *Monumenta Juris Canonici*, Series C: Subsidia, vii (1985), 467–78.

family in question became for a time unable to keep itself and might well have its whole future reshaped by a fortuitous event, such as the onset of chronic illness or the death of its principal bread-winner. Thus a poor family with several children, none of whom was of an age to contribute to the family income, might depend for a considerable number of years on the assistance of the kin or local community. If, however, the bread-winner died in this period, the family household might well break up altogether.[52]

Monastic corrodians are rarely to be numbered among the truly poor. Some, however, were poorer than others, and some evidently entered into their bargains with the monastery in question at a time when the risks to their economic survival were greater than usual. Indeed, this may be true of the widows of whom Latimer wrote with so much disapproval. Since they had evidently given up all hope of remarrying, it is possible that they were rather old; and old age, with its progressive incapacity for work, is one of the classic phases of high risk. Simon Payne was perhaps in a dangerous phase of a different kind when, in 1290, he took up the offer of a corrody at the expense of the canons of Bayham, for to have too many children was to be as much at risk as to be old—and in the thirteenth century to have seven children, if possessed of only a small estate, was to have too many.[53] When Robert of Torpel made his agreement with Peterborough Abbey, in 1147, he probably possessed an adequate income, for at an earlier juncture he had paid 40 marks (£26 13s. 4d.)—a large sum for the period—for the lands which he now made over to the monks. What Robert lacked was not the means to live independently, but the physical capacity to do so, for he was a leper.[54]

Yet when we have made due allowance for these factors, we are left, quite often, with transactions where it is hard to acquit the monks of putting pressure on a reluctant tenant to surrender his land in exchange for a corrody: they uncovered a weakness in his title and exploited the discovery. One casualty of this practice was perhaps a corrodian who has already been mentioned—Ernulf of Seint Oweyn.[55]

Ernulf was no peasant: he held an estate in Wiltshire comprising the vill of Chelworth, with fifteen hides of 'good land', with woodland and pastures appurtenant, and other lands in addition to these. However, in the 1140s or 1150s, he surrendered the entire estate to Malmesbury Abbey, which agreed to discharge the service of one knight owing to the king. In exchange he received a monk's corrody, with wine and flans, the promise of winter and summer clothing each year, and confraternity with the monks, who

---

[52] R. M. Smith, 'Some issues concerning families and their property in rural England 1250–1800', *Land, Kinship and Life-Cycle*, 1–86, at 68–85; T. Wales, 'Poverty, poor relief and the life-cycle: some evidence from seventeenth-century Norfolk', ibid. 351–404, at 367–81. In both essays, the assistance from kin is judged of marginal significance.          [53] Above, p. 185.
[54] King, *Peterborough Abbey, 1086–1310*, 28.          [55] Above, p. 182.

undertook to pray for him daily at Mass. The agreement stipulated that Ernulf should move from the manor house (*curia*) at Chelworth, and live in that at Cole Park, until the monks should have found him a fitting tenement and a virgate of land to go with it—a condition unfulfilled for ten years or more. His need for fuel was met by a clause permitting a man of his to go three times a day into the woods at Cole Park, to collect firewood. The grant was to be enjoyed by Ernulf and his lawful heirs, and the tenement and virgate were to be held on the same heritable terms. Moreover, we know that Ernulf actually had sons, for the monks promised to see that his *pueri* were promoted to holy orders, and a son named Robert, who was presumably his heir, was later said to have been associated with him in the surrender of his lands.[56]

A corrodian possessed of a substantial estate and male heirs to inherit it, who nevertheless surrendered all his property and agreed to leave his own residence, before it was known where his permanent home for the future would be, deserves our attention. To monks with long memories, however, Ernulf of Seint Oweyn's situation was not quite as secure as it may have appeared to most people to be at the time. Security, in fact, was the great prize which he gained by his transaction with the monks of Malmesbury.

The nucleus of Ernulf's property was probably the estate of four hides in Chelworth which a tenant named William held, not in chief, but of Malmesbury Abbey in 1086, William being, almost certainly, Ernulf's grandfather.[57] However, these hides had a long history. They lay in Crudwell, which was itself part of a much larger estate centred on Kemble, now in Gloucestershire, and allegedly given to the church at Malmesbury by Caedwalla of Wessex at the end of the seventh century.[58] If the church possessed them at this early date, she evidently lost possession later, for at the end of the ninth century Alfred gave them to his minister Dudi for four

---

[56] *Reg. Malm.* ii. 323–4, 326–8. Ernulf surrendered his 15 hides *temp.* Abbot Peter Morant (1141–61); he received the virgate *temp.* Abbot Robert (1171/2–c.1180). For the abbots, see *Heads of Religious Houses*, 55; and I am also indebted here to Dr. N. P. Berry.

[57] *DB* i. 67ᵃ (*VCH Wilts.* ii. 126 [77]); and for Ernulf's grandfather, William, *Reg. Malm.* ii. 324. In the following account, I have tried to make sense of evidence which contains some apparent inconsistencies. Some of the difficulties are eased if it is assumed that words have been lost from the grant of the corrody to Ernulf, which survives in cartulary copies. See the puzzling *que quidem terra continet quindecim hydatas bone terre unde Willelmus avus meus habuit ex dono domini regis* (PRO E 164/24 (= KR Misc. Bks. i. 24), fo. 284ᵛ; BL Lansdowne MS 417, fos. 203–204ᵛ; *Reg. Malm.* ii. 324). The missing words are needed after *unde*. For this suggestion, and for much generous help with this episode, I am indebted to Dr Pierre Chaplais. For an able account of Ernulf of Seint Oweyn and Malmesbury Abbey's estate in Chelworth, which differs in some respects from that given above, see N. P. Berry, 'The Estates and Privileges of Malmesbury Abbey in the Thirteenth Century' (Ph.D. thesis, University of Reading, 1989), i. 55–7.

[58] Sawyer, 231, 234. However, Malmesbury Abbey later attributed the gift of 10 hides at Kemble and 10 at Crudwell to Æthelwulf of Wessex (Sawyer, 305; and see *VCH Wilts.* ii. 89–90).

lives, with reversion to the church at Malmesbury.[59] This reversion implies
a continuing recognition of Malmesbury Abbey's right. The church obtained possession in 901, though at the price of relinquishing another estate,
for as many as five lives, and only, as it appears, to lose it again subsequently.[60] Ernulf claimed that the king had granted Chelworth to his
grandfather, and we can safely identify this king with the 'King William' for
whom Masses were endowed when the monks made their agreement with
Ernulf. He was probably William I. But the king's path may have been
smoothed by the co-operation of the abbot of Malmesbury for the time
being. If so, the abbot was probably Warin (1070–*c*.1091), formerly a monk
of Lire, in Normandy, who was remembered at Malmesbury as an abbot
who had alienated the goods of the house.[61] These circumstances explain the
existence in the Malmesbury archive of a crude twelfth-century forgery,
forbidding all men, not excepting the king or abbot, to alienate land in
Chelworth from the church.[62] Crude the forgery may have been, but the
principle that church lands were inalienable did perhaps play a part in per-
suading Ernulf of Seint Oweyn to exchange his ancestral estate for a corrody
at Malmesbury Abbey.

In 1185, thirty or forty years after Ernulf of Seint Oweyn's surrender to
the monks of Malmesbury, the abbot of Westminster made a final concord
in the king's court with two brothers, Richard and William de Paddington: it
concerned the tenement which Richard and William held in the manor from
which they were named.[63] Earlier, there had been a plea about the property.
Now, the two brothers surrendered the tenement, and accepted corrodies at
Westminster Abbey for themselves and their respective wives for life.
Moreover, the abbot and convent undertook to give the brothers the large
sum of 40 marks (£26 13s. 4d.). The prestigious names of the justices who
saw to this fine—among them, those of Ranulf Glanvill, Geoffrey de Luci,
and Hubert Walter—may indicate the real difficulty of the case, or the kind
of panel that a wealthy monastery of the period could interest in its pleas,
if it was so minded; or both circumstances may be indicated. At any rate,
the monks got the land, although their tenants had evidently been reluctant
to surrender it.

It is possible that when the legal status of peasant tenures was clarified in
the second half of the twelfth century, the land of Richard and William de
Paddington fell on what was, from the monks' point of view, the wrong

---

[59] Sawyer, 356; William of Malmesbury, *Gesta Pontificum Anglorum*, ed. N. E. S. A.
Hamilton (RS 1870), 394–5; *VCH Wilts*. iii. 213.

[60] Sawyer, 1205, 1797; *Reg. Malm*. i. 303–4.

[61] *Reg. Malm*. ii. 7; *Letters of Pope Innocent III (1198–1216) concerning England and Wales*,
ed. C. R. Cheney and M. G. Cheney (Oxford, 1967), no. 1061; and for Warin, see William of
Malmesbury, *Gesta Pontificum Anglorum*, 421, and *Heads of Religious Houses*, 55.

[62] *Reg. Malm*. ii. 316–17.     [63] WAM 16194; and see Appendix V, no. 5.

side of the line. In consequence, it was perhaps enjoyed for a time by its occupiers as a free tenement; but its status was not sufficiently clear to save them, in the end, from dispossession.[64] Seventy or eighty years later, another corrody granted by the monks of Westminster seems to belong in this very context: dispute about the status of a relatively modest holding. Osbert, a tenant of the Abbey at Stevenage, whose designation as a palmer may mean that he had made the pilgrimage to the Holy Land, surrendered a virgate of land in the manor, together with five acres of assarted land. He recognized that the virgate had once been customary land, and the monks, for their part, granted him a life-interest in his dwelling and in the croft and garden appurtenant to it, together with a corrody. The latter consisted of six quarters of wheat, two quarters of barley, and one quarter of oats per annum, four cartloads of wood for fuel, and a clothing allowance. Later, however, they relented and allowed Osbert a life-interest in the virgate itself, though not in the assart.[65] The restoration of the land to Osbert for his life tells us that he was not an old man, but active and still capable of working his land when he surrendered it to the monks.

The monastic campaign for the recovery of alienated property helps to explain the concern about acquisitions of land in mortmain which was voiced from time to time in the century before the enactment of the Statute of Mortmain in 1279.[66] Yet it sheds an ironic light on the statute and earlier attempts to grapple with the problem of mortmain. The main thrust of all this legislation was towards protecting the interests of the lords whose tenants wished to alienate. Monks, however, actually used their position as lords to promote the flow of property to the Church. If the suggestions made above are correct, some monks engaged in this work developed a rather predatory attitude towards tenants who combined small properties with vulnerable titles; and when this happened, the corrody system served their purpose.

Sometimes, of course, the monks overreached themselves in this kind of transaction. Indeed, the abbot and convent of Peterborough did so in the

---

[64] For the legal background see P. R. Hyams, *King, Lords and Peasants in Medieval England: The Common Law of Villeinage in the Twelfth and Thirteenth Centuries* (Oxford, 1980), 221–65.

[65] WD 213ᵛ–214; and see Appendix V, no. 10. See also ibid., no. 4, where the phrase *et quicquid juris in eadem villa habere videbatur* suggests that a dispute about title underlay Gilbert de Claygate's surrender of his land in part exchange for a corrody, *temp.* Henry II.

[66] Magna Carta (1217), cc. 39, 43; 'Petition of the Barons' (1258), c. 10; Provisions of Westminster (1259), c. 14 (*Select Charters and Other Illustrations of English Constitutional History from the Earliest Times to the Reign of Edward I*, ed. W. Stubbs (9th edn., rev. H. W. C. Davis, Oxford, 1921), 343; *Documents of the Baronial Movement of Reform and Rebellion, 1258–67*, ed. R. F. Treharne and I. J. Sanders (OMT 1973), 80, 144). For comment see P. A. Brand, 'The control of mortmain alienation in England, 1200–1300', in J. H. Baker (ed.), *Legal Records and the Historian* (London, 1978), 29–40; S. Raban, *Mortmain Legislation and the English Church, 1279–1500* (Cambridge, 1982), 12–16.

case of Robert Torpel. The lands which Robert made over to the monks in exchange for a corrody represented only a small part of the whole honour of Torpel. They had once been the marriage portion of his sister, and Robert had purchased them from her husband. The record of Robert's grant of these lands to Peterborough Abbey in 1147 stresses his freedom to execute it: when he received the lands, the king and many barons had agreed that they were his to hold or to alienate as he pleased.[67] But this very note in the record suggests that objections were anticipated; and evidently they occurred, for in Henry II's reign the Torpel family recovered Robert's lands for their own demesne.[68] But the Torpels were a powerful family—the premier family among the honorial baronage of Peterborough Abbey at this date. Few, perhaps, of the families whose fortunes as landholders were adversely affected by the traffic in corrodies could hope ever to recover their property, once surrendered.

### (iii) The balance of advantage

Even so, did monks actually gain from this kind of transaction? When they granted a corrody in return for real property, they pledged future income, represented by the annual cost of the corrody until the corrodian should die, in order to augment their landed estate—their chief capital asset. They could reduce the demands on income by making over to their corrodians victuals that were in principle set aside for charitable use.[69] They could even profess fewer novices for the time being and feed their corrodians on the victuals thus saved; and our sources sometimes hint at this practice.[70] Nevertheless, in the short run, the cost of the corrody might well exceed the rental value of the land in question. But this scarcely mattered, for if anyone has ever lived *sub specie eternitatis*, monks did so in the Middle Ages. In the long run, a monastery which exchanged a corrody for real property could scarcely lose, for it had the property.

## 5. Grants in Exchange for Money

### (i) A form of waste?

Why, then, were the risks to monasteries greater in the transactions involving the exchange of corrodies for money?

These transactions were characteristic of the system in the later Middle Ages, and contemporaries well placed to observe the consequences were apprehensive, if not censorious, about them. There was, for example, much of a disturbing kind to report about William de Drynghow, abbot of Meaux,

---

[67] King, *Peterborough Abbey, 1086–1310*, 27–8.
[68] Ibid. 38.        [69] Above, pp. 191–2.
[70] *Reg. Malm.* ii. 7; *Letters of Pope Innocent III concerning England and Wales*, ed. C. R. Cheney and M. G. Cheney, no. 1061.

who was deposed in 1353, for he left debts amounting to £1,000 at his resignation. Even so, the chronicler of Meaux, himself a monk, did not fail to record, among Abbot William's blunders, what may now appear the peccadillo of selling two corrodies for £50.[71] As for the bishops, most of them were now too realistic to think that Ottobuono's absolute prohibition on sales—as he intended it to be—could be enforced. Yet their disapproval was plain enough. In their injunctions for religious houses, they sometimes bracketed the sale of corrodies with that of woodland and trees—itself long recognized as a form of spoliation if practised to excess—and their concern extended to grants for a fixed term as well as those for life or in perpetuity.[72] They tried to insist that monks seek their permission before making any such grants; and Richard Flemyng, bishop of Lincoln 1420–30, added the further, remarkable, requirement that each proposal be considered in chapter over a three-day period.[73]

A landowner who cut down an excessive number of trees in his woods, in order to raise ready money, sacrificed a capital asset in return for present income: he wasted his asset. It is perhaps difficult to see how bishops found a parallel here for a monastery's sale of corrodies. In the latter case future income—the cost of the corrodian's benefits year by year—was, on the face of it, sacrificed in order to obtain a lump sum of money which was potentially a capital asset. But William Drynghow's case points to the explanation. The chronicler of Meaux had a good deal of sympathy for this abbot, whose income was stretched to cover not only the ordinary expenses of the monastery but also the cost of a number of pensions granted by his predecessor. Hard pressed, and led on by a wicked cellarer who desired his ruin, he sold the two corrodies, each for a life term, and chattels, for the down payments of money which could be obtained in this way; and we are told that he made imprudent leases for the same reason.[74] In fact it is most unlikely that William Drynghow invested the money which he raised by selling corrodies: we are meant to understand that he spent it as income. This outcome was surely what the bishops feared when monasteries under their jurisdiction sold corrodies: the use of the proceeds as income instead of capital. But were their suspicions well founded?

[71] *Chron. Melsa* iii. 85; see also ibid. 106, 245–6.

[72] *Visitations of Religious Houses*, i. 4, 10, 28, etc. Cf. *Chapters of English Black Monks*, ii. 88; and for an earlier episcopal attack on corrodies, whether granted in perpetuity or for a term, see *Register of John de Grandisson, bishop of Exeter (AD 1327–1369)*, ed. F. C. Hingston-Randolph (3 vols., London, 1894–9), ii *(1331–1360)*, 1192. For the offence of wasting woodlands etc., see *Documents of the Baronial Movement of Reform and Rebellion*, ed. Treharne and Sanders, 270; M. Howell, *Regalian Right in Medieval England* (London, 1962), 117–19, 144–5. (The references here are not necessarily to the *sale* of trees, but this does not affect the argument.) For Ottobuono's prohibition, see above, p. 180.

[73] *Visitations of Religious Houses*, i. 10; see also ibid. 47, 56.

[74] *Chron. Melsa* iii. 84.

## (ii) Transactions at Westminster Abbey, 1400–1540

### (a) The corrodians

The corrodies sold by Westminster Abbey for money in the fifteenth and early sixteenth centuries may shed some light on the disposal of the lump sums raised by the sale of corrodies. Moreover, they can also tell us something about the fastidious purchasers who preferred selective corrodies to the standardized arrangements exemplified in the so-called monk's corrody, for most of the corrodies exchanged for money at Westminster in this period were of the former kind.[75] Twenty such grants can now be traced, and with one exception all were made before 1500. The number actually made may have been larger than this, but it is unlikely that many made for a long term escape notice in the surviving sources.

By 1400 the corrody system at Westminster Abbey had been captured by the middle class, and on the whole by a middle class that was already on the Abbey's pay-roll or connected with the monastery in other ways. The list includes, for example, John Newborough, the Abbey's grammar-school master, and his wife, and William Thornwerk, a mason employed by the Abbey over a period of thirty-five years, and his wife.[76] John Gedney, a London draper who supplied clothing to the Abbey for distribution as livery, was a corrodian; so, too, John Randolf, who was one of the two servants of the rank of valet in charge of the monastic refectory, and his wife.[77] Moreover, several corrodians already occupied houses or tenements in the precinct when they made their agreement with the monastery. If we are tempted to doubt that the corrodians of this period were in general people of some little substance, a glance at the properties in question will reassure us. Remissions of rent for properties held of the Abbey were a feature of corrodies in this period, and sums of two, three, and four pounds per annum are mentioned. Yet this was a period when a single shop or cottage could be leased from the monks for a few shillings per annum. The rents remitted related to substantial properties which were evidently not merely residences, but also sources of income to those holding them of the Abbey.[78] We can assume, for example, that the house ('domus') which the Newboroughs held free of its former rent of £2 13s. 4d. per annum for the duration of their corrody was a sizeable property: John's wife may have been gainfully employed here while John himself taught the grammar-school

---

[75] For the list see Appendix V, nos. 51–69. In nos. 53, 55, and 64, the allowance of victuals probably derived, in each case, from a monk's corrody, but the latter had evidently been adapted to suit the wishes of the corrodian in question. For another possible case of this kind, see ibid., no. 59.

[76] Ibid., nos. 57, 63.       [77] Ibid., nos. 56, 62.

[78] For an authoritative account, see Rosser, *Medieval Westminster*, 55–96. c.1450 the Abbey disengaged from direct exploitation of its urban properties, and ceased to ask economic rents of its tenants. This, however, does not affect the argument in the text.

boys.[79] The tenement in King Street, and the meadow and pasture in Mauduit's garden, on or near Tothill Street, which John Gedney held rent-free as a corrodian in the 1420s, were only two among several properties which he currently held of the Abbey. Yet the rent of £4 per annum marks them out as, in themselves, no mean properties.[80]

## (b) The allowances

It was of the essence of a corrody that it included allowances in kind—a term used here to include free housing. Yet the actual importance of these allowances in the corrodies granted by Westminster Abbey varied greatly in the individual case. As far as we know, some corrodians received nothing except allowances in kind.[81] But it is a sign of the extent to which the system had been affected, over a long period of time, by the commercialization of relationships of all kinds between the monastery and its dependants that some entirely different arrangements are recorded. John and Joan Chertsey, who purchased their corrody in 1418, apparently received nearly 50 per cent of their benefits in money; Thomas and Joan Stone, who purchased theirs in the same year, received more than 50 per cent of theirs in this form.[82]

The allowances in kind that were included in these corrodies illustrate the domestic economy and housekeeping worries of some comfortably-off residents of Westminster and its environs at this time. Yet the evidence, incomplete as it is, must be used cautiously.

The most unusual corrodian in the entire list was Thomas Huntyngdon, the physician, who purchased the so-called portion—to be understood as the cooked food—of a deceased monk, Richard Tedyngton, for much of the year in which, by custom, it should properly have been given to the poor.[83] He was unusual in wanting cooked food, for of all the benefits now available to the Abbey's corrodians, this, it appears, was least in demand: as a rule, not even corrodians residing in the precinct were tempted to eat food provided by the Abbey kitchen; and some who were entitled to do so preferred to receive cash in lieu.[84] It is possible that Mr Thomas had a thriving practice in Westminster but did not actually live near at hand, and for these reasons found it useful to dine in the monastery.

Fuel was probably a more popular item than cooked food with the

---

[79] The house was one of the Knowle chantry houses, for which see Rosser, *Medieval Westminster*, 74–5.

[80] WAM 18568–76. For the other tenements, see Rosser, *Medieval Westminster*, 379, and for Tothill Street, ibid., fig. 4. Mauduit's Garden was named after the family which put together a property on this site in the 12th cent.

[81] Appendix V, nos. 56, 58, 62 (i), 63, 67, 69; of which no. 67 relates to a short-term arrangement. Note, however, that at Westminster and elsewhere benefits originally received in kind may have been commuted into money payments subsequently without leaving traces of the change in the surviving sources.

[82] Ibid., nos. 52, 54.     [83] Ibid., no. 67.     [84] Ibid., nos. 53, 55, 59, and 64.

corrodians of this period. Even so, only five of the surviving grants mention this item, and this low number suggests that fuel supplies were not yet, if they ever became, a cause of real anxiety to townsmen of Westminster. The grants that included fuel specify faggots as well as charcoal. Charcoal was fuel for a brazier, faggots for a hearth, and evidently the corrodians in question were providing for both needs.[85] In an earlier grant, that to Thomas Gynes in 1373, the monks undertook to deliver fuel to the corrodian's door. Gynes, however, was in a position to drive a hard bargain, for his corrody represented the price at which he agreed to surrender his perpetual rights in the office of servant in the Abbey kitchen: it had long been the Abbey's policy to redeem such perpetual serjeanties when it could, and on this occasion the monks were probably more anxious to grant a corrody to Thomas Gynes than he to receive it.[86] We do not hear of a similar promise on their part to pay delivery costs in the fifteenth or early sixteenth centuries.

With fuel, one or two corrodians also received candles. Thomas and Joan Stones's 24 lbs. of candles per annum, if kept for the darker months of the year, would have provided at least 1 lb. per week then, or, reckoning sixteen candles to the pound, two candles per night during that season.[87] John and Agnes Pykeworth, with their 20 lbs. per annum, could have used two candles per night for nearly six months each year.[88] The Stones and the Pykeworths, however, were in possession of quite substantial properties, as we can infer from the level of the rents which they owed to the Abbey for the latter and which were rebated as part of the new arrangements: the Stones owed £2 per annum and the Pykeworths £2 13s. 4d. per annum. For such corrodians an allowance of two candles per night or thereabouts in the darker months seems little enough. The modest scale of the allowance, together with the omission of candles from most of the Abbey's grants, suggests that homelier methods of lighting—as, for example, rushes soaked in fat—were still in common use in small middle-class households of the period, and that candles were still regarded there as a luxury.

Several corrodians received clothing, and in these cases squire's livery of a robe with furs of lambskin seems to have been the normal provision.[89] Corrodians, in fact, might have the same livery as servants and officials of

---

[85] Ibid., nos. 52–4, 57, and 59. See also no. 66, where an entitlement to fuel is commuted into a money payment. I am indebted to Dr E. A. Wrigley for drawing my attention to the special difficulties which urban householders might experience in obtaining fuel supplies.

[86] Appendix V, no. 47.

[87] Ibid., no. 54. For late medieval lighting, see Rogers, *History of Agriculture and Prices in England*, iv (1401–1582), 367–8, and for candle prices, ibid. 376–81. For the difference between candles of Paris, which were of tallow, and the superior candles made of wax, see H. Swanson, *Medieval Artisans: An Urban Class in Late Medieval England* (Oxford, 1989), 16. It is likely, although never stated, that the Abbey's corrodians had wax candles if they had any.

[88] Appendix V, no. 53.

[89] Appendix V, nos. 52, 54, 56, 57, 61, 62, 68. For the superior livery of a very superior clerk, see ibid., no. 49.

the highest rank in the monastery, if only they would pay for it. In cases of jointure, the female spouse was sometimes provided with livery of her own.[90]

Yet the most popular items in a corrody of this period at Westminster were probably bread and ale, and, after these two, free housing. The Abbey's corrodians no longer aspired to accommodation in the monastery itself, or, if they entertained hopes of this kind, it was only to be disappointed. But eight or nine (40 or 45 per cent) of the twenty grants surviving from the fifteenth and early sixteenth centuries included remissions of rent for property already held on lease from the Abbey: evidently, the corrodians in question wished to disburden themselves of this item in the cost of living.[91] Allowances of bread and ale are more likely to escape notice in our sources than remissions of rent. Even so, they were probably features of ten (50 per cent) of the twenty grants, and in one or two cases these were the only items covered by the agreement. Thus, in 1427–8, John Clerk, a skinner who possessed several properties in the precinct, paid £10 for a corrody of bread and ale; and in 1455–6 William Thornwerk, the Abbey's master mason, paid £13 6s. 8d. for a corrody of this kind.[92] The normal allowance was probably one conventual loaf and one gallon of best ale per day, but, exceptionally, more or better was sometimes promised. John and Margaret Randolf, who were entitled to ten loaves and ten gallons of ale per week, were also promised wastel bread on the Abbey's principal feasts.[93] John Gedney preferred to receive corn and malt in lieu, and his corrody included an allowance of three quarters, two bushels of wheat and six quarters of malt per annum.[94]

If a corrody was to be sold, it was necessary to value the items comprised in it, in however rough and ready a way. The prices used by the monks of Westminster for this purpose reflect the remarkable stability of prices of consumables in general from end to end of the fifteenth century. Over the entire century, a conventual loaf, weighing perhaps a little over two pounds, was valued for these and other purposes at $^3/_4 d.$, and a gallon of best ale at $1^1/_4 d.$ Over this period, therefore, the typical allowance of one loaf and one gallon of ale per day had an annual value of c.£3.[95] The short faggots used in corrodies were normally valued at 3s. or 3s. 4d. per 100, and a squire's

[90] Ibid., nos. 54, 57.
[91] Ibid., nos. 52–7, 60, 64, and 66. It is not certain that the property in no. 66 was held of the Abbey.
[92] Ibid., nos. 58, 63. See also nos. 53, 55, 59, 62 (2 grants), 64 (2 grants), and 68–9.
[93] Ibid., no. 62; see also no. 68.    [94] Ibid., no. 56.
[95] For the early 16th-cent. values of the loaf and gall. of ale, see WAM 5919*. A monk received one such loaf and gall. of ale daily; for the annual value of £3 set on this, the so-called monk's corrody in the cellar, c.1400, see WAM 19881.

In WAM 5919*, 'Domina Cotton' is Margaret Cotton, who held the hereditary serjeanty of the almonry 1503/4–33 (WAM 19114–48). Margaret Randolf, who is also mentioned, apparently died 1524–5. The outer dates for the document are, therefore, 1503 × 25. On the bread and ale, see also above, p. 58 n.; and for Margaret Randolf, below, Appendix V, no. 62.

robe at 13s. or 14s.[96] Actual values cannot have been as stable as this from
year to year, but evidently these did not change sufficiently for a revision
of those used for accounting purposes to be necessary. In the few cases
where we can estimate the total value of the corrody, the range was wide:
c.£5 to c.£11 per annum.[97] The lower of these figures probably lay within
the range of earnings of one of the Abbey's servants ranking as a groom; the
higher represented an income considerably in excess of the maximum earnings
of a valet there.[98] Allowances in kind—among which we must include
remissions of rent—also varied in importance in the individual case: they
accounted for not less than 40 per cent or more than 80 per cent of the total
value where the latter can be estimated.

   To cost the annual benefits was, for the monks, an easy task. To calculate
the lump sum which should be asked of an applicant wishing to enjoy them
for life was, on the face of it, much more difficult, for, in a business-like
deal, life-expectancy had to be taken into account; and the difficulty was
compounded if a spouse was also involved. No doubt this factor helps to
explain some apparent inequalities in the sums of money changing hands at
Westminster Abbey. Thus, in 1418, John Chertsey paid £133 6s. 8d. for a
corrody probably worth about £10 13s. 4d. per annum: he paid 12.5 times
the annual value of what he and his wife were to receive from the monastery, or 12.5 years' purchase. In the same year, John Pykeworth paid £40 for
a corrody worth £8 8s. per annum: he paid less than five years' purchase for
what he and his wife were to receive. However, both Pykeworths died
within eight years of becoming corrodians, but one of the Chertseys lived
to enjoy their corrody for some forty-eight years.[99]

   Yet it is most unlikely that the monks of Westminster approached any
corrody agreement in the spirit of actuaries, trying to get the calculation
right. In nearly every case, as we have seen, they were already involved in
a relationship with the would-be corrodian; and in these circumstances refined calculations may have seemed inappropriate.[100] This, of course, is not
to say that the monks were constantly tempted to be generous, lopping a
year or two off the purchase-price here and adding an extra loaf or two to
the ration there. On the contrary, in such cases the corrodian may sometimes have offered more than was strictly owing for the benefits in prospect.

---

[96] For the faggots, which also featured in the corrodies of senior monks living in chambers,
see WAM 19913, 19915, 19931, 19945, etc. Talwood, also used in fuel liveries, were normally
valued @ 6s. or 6s. 8d. per 100, candles @ 1½ d. per lb., and charcoal @ 7d. or 7½d. per quarter.
(For the equation, one faggot = ½ talwood, in the royal household, see *Household of Edward
IV*, ed. Myers, 128, 138.) For the value set on squire's livery in the monastery, see WAM
19884 ff. It is to be understood that the first group mentioned each year in the livery section
of these accounts ranked as squires. However, the prior's squire normally had livery @ 20s. p.a.
[97] Appendix V, nos. 52–4, 62, and 64.         [98] Fig. V.1.
[99] Appendix V, nos. 52–3; and for the purchase-price of corrodies at Peterborough Abbey
in the 15th cent., see Thompson, 'Corrody', 119 and n.                [100] Above, p. 200.

We are simply to understand that neither party regarded the transaction as an economic one in the straightforward sense of the term, and to remember this when we try to discover who actually gained and who lost in the individual case.

### (c) *What was done with the proceeds?*

Invested in real property—and monastic communities rarely invested in anything else—the initial down-payment for a corrody would probably have yielded 5 or 6 per cent per annum in an average year in the fifteenth century; and towards the end of the century, the monks of Westminster could have obtained a considerably higher return than this had they chosen—as in general they did not—to exploit the growing demand for property in the town of Westminster.[101] In some cases, to our knowledge, the annual value of the Abbey's corrodies exceeded 6 per cent of the down-payments. Thus a 6 per cent return on the sum of £133 6s. 8d. paid by John and Joan Chertsey would have amounted to £8 per annum, leaving a shortfall of £2 13s. 4d. per annum on the theoretical cost to the monastery of their corrody; and with 6 per cent per annum on the initial down-payments made by the Pykeworths and Stones, the monks would have had a shortfall in these cases too.[102] If, however, we take into account the fact that some of the victuals in question would have been given to the poor had they not been consumed by corrodians, the difference narrows; if we remember the waste that occurred, willy nilly, every day in a great household such as the Abbey's, it becomes, in any case, insignificant. Moreover, provided that the lump sum normally paid by a corrodian of this period was properly invested, the monks had no cause to worry if he or his spouse lived longer than anticipated when the agreement was made, for death, however long delayed, would leave them with the investment. Not even Margaret Randolf, John Randolf's wife, need have been an embarrassment to them. Margaret died in the mid-1520s, still enjoying the corrodies of bread, ale, and livery of clothing which she and her husband had obtained seventy years before.[103]

But did the abbot and convent of Westminster actually invest the money

---

[101] K. B. McFarlane, 'The investment of Sir John Fastolf's profits of war', *TRHS* 5th ser. vii (1957), 91–116, at 110–14; reprinted in McFarlane, *England in the Fifteenth Century* (London, 1981), 175–97. See, however, on Fastolf's expenditure on litigation, A. Smith, 'Litigation and politics: Sir John Fastolf's defence of his English property', in A. J. Pollard (ed.), *Property and Politics: Essays in Later Medieval English History* (Gloucester, 1984), 59–75, at 60. On rents in Westminster, see Rosser, *Medieval Westminster*, 89–92. Cf. A. F. Butcher, 'Rent and the urban economy: Oxford and Canterbury in the later Middle Ages', *Southern History*, i (1979), 11–43, at 42–3; and M. Bonney, *Lordship and the Urban Community: Durham and its Overlords, 1250–1540* (Cambridge, 1990), 111–31.

In the following paragraphs I am particularly indebted to Sir Richard Southern. However, for the conclusion reached, I am solely responsible.

[102] Appendix V, nos. 52–4.

[103] Ibid., no. 62. John Randolf, her husband, died in 1490.

received in exchange for corrodies—or did they spend it as income? The question is not quite as easy to answer as we may expect.

The finances of Westminster Abbey in this period were deeply affected by the cost of the new work in the nave which had first been taken in hand in 1375 but was not completed until 1528. This enterprise cost at least £21,000—a sum representing more than eight times the annual income of the monastery for most of the intervening period—and the monks themselves raised most of this amount.[104] Moreover, from 1440 to 1469 the monastery experienced the singular misfortune of being ruled by two incompetent abbots in succession: Edmund Kyrton (1440–62) and George Norwich (1462–9). When Abbot Norwich went into obligatory retirement two years before his death, the monastery owed debts amounting to £2,025.[105] It will be clear that the sale of twenty corrodies, or thereabouts, can have done very little either to create or to solve problems of this order of magnitude.

Nevertheless, the problems which have just been described do explain why the abbot and convent of Westminster, who had previously been very reluctant to sell corrodies unless in exchange for real property, now, in the fifteenth century, sold them for money. They sold half a dozen on these terms in the years around 1420, and the date is significant. The new work on the nave was resumed at the beginning of Henry V's reign after a decade of inactivity, but it soon became clear that Henry's promise of 1,000 marks (£666 13s. 4d.) per annum for this purpose was not to be honoured in full.[106] By 1420 the Abbey's own revenues were taking much of the strain. Although, as far as we know, none of the proceeds of the sale of corrodies at this time were applied directly to the new work, in a general sense they helped the latter by relieving the pressure on revenues as a whole. This pressure is evinced by heavy overspending on the part of the conventual treasurers at this time.[107] Since new work in the nave was calculated to bring visitors to the Abbey on its completion, and visitors occasionally made offerings, it can even be said that the proceeds of these transactions were productively invested.

In the same general sense, some of the corrody agreements made by Abbot Kyrton and his monks in the mid-fifteenth century eased the strain imposed on Abbey revenues by building expenses. Under Kyrton, the new work in the nave proceeded at a very slow pace. However, both the monks' dormitory, which was set on fire in 1447 by the incautious act of a novice,

---

[104] R. B. Rackham, 'The nave of Westminster', *PBA* (1909), 3–64, at 57; cf. Colvin (ed.), *History of the King's Works*, i. 151; and for the Abbey's income, Harvey, *Estates*, 63.

[105] Widmore, *Enquiry*, 193; Harvey, *Estates*, 67. Two corrodians, Robert Drope and John Randolf, are named among the Abbey's creditors on this occasion.

[106] Rackham, 'The nave of Westminster', 14–15; and for the corrodies sold c.1420, see Appendix V, nos. 52–7.

[107] WAM 19905–22. The proceeds of the sales of corrodies were made over to the conventual treasury in this period. The relevant accounts of the new work are WAM 23479–97.

and the rose window in the south transept of the Abbey church needed costly attention during his abbacy.[108] A better man of business than Kyrton might, even so, have avoided the sale of corrodies at such a juncture. Kyrton and his monks sold at least nine, and several cash annuities beside; five of the corrodies were sold in the years 1447–62, when work on the dormitory or the rose window was in hand.[109] Margaret and John Randolf purchased the first of their two corrodies in the year (1449–50) when the dormitory was rebuilt.

As an exempt house, directly subject to the see of Rome, Westminster Abbey was never formally visited by a bishop in his capacity as diocesan. Had such a visitation taken place at this time, or earlier in the years around 1420, the bishop could not have failed to note with disapproval the monastery's increasing burden of debt. In the 1450s and 1460s he might have noticed, too, that some of its creditors were among those who seized the opportunity of becoming corrodians. In 1467, when Abbot Norwich was demoted, the Abbey owed John Randolf the considerable sum of £185.[110] Yet it is a nice question whether the abbot and convent of Westminster spent or invested the proceeds of their sales of corrodies in this period. And when visiting bishops put this question, *mutatis mutandis*, to other monastic communities about the proceeds of *their* sales of corrodies, the truth must often have been as finely balanced.

## 6. The Age and Marital Status of Corrodians

Were corrodians on the whole elderly people? Clearly, we must interpret age and the ageing process in their terms and not our own. The medieval elderly were those who had passed the peak of their working life and were, or would soon become, unproductive members of society. In medieval England, anyone over the age of 60 was probably old in this sense.[111] Some,

---

[108] Rackham, 'The nave of Westminster,' 24–8. For the main repairs to the dormitory, in 1449–50, see WAM 23515. For intermittent repairs to the rose window, 1451–62, see WAM 23517, 23522, 23525–6.

[109] Appendix V, nos. 59–65. The grants mentioned in nos. 59–60 fall outside the years 1447–62. Nos. 62 and 64 relate, in each case, to multiple grants. For the annuities, which were for short terms, see WAM 19964, 23510. The sale of short-term annuities is also recorded c.1470–4, during the abbacy of Thomas Millyng (WAM 23535, 23537, 23539, 23541).

[110] For references, see Appendix V, no. 62; and for a loan of £100 from John Randolf in 1461, WAM 19966.

[111] A simplification of a complex situation to which M. Pelling and R. M. Smith, 'Introduction', in Pelling and Smith (edd.), *Life, Death, and the Elderly: Historical Perspectives* (London and New York, 1991), 1–38, and Smith, 'The manorial court and the elderly tenant in late medieval England', ibid. 39–61 provide the essential introduction. For 60 as a significant age, see also *Land, Kinship and Life-Cycle*, 75–7; and for the suggestion that a degree of correlation existed between widowhood and old age in early modern England, ibid. 360. Cf., for an earlier period, J. Z. Titow, 'Some differences between manors and their effects on the condition of the peasant in the thirteenth century', *AHR* x (1962), 1–13, at 7; reprinted in W. E. Minchinton (ed.), *Essays in Agrarian History* (Newton Abbot, 1968), 37–51, at 45.

however, may have reached the critical point when they were younger in years. Of course, at the higher levels of society, many spent an entire lifetime unproductively, but such people did not normally end their days as corrodians: for the latter, the definition will serve.

We may first note that some of Westminster Abbey's middle-class corrodians in the fifteenth century were demonstrably not old or on the threshold of old age, as defined above, when they acquired their privileges. John Randolf did not live as long as his remarkable wife; but he did live for forty years after buying his first corrody in 1450.[112] Robert Drope lived for about twenty-six years after buying his first corrody in 1460, and his period of service as an alderman of the City of London did not begin until 1468.[113] John Thirsk, who became a corrodian in 1445–6, when he was the Abbey's master mason, was still sufficiently vigorous three or four years later to be appointed master mason at Windsor Castle.[114]

It has perhaps been too readily assumed that corrodians were in general rather old. To have a defective title to land is not to suffer from an age-related condition. And to feel the burden of too many children is not normally to be old, but to have a young family which has not yet reached the stage of contributing to the family income. Yet these, as we have seen, were circumstances that sometimes brought monasteries and prospective corrodians together.[115] Like most people in most situations, men and women purchasing a corrody had more than one thing in mind. Not the least important was a desire to provide against incapacity to earn at whatever point in the life-cycle this should come about—and under medieval conditions that point was not easily predicted. In many cases, however, the main purpose of the transaction in the eyes of the male corrodian was surely to provide a degree of security for his spouse, were she to be the survivor, and to give her a modest competence that did not depend on support by the children of the marriage, if any. Hence the remarkably early appearance, in arrangements relating to corrodies, of joint tenancies for husband and wife, with remainder to the survivor. Jointure of this kind begins to be mentioned in corrody agreements in the first half of the thirteenth century—rather ahead, it seems, of the common use of jointure in land transactions at any level of society. In their own way, and in a wide variety of situations, corrodies seem a little to have anticipated the improvement in women's rights of property which Richard Smith has traced, particularly in rural society, in the early fourteenth century.[116]

---

[112] Appendix V, no. 62.   [113] Ibid., no. 64.
[114] Ibid., no. 60.   [115] Above, pp. 193–4.
[116] R. M. Smith, 'Women's property rights under customary law: some developments in the thirteenth and fourteenth centuries', *TRHS* 5th ser. xxxvi (1986), 165–94, at 184–6. For jointure in grants of corrodies in the early or mid-13th cent., see e.g. *Calendar of Charters and Documents relating to Selborne and its Priory*, ed. W. D. Macray (2 vols., Hants Record Soc.,

## 7. Conclusions

Throughout the Middle Ages, the typical corrodian was perhaps somewhat younger and more active, and corrodians in general less numerous, than historians have commonly supposed. Even so, corrodians evidently changed a good deal in the course of this long period, for the typical corrody itself changed. What began as a livelihood, comparable to that of a monk, for one who would become a resident member of the monastic household, ended, more often than not, as a basketful of consumables for one who need never actually put in an appearance in the monastery. Moreover, it was not only at Westminster that the system was to a large extent captured by the middle class: inevitably, cash transactions, involving large sums of money payable in advance, had this outcome wherever they were introduced. Did monks ever reflect on the fate of their corrodies, or even notice what was happening, as entrepreneurs and officials with large savings supplanted peasants and minor gentry in the queue? If they did so, it was perhaps only to find the changes natural and entirely acceptable, for, after all, from the twelfth century onwards, many monks probably came from the middle class: the middle-class corrodian was simply a projection of the monastic community itself.

1891–4), i. 34–5; and Heales, *Records of Merton Priory*, Appendix, p. xxix. Cf. Appendix V, no. 5, where, in 1185, two pairs of spouses are provided for by four *several* corrodies.

In cases of jointure, it was a common, though not invariable, practice to reduce some of the allowances enjoyed by the survivor; for such a reduction of livery, see Appendix V, no. 54.

The importance to the corrodians of the spouse's jointure was noticed in Thompson, 'Corrody', 118.

# Epilogue

WHEN Benedictine monks looked at the world outside the cloister, at any time from the twelfth century onwards, they liked much of what they saw and paid it the compliment of imitation. The effects on their mode of life were cumulatively very large. In the later Middle Ages, the monks of Westminster, who have provided the principal case-study for this book, ate flesh-meat almost as frequently as their equals in secular society; as many of them as possible made use of private chambers, in preference to sleeping in the common dormitory; and they moved in and out of the monastery quite freely. They allowed themselves substantial wages, or personal incomes, and the cost of these absorbed c.20 per cent of the entire net income of the monastery.[1] They employed professional cantors to sing their services, and schoolmasters to teach in their schools.[2] Already, in fact, there was a pragmatic resemblance between the community at Westminster and a collegiate establishment, in which canons enjoyed prebends but employed others to perform duties which they were not always present to perform themselves.

The canonical hours shaped the monks' day—and, to some extent, their night, too—but in the later Middle Ages their ceremonial life found its actual focus in the Mass. They said many Masses for the dead, on anniversaries or as daily chantries. Since the thirteenth century, all monasteries had faced serious competition from other churches for the patronage of benefactors intending to endow post-obit Masses of this kind. Yet the Abbey's life was still strongly influenced, as it had been since the eleventh century, by the contemporary belief in a Purgatory where the expiation of the consequences of sin could be assisted in this way.[3] Directly or indirectly, the monks of Westminster owed most of their endowments to their place in this penitential system, and other features of their life were affected too. For example, because they said Masses for the royal and noble dead, they were involved in the distribution of alms on a notable scale.[4] The place of the Mass in a more general sense in their lives is well illustrated by the practice, which

---

[1] i.e. c.£550 p.a. Most of this sum came from the surplus income of the royal foundations. For individual shares see above, p. 153 n.

[2] For the cantors, see LNQ 86ᵛ, and for the schoolmasters, Appendix I, n. 7.

[3] For the doctrine of Purgatory, see R. W. Southern's review of J. Le Goff, *La Naissance du Purgatoire* (Paris, 1981), in *Times Literary Supplement* (18 June 1982), 651–2, and for a helpful summary, Burgess, '"By quick and by dead"', 838. For some memorable material consequences of the doctrine, see H. M. Colvin, *Architecture and the After-Life* (New Haven, Conn., London, 1991), ch. ix. 

[4] Above, pp. 24–7.

they seem to have followed, of presenting novices to a bishop for ordination as soon as they reached the canonical age, however short the period elapsing since profession.[5]

If we did not know from other evidence that many Benedictine houses followed essentially the same kind of life, we could conclude this from the Injunctions of 1535–6.[6] The Injunctions, the work of Thomas Cromwell, were compiled before the Visitors began their circuit of monasteries. Nevertheless, they display a sound acquaintance with irregular practices in Benedictine houses. Indeed, they are so well informed that we can probably regard the absence of comment on a particular practice as deliberate and not arising from ignorance.

Cromwell did not attempt to prohibit the practice of giving monks wages. However, by prohibiting excursions outside the precinct, he ensured that monks would have fewer opportunities than previously for spending what they received. He did not prohibit the consumption of flesh-meat. But he did insist that the practice of using more than one room at meal-times, which had developed concurrently with meat-eating, should cease.[7] Monks were to take their meals together in one room, and that the misericord. They were to leave the distribution of leftovers after their meals to the almoner—an implicit condemnation of the practice, hinted at earlier, whereby each monk chose a recipient for his own leftovers.[8] They were to sleep in a common dormitory at night, and enter the infirmary when sick—the latter rule was evidently directed at the occupants of private chambers who stayed where they were when sick.[9] The requirement that each house send one or two monks to a university, the better to teach and preach the Word of God on their return, has perhaps the flavour of the new beliefs of the period rather than the old. In fact, the Benedictine General Chapter had for centuries encouraged such a practice, though, unlike Cromwell, it recognized that a monk preparing a sermon needed a private chamber in which to prepare it.[10]

Cromwell assumed that monks who were priests would say Mass every

---

[5] Above, pp. 119–20.

[6] Wilkins, *Concilia*, iii. 789–91; Youings, *Dissolution of the Monasteries*, 149–52; and for comment, *RO* iii. 275–8. Injunctions for Westminster Abbey were issued in 1536 (WAM 12787). For lay attitudes to monasteries at this time, in a regional context, see Haigh, *Reformation and Resistance in Tudor Lancashire*, 63 ff.

[7] For the rota involving more than one room for eating, see above, p. 40. In some houses, however, a sole room, except on major feasts, was already in use in the later Middle Ages.

[8] Above, pp. 20–1.

[9] For this practice see above, pp. 100–1. The Injunctions for Westminster provided an income for the infirmarer, on a per capita basis, to enable him to meet the expense of universal use of his resources—a sign that this point had been raised at the Visitation of this house (WAM 12787).

[10] *Chapters of English Black Monks*, i. 27, 75, etc.; ii. 11–12, 76, 120. Benedict XII's encouragement of the practice of sending monks to the university would have given Cromwell less satisfaction.

day, and directed that each Mass should include prayers for the king and queen. He said nothing explicit about Masses for the dead and perhaps felt no need to mention such a well-established feature of monastic life. Yet, given the Scriptural emphasis of the Injunctions as a whole, his very silence on this point may be significant, for the doctrine of Purgatory, which was so closely associated with all forms of prayers for the dead, has only slender support in Scripture.[11] If he was silent about Masses for the dead, he expressed himself somewhat equivocally about the value of the monastic life itself to English spiritual life in a more general sense. The Injunctions are not, indeed, in the tradition of the Lollards, who rejected the monastic life as a form of 'private religion', lacking the authority of Scripture.[12] But not a great deal was claimed for it, even so, and the description of monastic ceremonies as only 'the first letters or principles and certain introductions to true Christianity' strikes a very different note from St Benedict's description of his Rule as 'a little Rule for beginners'.[13] A disparaging reference to 'uprising in the night' suggests that Cromwell may not have known that the night office rested on biblical foundations.[14] The Injunctions, in fact, combined a high claim for discipline with a rather low claim for the end for which that discipline was undertaken. The communities which received them can hardly have doubted that something more extreme might well occur shortly.

Five years later, in January 1540, the monastic foundation at Westminster Abbey was dissolved. By the end of that year, however, a cathedral, served by a collegiate body, was in existence there. William Benson, the last abbot, became the first dean, and ten of the twenty-four monks who had signed the deed of surrender became either prebendaries or minor canons in the new foundation.[15] The Dissolution of the monastic foundation did not, of course, bring to an end traditional forms of service in the Abbey church— or traditional forms suitably adapted for the times. In 1548, as Wriothesley notes, the anniversary Mass for Henry VII was sung here in English, and omitting all the Canon after the Creed except the Pater Noster.[16] Moreover, the quick replacement of the former monastery by a cathedral and collegiate foundation must mean that the social and economic consequences of the Dissolution for the townsmen of Westminster were less severe than for many other urban communities.

---

[11] For the controversy in London in the 1530s, see S. Brigden, *London and the Reformation* (Oxford, 1989), 258–9.

[12] Hudson, *The Premature Reformation*, 349–50.     [13] *Rule*, cap. lxxiii.

[14] Southern, *Western Society and the Church in the Middle Ages*, 221.

[15] E. Carpenter (ed.), *A House of Kings: The History of Westminster Abbey* (London, 1966), 110–13.

[16] Wriothesley, *Chronicle of England*, ii. 2; cited in Brigden, *London and the Reformation*, 435.

If we were to assess these consequences, we would have to ask how far the more numerous, but smaller, households of the new bishop of Westminster and the dean and prebendaries could compensate, as consumers and employers, as almsgivers, and in the other roles which they now assumed, for the disappearance of the vast monastic household and the lesser households associated with it—those of the abbot, the prior, and the monk-bailiff. Some of the chapters in this book may serve to show—if any demonstration is needed—that the answer to this question does not lie on the surface of events. We cannot, for example, understand the scope and quality of monastic almsgiving before the Dissolution if we look only at the formal obligations resting on monasteries, and neglect to ask how these were actually carried out.[17] Nor can we estimate the number of servants who had to look for new sources of livelihood after the Dissolution without scrutinizing the structure of the households in which they served previously.[18] How far below the surface did the government contrive to look, as it grappled with problems which it had itself done so much to create? I leave these questions, with so many others, unanswered.

[17] Above, pp. 30–3.    [18] Above, pp. 151–3.

# APPENDIX I

## Charitable Giving at Westminster Abbey, *c.*1510–*c.*1530

### Average Annual Expenditure

| Type or destination of alms | £s |
|---|---|
| Doles | |
|    post-obit[1] | 195 |
|    other[2] | 15 |
| Henry VII's almshouses[3] | 84 |
| Knights of St Edward[4] | 1 |
| Lay brethren[5] | 23 |
| Nuns of Kilburn[6] | 18 |
| Grammar school and song school[7] | 60 |
| Other[8] | 5 |
| TOTAL | 401 |

[1] Of the sum of £195 p.a., £90 p.a. was distributed on the yearly anniversaries commemorating, respectively, Eleanor of Castile, Richard II and Anne of Bohemia, Henry V, Henry VII, and Margaret Beaufort, £75 p.a. on the weekly anniversaries also commemorating several in this list, and £30 p.a. on the yearly anniversaries of private benefactors. These figures exclude the sums totalling *c.*£14 p.a. which were now deflected to the Abbey's song school from Henry VII's weekly anniversary (above, p. 32.).

[2] The estimated sum includes 14*s.* p.a. representing the almoner's outlay on 2 qu. 2 bus. beans and peas for pottage for the poor during Lent, and the following cash doles: £1 10*s.* p.a. on Maundy Thursday, a total of £3 p.a. on the Rogation days, a total of £1 13*s.* 4*d.* p.a. on the feasts of All Souls and Holy Trinity, and 6*s.* 8*d.* p.a. on the feast of SS Peter and Paul. A sum has also been included for doles which were probably distributed on other major feasts but without leaving traces in our sources. The doles on Maundy Thursday were distributed to 120 poor persons @ 3*d.* per person, and the use of bags, specially made each year, points to a ritualized occasion. See WAM 19112 ff., 19764 ff., 23161 ff.; and for the Maundy bags, mentioned from *c.*1515, WAM 18800 ff.

The distribution of beer or ale on Saturdays and the vigils of principal feasts, mentioned in Rosser, *Medieval Westminster*, 298, was not in fact a charitable outlay but a pittance for the monks themselves, the days in question being days on which they did not eat a full supper but had, instead, an evening collation with a special allowance of drink.

[3] For the almshouses built within the Abbey precinct *c.*1504 for a priest, 12 almsmen, and 3 almswomen, see ibid. 297. In addition to a common allowance of fuel @ £3 p.a., the inmates received the following emoluments: priest: wages 2*s.* 4*d.* per week, clothing @ *c.*£1 p.a.; other almsmen: wages @ 1*s.* 5¹/₂*d.* per week; clothing @ *c.*14*s.* 6*d.* p.a.; almswomen: wages @ 1*s.* 4*d.* per week; clothing @ *c.*14*s.* 6*d.* p.a. See WAM 24236 ff.; cf. *VE* i. 420. But the inmates were also eligible for doles on the royal anniversaries and each could expect to receive an additional 2*d.* per week from this source.

In 1541, as a member of the cathedral and collegiate foundation at Westminster, each almsman was allowed £6 13*s.* 4*d.* p.a. for all purposes (WAM 6478, fo. 4ᵛ). There were no women on the new foundation. However, Anne Jurye and Anne Birde, who received pensions of £6 13*s.* 4*d.* for life from the Court of Augmentations, were probably the last surviving almswomen on the old foundation. They were said to be poor who had lived in the monastery. PRO LR 6/61/1–2.

⁴ Formerly known as the brethren or poor of St Edward; and in the 13th and early 14th cents., sisters of St Edward are also mentioned. The term *milites* is first used in 1492–3 (WAM 19103).

The only recorded emoluments of the knights, who may have been respectable poor of the town of Westminster, were wages @ 3s. 8d. p.a. ( = 11d. per quarter), and these were virtually unchanged since the late 13th cent. There were now 6 knights, but formerly 13 knights and sisters. See WAM 18962* ff., 19112 ff.; *Customary*, ii. 177.

⁵ At the beginning of the 16th cent. there were 6 brethren, but subsequently, with the help of £5 p.a. from Margaret Beaufort's foundation, 9. Each received 2s. 6d. p.a. in cash; clothing @ 13s. 4d. p.a.; and food and drink in the refectory, consisting in part of leftovers from the monastic meal, valued @ £1 p.a. in *VE* i. 421, but probably worth more—say £1 5s. p.a. In addition, each was eligible for doles on the royal anniversaries and probably received at least 9s. 6d. p.a. from that source. The large clothing allowance, comparable to that of one of the Abbey's squires, suggests that the lay brethren now had ceremonial duties for which they were expected to be well dressed. See WAM 19112 ff., and for earlier references to doles for the lay brethren on royal anniversaries, WAM 23712, 23714, 23716. For their food, see also above, pp. 68–9.

In and after 1541, some lay brethren received £3 6s. 8d. per person p.a. for all purposes from the cathedral foundation at Westminster. However, as these survivors of the old regime died or moved away, they were not replaced (PRO LR 2/111, fos. 57ᵛ, 59ᵛ, 63, 66).

⁶ For the corrodies of the nuns of Kilburn, which dated from the 12th cent., see Appendix V, no. 2.

⁷ The schools originated in the 14th cent. and had separate identities from the 1380s. Until the 1460s, both were housed in the almonry, but then the grammar school moved to new quarters in the cellarer's range of buildings. In the early 16th cent. there were c.30 boys in the grammar school and 6 in the song school, and a master for each group. Some food was purchased for the boys, but their main sustenance was probably the leftovers of the monastic meal in the misericord. The low level of the cash emoluments of the masters suggests that each was also entitled to food and drink, despite the absence of explicit references to these corrodies in our sources.

The sum of £60 p.a. contains an element of conjecture and is made up as follows: grammar-school master: stipend £2 p.a., clothing @ 13s. 4d. p.a., food and drink @ £6 p.a. (an estimate); song-school master (who was not entitled to livery of clothing): stipend 13s. 4d. p.a., food and drink @ £4 p.a. (an estimate); for the boys: cost of leftovers (@ ½d. per day) £27, cost of additional food, clothing (of a superior kind for the singing boys), laundry, etc. £20 p.a. See WAM 19112 ff., 33301.

If these estimates are of the right order of magnitude, the two masters may have been well served, initially, by the Dissolution, despite the loss of their allowances in kind. As members of the cathedral establishment, the grammar-school master received a stipend of £20 p.a., and the song-school master a stipend of £10 p.a. Moreover, an usher was now provided for the grammar school at a stipend of £10 p.a.: previously, if the master had help he probably paid for it himself. In addition, the sum of £3 6s. 8d. p.a. was now allowed for each grammar-school boy and each singing boy. See WAM 6478, fo. 3; PRO LR 2/111, fos. 56ᵛ ff., and for the context of the changes c.1540, C. S. Knighton, 'The provision of education in the new cathedral foundations of Henry VIII', in D. Marcombe and C. S. Knighton (edd.), *Close Encounters: English Cathedrals and Society since 1540: Studies in Local and Regional History no. 3* (University of Nottingham, Department of Adult Education, 1991), 18–42. On the Abbey's grammar school see also Rosser, *Medieval Westminster*, 207–9, and J. Field, *The King's Nurseries: The Story of Westminster School* (London, 1987), 14–16.

⁸ A catch-all, allowing for e.g. the distribution of 6s. 8d. in alms by the infirmarer on the death of a monk; for such casual alms as the abbot and prior gave from their separate portions; and for alms given by obedientiaries from petty cash funds which have left little trace in our sources. These sums, too, were probably distributed in doles.

# APPENDIX II

## Catering in the Refectory and Misericord at Westminster Abbey c.1495–c.1525: Numbers and Messes

Monastic households accepted waste as a fact of life and made no attempt to achieve an exact daily match between the numbers catered for at meals and the numbers actually present to eat what was provided. Indeed, they were committed to a degree of mismatch, since surpluses went to the poor, whose claims might not be denied. Yet, at the end of the Middle Ages, monastic waste was a mere shadow of what it had been earlier, and the share of the poor correspondingly reduced. At Westminster Abbey, the kitchener of this period, though careless enough about tiny fluctuations in numbers, responded as soon as this margin was exceeded. The numbers for which he catered varied within a remarkably small range, and this reflects mainly the stability in numbers achieved by the monastic community itself. The optimum number of monks at Westminster was now considered to be 48, and the actual number was close to this: in the exact period covered by the surviving kitchener's accounts (1497–1522), the average number at Michaelmas (29 Sept.) each year was 46; the lowest number recorded at that point in the year was 40; the highest, 51.[1] Few seculars were now entitled to corrodies in the conventual kitchen—that is, to portions of cooked food as served to the monks—and, as far as we know, the number so entitled varied little from year to year. Nor, in the conventual household, were guests numerous. In these respects, too, therefore, numbers were relatively stable.

The stability of numbers in the refectory and misericord provides an essential clue to the interpretation of the kitchener's accounts, the principal source for monastic diet in this period. Every kitchener tended to use conventional prices in his account, in preference to the actual prices obtaining in the market in the week or month in question. But in some other important respects the accounts vary with the kitchener. Some kitcheners entered the precise numbers of eggs or fish used in dishes of these foods; others were content to round numbers up or down. Some recorded the precise cut used in meat dishes, the quantity thereof, and the cost; some only the cost. In 1506–9 and again in 1520–1, for example, the meat used for mortress was identified as fillet of pork and costed at 1d. per fillet.[2] But in 1516–17 the

---

[1] WAM 19994 ff., 23903 ff. (where, however, the lists omit the abbot); and see above, p. 74.
[2] e.g. WAM 33322, fos. 1ᵛ, 2ᵛ, 6, etc.; WAM 33323, fos. 2ᵛ, 3, 3ᵛ, etc.; WAM 33329, fos. 1ᵛ, 2, etc. Even in these years, however, the quantity of meat for this dish is often omitted.

kitchener entered the total cost of 'mortress flesh' in his account on the appropriate days—and the sum was usually 4*d*. on each occasion—without any further details.[3] Knowing, however, that every kitchener was catering for approximately the same numbers and using conventional prices that varied little if at all from year to year, we can use the more informative accounts to interpret the less informative. The entries relating to mortress illustrate this point. This dish was normally made at Westminster Abbey with fillets of pork, and evidently 1*d*. per fillet, the price mentioned in 1506–9 and again a dozen or so years later, was the conventional price in the kitchen for this cut of meat. When, therefore, the kitchener entered an outlay of 4*d*. on mortress flesh in his account, we are to understand that he used four fillets of pork on the day in question.

How many messes of food did the kitchener provide at each meal, and for how many persons was each mess intended? It is only sensible to assume that the total numbers for which he catered on meat days, on the one hand, and on fasts, on the other, were very similar, if not identical. Meat days and fasts, however, throw up different kinds of evidence. In both cases, it will be convenient to consider first the period down to and including 1509.

At dinner on meat days in this period, the kitchener normally served 8 messes of meat in the misericord and recorded this fact explicitly in his account.[4] We are not told explicitly how many messes were served at this meal on meat days in the refectory. However, in the listing of the ingredients used in some dishes served in this room, the number 5 occurs often enough for us to conclude that it provides a clue to the number of messes served here. When, for example, mortress was served, the kitchener used 5 fillets of pork in this dish on an average day, and similarly, if 'umbles' was served, he used 5 sheep's 'gathers'. If we can assume that one fillet of pork was used per mess of mortress, and one sheep's 'gathers' per mess of 'umbles'—and the conventions of the accounts suggest that this is probably how we should understand such entries—it will follow that the kitchener served 13 messes in all on meat days at this time: 5 in the refectory and 8 in the misericord. But do arrangements on fasts suggest that this hypothesis is well founded and shed light on the number catered for in each mess?

[3] WAM 33327 *passim*.

[4] Explicitly in the case of beef, whatever the year, and in 1497–8 and 1501–3 in the case of boiled meat too (WAM 33318, 33321). In the case of roast meats messes are not specified. However, the number '8', as in '8 conies', and factors of 8 occur frequently, and there is no reason to think that the number of messes was different for these dishes. From 1516, a small outlay on meat for servants at dinner is specified, and in some years the meat in question is described as a mess of beef. We should probably understand that a similar provision was made for servants before 1516 but not charged against the kitchener's daily allowance, and therefore not entered in his account. Occasionally, the normal messes of meat were reduced by one or two, with the explanation that a seyney (blood-letting) was taking place. The reduction seems to apply consistently in the case of beef and boiled meat, but not always in that of roast meat. See e.g. WAM 33322, fos. 23[v], 36, 49, 50[v]; WAM 33323, fos. 4[v], 9, 22, 34.

Fish could be, and frequently were, counted in and out of the pot and thus lent themselves to a precise reckoning of individual shares; and, *mutatis mutandis*, the same is true of eggs, another staple food of fasts.[5] If eggs are used as indicators of the number of messes, it is essential to compare the numbers used on days of the week subject to the same dietary rules and at the same meal; and similarly, if fish are used for this purpose, it is essential to be aware of seasonal variation in the size of messes and of variation as between main courses and pittances. But with these precautions taken, the account of a kitchener who liked to enter precise numbers in his account can reveal the exact numbers catered for in particular dishes on fast days. Br. Henry Jones, who was kitchener in 1506–7, was evidently such a man, for his account contains a considerable number of exact figures, and they have the ring of actuality. When, for example, Br. Henry records the use of 117 eggs or 127, or 137,[6] it is hard to doubt that he actually used this number: other kitcheners might have been content to enter '120', '130', or '150'.

Henry Jones's account suggests that he normally catered for 52 persons or thereabouts at dinner. On 3 Dec. 1506, for example, and again two days later, he explicitly records the service of 52 messes of eggs as a 'service' (main course) at this meal.[7] From the cost of this item, 2*s.* 6½*d.*, and from our knowledge of the price at which the kitchener normally costed eggs at this time, we can infer that 260 eggs ( = 5 per mess) were used on each occasion. This number of eggs was used quite frequently for egg dishes this year, and we can assume that the number made 52 messes on these other occasions too.[8] Br. Henry's repeated use of 208 white herring when he served this dish during Lent suggests that he made up 52 messes, each of 4 fish, on these occasions.[9]

If the kitchener was catering for 52 at dinner on a normal fast at this time, he was probably doing the same on normal meat days. If so, the hypothesis that he served 13 large messes on meat days—8 in the misericord and 5 in the refectory—this year, and in other years down to *c.*1509, is vindicated, provided that we allow 4 persons to a mess (13 × 4 = 52). In a monastic context, 4 to a mess would not be an unusual arrangement in this period. Indeed, the Injunctions of 1535–6 prescribed this arrangement, though some communities seem to have considered such a rule rather niggardly: they

---

[5] But eggs were not eaten during Lent. We should also note that the number of eggs entered in the kitchener's account sometimes conflates the number used in dishes and the number given to corrodians in lieu of cooked food on meat days. The corrodians' allowances were known as 'liveries', and this word is used of the conflated totals too.

[6] i.e. (for the long hundred was used for eggs): 'di. C quart', xxvij', 'C vij', and 'C xvij'. See WAM 33322, fos. 13ᵛ, 14, 14ᵛ.                          [7] WAM 33322, fo. 7.

[8] Ibid., fos. 6ᵛ, 7ᵛ, 8, etc. However, we should note that in the vocabulary of the kitchen at Westminster, 'mess of eggs' sometimes describes 5 eggs as a quantity, whether or not they formed a mess for one monk, as at supper on Wed., 2 Feb. 1502, when 24 eggs used in the *cawagium* and 32 in the misericord are said to make 11 messes and 1 egg (WAM 33318, fo. 59).                                          [9] Ibid., fos. 16 ff.

were evidently accustomed to a smaller number per mess and to larger individual shares of the food in question.[10] The hypothesis of 4 to a large mess and messes for 52 in all does not imply that every person eating dinner in the refectory or misericord participated in each of the dishes brought to the table, or had a whole individual mess or a quarter share of a large mess when he did so. The kitchener reckoned in terms of what a *monk* could eat or must at least be offered. Some seculars, however, were entitled to rather less than the number of dishes served to a monk and to less than a monk's mess of the dishes to which they were actually entitled. The example of the garden servants in Abbot Ware's monastery *c*.1270 reminds us that a secular person's entitlement might be limited in other ways too: some of these had two dishes a day for 40 days in the spring and 66 in the summer and autumn; others, one dish on every meat day in the year, but nothing on fasts.[11] We are to understand that *c*.1500 the kitchener normally thought in terms of 52 messes as served to a monk and 13 large messes as served to every four monks, and found that he could meet the needs of all eating in the refectory or misericord in this way.

Yet Henry Jones's account in 1506–7 also shows that the number for which he catered on fasts fluctuated over periods of months, weeks, and even days: on some days for herring in Lent he used, not 208 fish, but 200, 212, or 220, and was probably catering for 50, 53, or 55.[12] Given these fluctuations, we can the better understand arrangements on meat days, when the number of messes in use was apparently stable over long periods of time. This number represents a somewhat formalized method of accounting, in itself well attested in general in our sources: on occasion the kitchener made up one or two more messes than he confessed to, and on occasion one or two less. Normally, however, down to *c*.1509 he catered at dinner on meat days, as on fasts, with the number 52 in mind.

In essentials, this system was unchanged after 1509, but by 1516–17, the next year for which the kitchener's day-account survives, it had evidently been modified in one respect. The change is betrayed by an alteration in the quantities of flesh-meat and entrails used in two dishes which have already been mentioned: mortress and umbles. For mortress, instead of 5 fillets of pork, the kitchener now normally used only 4, and for umbles he now used 4 sheep's 'gathers' instead of 5.[13] We can probably conclude that he now served only 4 large messes of these dishes instead of the former 5; and in later years the evidence suggests that only 3 were normally served.[14] If each

---

[10] Wilkins, *Concilia*, iii. 790; cf. *L & P Henry VIII*, ix, no. 879.
[11] *Customary*, ii. 73–4.     [12] WAM 33322, fos. 19, 19ᵛ.
[13] WAM 33327, fos. 1, 1ᵛ, 2, 2ᵛ, 3, etc. In the case of mortress, the number of fillets has been inferred from the kitchener's outlay: 4*d.* for mortress meat indicates the use of 4 fillets of pork. In the case of umbles, the use of 4 sheep's gathers is mentioned explicitly.
[14] WAM 33328, fos. 2, 3, 4, etc., where 3*d.* indicates the use of 3 fillets of pork.

mess was indeed for 4 persons, he was now catering not for 20 persons when he served these dishes but for 12 or 16. Yet our sources, though recording many short-term fluctuations, do not point to a general reduction in the number of messes served at dinner in this period, whether on meat days or on fasts. Why, then, did he reduce the number of messes in the case of mortress and umbles?

Both these dishes were served between mid-September and the beginning of Lent, and served with great regularity then: umbles on virtually every Sunday and Tuesday, and mortress on every Monday and Thursday. The umbles on Sunday and Tuesday were accompanied by froise, the mortress on Monday and Thursday by pudding. On each of the four days in question, every monk eating in the refectory was entitled to both dishes of the day. However, as we have seen, not every secular person eating with the monks in this room was entitled to both. It seems clear that the number of seculars entitled to one dish in the refectory on meat days, and precisely to umbles on Sundays and Tuesdays and mortress on Mondays and Thursdays, fell between 1509 and 1516: in the former year, the old number of messes was still being served; in the latter, the smaller numbers were in use. But this change affected only one of the main dishes served at dinner in one of the rooms used for eating and in one season of the year. The kitchener still made up most dishes at dinner with *c.*50 persons in mind and still reckoned 4 to a mess.

Most suppers provided by the kitchener occurred on meat days, and the numbers catered for at this meal were evidently smaller than numbers at dinner. It must be emphasized that no hypothesis about the arrangements fits all the evidence: we simply have to balance probabilities.[15]

As at dinner on meat days, so at supper, the monks were divided into two groups, and these ate in different rooms. In the misericord, the kitchener probably served 5 messes, together with a sixth, normally of mutton or pork, for the servants entitled to the meal. Hence the considerable number of entries recording the use of 5 hens, ducks, or conies, together with pork or mutton for the servants, at a meal which is explicitly, or by implication, identified as supper.[16] Shoulder of mutton was considered a suitable dish for

[15] The fact which most awkwardly distances itself from the suggestions made in the following paragraphs is the frequent use of 56 eggs at supper on Wednesday, especially if a very few references to a division in the proportions 24 : 32 between the *cawagium* and the misericord reflect normal practice; for an example, see n. 8 above. However, 'supper' on Wed., a fast day, was not a full meal, but a collation or pittance, and it is possible that arrangements were peculiar to the day. For the possibility that the kitchener provided 56 hard-boiled eggs at breakfast on Easter morning see n. 22 below: in certain circumstances, 56 was perhaps the established number for a pittance.

[16] e.g. WAM 33323, fos. 11, 25ᵛ, 28, 29ᵛ, 46ᵛ. However, in 1516–17 the servants seem often to have been given the same meat as others at supper, whatever the meat: hence references to 6 conies etc. at this meal (WAM 33327, fos. 2ᵛ, 4, 15, etc.).

supper, and on days when everyone ate mutton, the use of 6 shoulders, implying 6 messes, is sometimes recorded.[17] The amount of edible flesh provided by hens, ducks, and conies at this time was almost certainly too small for more than a single mess to be made from each carcass, and we can assume that each of the 5 messes was for 4 persons. If so, servants apart, the kitchener catered for 20, other than servants, in this room. However, at supper, as at dinner, the actual number of messes provided was sometimes smaller and sometimes larger than the conventional number.

How many were catered for at supper in the refectory or *cawagium*, the chamber inside the refectory? Since, as far as we know, even the strictest rota in use in black monk houses in the later Middle Ages permitted at least half the community to eat in the misericord, we can assume that not more than 20 monks or thereabouts were normally catered for at the second meal in these rooms. Again, it is important to remember that the conventional number would sometimes have been superseded by an actual number that was different. Such variations are in fact suggested by the number of eggs used in egg dishes that were probably served in the rooms in question. In 1517–18, for example, this evidence suggests that the actual number catered for varied quite regularly in the range 20 to 26.[18]

How, then, was it that the conventional numbers used in catering were normally lower at supper than at dinner? We must conclude that most of the seculars who were entitled to dinner were not entitled to supper. Of the 13 large messes served at dinner on a meat day, 3 were probably for seculars, and only 10—5 in the refectory and 5 in the misericord—for monks. If so, the kitchener normally catered for only 40 monks or thereabouts in the one room or the other at dinner or supper. Yet the community actually included a larger number of monks: clearly, the kitchener assumed that some would absent themselves from the common meals. This hypothesis is credible on general grounds, for the common life was at a low ebb in black monk houses of this period. But it is confirmed for Westminster by more particular evidence. The monastic ration of bread, consisting of one conventual loaf per monk per day, was delivered by the baker to the refectorer, and the number of loaves required by the latter each day indicates the number of monks participating, however erratically, in the common meals, whether in the refectory itself or in the misericord. Baker's accounts surviving from the period immediately following that covered by the kitchener's

---

[17] e.g. WAM 33323, fos. 42ᵛ, 50; WAM 33327, fo. 8; and for 6 'joints' of mutton at supper, see WAM 33330, fo. 21ᵛ.

[18] An inference from the various numbers of eggs used at supper on Sundays in the refectory: 60 ( = 3 × 20), 69 ( = 3 × 23), 78 ( = 3 × 26), 84 ( = 4 × 21), 92 ( = 4 × 23), 100 ( = 4 × 25). 78 occurs more frequently than any other number and on 15 of a total 36 occasions. See WAM 33328. On Sun., 20 Dec. 1517, 152 eggs ( = 4 × 38) were used at supper, but the egg dish on this Sun., which fell in Advent, was probably intended for all monks eating supper.

accounts show that *c*.40 loaves, and no more, were needed daily for the monks at this time.[19]

On several occasions in the year the kitchener catered for considerably fewer than usual. Paradoxically, numbers fell most dramatically on some of the very days in the year when we might expect attendance at the common meals to be very good—on some of the principal feasts of the monastic year and during the twelve days of Christmas (25 Dec. to 6 Jan.). During the latter period, when, following long-established custom, the misericord was closed and flesh-meat excluded from the official diet, monks seem to have felt quite free to desert the common meals altogether: the absentees ate, no doubt, at the abbot's table or with one of the obedientiaries having a household of his own. The kitchener evidently knew that this would happen, for his own provision of food in this season was smaller than usual.[20] Similarly, the misericord was closed on some of the monastery's principal feasts, including the dedication feasts of SS Peter and Paul (29 June) and St Peter in Chains (1 Aug.). On these days, too, the kitchener knew that it was safe to reduce the number of messes at the common meals.[21] These arrangements will not surprise anyone familiar with the general way of life of Benedictine monks at the end of the Middle Ages. It is more surprising to find little or no evidence of an increase in the normal number of messes on major feasts when the misericord was open and its saving diet of flesh-meat available, for we might expect an unusually large attendance of monks on these days.[22]

Whatever the actual number in the kitchener's calculations for the day, on meat days, when the refectory and misericord were both in use, a rota was needed which should assign each monk to one or other of these rooms. It has been suggested in this appendix that the kitchener catered on a normal day for *c*.40 monks but provided messes for only half this number in the

---

[19] The daily average was 41 in 1520–1, 42 in 1526–7, and 40 in 1528–9. The actual range was 42 to 44 loaves daily in 1520–1, 41 to 44 in 1526–7, and 37 to 42 in 1528–9. See WAM 33315, 18941, 31916. The refectorer drew, additionally, 2 loaves daily for the poor eating in the refectory—i.e. for the lay brethren. These numbers exclude loaves provided for monks living privately in chambers.

For explicit evidence of absenteeism from the common meals, see above, pp. 68–9.

[20] See e.g. the 12 days of Christmas 1507–8: for mortress in this period the kitchener used only 3 fillets of pork instead of the normal 5, and for froise only 120 to 150 eggs instead of the normal 180 (WAM 33323, fos. 2–3ᵛ).

[21] WAM 33323, fos. 25, 29. We should allow for similar behaviour on the deposition and translation of St Edward the Confessor (5 Jan. and 13 Oct.), Easter, and Christmas Day. The misericord was now open on the remaining principal feasts: Pentecost, Holy Trinity, and the Assumption of the BVM.

[22] On the principle that there must have been *some* increase, I have allowed for 56 individual messes or 14 large ones for certain dishes on such days. In fact, the 60 hard-boiled eggs said to have been provided for breakfast on several Easter mornings in this period may actually represent the rounding up of 56. And similarly, the '90' or '120' eggs provided by more generous kitcheners on this occasion may conceal 84 ( = 1½ × 56) and 112 (2 × 56).

misericord. It follows, therefore, that the rota in use at Westminster Abbey *c.*1500 divided the relevant number of monks equally between the two rooms in use. It will be clear, even from details given in this brief discussion, that the monks of this period found ways and means of evading the requirements of the rota when it suited them to do so. Indeed, the whole economy of the kitchen depended on this fact, which meant that on most days in the year there were portions to spare for visitors and others for whom no formal provision was made.[23] In principle, however, the rota permitted only half the community to eat in the misericord on a meat day. *Circa* 1500, in fact, the community at Westminster still adhered to the letter of the compromises hammered out in the early fourteenth century: then, Benedict XII decreed that black monks might eat flesh-meat, provided that, even on meat days, at least half the community in each house remained in the refectory, there to eat regular food.[24] In reckoning the half, it had long been permissible to disregard those who could plead an excuse for not eating the common meal on the day in question. However, the use of *c.*40 as the number at Westminster Abbey (80–90 per cent of the total number of professed monks) suggests that only monks residing, for the time being, outside the precinct were disregarded.

It will be clear that the total number, including seculars as well as monks, for whom the kitchener of Westminster catered at the end of the Middle Ages fluctuated. However, it has been suggested in this appendix that there was even so a norm, and that this was 52 or thereabouts at dinner and 40 or thereabouts at supper. Even when the actual number catered for was different from the norm, the use of a somewhat formalized system of accounting ensured that the quantities of food recorded by the kitchener were often those of the norm. It seems clear too that the large mess used on meat days was for four monks. With these vital clues to guide us, we are in a position to estimate, very tentatively, the size of the messes in use for many of the dishes of fish or meat which appeared on the tables in the refectory or misericord in this period. Such estimates must be made in two stages: the first relates to the weight of the whole fish or carcass of meat in question; the second to the weight of the messes which fish or carcass provided.

Estimates for fish at each of these stages are shown below in Table A. They relate to the main dishes paid for by the kitchener and therefore exclude most varieties of expensive fish: these were normally served as extra dishes and paid for out of other funds.[25] Nor has it been possible to include every variety of common fish eaten by the monks of Westminster. However, the varieties included in the table made up more than 90 per cent of the total

---

[23] Above, p. 69.    [24] Above, p. 40.
[25] For the kitchener's main dishes, see above, p. 43.

number of main dishes at dinner—and fish, other than molluscs, were not eaten at supper.

Fish weights have been arrived at by reference to fish-bone evidence from excavated sites, to the price of the fish in question—for the prices in our sources, though conventional, were related to actual prices in the market[26]— or to equivalents used by the kitchener himself, as, for example, his equa- tion, give and take a little here and there, of one ling with 1.4 haburdens or green fish. Allowances for waste, which must be made before the weight of the edible flesh of each variety of fish can be estimated, are normally based on information in M*Cance and Widdowson's Composition of Foods.*[27] But in some cases it has been necessary to improvise. Where a choice is neces- sary, I have preferred to make the larger allowance for waste.

As noted above, the kitchener records the precise number of fish which he used for a main dish somewhat erratically. For cod in its several forms he gives the number more often than not, but for whiting only in 1497–8 and 1501–3, and for herrings only in 1506–9 and 1516–18. The estimates of mess weights derive from these detailed entries, when they occur. They assume that the kitchener normally catered for 52 at dinner, but for 56 in the case of certain dishes on major feasts.

The estimates for meat in Table B relate to the main dishes of flesh-meat served in the misericord, the room set aside for the consumption of that food. In the present context, meat poses even greater problems than fish. Most of the varieties of fish served by the kitchener grew in the wild, and estimates of their weight can be compared to the known weights of fish which have grown under similar circumstances today. But very few of the animals providing meat for the kitchener's dishes were wild game: nearly all were reared for the table, in conditions which have changed fundamentally since the end of the Middle Ages. Stouff's analysis of carcass weights in markets in late medieval Provence[28] provides valuable indications of weights at a time that was not very distant *c.*1500, and wherever possible these have been followed. In other cases, equivalents which the kitchener seems to have had in mind have been useful—as, for example, that between one fat pig and one quarter of a mature pig—and, in others still, prices have provided clues. Again, appropriate allowances have been made for waste. For beef cattle and sheep, estimates relating to pre-improvement animals in Scotland have been useful;[29] but, again, in some cases it has been necessary to improvise.

In the misericord, meat was served at supper as well as dinner. It is

---

[26] Where appropriate, prices recorded in the day-accounts of the abbot of Westminster's household for this period have been utilized, as well as those in the kitchener's accounts.

[27] Revised edn., ed. A. A. Paul and D. A. T. Southgate (1978).

[28] Stouff, *Ravitaillement et alimentation en Provence*, 186–9, 301–15.

[29] A. J. S. Gibson, 'The size and weight of cattle and sheep in early modern Scotland', *AHR* xxxvi (1988), 162–71, at 165 and 169.

assumed that the kitchener normally made up 8 messes, each for 4 monks, for each dish at dinner and 5 messes, each for 4 monks, for each dish at supper. Our sources imply that the weight of a mess of flesh-meat was approximately the same at supper as at dinner.

It will be clear that all the estimates given in the following tables are subject to a very considerable margin of error. Nevertheless, they probably indicate the order of magnitude of messes of fish and meat at Westminster Abbey towards the end of the Middle Ages.

TABLE A. Messes of Fish in the Refectory at Westminster Abbey c.1495–c.1525

| | 1. Weight per fish | | 2. Edible matter as % of (1) | 3. Weight of edible matter per fish | | 4. Mess for 1 monk | | |
| --- | --- | --- | --- | --- | --- | --- | --- | --- |
| | | | | | | No. or portion of fish | Weight of edible matter | |
| | lbs. | g. | | lbs. | g. | | lbs. | g. |
| *White fish* | | | | | | | | |
| Cod family[a] | | | | | | | | |
| cod | 6.60 | 2,996 | 66 | 4.36 | 1,979 | 1/6 (0.17) | 0.73 | 331 |
| green fish[b] | 4.70 | 2,134 | 66 | 3.10 | 1,407 | 1/4 (0.25) | 0.78 | 354 |
| haburdens[c] | 4.70 | 2,134 | 66 | 3.10 | 1,407 | 1/4 (0.25) | 0.78 | 354 |
| ling | As for cod | | | | | | | |
| stockfish | 4.40 | 1,998 | 66 | 2.90 | 1,317 | 1/4 (0.25) | 0.73 | 331 |
| Pike[d] | 3.30 | 1,498 | 55 | 1.82 | 826 | 1/4 (0.25) | 0.46 | 209 |
| Plaice[e] | 2.00 | 908 | 42 | 0.84 | 381 | 1/2 (0.50) | 0.42 | 191 |
| | | | | | | or | | |
| | | | | | | 3/4 (0.75) | 0.63 | 286 |
| Roach[f] | 1.40 | 636 | 55 | 0.77 | 350 | 1 | 0.77 | 350 |
| Whiting[g] | 1.10 | 499 | 50 | 0.55 | 250 | 2 | 1.10 | 499 |
| *Fatty fish* | | | | | | | | |
| Eel[h] | | | | | | | | |
| conger | 5.00 | 2,270 | 67 | 3.35 | 1,521 | 2/13 (0.15) | 0.50 | 227 |
| other | 0.80 | 363 | 67 | 0.54 | 245 | 1 | 0.54 | 245 |
| Herring[i] | 0.50 | 227 | 55 | 0.28 | 127 | 4 or 5 | 1.26[j] | 572[j] |
| Mackerel[k] | 1.40 | 636 | 56 | 0.78 | 354 | 1 | 0.78 | 354 |

[a] For the weight of cod see Wheeler, 'Fish bone', 407–8. The small cod represented in the King's Lynn sample examined by Wheeler clustered in the range c.60 to c.80 cms. The weight of a cod at the mid-point of this range is estimated at 2.99 kgs. (6.6 lbs.).

In our sources, so-called cod is to be identified as fresh cod. So-called ling was the commonest variety of preserved cod served in the refectory, but 'green fish', 'haburdens', and 'stockfish' were served on occasion instead. When the kitchener needed to make up dishes containing more than one kind of cod, he seems to have used the following equation:

$$1 \text{ ling} = 1.4 \text{ haburdens or green fish or } 1.5 \text{ stockfish.}$$

Nevertheless, messes of, respectively, haburdens, green fish, and stockfish, served on their own, consisted of approximately identical portions of the fish in question.

[b] i.e. fish pickled in brine.

[c] Sometimes referred to as Scarborough fish; for examples, see WAM 33327, fos. 1$^v$, 2, 3$^v$.

[d] A fish served only on special days, when a mean number of c.14 was used, probably in messes for 56. The number of fish used suggests that they were in fact small pike and scarcely more than large pickerel. For the suggestion that most pickerel weighed less than 1.5 kg. (3.3 lbs.), see Dyer, 'The consumption of fresh-water fish in medieval England', 31. Pike is a bony fish; hence the relatively large allowance for waste.

[e] The weights of, respectively, place, mackerel, and roach have been estimated from the prices paid for these fish and on the assumption that, in this period, $\frac{1}{2}d$. normally purchased 1 lb. of common sea-fish, other than herring, or common freshwater fish; cf. Dyer, loc. cit.

The abbot's household accounts regularly distinguish between small and large plaice. The former normally cost $\frac{3}{4}d$. to $1\frac{1}{4}d$. per fish; the latter, at least twice as much. The distinction between small and large can be glimpsed in the accounts of the kitchener, who seems to have purchased small plaice for ordinary days and large ones for special days. The weight given in the table is the estimated weight of small plaice. See also above, p. 50 and n.

The actual number of plaice used per dish is never specified. However, the kitchener's outlay on this fish suggests that on ordinary days other than Fridays a mess consisted of ½ a small plaice. On Fridays, when only 2 dishes of fish were served at dinner instead of the usual 3, it consisted of ¾ of a small plaice, and on special days such as solemn vigils, of ½ a large plaice. The messes in the table relate to ordinary days.

[f] The mature fish; for the weight, see previous note. Mature roach was served less frequently than rochets (small roach) or rochets and dace. However, there is a little evidence to suggest that a mess of the former for 1 monk contained 1 fish or a little more, and this allowance probably indicates the weight of the mess on the other occasions.

[g] For the weight of the fish see Wheeler and Jones, 'Fish remains', 218–19. The size of the mess is that implied most frequently in our sources; the actual number of whiting per mess varied in the range 1 to 3.5.

[h] Our sources provide the following clues to mess weights of this fish. A salted eel made a mess for 1 monk; 7 to 10 conger eels, messes for 52 or 56; a wey, said to contain, variously, 40 lbs. or 48 lbs., made a dish of stewed eel for 52 or 56; and ½ wey (20 or 24 lbs.) made a dish of baked eel for 52. It seems probable that the per capita allowance of eel before wasting indicated in the case of stewed eel (0.80 lbs./363 g.) indicates the approximate allowance whenever eel was served on its own and not (as when baked) in pastry. If so, the salted eel making a mess for 1 was of this weight, and conger eels were of a weight to produce messes of similar size.

Eel for baking is sometimes identified as shaft eel; eel for stewing, as stub eel.

[i] Herrings, whether fresh or preserved, were much cheaper than the other fish mentioned in n. e above: the kitchener seems to have costed them at 1$d$. for 6 or 7. But it would not have made sense to cook and serve such a bony fish weighing less than c.½ lb.; on the other hand, if the normal weight was larger than this, the allowance of 4 to 5 per mess would appear incredible. The number of herrings used per dish, from which the size of the mess has been derived, is given only in Lent, when this fish was normally served 3 times per week.

[j] The values assuming 4.5 fish per dish.

[k] The mess weight of this fish may be underestimated: the kitchener's normal outlay suggests that he used 50 to 60 mackerel per dish, but the evidence is slender.

TABLE B. Messes of Meat in the Misericord at Westminster Abbey, c.1495–c.1525

| | 1. Weight per carcass | | 2. Edible meat[a] as % of (1) | 3. Weight of edible meat per carcass | | 4. Mess for 4 monks | | |
| --- | --- | --- | --- | --- | --- | --- | --- | --- |
| | | | | | | Portion of carcass | Weight of edible meat | |
| | lbs. | g. | | lbs. | g. | | lbs. | g. |
| Beef cattle[b] | | | | | | | | |
| mature | 308.00 | 139,832 | 78 | 240.24 | 109,069 | 1/80 (0.0125) | 3.00 | 1,362 |
| veal[c] | 57.00 | 25,878 | 66 | 37.60 | 17,070 | 1/16 (0.0625) | 2.35 | 1,067 |
| Pig[d] | | | | | | | | |
| mature | 72.00 | 32,688 | 70 | 50.40 | 22,882 | 1/16 (0.0625) or 1/20 (0.05) | 3.15 / 2.52 | 1,430 / 1,144 |
| young | 18.00 | 8,172 | 70 | 12.60 | 5,720 | 1/4 (0.25) | 3.15 | 1,430 |
| Sheep | | | | | | | | |
| mutton[e] | 31.00 | 14,074 | 78 | 24.18 | 10,978 | 1/8 (0.125) | 3.02 | 1,371 |
| lamb[f] | 11.50 | 5,221 | 78 | 8.97 | 4,072 | 1/8 (0.125) | 1.12 | 508 |
| Poultry[g] | | | | | | | | |
| chicken | 1.50 | 681 | 64 | 0.96 | 436 | whole carcass | 0.96 | 436 |
| duck | 4.00 | 1,816 | 55 | 2.20 | 999 | whole carcass | 2.20 | 999 |
| goose | | | | | | | | |
| fat | 8.00 | 3,632 | 55 | 4.40 | 1,998 | 1/4 (0.25) | 1.10 | 499 |
| green | 2.00 | 908 | 55 | 1.10 | 499 | whole carcass | 1.10 | 499 |
| hen | 4.00 | 1,816 | 64 | 2.56 | 1,162 | whole carcass | 2.56 | 1,162 |
| Game | | | | | | | | |
| cony[h] | | | | | | | | |
| mature | 4.00 | 1,816 | 62 | 2.48 | 1,126 | 1/2 (0.50) | 1.24 | 563 |
| young | 2.00 | 908 | 62 | 1.24 | 563 | whole carcass | 1.24 | 563 |

ᵃ Including fat.

ᵇ For carcass-weight, see Stouff, *Ravitaillement et alimentation en Provence*, 186–9, 301–15. However, this and other weights in the table have been corrected to allow for the use by Stouff's sources of a lb. avoirdupois equivalent to only 400 g. Cf. Gibson, 'The size and weight of cattle and sheep in early modern Scotland', 168, where the lowest estimate for the carcass weight of pre-improvement cattle is almost identical with the figure suggested here.

The estimate of mess weight for this meat is conjectural. A mess of beef was normally costed at 2*d.* or 2¹/₂*d.* The median price paid for beef cattle for the abbot's household in this period was c.13s. 4*d.*, and this suggests that a mess costing c.2*d.* represented c.1/80 of a carcass. For an earlier convention that a beef carcass made 40 messes of meat, each for 2 soldiers on garrison duty, see M. Prestwich, 'Victualling estimates for English garrisons in Scotland during the early fourteenth century', *EHR* lxxxii (1967), 536, and for the division of a beef carcass into 60 pieces for the diet of the master and students of St Leonard's College, St Andrews, in 1671, Gibson, op. cit. 162.

ᶜ The invariable term for young beef cattle in our sources. I have assumed that the kitchener's 'veals' were slaughtered soon after birth; see Stouff, *Ravitaillement et alimentation en Provence*, 187.

On several occasions in 1522, 'one veal' provided 8 messes of roast meat at dinner. However, the price at which the kitchener costed this item, which rarely exceeded 1s. 8*d.* and was often lower, and which, moreover, approximated to that used in the abbot's household for what is there explicitly described as '4 joints', suggests that his own entries actually refer to ¹/₂ carcass. If so, ¹/₂ carcass made 8 messes. On one occasion, however, veal for roasting is described as '4 joints', and the equation 4 joints = ¹/₂ carcass may have been normal. See WAM 33320, fos. 11ᵛ, 15, 17, etc., WAM 33324, fos. 5, 5ᵛ, 7ᵛ, WAM 33330, fos. 21ᵛ, 22–23ᵛ; cf. Rogers, *History of Agriculture and Prices*, iv (1401–1582), 355.

ᵈ The carcass weight suggested for mature pigs derives from the average weight of pigs slaughtered at Carpentras in 1422–3 (Stouff, *Ravitaillement et alimentation en Provence*, 301 ff.). I have preferred this figure to the higher one relating only to pigs slaughtered in autumn and winter (ibid. 189).
A whole pig, if mentioned in the kitchener's accounts, is to be identified as a young or fat pig, and sometimes the term 'fat pig' is used. I have assumed that, then as now, the weight of a fat pig was 25% that of a mature pig. However, this may be to assume a stable relationship between the weights in question which did not in fact exist. See Rogers, *History of Agriculture and Prices*, iv (1401–1582), 340–1. In each case, the edible weight in this table excludes head and feet.

The larger of the 2 mess weights shown seems to have been used for roast, the smaller for boiled pork. Thus, in the case of roast dishes, 1 loin of the mature animal made 4 messes of roast pork and was equated for this purpose with the whole carcass of a young pig. See e.g. for the loins, WAM 33322, fos. 1ᵛ, 2ᵛ, 3; and for the young pigs, which were always roasted and never boiled, WAM 33330, fos. 7ᵛ–8, 9ᵛ. In the case of boiled dishes, 1 chine made 4 messes of boiled pork. But this joint was sometimes costed more cheaply than loin of pork; see e.g. WAM 33322, fos. 1ᵛ, 2, 2ᵛ, etc.), where chine is costed at 5*d.* but loin at 6*d.* Chine, in fact, provided less meat than loin, and, if so, a mess of boiled meat contained less than a mess of roast; say c.80% of the latter.

The entries for pork, like those for mutton, suggest that the kitchener used the word 'loin' of a somewhat larger part of the carcass than is intended in modern usage.

T ABLE B. (notes cont.)

e For carcass weight see Stouff, *Ravitaillement et alimentation en Provence*, 187. Cf. Gibson, op. cit. 169, where the carcass weight of unimproved Scottish breeds is estimated at 30 lbs.

'One mutton' made 8 messes of boiled meat or 8 of roast at dinner; see e.g. WAM 33330, fos. 2–3. 'Four loins' also occurs frequently as provision for 8 messes of roast mutton, and seem to be equated with 1 carcass. 'Four legs, 2 breasts and 2 necks' occurs once as provision for 8 messes of boiled mutton (WAM 33318, fo. 109). The kitchener's prices for, respectively, mutton for boiling and mutton for roasting were normally identical, and this suggests that he served approximately the same amount of meat in each dish. His prices also suggest that when this meat was served on its own at supper, messes were of the same size as those served at dinner. If served with chicken, however, the messes were smaller—perhaps half the normal size—and this was probably the case also when mutton was served with pigeon.

f It has been assumed that the lambs used by the kitchener were only a few weeks old when slaughtered; see Stouff, *Ravitaillement et alimentation en Provence*, 187.

g Estimates of poultry weights represent mainly guess-work, with attention to both modern weights and hints in our sources. For chicken and goose see also Dyer, 'Changes in diet in the late Middle Ages: the case of harvest workers', 37. In the misericord chicken, unlike hen, was served, not on its own, but with mutton.

The kitchener normally equated a fat or stubble goose with 4 green geese.

In the case of goose and duck, it can be assumed that much of the fat which would not now be eaten at table was eaten in the late medieval misericord.

h Our sources normally equate a mature cony with 2 young conies or rabbits. The former was costed at 2d. or 2¹/₂d., a young cony at 1¹/₂d. or 2d. These were relatively modest prices for the period if the conies were supplied by a butcher or poulterer. But it seems likely that the kitchener would have aimed to provide per capita allowances of not less than 4 to 6 oz. of this meat—which was no longer an uncommon dish, in season—or 1 to 1.5 lbs. per mess for 4, and the carcass weights suggested here are based on this assumption. See Rogers, *History of Agriculture and Prices*, iv (1401–1582), 717; M. Bailey, 'The rabbit and the medieval East Anglian economy', *AHR* xxxvi (1988), 1–20, at 11–15. Young conies are sometimes referred to in our sources as 'runners'.

# APPENDIX III

## Apothecaries, Physicians, and Surgeons Employed by the Abbot and Convent of Westminster c.1300–1540[1]

### Apothecaries

1. GUY, MR. Supplied medicines in 1305–6. WAM 19319.

2. J. BOSEVILL'. Supplied medicine—probably a solution for bathing the affected limb—in a case of *tibia* in 1356–7. WAM 19336; above, p. 109.

3. J. DE CANTUARIA. Supplied medicine in 1305–6. WAM 19319. The date seems too early for an identification with the physician Jordan of Canterbury, for whom see *MPME* 198–9, and Getz, 'Medical practitioners in medieval England', 269.

4. J. DE SUDWERK. Supplied medicines in 1305–6. WAM 19319. Probably not identical with John of Southwark, a London barber of the period, for whom see Getz, op. cit. 267.

5. JOHN DE BOVENDEN. Supplied medicines on physician's prescription in 1354–5; described as spicer and apothecary. WAM 19334.

6. JOHN HOLDY. Received 15s. 11d., presumably for medicines, in 1443; described as 'apothecary'. WAM 19420.

7. JOHN HOO. Supplied medicines in 1425–6. WAM 19414.

8. JOHN DE KENT. Supplied medicines in a surgical case in 1297–8. WAM 19318.

9. JOHN DE NOTEGARSHALE. Supplied medicines in 1305–6. WAM 19319.

10. LAURENCE, MR. Supplied medicines in a surgical case in 1297–8. WAM 19318.

11. POPHAM. Received 4d. in 1309–10 for a *decoctio* for a case of *tibia*; the case was also treated by Richard de Reding (q.v.). WAM 19320. For *decoctio* as a term for a medicinal remedy including, on occasion, vinegar as an ingredient, see also WAM 19328. However, Popham may have been an Abbey servant with healing skills, not a professional apothecary.

12. RICHARD DE REDING. Treated a case of *tibia* in 1309–10; described as an apothecary. WAM 19320.

13. ROGER DE ARCUBUS. Supplied medicines in 1322–3. WAM 19324.

14. THOMAS DE ELY, MR. Supplied some medicines, and made up others in the infirmary, in 1305–6. WAM 19319.

[1] The functions of apothecary, physician, and surgeon were not always distinguished in this period, although they were more often distinguished at the end than the beginning. In the following lists, some names may be in the less appropriate of two or three possible categories, and it is possible that some names should appear in more than one category. For the employment of an apothecary-surgeon in the infirmary at Westminster in the mid-14th cent. see above, p. 84 n.

15. THOMAS DE WALDEN, SEN. Supplied medicines 1339–53 and 1355–6, and was in some of these years the monastery's principal apothecary. WAM 19326, 19328, 19331–3, 19335. Citizen and spicer of London; MP, 1346; City chamberlain, 1349–c.1359. Beaven, *Aldermen*, i. 266; B. R. Masters, *The Chamberlain of the City of London, 1237–1987* (1988), 107. Founded a chantry in Westminster Abbey with the sum of £100. Harvey, *Estates*, 395.

16. THOMAS DE WALDEN, JUN. Son of no. 15 above. Supplied medicines on a regular basis in 1354–7; described as an apothecary. WAM 19334–6.

## Physicians[2]

17. ANDREW, MR. Convent's physician 25 Mar. to 25 Dec. 1340. Received a fee of 13s. 4d. per quarter ( = £2 13s. 4d. per annum) during that period. WAM 19326, 19328–9. Cf. *MPME* 16.

18. FREEMAN, DR. Received a fee of £1 6s. 8d. in 1536–7; probably convent's physician. WAM 19502.

19. GEOFFREY, MR. A reference to the supply of medicines by 'Mr Geoffrey' from Easter to 29 Sept. 1389 means, in the context, that a practitioner of this name was convent's physician during that period. WAM 19373. Possibly, though not certainly, identical with no. 20 below.

20. GEOFFREY, MR. Called in in the case of Br. Robert de Hermondesworth in 1393–4 and received a fee of 6s. 8d. for 4 visits. WAM 19380. Convent's physician, 24 June 1395 to 29 Sept. 1409. During that period, received a fee of £2 13s. 4d. per annum, and a robe, with furs of lambskin, per annum costing 12s. 4½d. to 14s. 2½d. Frequently supplied medicines: these he may or may not have dispensed himself. For references, see *MPME* 51, where, however, it is assumed that Mr Geoffrey himself dispensed the medicines. See also no. 19 above, and above, p. 82.

21. HENRY DE WYGNESTON, MR. Received a fee of £2 13s. 4d. in 1353–4, when he is described as *medicus*. WAM 19849. The fee identifies him as convent's physician, and in that capacity he doubtless received a robe as well. We can safely identify him with 'Mr Henry', a physician, who, with the apothecary, Thomas de Walden, sen., attended a session with the infirmarer in London in 1352–3, to settle the account for a year's prescriptions. WAM 19333. If so, Henry de Wygneston was already convent's physician in that year. He may have continued in this capacity until c.1360. See *MPME* 73, s.n. 'Henry'.

22. JOAN. A reference to the cost of medicines in the period 29 Sept. 1388 to Easter (18 Apr.) 1389, as occurring *tempore Johanne fisiciane* implies that a woman named Joan was convent's physician at the time. Possibly identical

---

[2] Some physicians in the following list held the office of 'convent's physician', for which see above, pp. 82–3; some were consulted by the monks *ad hoc*.

with the woman, described as a physician, who was paid 40s. in 1386–7 for her 'labour' and for dispensing medicines. WAM 19370, and see above, p. 83. Cf. the treatment of a case of *tibia* by a woman in 1374–5; this, however, was normally regarded in the monastery as surgeon's work, and the woman was probably a surgeon. WAM 19351. See above, pp. 85–6.

23. JOAN DE SUTTON. Dispensed medicines in 1407–9; described as a leech. *MPME* 100; and for the identification as Joan de Sutton of Westminster, Getz, 'Medical practitioners in medieval England', 263.

24. JOHN, MR. Convent's physician for the year beginning 24 June 1394; received a fee of £5 per annum. Possibly identical with no. 25 below. WAM 19380–2.

25. JOHN EMME, MR. Called in for Br. John Stowe in 1393–4; received a fee of 3s. 4d. Possibly identical with no. 24 above. If so, as the *ad hoc* fee shows, the consultation in Stowe's case occurred at a point in the year before he became convent's physician. WAM 19380; and for John Emme, see *MPME* 142.

26. JOHN LE GROS, MR. Received a fee of 40s. for a visit to the terminally ill Abbot Wenlok at Pyrford in 1307. *Walter de Wenlok*, 212.

27. JOHN DE HOWGATE alias HUGATE. Convent's physician, 1376–8. Received a fee of £4 per annum and a robe with 2 furs costing c.£1 per annum. WAM 19352–4; cf. *MPME* 157.

28. JOHN MIDDLETON. Called in, with other physicians and surgeons, in 1390–1. Then, or soon after, physician to Richard II. WAM 19375; *MPME* 172; Rawcliffe, 'The profits of practice', 64, 71 n.

29. MANUEL, MR. Received a fee of 26s. 8d. for the period Easter (24 Mar.) to 24 June 1364; it is implied that he had succeeded Mr William de Pyl (no. 41 below) as convent's physician; however, the arrangement did not last long, and William de Pyl was probably in post again from 24 June. WAM 19343; *MPME* 207.

30. NICHOLAS, MR. Received a stipend of 20s. for the last quarter of 1362–3; one of four physicians, including one from Lombardy and one from Ireland, who received stipends, in each case for a quarter, this year; none of the four is referred to as convent's physician. WAM 19342; *MPME* 217.

31. PAUL, MR. Probably Paul de Monte, physician to Richard II. Received 7s. 6d. for prescribing medicines for Br. John de Canterbury, a terminal case, in 1399–1400. WAM 19390; *MPME* 240.

32. PETER LOMBARD, MR. In 1360–1, prescribed medicines which were dispensed *apud apotecarios suos de Lombardia*; received 6s. 8d. for his own services. WAM 19340; *MPME* 249.

33. PHILIP, MR. Received stipends for short periods of service on several occasions, 1363–76. After the expiry of one such term, 24 June to 1 Aug. 1364, received 6s. 8d. for prescribing medicines. WAM 19343; *MPME* 254.

34. ROBERT DE RENHAM, MR. Visited the terminally ill Abbot Wenlok at Pyrford on two occasions in 1307: received 20s. in a silk purse for the one visit and £5 for the other. *Walter de Wenlok*, 208, 212; *MPME* 298.

35. ROBERT OF ST ALBANS. Convent's physician 1320–3; received a fee of £2 13s. 4d. per annum. *MPME* 299.

36. T. HUNTYNGDON. Received a fee of 40s. per annum from 18 Jan. 1483 to 29 Sept. 1484 and 10s. for Christmas term 1486–7; described as *physicus*; probably convent's physician throughout this period. WAM 18673–4, 19980. See also Appendix V, no. 67.

37. THOMAS COLCHESTER, MR. Convent's physician 29 Sept. 1409 to 24 June 1413. Received a fee rising from 13s. 4d. to 40s. per annum. WAM 19403–7; *MPME* 337.

38. THOMAS DE WALCOTE. Convent's physician 1347–8; received a fee of £2 13s. 4d. WAM 19330. Cf. *MPME* 193, where the first name is 'John'.

39. WILLIAM, MR. Convent's physician 1351–2, probably for the whole year, though only a quarter's fee is recorded. In course of that year, attended a session in the infirmary, with the apothecary, Thomas Walden, sen. (no. 15 above) to settle the account for a year's prescriptions. WAM 19332. Probably identical with no. 43 below.

40. WILLIAM. Convent's physician; received a fee of 26s. 8d. in 1505–6. *MPME* 380.

41. WILLIAM DE PYL, BM. Convent's physician 1361–5, but with some interruptions which were probably occasioned by his absence from Westminster and London. For a full year's service, William was entitled to a fee of £4, a robe with 2 furs of budge costing 26s. 8d., and a cartload of hay for his horse. In 1361–2 he forfeited the robe and a quarter's fee on account of absence; the failure to give him a robe in 1363–4 is probably to be explained in the same way. WAM 19340–1, 19343–4; *MPME* 411; *BRUO* ii. 1133.

42. WILLIAM TANKERVILLE, MR. Convent's physician, 1358–61 and 1366–70. Received a fee of 40s. per annum 1358–61 and £4 per annum 1366–70. The annual robe to which he was entitled was also priced more highly in the later period: it was now a 'large' robe with 3 furs, such as the Abbey gave to its squires; in 1369–70 it used a third of a [broad]cloth (i.e. *c*.8 yards of cloth) and cost, with furs, 30s. WAM 19340–7; *MPME* 417.

43. WILLIAM WALLERAM. Convent's physician 1350–1. Received a fee of £2 10s. per annum. WAM 19331, 19847; and see no. 39 above. Cf. *MPME* 418.

## Surgeons[3]

44. JOHN BRADMORE. Called in, with other surgeons and physicians, in 1390–1. In 1401–2 received 6s. 8d. for treating Br. William Ashwell. A

---

[3] John Arderne, who received a stipend and robe from the infirmarer in 1378–9, was, it appears, the infirmary butler, not the surgeon of that name (WAM 19355–6).

licensed surgeon. WAM 19375, 19392; *MPME* 123–4; and see also above, p. 86; Rawcliffe, 'The profits of practice', 69; and S. J. Lang, 'John Bradmore and his book Philomena', *Social History of Medicine* v (1992), 121–30.

45. WILLIAM DE OTEWYK, alias OTEWYCH. Treated a case of *tibia* in 1309–10. The nature of the case makes it likely that he was a surgeon, not a physician, and this identification is confirmed in other sources. WAM 19320; *MPME* 409; Getz, 'Medical practitioners in medieval England', 282.

46. WILLIAM WADESWORTH. Called in, with other surgeons and physicians, in 1390–1. WAM 19375.

47. WILLIAM DE WODESTRET. Received 2s. for surgery on a monk in 1322–3. WAM 19324.

# APPENDIX IV

## Estimating the Life-Expectancy of the Monks
## of Westminster

### by Jim Oeppen

If the complete life-histories of all the members of a cohort of individuals are known, it is a simple matter to calculate their average life-expectancy at each year of life. The sum of the remaining lifetimes or person-years at any given age is divided by the number of individuals who are still alive to give the average life-expectancy at that age. The data for the monks of Westminster cannot be analysed in this simple way for three reasons.

First, not all dates of death are known. Some monks left the monastery, so that if the simple method of calculation were followed, life-expectancy would be underestimated, as the part of their lifetimes spent outside Westminster, after their departure, could not be added to the numerator. This problem is referred to in the statistical literature as right-censoring—the situation where it is only known that a death must have occurred after a certain date.[1] An allowance for this problem is particularly important in the last two cohorts, where the proportion of individuals lost to observation rises to a half as a result of the Dissolution in 1540. Four deaths are known after this date, the data-set terminating with the death in 1577 of the oldest of the four. In a minor way, the same problem may affect other cohorts, as monks were sometimes absent from the monastery temporarily, for short or long periods.

The second problem concerns the fact that not all the monks joined at the same age. This is known as left-truncation of the data. For the calculation of life-expectancy at a particular age to include all the data above that age, an allowance must be made for the fact that some monks may have been living in another mortality environment which, by definition, did not result in their death. For example, Richard Southbrooke had already spent some time at Oxford and was probably about 30 on his profession at Westminster.[2] If he had died in Oxford, he would never have appeared in the data—his inclusion is conditioned on his surviving to move to Westminster and

---

[1] For an introduction to event-history analysis see J. D. Kalbfleisch and R. L. Prentice, *The Statistical Analysis of Failure Time Data* (New York, 1980).
[2] Southbrooke became a scholar of New College in 1397 and entered the monastery in 1412–13. According to the statutes of New College, scholars were to be between 15 and 20 years of age. *BRUO* iii. 1733–4; J. McConica, 'The rise of the undergraduate college', in McConica (ed.), *The History of the University of Oxford*, iii (Oxford, 1986), 1–68, at 2–3.

enter the monastery. Without the necessary adjustment, he would be contributing 10 person-years to the data underlying life-expectancy at age 20,
in a period when it was impossible for him to contribute a death. Life-
expectancies calculated for ages 30 and above would need no such adjustment, because his death could then appear in the data.

To overcome these two problems, the life-expectancy estimates were
calculated using a method developed by Turnbull.[3] It is based on Efron's
*self-consistency algorithm*[4] and is appropriate to a wider class of problems
that historians might face in analysing life-history data than the one considered here. The procedure can be understood intuitively in the following
manner. Suppose that 100 monks entered at age 20 and had death ages spread
over the next 80 years. The simple method of calculating life-expectancy, or
any other life-table curve, would apply. At each age from 20 onwards, the
proportion left alive or survivorship curve could be calculated. Imagine that
there was one more monk who entered at 30 and left at 50, thus combining
the first two problems identified in the Westminster data. Intuitively, this
additional piece of data must lead to a slightly improved estimate of life-
expectancy after 30. How can it be combined efficiently with the estimates
based on the 100?

Turnbull proposed that the individual should be 'phased in' from 20 to
30 and 'phased out' after 50 according to the survivorship curve of the 100
individuals with the full data. In order to get exactly 1 person at age 30, more
than 1 person, say 1.2, would have to enter at 20 and be subjected to the
mortality regime of the 100. The survival curve for the 1.2 monks would fall
to 1 by age 30, but remain at 1 to 50 before falling again. With suitable
weighting, the survivorship curve for the 100 individuals can be combined
with that for 1.2 'monks' using the simple method. The outcome would
probably be slightly different from the original curve based on 100, so the
procedure of inferring the complete curve for the 'problem' monk and
combining it with the rest is repeated, with the output curve being used as
the input at each successive iteration. When the output is effectively the
same as the input, the estimates are self-consistent in Efron's terms. Turnbull
proved that the iteration always converges and that the estimates have certain
desirable statistical properties.

The final problem with the data concerns the lack of known ages at entry.
If one were only concerned with elapsed time after entry to the data-set, as
might be the case with heart-transplant survivors, for example, then there is
no problem: the time-scale would start at entry. However, for these data the
scale of interest is calendar-age, so that each individual's lifetime is the sum

[3] B. W. Turnbull, 'The empirical distribution function', *Jnl. of the Royal Statistical Society*,
Series B (1976), xxxviii. 290–5.
[4] B. Efron, 'The two-sample problem with censored data', *Proc. of the Fifth Berkeley Sym-
posium Math. Statist. Prob.* iv (University of California Press, Berkeley, Calif., 1967), 831–3.

of two intervals: birth to entry, which may be unknown, and entry to death or departure. Thus any alteration in the assumed age at entry of one or more of the individuals will naturally affect the estimates of average life-expectancy for the monks. Fortunately, the nature of the calculations makes the possible biases behave in a manner that is likely to be predictable.

The two intervals that form the lifetime of each monk are clearly additive and can be assumed to be statistically independent. Therefore, taking the data on the monastic interval as given, adding one year to all ages at entry will increase life-expectancy by one year. Similarly, if the trend in the fall in age at entry has been underestimated, then the fall in life-expectancy at each age over time has also been underestimated to the same degree. Simple changes in all ages at entry have easily predicted effects because the relative positions of individual monastic lifetimes are unchanged. However, a change affecting a sub-set of the monks, for example, to the small group ordained before entry, would lead to smaller but less predictable change. Fortunately the number of individuals whose ages at entry are unknown—i.e. cannot be estimated from the ordination data—is relatively small.[5]

Finally, it should be borne in mind that, because of the small number of individuals available in this data set, the confidence intervals around the estimates must be relatively large. Random variation about the assumed age of entry must, even if the expected value is unaffected, lead to widening of the confidence interval surrounding each estimate. Nevertheless, the dramatic scale of the changes is likely to swamp small changes in the data and this, together with the broad coincidence in both levels and trend between the Westminster and Canterbury estimates in their common period, forces one to conclude that there was a significant decline and recovery in the survivorship of the monks. That this should have happened to an adult group living in a relatively unchanging internal environment distinguishes it from the only other quantified change of this magnitude in England: the improvements in the nineteenth century associated with changes in urban public health.

---

[5] Above, pp. 118–21.

# APPENDIX V

## Corrodians of Westminster Abbey, 1100–1540[1]

1. AIMAR THE HERMIT. A corrodian who evidently died in or before c.1130; see below, no. 2.

2. ANCHORESSES, LATER NUNS, OF KILBURN. 1127 × 34 three women, the nucleus of the community, were granted in perpetuity (i) the corrody of bread, ale, mead, wine, and pittances formerly held by Aimar the hermit for his life, and (ii) the corrody given daily in alms for monks of Westminster and Fécamp, living and deceased (*Westminster Abbey Charters*, no. 249). (iii) 1138 × 57, the nuns of Kilburn were granted in perpetuity the corrody given daily in alms for Abbot Gilbert Crispin, with claret [*sc.* on feasts and

---

The following terms are used in our sources and in this appendix: (Ale) *conventual ale*: best ale, as given daily to each monk; *meyne ale*: second-best ale, as given to many servants; *nuns' ale*: ale, inferior to conventual ale, and of the quality given to the nuns of Kilburn. (Bread) *conventual loaf*: a loaf, sometimes described as 'white', made from relatively fine flour and of the quality and weight given daily to each monk; *meyne bread/loaf*: bread/loaf, sometimes described as 'black', made from relatively coarse flour and given to servants; *myche loaf*: a large conventual loaf; *pumpe loaf*: probably a conventual loaf; *wastel bread*: bread for festal occasions, made from very fine flour and baked in a very hot oven. (Corrodies) *monk's corrody*: a daily allowance of victuals, as given to a monk, sometimes broken down into its component parts, the corrody in the cellar, and the corrody in the kitchen or refectory; *monk's corrody in the cellar*: a daily allowance of one conventual loaf and, until *c.*1350, one *gazo* (q.v.), but thereafter one gallon, of conventual ale; *monk's corrody in the kitchen or refectory*: a daily mess of each of the two main courses, known as 'generals' (*generalia*) served at dinner to monks eating in the refectory, but sometimes commuted, for corrodians, into a money pension; *servant's corrody*, sometimes referred to as *a free servant's corrody*: the daily allowance of victuals of a servant with an established position in the household; this always included bread and ale ('the corrody in the cellar'), but did not necessarily include cooked food ('the corrody in the kitchen or refectory') as well. (Other) *gazo*, pl. *gazones*: a measure of ale, equivalent to $1^1/_2$ gallons (WAM 5917, 18887; WD 218); *livery*: in the present context, an allowance of clothing or cloth in lieu.

The following abbreviations are used in this appendix: *a. and c.* abbot and convent; *conv.* conventual; *d.* daughter; *gall.* gallon; *p. and c.* prior and convent; *s.* son; *yd.* yard. Square brackets indicate that a corrody was requested for the person in question but that the outcome of the request is uncertain.

[1] The list excludes officials and servants who held corrodies *ex officio*, the parochial chaplains of Paddington and Tothill, who were also corrodians, and pensioners receiving only cash benefits. Among the latter were the beneficiaries of the claim advanced by Edward I, Edward II, and Edward III that the Abbey was bound to find a suitable benefice for a royal clerk on every new creation of an abbot, and to provide the clerk with a pension until the benefice was found; for this claim, see *Cal. Cl. R., 1313–18*, 452, and ibid. *1343–6*, 566. For the chaplains see WAM 5919* and *Customary*, ii. 73, 79. The king also claimed corrodies in the cellar for 3 Exchequer or Chancery clerks; for references to these see WAM 18887, 33315.

The practice of giving the corrody of a deceased monk to a poor secular priest for a chantry in the year after death is mentioned in the 13th cent., may have been long-lasting, but, even so, was probably superseded by the late 15th cent. None of these corrodians is known by name. WD 637ᵛ–638, and below, no. 67.

anniversaries] (ibid., no. 264, and for the wine, *Customary*, ii. 79). Since Gilbert was abbot, his corrody would have included double rations: i.e. the nuns now had the equivalent of 4 corrodies. In the early 16th cent., they are said in an Abbey source to be entitled to 28 conv. loaves @ ³/₄*d.* and 45 galls. conv. ale per week @ 1¼*d.* and to cooked food @ £1 6*s.* 8*d.* per annum. Total value per annum of corrodies according to this source: £20 9*s.* 1*d.*; actual total according to the stated values of the several items: £18 1*s.* 5*d.* (WAM 5919*; cf. *VE* i. 432). A reference to 'nuns' ale' in the 13th cent. (below, no. 13) shows that the nuns had not always been given the best brew. For Kilburn Priory see Thompson, *Women Religious: The Founding of English Nunneries after the Norman Conquest*, 25–6, 63.

3. THE ABBEY'S JANITOR. *Temp.* Abbot Herbert (1121–36), purchased a corrody of 2 messes of cooked food per day in fee; this was additional to the corrody to which the janitor was entitled *ex officio* (*Customary*, ii. 73).

4. GILBERT DE CLAYGATE. *Temp.* Henry II, Gilbert was granted in fee a corrody consisting of 1 qu. wheat, 1 qu. rye, 2 qu. oats, and 2 qu. barley per annum, together with the office of servant in the almonry and the corrody annexed to the latter, also 2 houses in the precinct on the land formerly belonging to Alice Picot—those nearest the monastery are specified—in exchange for the quitclaim to the a. and c. of his estate in Claygate (Surr.) *et quicquid juris in eadem villa habere videbatur*, and his land in Kingscroft (WD 465ᵛ, LNQ 78). The transaction may have concluded a long-drawn-out attempt by the Abbey to recover seisin of land in Claygate whose loss is implied 1155 × 1158 in *Westminster Abbey Charters*, no. 125. For the liveries of grain see WAM 18965 ff.

5. RICHARD DE PADDINGTON AND WIFE, and WILLIAM DE PADDINGTON AND WIFE. In 1185, in a final concord terminating a plea in the king's court, they were granted 4 corrodies and the sum of 40 marks of silver (£26 13*s.* 4*d.*). Richard and William, who were brothers, were each to hold 1 corrody for 12 years, their wives 1 each for life. The wives' corrodies included pittances. In exchange, Richard and William quitclaimed to the abbot their tenement in Paddington *et quicquid juris in eo habebant*. WAM 16194; WD 470ᵛ.

6. MATILDA d. of SIMON S. of OSMAR, also called MATILDA PARIS. *c.*1200 she was promised a sufficiency of food and clothing in exchange for the gift to the Abbey in pure and perpetual alms of 1½ hides in Harrow (*Herghes*), belonging to fee of the archbishop of Canterbury, to whom the Abbey was to render 5*s.* per annum (WD 502–502ᵛ).

7. BELA DE LONDON, widow of AUGUSTINE FITZ EUSTACE, mercer, and d. of JOCE LE PELUR. In the mid-13th cent. Bela was granted a monk's corrody in the cellar and kitchen, probably in exchange for the quitclaim to the a. and c. of land, with houses on it, in parish of St Laurence, Candlewick Street, which she and Augustine had sold to William Chenduit, rector, and which the latter had granted to the a. and c. in free alms *c.*1230, the grant to take

effect after his death. A plea of right, brought by Bela, in Guildhall, London, is mentioned and probably preceded the exchange. In 1276, after further litigation, Thomas, her s., quitclaimed the property and the corrody to the a. and c. WD 488ᵛ–489; Harvey, *Estates*, 390 and n.

8. ROBERT DE BEVERLEY. A master mason, occurring frequently in witness lists at the Abbey in the mid-13th cent. (WD 459, 522ᵛ, 524, etc.). For his monk's corrody, see *Customary*, ii. 79.

9. LAURENCE DE WANDLESWORTH. Said in 1258 to hold corrodies which had been granted in return for land in Pensham (Worcs.); accommodation in the infirmary is implied (*Customary*, ii. 244). The grants were probably connected with the Abbey's assumption, c.1248, of responsibility for his debt to Moses s. of Benedict Crespin. Eventually, the Abbey acquired the whole of Laurence's estate in Worcs. and Glos., but, for a time, he held land of it in Todenham (Glos.). WAM 5079; Harvey, *Estates*, 170 and n.

10. OSBERT DE STEVENAGE. Described as a palmer (i.e. pilgrim). In 1258, during the vacancy after Abbot Crokesley's death, Osbert was granted a corrody, for life, consisting of 6 qu. wheat, 2 qu. barley, and 1 qu. oats per annum from the grange at Stevenage, 4s. per annum, payable at Mich. (29 Sept.) and Easter, for clothing, and 4 cartloads of brushwood per annum. In exchange, he quitclaimed to the p. and c. his tenements in Stevenage, including houses, croft, and garden, a virgate of land said to have been formerly customary land (*que quondam terra consuetudinaria fuit*), and 5 acres of assarted land near the wood at Stevenage, though he retained a life-interest in the houses, croft, and garden. *Temp.* Abbot Ware (1258–83), these arrangements were altered: Osbert, though recognizing that his former tenements belonged to the Abbey's demesne, was granted a life-interest in the whole property, excepting only the assart; and his wife, if the survivor, was promised reasonable dower in the land, now described as 3 acres on west side of the highway and 2 acres on east side. WD 213ᵛ–214.

11. MATILDA, d. of ADAM DE DEORHURSTE. In mid-13th cent. Matilda was granted a monk's corrody in the refectory, including wine and pittances, and, additionally, in the cellar, 1 *pumpe* loaf, 1 *meyne* loaf, and 1 *gazo* 'church' (i.e. conv.) ale per day, together with a servant's mess of cooked food there, in exchange for her inheritance in Battersea, which the a. and c. were to hold of her and her heirs for a quit-rent of 1 lb. cumin per annum. Matilda, a widow, also received 12 marks (£8) towards the marriage of her 2 ds. Adam de Deorhurste is mentioned c.1225 as the free tenant of 3 virgates of land in Battersea. WD 162–162ᵛ; Harvey, *Estates*, 110 n.

12. RALPH DE FREMINGHAM, MR. Occurs as a royal justice (WD 599–600). By 1265, held a monk's corrody, including wine on feast days and anniversaries, and flans, and a free servant's corrody in the cellar and kitchen, for life. A connection between this grant and the Abbey's acquisition of land at Combe (Kent), 1245 × 1257, is possible. WD 591ᵛ–592; *Customary*, ii. 79.

13. JOHN S. of ROBERT HUMPHREY. In 1275 John was granted, for life, a corrody consisting of 1 white (i.e. conv.) loaf, 2 servants' loaves, 1 *gazo* good (i.e. conv.) ale, 1 *gazo* nuns' ale, and 2 messes of cooked food—all per day; 10s. per annum; and a house outside the precinct, which the a. and c. were to keep in repair; 4 cartloads of wood per annum, or 2s. in lieu; and 2 trusses of hay per annum. The victuals are described as a monk's corrody. The a. and c. undertook to find employment for his s. In exchange, John quitclaimed to them his tenement in Stevenage and the reversion of his mother's dower there on her decease. The lands in question no doubt included the arable field, 21½ measured acres in extent, which belonged to the demesne of Stevenage in the early 14th cent. and was then known as *Umfrayesfeld*. WD 218; CUL, MS Kk. 5. 29, fo. 79; and for the nuns of Kilburn, above, no. 2.

14. JOAN, widow of GEOFFREY DE BOLSCHAMELE. In 1282 Joan was granted a corrody including 6 bus. wheat and 6 bus. oats per annum for life, the wheat to be paid at Mich. (29 Sept.) and the oats at feast of Purification (2 Feb.). In exchange, Joan surrendered her dower in lands in Feering (Essex), which her husband had demised to the a. and c. (WD 248). In 1289 Geoffrey's lands are described as a messuage and 34 acres of arable and meadow (CUL, MS Kk, 5. 29, fo. 100). In 1295 Joan quitclaimed her corrody to the a. and c. (WD 248; see also WAM 25582 ff.).

15. ROGER LE PRESTENDEN. Was granted a so-called servant's corrody consisting of 1 loaf of *meyne* bread and 1 *gazo* second-best (i.e. *meyne*) ale per day, *temp.* Abbot Wenlok (1283–1307), to whom he was related. Roger quitclaimed the corrody to the p. and c. in 1309, in the vacancy following Wenlok's death. WAM 31754; *Walter de Wenlok*, 247 n.

16. ROBERT TIPTOFT/TYPETOT. A royal servant employed by Edward I in Wales and on the Continent. A reference to the repair of his chamber in the infirmary in 1297 or 1298, possibly after the fire in the infirmary in the latter year, provides the only, but sufficient, evidence that Robert was a corrodian. Died 22 May 1298, at his manor of Nettlestead. WAM 19318; *DNB* xix. 894.

17. ALICE, widow of EBORARD LE PARKER. In 1299–1302 Alice received small liveries of wheat (2 or 3 bus. per annum) from the grange at Birdbrook (Essex). These were probably part of a corrody intended to compensate her for the taking of Eborard's land into the demesne after his death in 1298 or 1299, and the denial to her of continued residence in the dwelling appurtenant to it. In 1299–1300 Beatrice, Eborard's d., also received some wheat. Alice married, secondly, Philip le Archer, who took part in an unsuccessful attempt to prevent her ejection from the house, where he may have been cohabiting at the time. WAM 25401–7. (I am indebted to Dr Phillipp Schofield for these references.)

18. [HENRY DE MONTPELLIER.] A royal serjeant and wardrobe clerk (Tout,

*Chapters*, ii. 23–4, 41 and n.). In 1303 Edward I requested the grant of a corrody of food and clothing for Henry and his groom, for the term of Henry's life, the grant to be made under the common seal of the Abbey (*Cal. Pat. R., 1301–7*, 188).

19. SIMON BOLEBEK. Said to be of Kingsey (Bucks.) and Oxon. In or before 1304, Simon was granted a corrody at the request of Margaret of France. It included annual livery of a robe on All Saints' Day, or £1 in lieu. WAM 19841–2, 29234, 29306, 29336.

20. JOHN DE SOMERSET. A corrodian nominated by Edward I; deceased in or before 1315 (below, nos. 26–7).

21. AGNES CAPOUN. A corrodian nominated by Edward I; deceased in or before 1324 (below, nos. 34 and 40).

22. THOMAS SEMAN. A bailiff employed on manorial duties; later bailiff of Westminster (*Walter de Wenlok*, no. 258 and n.; Rosser, *Medieval West-minster*, 329). In 1312 Thomas quitclaimed to Abbot Kedyngton a so-called servant's corrody consisting of 1 loaf of *meyne* bread, and 1 *gazo meyne* ale per day, which he had earlier been granted, probably in the vacancy (1307–10) after Abbot Wenlok's death. WAM 31756.

23. HENRY LE AVENER. Held, by 1311, a monk's corrody in the cellar, and later a full monk's corrody; also 20s. per annum in lieu of a robe. A royal nominee, and said to be of Watford. Payment of the fee continued until 1333. PRO C 270/6/23–4; WAM 29447, 29459, 29466, etc.

24. [STEPHEN LE BARBER]. See below, no. 25.

25. [ROBERT WHITHEVED.] Described as a servant to Edward I and Edward II. In 1311, and again *temp.* Abbot William de Curtlington (1315–33), Edward II requested a corrody for him, such as Stephen le Barber, now deceased, had enjoyed in the monastery at the request of Edward I. The a. and c. denied that Stephen le Barber had ever held a corrody in their house, and there is no evidence that Robert Whitheved was more successful. PRO C270/6/23; WAM 5883.

26. [RALPH DE LA PANETRIE.] In 1315 Edward II requested a corrody for him, identical with that granted by the a. and c. to John de Somerset, now deceased, at the request of Edward I, whom Ralph also served (*Cal. Cl. R., 1313–18*, 233; and see above, no. 20.

27. [MATILDA DE HAUKESEYE.] A royal laundress, for whom, in 1317, and on account of her long service, Edward II requested a corrody identical with that of John de Somerset, now deceased (*Cal. Cl. R., 1313–18*, 453; and see nos. 20, 26).

28. JOHN DE MOCKYNGE (alias MACCHYNG), and IDONEA, his wife. In 1317 John, said to be of Somerset, and Idonea were granted a corrody consisting of 2 conv. loaves and 1 *gazo* conv. ale [*sc.* per day], for their joint and several lives, the loaves and ale to be collected once or twice a week, as they should choose (WAM 5891). For a 15th-cent. reference to John Macchyng's house

in the precinct, the garden of which extended to the south side of St Margaret's church, see WAM 17736. The endorsement to WAM 5891, *Registratur*, is of interest, suggesting as it does that in this period the monastery entered such grants in a register or cartulary other than those which have survived: the latter do not contain this grant.

29. GILBERT DE CONEHAM. In 1319 Gilbert purchased a corrody for an unspecified cash sum. It consisted of 1 conv. loaf and 1 *gazo* conv. ale, also 1 *meyne* loaf, 1 *gazo meyne* ale, together with 2 dishes of cooked food and pottage as served to a monk in the refectory—all per day (WAM 5912). (The whole represented a monk's corrody in the cellar and kitchen, and a servant's corrody in the cellar, but these terms are not used.) Gilbert was to be permitted to collect the food daily or once or twice a week, in person or by deputy. He probably held property in Tothill, Westminster (WAM 17567).

30. THOMAS DE COVENTRY. Described as a chaplain. On 22 Feb. 1319 Thomas was granted a corrody consisting of 7 conv. loaves and 7 galls. conv. ale per week, to be taken from the cellar on Saturdays, until the a. and c. should present him to a fitting benefice. On 25 Feb. 1319 he acquitted the a. and c. of arrears for 26 years of a pension of £2 per annum. This pension was also to cease when he obtained the benefice. See WAM 5913–14, 29395. Thomas was later presented to St James, Garlic Hythe, of which he was incumbent at his death in or before 1331 (*Registrum Radulphi Baldock, Gilberti Segrave, Ricardi Newport, et Stephani Gravesend, episcoporum Londoniensium*, AD *MCCCIV–MCCCXXXVIII*, ed. R. C. Fowler (CYS 7, 1911), 295.

31. [JOHN LESCUREL.] In 1319 Edward II requested a corrody of food and drink for John, a serjeant-at-arms, said to have served both the king and his father at home and abroad but now to be old and weak. The corrody was to be appropriate to his status. WAM 5882.

32. WILLIAM S. of RICHARD MARY. Said to be of Addington (Berks.). In 1319 William was granted a monk's corrody, itemized as 1 conv. loaf, 1 *gazo* conv. ale, and 2 dishes of 'generals' from the kitchen—all per day. The bread and ale might be collected once a week, if William desired, in person or by his assign; the cooked food was to be received daily. WAM 5917.

33. ADAM MASCHEBERY, and ISABELLA, his wife. In 1319 they were granted a corrody consisting of 3 conv. loaves and 2 *gazones* conv. ale per day, to be received once or twice a week, if desired, in London or elsewhere. WAM 5911.

34. [WILLIAM BALSHAM.] In 1324 Edward II requested that William be granted maintenance identical with that formerly enjoyed by Agnes Capoun, now deceased; William is described as a servant of long standing of Edward and Isabella (WAM 5880; *Cal. Cl. R., 1323–7*, 176; and see above, no. 21).

35. ROGER GERARD. In 1325 Roger was granted a corrody with a life-term. It consisted of 2 conv. loaves and 2 *gazones* conv. ale per day, to be

collected either daily or once or twice a week, and in person or by deputy (WAM 5896). He is mentioned on occasion as selling corn to the Abbey (WAM 19155, 19845, etc.). In 1362–3 the Abbey acquired a substantial property in Hendon which had belonged to him (Harvey, *Estates*, 172).

36. WALTER LE FRAUNCEYS and JULIANA, his wife. Said to be 'of Westminster'. On 28 Oct. 1325, when Walter surrendered the office of summoner at the Abbey, which he had held in serjeanty, and the corrody annexed to it, he and Juliana were granted a corrody consisting of 1 conv. loaf, 1 *meyne* loaf, 1 *gazo* conv. ale, and 2 dishes from the kitchen per day, and supper when other seculars received supper from the convent's kitchen; this was to be held for their joint and several lives. WAM 5887.

37. WILLIAM DE WESTON. In 1327 William, a baker, purchased a corrody consisting of 1 *myche* loaf, 1 *meyne* loaf, and 1 *gazo* best (i.e. conv.) ale per day, for a sum which is not specified. The bread and ale were to be collected once or twice a week, personally or by deputy. WAM 5915.

38. [WILLIAM DE LA CORNERE.] In 1330 William obtained privy seal letters requesting that a sufficient maintenance (*sustentacio*) be found for him: food, clothing, shoes, and all other necessities were to be provided, the grant to be made under the Abbey's common seal. He is described on this occasion as chamberlain to Robert de Fiennes, who was formerly Queen Isabella's seneschal in Ponthieu. WAM 5881; Tout, *Chapters*, v. 277–8.

39. [RICHARD DE LUDA.] A royal clerk and Exchequer official, said to have served Edward I, Edward II, and Edward III. In 1331 Edward III requested a corrody for him, with a life-term: it was to include food, drink, clothing, and shoes, for himself and his yeoman, together with a chamber in the Abbey enclosure, and candles, fuel, and other necessities appropriate to the maintenance of a royal clerk. The grant was to be under the common seal, and the a. and c. were to send their reply by the bearer of the king's letter. The king's letter, dated 12 Jan. 1331, was received by the a. and c. on 28 Feb. In their reply, dated 2 Mar., the a. and c. pleaded the existing burden on their resources represented by 2 corrodies in the cellar for Exchequer clerks, the corrody of Henry le Avener, and by the pensions—respectively £5 and £3 6s. 8d. per annum—of Simon de Monte Acuto and John de Nassington, who were evidently royal nominees. PRO C260/6/24; *Cal. Cl. R., 1330–3*, 183–4; above, no. 23; and for Richard de Luda, see M. Prestwich, *Edward I* (London, 1988), 431–2, s.n. Louth.

40. [JOHN DE WHITCHURCH.] A yeoman of the queen's chamber. In 1334 Edward III requested maintenance for him identical with that formerly enjoyed, at Edward I's order, by Agnes Capoun, now deceased; it was to be held for a life-term. *Cal. Cl. R., 1333–7*, 317; and see above, no. 21.

41. RICHARD COUNCEDON. Was granted a corrody with a life-term c.1336, at the request of Edward III, who released the a. and c. from any obligation to receive another corrodian in Richard's place when he should die (*Cal. Pat. R., 1334–8*, 261).

42. WILLIAM BROUN and THOMAS MORLEE. On 25 Apr. 1341 were granted a corrody, described as a monk's corrody, but itemized as 2 conv. loaves, and 1 *gazo* conv. ale per day, with £1 per annum in rents in Westminster, Knightsbridge, and Paddington. (The latter sum was probably in lieu of cooked food.) William and Thomas and their assigns, and the heirs of Thomas, were to enjoy the corrody for the term of William's life. See WAM 5889–90. In addition, William and Thomas were granted £6 13s. 4d. per annum in rents in the same manors (WAM 17628). On the same day, William granted to nominees acting on behalf of the a. and c. all his tenements in Eye, Knightsbridge, and Westbourne, and the reversion of those which were on lease to John le Holbourn and Robert de Capella for a term of years. Subsequently, these tenements were demised to William and Thomas for a term of 3 years, with provision for the death of either within the term. WAM 16206, 16226, 16231; cf. WAM Loan 5.

43. JOHN DE TOTHALE. A monk of Westminster who left the Abbey in 1338 to become prior of its cell at Hurley. In 1352, at Edward III's request, the a. and c. granted him a full monk's corrody and occupancy of a chamber in the infirmary for life; the grant was not to be regarded as a precedent. *Cal. Pat. R., 1350–4*, 255; and see *Monks*, 77–8.

44. IVO DE FULHAM. In 1360 Ivo purchased a corrody, with a life-term, consisting of 2 *myche* loaves and 2 galls. conv. ale per day, as served in the refectory, for a sum which is not specified. The bread and ale were to be collected once or twice a week, according to Ivo's preference. If the corrody were to be withheld for more than 3 months, Ivo might distrain in the Abbey's manor of Knightsbridge or elsewhere in Middx. WAM 5910.

45. THOMAS DOLSALY. Son of Henry Dolsaly, a London pepperer. In 1362 Thomas purchased the bread and ale belonging to the corrody of Br. William de Yepeswich, then studying at Oxford, for the period 22 Feb. to 29 June (WAM 19855). At the time, Thomas was in receipt of a pension of £40 per annum and yearly livery of a robe, these having been granted by Abbot Langham (1349–62), in each case for Thomas's life. In 1364 Thomas quitclaimed both pension and robe to the a. and c. The size of the pension, which has no parallel among the Abbey's ordinary arrangements relating to pensions, suggests that it was part of a loan agreement. WAM 5909.

46. RICHARD DE HEYLE. On 25 June 1367 Richard was granted a corrody, with a life-term, consisting of 2 conv. loaves and 2 galls. conv. ale per day, annual livery of a squire's robe with furs, a pension of £20 per annum, and occupancy of the house in the precinct formerly occupied by Sir John Molyns, knight, the a. and c. to be responsible for repairs. In exchange, Richard demised the manor of Chelsea to the a. and c. for the term of his own life: this manor had been alienated *temp.* Abbot Gervase de Blois in the mid-12th cent. for a rent, now remitted, of £4 per annum. However, the arrangement was short-lived, because Richard died in or about 1369. WAM 19861 ff.; *Cal. Cl. R., 1364–8*, 385–6; Harvey, *Estates*, 167 and n.

47. THOMAS GYNES and MATILDA, his wife. An annual allowance of fuel (100 talwood and 100 faggots) to Thomas and Matilda is mentioned in 1386 and subsequently, and was, no doubt, part of a larger corrody; the fuel was to be delivered to their door. The corrody was probably granted in 1373, when Thomas surrendered the office of servant in the convent's kitchen, which he had held in perpetuity and to which a corrody was annexed. Thomas, who survived his wife, died in 1411. WAM 5906, 18520–48.

48. THOMAS SOUTHAM. A pluralist, whose benefices included the archdeaconry of Oxford; to the Abbey, an important person, since he was an executor of the will of Simon Langham (d. 1376) (*BRUO* iii. 1733; Widmore, *Enquiry*, 189). His corrody included 2 conv. loaves and 2 galls. conv. ale per day, annual livery of 10 yds. of cloth and furs of strandling, with, on occasion, additional livery for a squire, and occupancy of a chamber in the monastery. Thomas was probably a corrodian from 1378 to 1404 but may have ceased to reside by 1401, when a reference occurs to the chamber *nuper Thome Southam*. He died in 1404. WAM 18886–7; and for the Abbey's loan of books to Southam in 1369, see J. Armitage Robinson and M. R. James, *Manuscripts of Westminster Abbey* (Cambridge, 1909), 8 n.

49. WALTER METTECOMBE, alias MYDLECOMBE, and MARGARET, his wife. A corrody including 2 conv. loaves and 2 galls. conv. ale per day, 2 galls. wine on the feast of SS Peter and Paul (29 June) and again on that of St Peter in Chains (1 Aug.), 1 cartload of straw, 400 talwood, 6 qu. charcoal, and 12 lbs. of candles per annum, together with annual livery of robes with furs of lambskin and budge, and an allowance of £6 1s. 8d. per annum ( = 4d. per day) in lieu of cooked food, is mentioned from 1379–80. The corrody was probably part of a transaction in real property involving the warden of Eleanor of Castile's manors, and this obedientiary bore the main cost. In 1403–4 Walter is said to have been formerly seised of the manor of Stangraves (Kent). Margaret died in 1387–8, when the warden met some of the expenses of her burial. William subsequently remarried; his second wife was alive at his death in 1407 and received an *ex gratia* livery of 5 yds. of cloth; thereafter the corrody lapsed. WAM 18887, 23707–48.

50. ROBERT ALEYN, and MATILDA, his wife. Robert was a London fishmonger and a knight. He and Matilda were granted a corrody consisting of 14 conv. loaves and 14 galls. conv. ale per week, together with a pension of £6 13s. 4d. per annum, in 1392, for their joint and several lives; in exchange, they granted to the a. and c. land and a mill at Stratford (Essex). Robert died in 1401 or 1402; Matilda, in 1405. LNQ 88; WAM 19876 ff.; Harvey, *Estates*, 424.

51. WILLIAM BARBOUR, and MARGERY, his wife. In 1411 William paid £120 for a corrody for their joint and several lives. It included a pension of £5 per annum; other details are not recorded. William, the survivor, probably died in 1442–3, when payment of the pension ceased. He is said to be of Fleet Street, London. WAM 17768, 19900–45.

52. JOHN CHERTSEY, and JOAN, his wife. In 1418 they were granted a corrody for their joint and several lives. It comprised 100 long faggots and 18 qu. charcoal per annum, a pension of £5 per annum, annual livery of a squire's robe with furs of lambskin, and remission of rent of £4 per annum owing for property in the precinct held on lease by the Chertseys. Approximate annual value of the corrody in 1418: £10 13s. 4d. It can be assumed that the sum of £133 6s. 4d. received from John in that year was the payment for the corrody, though this point is not made explicit. John died in 1425; Joan in 1465–6. WAM 19912 ff.

53. JOHN PYKEWORTH, and AGNES, his wife. In 1418 John, described as a squire, paid £40 for a corrody comprising 400 faggots, 12 qu. charcoal, and 20 lbs. candles per annum, a pension of 1d. per day ( = £1 10s. 5d. per annum) in lieu of cooked food, and remission of rent of £2 13s. 4d. per annum owing for property leased from the Abbey in the sanctuary. The pension of 1d. per day was probably a conventional allowance in lieu of 'generals', the main courses at the monastic dinner; if so, it can be assumed that John and Agnes held a monk's corrody and were therefore entitled, additionally, to 1 conv. loaf and 1 gall. conv. ale per day. Approximate annual value of the corrody, on this assumption, in 1418: £8 7s. 11d. On John's death in 1420 or 1421, the corrody was transferred to Agnes, whom he may have married after purchasing it; she died in 1426. WAM 19913–25, 19664–7.

54. THOMAS STONE, and JOAN, his wife. In 1418 Thomas paid £150 for a corrody for their joint and several lives. It comprised 500 faggots, 24 lbs. candles, and 14 qu. charcoal per annum, a pension of £5 6s. 8d. per annum ( = 3½d. per day), annual livery of 2 squire's robes, and remission of rent of £2 per annum owed by the Stones for property leased from the Abbey. Approximate annual value of the corrody in 1418: £10 2s. 6d. Thomas died in 1426; Joan, in 1434. During her widowhood, the livery was reduced to 1 robe per annum. WAM 19913–31.

55. WILLIAM KEWE, and MARGERY, his wife. In 1421 William paid £40 for a corrody for their joint and several lives. It included a pension of 8d. per week ( = £1 14s. 8d. per annum) in lieu of cooked food, and remission of rent of £2 13s. 4d. per annum owed by the Kewes for property leased from the Abbey in the sanctuary. The pension probably represented a conventional payment in lieu of 'generals' at dinner (cf. no. 53 above), and perhaps pottage as well. If so, it can be assumed that William and Margery had a monk's corrody and were therefore entitled, additionally, to 1 conv. loaf and 1 gall. conv. ale per day. Margery died in 1432 or 1433; William, in 1437 or 1438. WAM 19917–37, 19664–79.

56. JOHN GEDNEY. A draper, alderman and mayor of London, who supplied cloth and garments to the Abbey for livery. In 1423 he was granted a corrody including 3 qu., 2 bus. wheat and 6 qu. malt per annum, together with annual livery of a squire's robe with furs, and remission of rent of £4

per annum owing for properties leased from the Abbey in the precinct and elsewhere. In the final year, bread and ale were given in lieu of grain and malt. No payment for the corrody is recorded: it was probably granted in part settlement of debts owed by the Abbey to John. Joan, his wife, was not explicitly included in the arrangements. John died in 1449. WAM 18568–74; Rosser, *Medieval Westminster*, 378–9.

57. JOHN NEWBOROUGH, and MARGERY, his wife. In or about 1424, they were granted, presumably for a down-payment, a corrody which included 400 faggots and 14 qu. charcoal per annum, annual livery of a robe for Margaret @ 12s. or thereabouts, and remission of rent of £2 13s. 4d. per annum owing for a house, belonging to the Knowle chantry, in the sanctuary. John, who was the Abbey's grammar-school master (*magister scolarium*), died in 1436; Margaret, in 1444 or 1445. WAM 19666–94, 19922–48; and for the Knowle chantry, Rosser, op. cit. 74–5.

58. JOHN CLERK, and ISABELLA, his wife. In 1427–8 John gave £10 for a corrody of bread and ale for their joint and several lives; quantities are not recorded. He was a skinner, who held property of the Abbey in the precinct and elsewhere in Westminster. WAM 19926; Rosser, op. cit. 374.

59. JOHN MALTON. In 1442 John paid £80 for a corrody which included 400 talwood, 600 short faggots, and 26 qu. charcoal per annum, and a pension of £4 6s. 8d. per annum ( = 20d. per week) which may have been in lieu of cooked food. If so, John probably held a variety of 'monk's corrody', and we can assume that he was entitled, additionally, to 1 conv. loaf and 1 gall. conv. ale per day. Payments ceased in 1447. WAM 19943–53.

60. JOHN THIRSK. Master mason of Westminster Abbey c.1429–50, and of Windsor Castle 1449–52. In 1445–6 John was granted occupancy, for life, of his house in the precinct free of rent (hitherto £2 per annum) and of the cost of repairs, and this arrangement may have been part of a more comprehensive corrody, distinct from that enjoyed by the master mason *ex officio*. However, the arrangement lapsed when John left the Abbey's employment. WAM 23510, 23512–13, 23516; Colvin (ed.), *History of the King's Works*, ii. 1053.

61. RICHARD WALSHE. The Abbey's janitor and chief steward 1449–65, and one of its auditors 1427–65. In 1450–1 Richard was granted, under the common seal, livery of a tunic or robe, in addition to the livery which he enjoyed *ex officio*. The livery, valued @ 13s. 4d. or 14s. per annum, was evidently that of a squire. The arrangement may have been part of a more comprehensive corrody. WAM 19956–72.

62. JOHN RANDOLF, and MARGARET, his wife. (i) In 1450 John paid £40 for a corrody of bread and ale for their joint and several lives; quantities are not recorded. (ii) On 7 Apr. 1451, in a grant which probably superseded (i), John and Margaret were granted a corrody consisting of 10 conv. loaves and 10 galls. conv. ale per week—but wastel loaves on each of 10 principal feasts

in the Abbey's calendar—and annual livery of a gentleman's robe with fur, or 10s. in lieu at Christmas, for their joint and several lives, with the right to distrain on the manor of Hendon if payments of the corrody were more than one week in arrears. Approximate annual value of the corrody in 1467: £4 16s. 6d. For this they gave a cash sum which is not specified. John, a squire of the king's household, and a minor Exchequer official, was also one of two servants of the refectory at the Abbey, and an occasional source of substantial loans to the latter: at Abbot Norwich's retirement in Nov. 1467, the sum of £105 was owing to him by instruments bearing Norwich's own seal, together with the sum of £80, said to represent 'excess' on his account to the Abbey—i.e. expenditure on the Abbey's behalf for which he had allegedly dipped into his own resources. John died in 1490; the last payment of 10s. to Margaret, in lieu of a robe, was made in 1524–5. WAM 5904, 19955–23058; Widmore, *Enquiry*, 193. For a late reference to Margaret as a corrodian, entitled to 10 loaves and 10 galls. ale per week, see WAM 5919*.

63. WILLIAM THORNWERK, and ELIZABETH, his wife. In 1455–6 William paid £13 6s. 8d. for a corrody of bread and ale for their joint and several lives. The grant was made under the common seal, but quantities are not recorded. William, a mason in the Abbey's service from the mid-1420s until 1458, and a rent-collector for the Abbey in Westminster, held property on lease in the precinct, and may have made a number of small loans to the Abbey. At his death c.1460, he was survived by his widow. WAM 19961, 23236 ff., 23497 ff.; Rosser, *Medieval Westminster*, 402. For a so-called annuity of £13 6s. 8d. per annum for 4 years, granted by the keeper of the new work to William and an associate in 1445–6, which may represent the repayment of a loan, see WAM 23511.

64. ROBERT DROPE, and ALICE, his wife. (i) In 1460 Robert paid £100 for a corrody for their joint and several lives. It included a pension of £1 14s. per annum (= 8d. per week) which was probably in lieu of cooked food. If so, it can be assumed that Robert and Alice held a monk's corrody and were entitled, additionally, to 1 conv. loaf and 1 gall. conv. ale per day (WAM 19966–79, and for the pension cf. no. 55). (ii) On 12 May 1467 Robert and Alice were granted, under the Abbey's common seal and for their joint and several lives, a corrody consisting of 7 conv. loaves and 7 galls. conv. ale per week, and the remission of the rent of £4 per annum owing for the messuage and garden which they leased from the Abbey in the sanctuary. Approximate annual value of the corrody in 1467, £7 0s. 8d. No payment is recorded: the corrody may have been part of a loan agreement. WAM 17795, 23242–60; and for the debt of £60 owing to Robert *ex penalitate pro defectu solutionum* at Abbot Norwich's retirement in Nov. 1467, see Widmore, *Enquiry*, 193. Robert, a London draper, and, from 1468, an alderman of London, died the survivor, in 1486–7. He was probably a kinsman of Br.

John Drope, who was a monk of Westminster 1462–3 to 1500 (Rosser, op. cit. 261 and n.).

65. RICHARD SAXILBY. In 1460–1 paid £20 for a corrody with a life-term; the details are not recorded (WAM 19966). Richard, who is described as a chaplain, was granted a lease of the church of St Margaret's, Westminster—i.e. the curacy there—in 1440, for life; he died in 1477 (Rosser, op. cit. 335 and n.).

66. WILLIAM TAPICER. His status as a corrodian is implied by his receipt, 1478–81, of 2s. 6d. or 3s. per annum from the almoner in lieu of 6 qu. charcoal, and 6s. 8d. per annum for the rent of his house (*mansio*); the latter may have been leased by William from another of the Abbey's obedientiaries. WAM 19086–9.

67. THOMAS, MR. Purchased the 'portion' (i.e., in this context, the cooked food) of Br. Richard Tedyngton for *c.*270 days in the year following the latter's death, for a total outlay of £3 0s. 4d. Described as a physician; probably to be identified as T. Huntyngdon, a physician retained by the monastery in the 1480s. WAM 33289, fo. 57$^v$; and see Appendix III, no. 36. The transaction suggests that the practice of giving the corrody of a deceased monk for the year after his death to a secular priest who should say a daily Mass for him had lapsed. WAM 637$^v$–638.

68. THOMAS DAGLAS. In 1494 Thomas, a chandler of London and Westminster, was granted a corrody consisting of 7 [conv.] loaves and 7 galls. [conv.] ale per week, and wastel loaves on principal feasts, together with annual livery of a 'gown' or 10s. in lieu, as part of an agreement whereby he undertook to supply tapers and torches for the anniversaries of Henry III, Eleanor of Castile, Richard II, and Henry V for 20 years; but the major item was a pension of £34 per annum (WAM Reg. Bk. i. 72$^v$–73). (The livery actually given was squire's livery.) Thomas died in 1500 or 1501. His widow received the livery, and presumably the bread and ale, until 1516, and it may be assumed that she carried on the business until then. WAM 23908–35. For a reference to Thomas's tenement in King Street, Westminster, see WAM 50768.

69. JOHN ATTWELL. He was granted a corrody of 10 conv. loaves per week in 1523, in recognition of 'good service past and to come', which he held until his death in 1530. Approximate annual value of the corrody in 1523: £1 12s. 5d. John was a chandler, who served the Abbey in various capacities and held substantial properties in Westminster. See Rosser, *Medieval Westminster*, 368–9.

# Bibliography

## I. MANUSCRIPT SOURCES

Muniment Room, Westminster Abbey, London

(i) *Accounts of abbatial officials*

| | |
|---|---|
| WAM 24510–48 | Accounts of steward and clerk of household, 1362–1466 |
| WAM 24411–26 | Accounts of steward of manors in Glos. and Worcs., 1399–1415 |
| WAM 24490 | Day account of steward of household, 1286 |
| WAM 33320, 33324 | Day accounts of household expenses, relating mainly to foodstuffs, 1500–2, 1509–10 |

(ii) *Accounts and memoranda of prior*

| | |
|---|---|
| WAM 33325 | Day account of household expenses, 1511–12 |
| WAM 33289 | Memoranda, 15th-cent. |

(iii) *Accounts of conventual officials*

| | |
|---|---|
| WAM 18962–19154 | Almoner, 1294–1539 |
| WAM 33301 | sub-almoner, 1514–25 |
| WAM 18829–940, 18942–5, 30724, 30909, 33311 | Cellarer, 1281–1535 |
| WAM 18941 | baker and brewer, 1526–7 |
| WAM 31916 | —— 1528–9 |
| WAM 33315 | —— 1520–1 |
| WAM 18717–827 | Chamberlain, 1291–1536 |
| WAM 18519–95, 23076–172 | Domestic treasurers, 1385–1532 |
| WAM 19155–310 | Granger, 1348–1529 |
| WAM 19318–502 | Infirmarer, 1297–1537 |
| WAM 33317 | Kitchener, expenses account, relating mainly to foodstuffs, 1491–2 |
| WAM 33318, 33321–3, 33327–9, 33330 | —day accounts 1497–1522 (*c.*10 years) |
| WAM 18627–716 | Monk-bailiff, 1413–1535 |
| WAM 23025* | monk-bailiff's butler, 1531–2 |
| WAM 33336, 33339–44, 33347, 33350–1 | Pittancer, 1528–35 |
| WAM 19503–616 | Refectorer, 1373–1537 |
| WAM 19618–810, 19813 | Sacrist, 1317–1535 |
| WAM 19811, 19816–30, 31863–4 | sub-sacrist, 1522–39 |

| | |
|---|---|
| WAM 19838–999, 23001–31, 23035\*, 30457, 33290, 33297–8 | Treasurers, 1297–1535 |
| WAM 33291 | Treasurer and monk-bailiff, 1496–7 |
| WAM 23452–626 | Warden of new work, 1341–1534 |
| | Wardens of royal foundations |
| WAM 23627–969 | Queen Eleanor of Castile, 1286–1534 |
| WAM 23970–24121 | Richard II and Anne of Bohemia, 1394–1534 |
| WAM 24122–235 | Henry V, 1437–1535 |
| WAM 24236–50 | Henry VII, 1502–32 |
| WAM 23179–316, 33314 | Warden of St Mary's chapel, 1298–1536 |
| WAM 33288 | Various officials, 1438–1502 |

(iv) *Cartularies and other registers*

| | |
|---|---|
| WAM Register Books i–ii | Lease-books, 1485–1536 |
| WAM Book i | Liber Niger Quaternus, late 15th-cent. |
| WAM Book xi | Westminster Domesday, early 14th-cent. |

(v) *Court rolls*

| | |
|---|---|
| WAM 50758–82 | Westminster manor, 1467–1523 |

(vi) *Deeds*

See index and calendar in the Muniment Room

(vii) *Inventories*

| | |
|---|---|
| WAM 31914 | Brewhouse, 1529–30 |
| WAM 6603, 18883A | Goods of deceased monks, 1396, 1400 |
| WAM 9480 | Hostelry, 1400 |
| WAM 6647 | Kitchen, 1491 |
| WAM 6597 | Misericord, 1509 |

(viii) *Ministers' accounts*

| | |
|---|---|
| WAM 25401–7 | Birdbrook (Essex), 1298–1303 |
| WAM 14859 | Islip (Oxon.), 1485–6 |

(ix) *Miscellaneous*

| | |
|---|---|
| WAM 37044 | Account for expenses of collegiate foundation at Westminster, 1544 |
| WAM 24846, 24859, 24861 | Accounts for repairs to conduit and main drain, 16th–18th-cent. |
| WAM 12787 | Draft injunctions for Westminster Abbey, 1536 |
| WAM 6478 | Draft scheme for collegiate foundation at Westminster, 1540 |
| WAM 6221 | Exhortation to prayer and processions, c.1403 |
| WAM 5919\* | List of corrodies, 1503 × 1525 |
| WAM 12890 | Notarial record of professions, 1501 |
| WAM 50684–98 | Records of Westminster fair, 1311–53 |
| WAM 25364 | Will, 1432 |

Other Repositories
*Cambridge, University Library*
CUL MS Kk. 5. 29, fos. 21ᵛ–128    A copy (late 14th cent. or early 15th cent.) of extents of convent's principal manors, 1289–1321

*London, British Library*

                                   Cartularies
Lansdowne MS 417                   Malmesbury Abbey, 14th-15th cent.
Harley MS 1708                     Reading Abbey, 13th cent.
Cotton Faustina A III              Westminster Abbey, *temp.* Edward I
Additional MS 27329,               Treatise on pestilence, 15th cent.
  fos. 236ᵛ–238ᵛ

*London, Guildhall Library*

                                   Ordinations
GL MS 9531/5, fos. 2–14            Reg. William Gray, bishop of London, 1426–31
GL MS 9531/8, 3rd ser., fos. 1–16  Reg. Thomas Savage, bishop of London, 1496–1501
ibid., 4th ser., fos. 3–11         Reg. William Warham, bishop of London, 1502–3
ibid., 4th ser., fos. 18ᵛ–24;      Reg. Richard Fitz James, bishop of London,
  GL MS 9531/9, iii,                 1506–22
  2nd ser. 156–84
ibid., 2nd ser., fos. 1–12ᵛ        Reg. Cuthbert Tunstall, bishop of London, 1522–30

*London, Public Record Office*
C 1/371/30                         Chancery petition, 1500 × 32
C 54/365, 372                      Close Rolls, 19 and 22 Henry VII
C 260/35/14                        Enquiry into allowances made by keepers during abbatial vacancies, 1325
C 270/6/23–4                       Replies of abbot and convent of Westminster to royal requests for corrodies, 1315–27
E 101/369/11, 400/4, 401/6         Royal wardrobe accounts, 1305–6, 1377–8, 1383–5
E 164/24 (= KR Misc. Bks. i. 24)   Cartulary of Malmesbury Abbey, late 13th cent.
E 315/24, fos. 5–6, 37–8, 81–86ᵛ   Draft schemes for a collegiate foundation at Westminster, 1540
LR 2/111                           Dissolution inventories for Westminster Abbey, and accounts for the collegiate foundation, 1541–2
LR 6/58/1–15, 61/1–2               Court of Augmentations, receivers' accounts, London and Middx., 1535–49
SC 6/1261/6                        Day account for abbot of Westminster's household, 1371–3

Oxford, Bodleian Library

MS Ashmole 1391, pp. 37–42        Treatise on pestilence, 15th cent.

## II. PRINTED SOURCES

*Account of the Great Household of Humphrey, First Duke of Buckingham, for the year 1452–3, The*, ed. M. Harris, with an introduction by J. M. Thurgood in *Camden Miscellany*, xxviii (Camden 4th ser. xxix, 1984), 1–57.

*Account-Book of Beaulieu Abbey, The*, ed. S. F. Hockey (Camden 4th ser. xvi, 1975).

*Annales Paulini*, in *Chronicles of the Reigns of Edward I and Edward II*, ed. W. Stubbs (2 vols., Rolls Series, 1882–3), i. 255–370.

BERNARD OF CLAIRVAUX, ST, *Sermones in cantica*, lxviii, in id., *Opera Omnia*, iv (*Patrologia Latina*, clxxxiii (1853), 1108–12).

*Book of St Gilbert, The*, ed. and trans. R. Foreville and G. Keir (Oxford Medieval Texts, 1987).

*Calendar of Charter Rolls* (HMSO, London, 1903–  ).

*Calendar of Charters and Documents relating to Selborne and its Priory*, ed. W. D. Macray (2 vols., Hampshire Record Society, 1891–4).

*Calendar of Close Rolls* (HMSO, London, 1892–  ).

*Calendar of Coroners Rolls of the City of London, AD 1300–1378*, ed. R. R. Sharpe (London, 1913).

*Calendar of Entries in the Papal Registers relating to Great Britain and Ireland Papal Letters*, xiii *(1471–84)*, 2 parts (HMSO, London, 1955).

*Calendar of Entries in the Papal Registers relating to Great Britain and Ireland, Petitions to the Pope*, i *(1342–1419)* (HMSO, London, 1896).

*Calendar of Patent Rolls* (HMSO, London, 1891–  ).

*Calendar of Plea and Memoranda Rolls preserved among the archives of the Corporation of the City of London at the Guildhall, AD 1323–64*, ed. A. H. Thomas (Cambridge, 1926).

*Calendar of Wills proved and enrolled in the Court of Husting, London, AD 1258–AD 1688*, ed. R. R. Sharpe (2 vols., 1889–90).

*Cartulaire de l'Abbaye cardinale de la Trinité de Vendôme*, ed. Ch. Métais (4 vols., Paris, 1893–1900).

*Cartularium Abbathiae de Whiteby*, ed. J. C. Atkinson (2 vols., Surtees Society, lxix, lxxii, 1879–81).

*Cartularium Monasterii de Rameseia*, ed. W. H. Hart and A. P. Lyons (3 vols., Rolls Series, 1884–94).

*Cartulary of Cirencester Abbey*, ed. C. D. Ross and M. Devine (3 vols., Oxford, 1964–77).

*Cartulary of the Priory of St Gregory, Canterbury*, ed. A. M. Woodcock (Camden 3rd ser. lxxxviii, 1956).

*Chronica Monasterii de Melsa*, ed. E. A. Bond (3 vols., Rolls Series, 1866–8).

*Chronicle of Battle Abbey, The*, ed. and trans. E. Searle (Oxford Medieval Texts, 1980).

*Chronicle of Bury St Edmunds, 1212–1301, The*, ed. and trans. A. Gransden (Nelson's Medieval Texts, 1964).

*Chronicle of Jocelin of Brakelond, The*, ed. and trans. H. E. Butler (Nelson's Medieval Texts, 1949). See also Jocelin of Brakelond.

*Chronicon Abbatiae de Evesham ad annum 1418*, ed. W. D. Macray (Rolls Series, 1863).

*Chronicon Monasterii de Abingdon*, ed. J. Stevenson (2 vols., Rolls Series, 1858).

*Close Rolls of the Reign of Henry III, 1227–1272* (14 vols., HMSO, London, 1902–38).

*Consuetudinum Saeculi x/xi/xii monumenta non-Cluniacensia*, ed. K. Hallinger (*Corpus Consuetudinum Monasticarum*, vii(3), 1984).

*Corrodies at Worcester in the 14th Century*, ed. J. M. Wilson and E. C. Jones (Worcestershire Historical Society, 1917).

*Councils and Synods, with Other Documents relating to the English Church* (2 vols.): vol. i, AD 871–1204 (2 parts, ed. D. Whitelock, M. Brett, and C. N. L. Brooke (Oxford, 1981)); vol. ii, AD 1205–1313 (2 parts, ed. F. M. Powicke and C. R. Cheney (Oxford, 1964)).

*Customary of the Benedictine Abbey of Bury St Edmunds in Suffolk, The*, ed. A. Gransden (Henry Bradshaw Society, xcix, 1973 for 1966).

*Customary of the Benedictine Abbey of Eynsham in Oxfordshire, The*, ed. A. Gransden (*Corpus Consuetudinum Monasticarum*, ii, 1963).

*Customary of the Benedictine Monasteries of Saint Augustine, Canterbury, and Saint Peter, Westminster*, ed. E. Maunde Thompson (2 vols., Henry Bradshaw Society, xxiii, xxviii, 1902–4).

Decretals of Gregory IX, in *Corpus Juris Canonici*, ed. E. Friedberg (Leipzig, 1879–81), ii.

*Discourse of the Common Weal of this Realm of England, A*, ed. E. Lamond (Cambridge, 1954).

*Documents Illustrating the Activities of the General and Provincial Chapters of the English Black Monks, 1215–1540*, ed. W. A. Pantin (3 vols., Camden 3rd ser. xlv, xlvii, liv, 1931–7).

*Documents Illustrating the Rule of Walter de Wenlok, abbot of Westminster, 1283–1307*, ed. B. F. Harvey (Camden 4th ser. ii, 1965).

*Documents of the Baronial Movement of Reform and Rebellion, 1258–67*, ed. and trans. R. F. Treharne and I. J. Sanders (Oxford Medieval Texts, 1973).

*Domesday Book, seu liber censualis Willelmi Primi Regis Angliae*, ed. A. Farley, H. Ellis *et al.* (4 vols., Record Commission, 1783–1816).

DORVEAUX, P., *L'Antidotaire Nicolas: Deux traductions françaises de l'Antidotarium Nicolai* (Paris, 1896).

—— (trans.), *Le Livre des Simples Medecines: Traduction française du Liber de simplici medicina dictus 'Circa Instans' de Platearius* (Paris, 1913).

DUGDALE, W., *Monasticon Anglicanum*, ed. J. Caley, H. Ellis, and B. Bandinel (6 vols., London, 1817–30).

Eadmer, *Historia Novorum in Anglia*, ed. M. Rule (Rolls Series, 1884).

—— *Life of St Anselm, Archbishop of Canterbury*, ed. R. W. Southern (Oxford Medieval Texts, 1962).

*Edward IV. The Household of Edward IV; The Black Book and the Ordinance of 1478*, ed. A. R. Myers (Manchester, 1959).

*English Episcopal Acta*: i, *Lincoln 1067–1185*, ed. D. M. Smith (London, 1980); ii, *Canterbury 1162–1190*, ed. C. R. Cheney and B. E. A. Jones (London, 1986); iii, *Canterbury 1193–1205*, ed. C. R. Cheney and E. John (London, 1986); iv, *Lincoln 1186–1206*, ed. D. M. Smith (London, 1986).

*English Wycliffite Sermons*, i, ed. A. Hudson (Oxford, 1983).

*Fabric Rolls of York Minster, The*, ed. J. Raine, jun. (Surtees Society, xxxv, 1859).

FLETE, JOHN, *The History of Westminster Abbey by John Flete*, ed. J. Armitage Robinson (Cambridge, 1909).

*Foedera, conventiones, literae et cujuscunque generis acta publica inter reges Angliae et alios quosvis imperatores, reges, pontifices, principes, vel communitates*, ed. T. Rymer (20 vols., London, 1704–35).

*Fountains Abbey Lease Book*, ed. D. J. H. Michelmore (Yorkshire Archaeological Society, Record Series, cxl, 1981).

*General Household Survey 1988* (Office of Population Censuses and Surveys: Social Survey Division, HMSO, London, 1990).

GERALD OF WALES, *De rebus a se gestis*, in *Giraldi Cambrensis Opera*, ed. J. S. Brewer, J. F. Dimock, and G. F. Warner (8 vols., Rolls Series, 1861–91), i. 3–122.

—— *Speculum ecclesie*, ibid. iv. 3–354.

and see Giraldus Cambrensis

GERVASE OF CANTERBURY, *Historical Works*, ed. W. Stubbs (2 vols., Rolls Series, 1879–80).

*Gesta Abbatum Monasterii Sancti Albani*, ed. H. T. Riley (3 vols., Rolls Series, 1867–9).

Giraldus Cambrensis, *The Autobiography of Giraldus Cambrensis*, trans. H. E. Butler (London, 1937).

and see Gerald of Wales

GOLTZ, D., *Mittelalterliche Pharmazie und Medizin dargestellt an Geschichte und Inhalt des Antidotarium Nicolai, mit einem Nachdruck der Druckfassung von 1471* (Stuttgart, 1976).

GRATIAN, *Decretum Gratiani*, in *Corpus Juris Canonici*, ed. E. Friedberg (Leipzig, 1879–81), i.

HALL, H., and NICHOLAS, F. J. (edd.), *Select Tracts and Table Books relating to English Weights and Measures (1100–1742)*, in *Camden Miscellany*, xv (Camden 3rd ser. xli, 1929), pp. i–xiv and 1–68.

HARIULF, *Chronique de l'Abbaye de Saint-Riquier (v<sup>e</sup> siècle–1104)*, ed. F. Lot (Paris, 1894).

HEALES, A., *Records of Merton Priory* (London, 1898).

HENRY VII, *The Will of Henry VII*, ed. T. Astle (London, 1775).

*Historiae Dunelmensis Scriptores Tres*, ed. J. Raine (Surtees Society, ix, 1839).

*Household Accounts from Medieval England*, ed. C. M. Woolgar, pt. i (Oxford, 1992).

*Household Papers of Henry Percy, Ninth Earl of Northumberland (1564–1632)*, ed. G. R. Batho (Camden 3rd ser. xciii, 1962).

JOCELIN OF BRAKELOND, *Chronicle of the Abbey of Bury St Edmunds*, trans. D. Greenway and J. Sayers (Oxford, 1989).

LANFRANC, *The Monastic Constitutions of Lanfranc*, ed. and trans. D. Knowles (Nelson's Medieval Texts, 1951).

and see *Vita Lanfranci*

LATIMER, HUGH, *Sermons and Remains*, ed. G. E. Corrie (2 vols., Parker Society, xvi, xx, 1844–5).

*Letters and Papers, Foreign and Domestic, of the Reign of Henry VIII*, ed. J. S. Brewer, J. Gairdner, and R. H. Brodie (21 vols. in 35, HMSO, London, 1862–1932).

*Letters of Pope Innocent III (1198–1216) concerning England and Wales*, ed. C. R. Cheney and M. G. Cheney (Oxford, 1967).

*Literae Cantuarienses*, ed. J. Brigstocke Sheppard (3 vols., Rolls Series, 1887–9).

LYNDWOOD, W., *Provinciale* (Oxford, 1679).

*Magnum Bullarium Romanum Augustae Taurinorum Editum*, ed. L. Cherubini *et al.* (10 vols., Luxemburg, 1727–30).

MATTHEW PLATEARIUS (attrib.), *Liber de simplici medicina dictus circa instans*, in *Practica vel Breviarium Johannis Serapionis* (Lyons, 1525), fos. ccxxiii–cclii. and see Dorveaux, P.

MORE, THOMAS, *The Apology of St Thomas More*, ed. J. B. Trapp (*The Complete Works of St Thomas More*, Yale, 1963– (in progress), ix, 1979).

NICHOLAS OF SALERNO (attrib.), *Antidotarium Nicolai*. See DORVEAUX, P., and GOLTZ, D.

NICHOLS, J. (ed.), *A Collection of all the Wills now known to be extant of the Kings and Queens of England etc.* (London, 1780).

*Observances in Use at the Augustinian Priory of S. Giles and S. Andrew at Barnwell, Cambridgeshire, The*, ed. J. W. Clark (Cambridge, 1897).

ORDERIC VITALIS, *The Ecclesiastical History of Orderic Vitalis*, ed. and trans. M. Chibnall (6 vols.: i and iii–vi, Oxford Medieval Texts, 1972–86; ii: ibid., corrected reprint, 1991, of first edn., 1969).

PETER THE VENERABLE, *The Letters of Peter the Venerable*, ed. G. Constable (2 vols., Cambridge, Mass., 1967).

—— *Statuta Petri Venerabilis abbatis Cluniacensis IX (1146/7)*, ed. G. Constable *et al.*, in *Consuetudines Benedictinae Variae (Saec. XI–Saec. XIV)* (*Corpus Consuetudinum Monasticarum*, vi, 1975).

*Reading Abbey Cartularies*, ed. B. R. Kemp (2 vols., Camden 4th ser. xxxi–xxxii, 1986–7).

*Recueil des Chartes de l'Abbaye de Cluny*, ed. A. Bernard and A. Bruel (6 vols., Paris, 1876–1903).

*Register of John de Grandisson, bishop of Exeter (AD 1327–1369)*, ed. F. C. Hingston-Randolph (3 vols., London, 1894–9).

*Register of St Augustine's Abbey, Canterbury, commonly called the Black Book, The*, ed. G. J. Turner and H. E. Salter (2 vols., London, 1915–24).

*Register or Chronicle of Butley Priory, Suffolk, 1510–1535, The*, ed. A. G. Dickens (Winchester, 1951).

*Registrum Malmesburiense*, ed. J. S. Brewer (Rolls Series, 2 vols., 1879–80).

*Registrum Radulphi Baldock, Gilberti Segrave, Ricardi Newport, et Stephani Gravesend, episcoporum Londoniensium, AD MCCCIV–MCCCXXXVIII*, ed. R. Fowler (Canterbury and York Society, vii, 1911).

*Regularis Concordia*, ed. and trans. T. Symon (Nelson's Medieval Texts, 1953).

RILEY, H. T. (ed.), *Memorials of London and London Life in the XIIIth, XIVth and XVth Centuries* (London, 1868).

*Rites of Durham, being a Description or Brief Declaration of all the Ancient Monuments, Rites and Customs belonging or being within the Monastical Church of Durham before the Suppression, written 1593*, ed. J. T. Fowler (Surtees Society, cvii, 1903).

*Rule of St Benedict, The*, ed. and trans. J. McCann (London, 1952).

Selby Abbey, *Monastery and Society in the Late Middle Ages: Selected Account Rolls from Selby Abbey, Yorkshire, 1398–1537*, ed. J. H. Tillotson (Woodbridge, 1988).

*Select Charters and Other Illustrations of English Constitutional History from the Earliest Times to the Reign of Edward I*, ed. W. Stubbs (9th edn., rev. H. W. C. Davis, Oxford, 1921).

STARKEY, THOMAS, *A Dialogue between Pole and Lupset*, ed. T. F. Mayer (Camden 4th ser. xxxvii, 1989).

*Statuta Capitulorum Generalium Ordinis Cisterciensis ab anno 1116 ad annum 1786*, ed. J.-M. Canivez (6 vols., Louvain, 1933–8).

*Statutes of the Realm* (11 vols., Record Commission, 1810–28).

STONE, JOHN, *The Chronicle of John Stone, Monk of Christ Church [Canterbury], 1415–1471*, ed. W. G. Searle (Cambridge Antiquarian Society publications, octavo ser. xxxiv, 1902).

THIRSK, J., and COOPER, J. P. (edd.), *Seventeenth-Century Economic Documents* (Oxford, 1972).

*Three Chapters of Letters relating to the Suppression of the Monasteries*, ed. T. Wright (Camden Society, xxvi, 1843).

*Two Cartularies of the Priory of St Peter at Bath*, ed. W. Hunt (Somerset Record Society, vii, 1893).

*Two Fifteenth-Century Cookery Books*, ed. T. Austin (Early English Text Society, Original Series, xlii, 1888).

ULRICH OF CLUNY, *Antiquiores Consuetudines Cluniacensis Monasterii* (*Patrologia Latina*, cxlix (1853), 635–778).

*Valor Ecclesiasticus temp. Henrici VIII, auctoritate Regia Institutus*, ed. J. Caley and J. Hunter (6 vols., Record Commission, 1810–34).

*Visitations in the Diocese of Lincoln 1517–1531*, ed. A. Hamilton Thompson (3 vols., Lincoln Record Society, xxxiii, xxxv, xxxvii, 1940–7).

*Visitations of the Diocese of Norwich, AD 1492–1532*, ed. A. Jessopp (Camden Society, NS xliii, 1888).

*Visitations of Religious Houses in the Diocese of Lincoln*, ed. A. Hamilton Thompson (3 vols., Canterbury and York Society, xvii, xxiv, xxxiii, 1915–27).

*Vita Gundulfi episcopi Roffensis*, in H. Wharton (ed.), *Anglia Sacra* (2 vols., London, 1691), ii. 273–92.

*Vita Lanfranci*, attrib. Miles Crispin (*Patrologia Latina*, cl (1854), 29–58).

WALTER DANIEL, *The Life of Ailred of Rievaulx*, ed. and trans. F. M. Powicke (Nelson's Medieval Texts, 1950).

WALTER MAP, *De Nugis Curialium: Courtiers' Trifles*, ed. and trans. M. R. James, rev. C. N. L. Brooke and R. A. B. Mynors (Oxford Medieval Texts, 1983).

*Walter of Henley and Other Treatises on Estate Management and Accounting*, ed. D. Oschinsky (Oxford, 1971).

*Westminster Abbey Charters, 1066–c.1214*, ed. E. Mason (London Record Society, xxv, 1988).

*Westminster Chronicle, 1381–94, The*, ed. and trans. L. C. Hector and B. F. Harvey (Oxford Medieval Texts, 1982).

WILKINS, D., *Concilia Magnae Britanniae et Hiberniae AD 446–1717* (4 vols., London, 1737).

WILLIAM OF MALMESBURY, *De antiquitate Glastoniensis ecclesiae*, in Adam de Domerham, *Historia de Rebus Gestis Glastoniensibus*, ed. T. Hearne (2 vols., Oxford, 1727), i. 1–122.

WILLIAM OF MALMESBURY, *Gesta Pontificum Anglorum*, ed. N. E. S. A. Hamilton (Rolls Series, 1870).

WRIOTHESLEY, C., *A Chronicle of England during the Reigns of the Tudors, from AD 1485 to 1559*, ed. W. D. Hamilton, i–ii (Camden Society, NS xi, xx, 1875–7).

## III. SECONDARY WORKS

AMULREE, LORD, 'Monastic infirmaries', in F. N. L. Poynter (ed.), *The Evolution of Hospitals in Britain* (London, 1964), 11–26.

AULT, W. O., *Open-Field Husbandry and the Village Community* (Transactions of the American Philosophical Society, NS, lv, pt. 7 (Philadelphia, 1965)).

—— *Open-Field Farming in Medieval England: A Study of Village By-Laws* (London, 1972).

BAILEY, M., 'The rabbit and the medieval East Anglian economy', *Agricultural History Review*, xxxvi (1988), 1–20.

BARLOW, F., *Thomas Becket* (London, 1986).

BARRON, C., 'The later Middle Ages: 1270–1520', in M. D. Lobel (ed.), *The City of London from Prehistoric Times to c.1520* (British Atlas of Historic Towns, iii, 1989).

BASKERVILLE, G., *English Monks and the Suppression of the Monasteries* (London, 1937).

BEAN, J. M. W., 'Plague, population and economic decline in the later Middle Ages', *Economic History Review*, 2nd ser. xv (1963), 423–37.

BEAVEN, A. E., *The Aldermen of the City of London temp. Henry III – 1912* (2 vols., London, 1908–13).

BEESON, C. F. C., *English Church Clocks, 1280–1850: Their History and Classification* (rev. edn., Ashford, 1977).

BINSKI, P., 'Abbot Berkyng's tapestries and Matthew Paris's Life of St Edward the Confessor', *Archaeologia*, cix (1991), 85–100.

BLACK, G., 'Excavations in the sub-vault of the misericorde of Westminster Abbey, February to May 1975', *Trans. London and Middlesex Archaeological Soc.* xxvii (1976), 135–78.

BOND, C. J., 'Monastic fisheries', in M. Ashton (ed.), *Medieval Fish, Fisheries and Fishponds in England* (2 parts, British Archaeological Reports, British Series, 182 (1988)), i. 69–112.

—— 'The fishponds of Eynsham Abbey', *The Eynsham Record*, 9 (1992), 3–17.

BONNEY, M., *Lordship and the Urban Community: Durham and its Overlords, 1250–1540* (Cambridge, 1990).

BOSL, K., 'Potens und Pauper: Begriffsgeschichtliche Studien zur gesellschaftlichen Differenzierung im Frühen Mittelalter und zum "Pauperismus" des Hoch-mittelalters', in his *Frühformen der Gesellschaft im mittelalterlichen Europa* (Munich, 1964), 106–34.

BRADFIELD, N., *Historical Costumes of England* (2nd edn., London, 1958).

BRAND, P. A., 'The control of mortmain alienation in England, 1200–1300', in J. H. Baker (ed.), *Legal Records and the Historian* (London, 1978), 29–40.

BRAUDEL, F., *The Mediterranean and the Mediterranean World in the Age of Philip II*, trans. S. Reynolds (2nd edn., 2 vols., London, 1972).

BRIGDEN, S., *London and the Reformation* (Oxford, 1989).

BRYDER, L., *Below the Magic Mountain: A Social History of Tuberculosis in Twentieth-Century Britain* (Oxford, 1988).

BULLOUGH, D. A., and STOREY, R. L. (edd.), *The Study of Medieval Records: Essays in Honour of Kathleen Major* (Oxford, 1971).

BURGESS, C., 'By quick and by dead: wills and pious provision in late medieval Bristol', *English Historical Review*, cii (1987), 837–58.

BUTCHER, A. F., 'Rent and the urban economy: Oxford and Canterbury in the later Middle Ages', *Southern History*, i (1979), 11–43.

CARPENTER, E. (ed.), *A House of Kings: The History of Westminster Abbey* (London, 1966).

CHARBONNIER, P., 'La consommation des seigneurs Auvergnats du xvᵉ au xviiiᵉ siècle', in 'Histoire de la consommation alimentaire du xivᵉ au xixᵉ siècle' (a 'dossier' presented by B. Bennassar and J. Joy), *Annales, Économies, Sociétés, Civilisations*, xxx (1975), 402–632.

CHENEY, C. R., 'Rules for the observance of feast-days in medieval England', *Bulletin of the Institute of Historical Research*, xxxiv (1961), 117–47.

CHENEY, M., 'The litigation between John Marshal and Archbishop Thomas Becket in 1164: a pointer to the origin of novel disseisin', *Law and Social Change in British History*, ed. J. A. Guy and H. G. Beale (London, 1984), 9–26.

—— 'Inalienability in mid-twelfth-century England: enforcement and consequences', *Monumenta Juris Canonici*, Series C: Subsidia, vii (1985), 467–78.

CLARK, E., 'Medieval labor law and English local courts', *American Journal of Legal History*, xxvii (1983), 330–53.

COLVIN, H. M., *The White Canons in England* (Oxford, 1951).

—— (ed.), *The History of the King's Works* (6 vols., HMSO, London, 1963–82).

—— *Architecture and the After-Life* (New Haven, Conn., and London, 1991).

COOPER, G. M., 'The Premonstratensian Abbey of Bayham', *Sussex Archaeological Collections*, ix (1857), 145–81.

COPPACK, G., *Abbeys and Priories* (English Heritage, London, 1990).

CORNWALL, J. C. K., *Wealth and Society in Early Sixteenth-Century England* (Cambridge, 1988).

COWDREY, H. E. J., *The Cluniacs and the Gregorian Reform* (Oxford, 1970).

CURRIE, C. K., 'Medieval fishponds in Hampshire', in M. Aston (ed.), *Medieval Fish, Fisheries and Fishponds in England* (2 parts, British Archaeological Reports, British Series, 182 (1988)), ii. 267–89.

DARLINGTON, R. R., 'Æthelwig, abbot of Evesham', 2 parts: i, *English Historical Review*, xlviii (1933), 1–22; ii, ibid. 177–98.

DAVIES, C. S. L., 'Les rations alimentaires de l'armée et de la marine anglaise au xviᵉ siècle', *Annales, Économies, Sociétés, Civilisations*, xviii (1963), 139–41.

DEBUS, A. G. (ed.), *Science, Medicine and Society in the Renaissance* (2 vols., London, 1972).

Department of Health, *Dietary Reference Values for Food Energy and Nutrients for the United Kingdom* (Report on Health and Social Subjects 41, HMSO, 1991).

Department of Health and Social Security, *Recommended Daily Amounts of Food Energy and Nutrients for Groups of People in the United Kingdom* (Report on Health and Social Subjects 15, HMSO, 1979).

DICKENS, A. G., *The English Reformation* (2nd edn., London, 1989).

*Dictionary of National Biography, The* (22 vols., London, 1908–9).

DOBSON, R. B., *Durham Priory, 1400–1450* (Cambridge, 1973).

DRUMMOND, J. C., and WILBRAHAM, A., *The Englishman's Food*, rev. D. Hollingsworth (London, 1958).

DUBY, G., 'Les pauvres des campagnes dans l'Occident médiévale jusqu'au xiii^e siècle', *Revue d'Histoire de l'Église de France*, lii (1966), 25–32.

DYER, C., 'English diet in the later Middle Ages', in T. H. Aston, P. R. Coss, C. Dyer, and J. Thirsk (edd.), *Social Relations and Ideas: Essays in Honour of R. H. Hilton* (Cambridge, 1983), 191–216.

—— 'Changes in diet in the late Middle Ages: the case of harvest workers', *Agricultural History Review*, xxxvi (1988), 21–37.

—— 'The consumption of fresh-water fish in medieval England', in M. Aston (ed.), *Medieval Fish, Fisheries and Fishponds in England* (2 parts, British Archaeological Reports, British Series, 182 (1988)), i. 27–38.

—— *Standards of Living in the Later Middle Ages: Social Change in England c.1200–1520* (reprint, 1990, of 1st edn., Cambridge, 1989).

EMDEN, A. B., *A Biographical Register of the University of Oxford to AD 1500* (3 vols., Oxford, 1957–9).

—— *A Biographical Register of the University of Oxford AD 1501 to 1540* (Oxford, 1974).

FIELD, J., *The King's Nurseries: The Story of Westminster School* (London, 1987).

FLINN, M. W., 'The population history of England, 1541–1871', *Economic History Review*, 2nd ser. xxxv (1982), 443–57.

FLINT, V. J., 'The early medieval "medicus", the saint—and the enchanter', *Social History of Medicine*, ii (1989), 127–45.

GASQUET, F. A., *Henry VIII and the English Monasteries* (8th edn., London, 1925).

GEDDES, J., 'Iron', in J. Blair and N. Ramsey (edd.), *English Medieval Industries: Craftsmen, Techniques, Products* (London, 1991).

*General Household Survey*, 1988 (Office of Population Censuses and Surveys: Social Survey Division, HMSO, London, 1990).

GETZ, F., 'Medical practitioners in medieval England', *Social History of Medicine*, iii (1990), 245–83.

GIBSON, A. J. S., 'The size and weight of cattle and sheep in early modern Scotland', *Agricultural History Review*, xxxvi (1988), 162–71.

GIBSON, M., *Lanfranc of Bec* (Oxford, 1978).

GILYARD-BEER, R., *Abbeys: An Illustrated Guide to the Abbeys of England and Wales* (HMSO, London, 1976).

GLASSER, R., *Time in French Life and Thought*, trans. C. G. Pearson (Manchester, 1972).

GOLDBERG, P. J. P., 'Urban identity and the poll taxes of 1377, 1379 and 1381', *Economic History Review*, 2nd ser. xliii (1990), 194–216.

GOODY, J., *Cooking, Cuisine and Class, a Study in Comparative Sociology* (Cambridge, 1982).

GOTTFRIED, R. S., *Epidemic Disease in Fifteenth Century England: The Medical Response and the Demographic Consequences* (New Brunswick, NJ, 1978).

—— *Doctors and Medicine in Medieval England, 1340–1530* (Princeton, NJ, 1986).

GRAY, H. L., 'Incomes from land in England in 1436', *English Historical Review*, xlix (1934), 607–39.

HAIGH, C., *Reformation and Resistance in Tudor Lancashire* (Cambridge, 1975).

HARRISON, M., 'The ordering of the urban environment: time, work and the occurrence of crowds 1790–1835', *Past and Present*, cx (Feb. 1986), 134–68.

HARVEY, B. F., 'The monks of Westminster and the University of Oxford', in F. R. H. Du Boulay and C. M. Barron (edd.), *The Reign of Richard II: Essays in Honour of May McKisack* (London, 1971).

—— 'Work and *festa ferianda* in medieval England', *Journal of Ecclesiastical History*, xxiii (1972), 289–308.

—— *The Estates of Westminster Abbey in the Middle Ages* (Oxford, 1977).

—— *Monastic Dress in the Middle Ages: Precept and Practice* (William Urry Memorial Trust, Canterbury, 1988).

HARVEY, J., *Medieval Gardens* (London, 1981).

HARVEY, P. D. A., 'The English inflation of 1180–1220', *Past and Present*, lxi (Nov. 1973), 3–30.

HARVEY, S. J. P., 'Taxation and the ploughland in Domesday Book', in P. Sawyer (ed.), *Domesday Book: A Reassessment* (London, 1985), 86–103.

HATCHER, J., 'Mortality in the fifteenth century: some new evidence', *Economic History Review*, 2nd ser. xxxix (1986), 19–38.

HEAL, F., *Hospitality in Early Modern England* (Oxford, 1990).

Hector, L. C., 'The beginning of the "natural day" in the late fourteenth century', *Journal of the Society of Archivists*, ii (1960–4), 87–9.

HORDERN, P., 'The death of ascetics: sickness and monasticism in the early Byzantine Middle East', in W. J. Shiels (ed.), *Monks, Hermits and the Ascetic Tradition* (Studies in Church History, xxii, 1985), 41–52.

HOWELL, M., *Regalian Right in Medieval England* (London, 1962).

HOYLE, R. W., 'Monastic leasing before the Dissolution: the evidence of Bolton Priory and Fountains Abbey', *Yorkshire Archaeological Journal*, lxi (1989), 111–37.

HUDSON, A., *The Premature Reformation: Wycliffite Texts and Lollard History* (Oxford, 1988).

HUNT, T., *Popular Medicine in Thirteenth-Century England* (Cambridge, 1990).

HYAMS, P. R., *King, Lords and Peasants in Medieval England: The Common Law of Villeinage in the Twelfth and Thirteenth Centuries* (Oxford, 1980).

JONES, M. K., and UNDERWOOD, M. G., *The King's Mother: Lady Margaret Beaufort, Countess of Richmond and Derby* (Cambridge, 1992).

JORDAN, W. K., *Philanthropy in England, 1480–1660* (London, 1959).

—— *The Charities of London, 1480–1660* (London, 1960).

KEALEY, E. J., *Medieval Medicus: A Social History of Anglo-Norman Medicine* (Baltimore, 1981).

KEIL, I., 'Corrodies of Glastonbury Abbey in the later Middle Ages', *Proceedings of the Somerset Archaeological and Natural History Society*, cviii (1964), 113–31.

KIMBALL, E. G., *Serjeanty Tenure in Medieval England* (Yale, 1936).

KING, E., *Peterborough Abbey, 1086–1310* (Cambridge, 1973).

KNIGHTON, C. S., 'The provision of education in the new cathedral foundations of Henry VIII', in D. Marcombe and C. S. Knighton (edd.), *Close Encounters:*

*English Cathedrals and Society since 1540: Studies in Local and Regional History, no. 3* (University of Nottingham, Department of Adult Education, 1991), 18–42.

KNOOP, D., and JONES, G. P., *The Mediaeval Mason* (3rd edn., Manchester, 1967).

KNOWLES, D., *The Monastic Order in England* (2nd edn., Cambridge, 1963).

—— *The Religious Orders in England* (3 vols., Cambridge, 1948–59).

—— and HADCOCK, R. N., *Medieval Religious Houses: England and Wales* (2nd edn., London, 1971).

KUSSMAUL, A., *Servants in Husbandry in Early Modern England* (Cambridge, 1981).

LANG, S. J., 'John Bradmore and his book Philomena', *Social History of Medicine*, v (1992), 121–30.

LANGENFELT, G., *The Historic Origin of the Eight Hours Day* (Stockholm, 1954).

LAPIDGE, M., 'Æthelwold as scholar and teacher', in B. Yorke (ed.), *Bishop Æthelwold: His Career and Influence* (Woodbridge, 1988), 89–117.

LASCOMBES, A., 'Fortunes de l'*ale*: à propos de Coventry, 1420–1555', in *Pratiques et Discours alimentaires à la Renaissance* (Actes du Colloque de Tours, 1979), ed. J.-C. Margolin and R. Sauzet (Paris, 1982), 126–36.

LAVER, J., *Concise History of Costume* (London, 1977).

LE GOFF, J., 'Labor time in the "crisis" of the fourteenth century: from medieval time to modern time', in id., *Time, Work, and Culture in the Middle Ages*, trans. A. Goldhammer (Chicago, 1980), 43–57.

LEWIS, R. G., 'The faculty of medicine', in J. McConica (ed.), *History of the University of Oxford*, iii (Oxford, 1986), 213–56.

MCCLURE, P., 'Patterns of migration in the late Middle Ages: the evidence of English place-name surnames', *Economic History Review*, 2nd ser. xxxii (1979), 167–82.

MCFARLANE, K. B., 'The investment of Sir John Fastolf's profits of war', *Transactions of the Royal Historical Society*, 5th ser. vii (1957), 91–116; reprinted in id., *England in the Fifteenth Century* (London, 1981), 175–97.

MCINTOSH, M., 'Local responses to the poor in late medieval and Tudor England', *Continuity and Change*, iii (1988), 209–45.

MCKITTERICK, R., 'Town and monastery in the Carolingian period', in D. Baker (ed.), *The Church in Town and Countryside* (Studies in Church History, xvi, 1979), 93–102.

MCLAUGHLIN, T. P., 'The teaching of the canonists on usury (xii, xiii and xiv centuries)', 2 parts, *Mediaeval Studies* (Toronto), i (1939), 81–147; ibid. ii (1940), 1–22.

MASTERS, B. R., *The Chamberlain of the City of London, 1237–1987* (London, 1988).

MAXWELL-LYTE, H. C., 'Glastonbury Abbey in 1322', *Collectanea*, i (Somerset Record Society, xxxix, 1924), 1–34.

MENNELL, S., *All Manners of Food* (Oxford, 1985).

MERTES, K., *The English Noble Household, 1250–1600: Good Governance and Politic Rule* (Oxford, 1988).

MICKLETHWAITE, J. T., 'Notes on the Abbey buildings of Westminster', *Archaeological Journal*, xxxiii (1876), 15–48.

—— 'On a filtering cistern of the fourteenth century at Westminster Abbey', *Archaeologia*, liii (1892), 1–10.

MOLLAT, M., 'La notion de la pauvreté au Moyen Age: position de problèmes', *Revue d'Histoire de l'Église de France*, lii (1966), 5–23.

—— *Les Pauvres au Moyen Age: Étude sociale* (Paris, 1978), trans. A. Goldhammer as *The Poor in the Middle Ages: An Essay in Social History* (Yale, 1986).

MOORMAN, J. R. H., *Church Life in England in the Thirteenth Century* (Cambridge, 1946).

MURRAY, A., 'Religion among the poor in thirteenth-century France: the testimony of Humbert de Romans', *Traditio*, xxx (1974), 285–324.

NEVEUX, H., 'L'alimentation du xiv⁰ au xviii⁰ siècle. Essai de mise au point', *Revue d'Histoire Économique et Sociale*, li (1973), 336–79.

NICHOLSON, R., 'The fish remains', in C. O'Brien, L. Brown, S. Dixon, and R. Nicholson, *The Origins of the Newcastle Quayside: Excavations at Queen Street and Dog Bank* (Society of Antiquaries of Newcastle-upon-Tyne, Monographs Series iii, 1988), 138–49.

PALMER, R. LIDDESDALE, *English Monasteries in the Middle Ages* (London, 1930).

PANTIN, W. A., 'Instructions for a devout and literate layman', in J. J. G. Alexander and M. T. Gibson (edd.), *Medieval Learning and Literature: Essays presented to Richard William Hunt* (Oxford, 1976).

PAUL, A. A., and SOUTHGATE, D. A. T. (edd.), *McCance and Widdowson's The Composition of Foods* (4th edn., HMSO, London, 1978).

PAYLING, S. J., *Political Society in Lancastrian England* (Oxford, 1991).

PEARCE, E. H., *The Monks of Westminster* (Cambridge, 1916).

PELLING, M., 'Illness among the poor in an early modern English town: the Norwich census of 1570', *Continuity and Change*, iii (1988), 273–90.

—— 'Old age, poverty, and disability in early modern Norwich: work, remarriage, and other expedients', in M. Pelling and R. M. Smith (edd.), *Life, Death, and the Elderly: Historical Perspectives* (Studies in the Social History of Medicine (London and New York, 1991)).

PHYTHIAN-ADAMS, C., *Desolation of a City: Coventry and the Urban Crisis of the Late Middle Ages* (Cambridge, 1979).

POOS, L. R., *A Rural Society after the Black Death: Essex 1350–1525* (Cambridge, 1991).

—— and SMITH, R. M., '"Legal windows onto historical populations?" Recent research on demography and the manor court in medieval England', *Law and History Review*, ii (1984), 128–52.

POUCHELLE, M.-C., *The Body and Surgery in the Middle Ages* (Oxford, 1990).

PRESTWICH, M., 'Victualling estimates for English garrisons in Scotland during the early fourteenth century', *English Historical Review*, lxxxii (1967), 536–43.

—— *Edward I* (London, 1988).

PULLAN, B., *Rich and Poor in Renaissance Venice* (Oxford, 1971).

—— 'Support and redeem: charity and poor relief in Italian cities from the fourteenth to the seventeenth centuries', *Continuity and Change*, iii (1988), 177–208.

RABAN, S., *Mortmain Legislation and the English Church, 1279–1500* (Cambridge, 1982).

RACKHAM, R. B., 'The nave of Westminster', *Proceedings of the British Academy* (1909), 3–64.

RAFTIS, J. A., *The Estates of Ramsey Abbey* (Toronto, 1957).

RAWCLIFFE, C., 'The hospitals of late medieval London', *Medical History*, xxviii (1984), 1–21.

RAWCLIFFE, C., 'The profits of practice: the wealth and status of medical men in later medieval England', *Social History of Medicine*, i (1988), 61–78.

RILEY, JAMES C., *Sickness, Recovery and Death: A History and Forecast of Ill Health* (London, 1989).

ROBERTS, R. S., 'The personnel and practice of medicine in Tudor and Stuart England', 2 parts: i, *Medical History*, vi (1962), 363–82; ii, ibid. viii (1964), 217–34.

ROBINSON, J. ARMITAGE, *Gilbert Crispin, Abbot of Westminster* (Cambridge, 1911).

—— *The Abbot's House at Westminster* (Cambridge, 1911).

—— and JAMES, M. R., *The Manuscripts of Westminster Abbey* (Cambridge, 1909).

ROGERS, J. E. THOROLD, *A History of Agriculture and Prices in England from the year after the Oxford Parliament (1259) to the commencement of the Continental War (1793)* (7 vols., Oxford, 1866–1902).

ROSSER, A. G., 'The essence of medieval urban communities: the vill of Westminster 1200–1540', *Transactions of the Royal Historical Society*, 5th ser. xxxiv (1984), 91–112.

—— *Medieval Westminster, 1200–1540* (Oxford, 1989).

ROSSER, G. See Rosser, A. G.

Royal Commission on Historical Monuments of England, *London*, i (*Westminster Abbey*) (London, 1926).

RUBIN, M., *Charity and Community in Medieval Cambridge* (Cambridge, 1987).

SALZMAN, L. F., *Building in England down to 1540* (Oxford, 1952).

SAUL, A., 'The herring industry at Great Yarmouth, c.1280–c.1400', *Norfolk Archaeology*, xxxviii (1981–3), 33–43.

SAVINE, A., *English Monasteries on the Eve of the Dissolution* (Oxford Studies in Social and Legal History, i, Oxford, 1909).

SAWYER, P. H., *Anglo-Saxon Charters: An Annotated List and Bibliography* (London, 1968).

SAYERS, J., '"Original", cartulary and chronicle: the case of the Abbey of Evesham', *Fälschungen im Mittelalter* (Monumenta Germaniae Historica, xxxiii(4)), 371–95.

SCARISBRICK, J. J., *The Reformation and the English People* (Oxford, 1984).

SEARLE, E., *Lordship and Community: Battle Abbey and its Banlieu, 1066–1538* (Toronto, 1974).

*Sharp Practice*, i (First Report of Soutra Hospital Archaeo-ethno-pharmacological Research Project, Edinburgh, 1987).

SHIELS, W. J. (ed.), *Monks, Hermits and the Ascetic Tradition* (Studies in Church History, xxii, Oxford, 1985).

SLACK, P., *The Impact of Plague in Tudor and Stuart England* (London, 1985).

—— *Poverty and Policy in Tudor and Stuart England* (London, 1988).

SMITH, A., 'Litigation and politics: Sir John Fastolf's defence of his English property', in A. J. Pollard (ed.), *Property and Politics: Essays in Later Medieval English History* (Gloucester, 1984), 59–75.

SMITH, R. M. (ed.), *Land, Kinship and Life-Cycle* (Cambridge, 1984).

—— 'Some issues concerning families and their property in rural England 1250–1800', ibid. 1–86.

—— 'Marriage processes in the English past: some continuities', in L. Bonfield, R. M. Smith, and K. Wrightson (edd.), *The World We Have Gained: Histories of Population and Social Structure* (Oxford, 1986), 43–99.

—— 'Women's property rights under customary law: some developments in the thirteenth and fourteenth centuries', *Transactions of the Royal Historical Society*, 5th ser. xxxvi (1986), 165–94.

—— 'The manorial court and the elderly tenant in late medieval England', in M. Pelling and R. M. Smith (edd.), *Life, Death, and the Elderly: Historical Perspectives* (Studies in the Social History of Medicine, London and New York, 1991), 39–61.

—— See also Poos, L. R., and Smith, R. M.

SNAPE, R. H., *English Monastic Finances in the Later Middle Ages* (Cambridge, 1926).

SOUTHERN, R. W., *Western Society and the Church in the Middle Ages* (Harmondsworth, 1970).

—— review of J. Le Goff, *La Naissance du Purgatoire* (Paris, 1981), in *Times Literary Supplement* (18 June 1982), 651–2.

SPUFFORD, M., *Contrasting Communities: English Villagers in the Sixteenth and Seventeenth Centuries* (Cambridge, 1974).

STONE, L., *The Crisis of the Aristocracy, 1558–1641* (Oxford, 1965).

STOUFF, L., *Ravitaillement et alimentation en Provence aux xiv<sup>e</sup> et xv<sup>e</sup> siècles* (Civilisations et Sociétés, xx, Paris, 1970).

SUTHERLAND, D. W., *The Assize of Novel Disseisin* (Oxford, 1973).

SWANSON, H., *Medieval Artisans: An Urban Class in Late Medieval England* (Oxford, 1989).

SWANSON, R. N., *Church and Society in Late Medieval England* (Oxford, 1989).

TALBOT, C. H., and HAMMOND, E. A., *The Medical Practitioners in Medieval England: A Biographical Register* (London, 1965).

TAYLOR, A. J., *The Jewel House, Westminster* (HMSO, London, 1965).

THOMAS, K. V., 'Work and leisure in pre-industrial society', *Past and Present*, xxix (Dec. 1964), 50–62.

—— 'Age and authority in early modern England', *Proceedings of the British Academy*, lxii (1976), 205–48.

—— *Man and the Natural World* (London, 1984).

THOMPSON, A. HAMILTON, 'A corrody from Leicester Abbey, AD 1393–4, with some notes on corrodies', *Transactions of the Leicestershire Archaeological Society*, xiv (1925), 113–34.

—— *The English Clergy and their Organization in the Later Middle Ages* (Oxford, 1947).

THOMPSON, E. P., 'Time, work-discipline, and industrial capitalism', *Past and Present*, xxxviii (Dec. 1967); reprinted in id., *Customs in Common* (London, 1991), 352–403.

THOMPSON, S., *Women Religious: The Founding of English Nunneries after the Norman Conquest* (Oxford, 1991).

THRUPP, S. L., *The Merchant Class of Medieval London [1300–1500]* (Chicago, 1948).

TIERNEY, B., *Medieval Poor Law: A Sketch of Canonical Theory and its Application in England* (Berkeley and Los Angeles, 1959).

—— 'The decretists and the "deserving poor"', *Comparative Studies in Society and History*, i (1958–9), 360–73.

TILLOTSON, J. H., 'Pensions, corrodies and religious houses: an aspect of the relations of Crown and Church in early fourteenth-century England', *Journal of Religious History*, viii (1974–5), 127–43.

Tɪᴛᴏw, J. Z., 'Some differences between manors and their effects on the condition of the peasant in the thirteenth century', *Agricultural History Review*, x (1962), 1–13; reprinted in W. E. Minchinton (ed.), *Essays in Agrarian History* (Newton Abbot, 1968), 37–51.

Tᴏᴜᴛ, T. F., *Chapters in the Administrative History of Medieval England* (6 vols., Manchester, 1920–33).

Tʀᴇᴠᴇʟʏᴀɴ, G. M., *English Social History: A Survey of Six Centuries, Chaucer to Queen Victoria* (3rd edn., London, 1946).

*Victoria History of the Counties of England* (in progress, London, 1900– ).

Vᴏɢᴜᴇ, A. ᴅᴇ, and Nᴇᴜꜰᴠɪʟʟᴇ, J., *La Règle de Saint Benoît* (7 vols., Paris, 1972–7).

Wᴀʟᴅʀᴏɴ, T., 'DISH at Merton Priory: evidence for a "new" occupational disease?', *British Medical Journal*, ccxci (1985), 1762–3.

Wᴀʟᴇs, T., 'Poverty, poor relief and the life-cycle: some evidence from seventeenth-century Norfolk', in R. M. Smith (ed.), *Land, Kinship and Life-Cycle* (Cambridge, 1984), 351–404.

Wᴇsᴛʟᴀᴋᴇ, H. F., *Westminster Abbey: The Church, Convent, Cathedral and College of St Peter, Westminster* (2 vols., London, 1923).

Wʜᴇᴇʟᴇʀ, A., 'Fish bone', in H. Clarke and A. Carter, *Excavations in King's Lynn, 1963–1970* (Society for Medieval Archaeology, Monograph Series, vii, 1977), 403–8.

—— and Jᴏɴᴇs, A., 'Fish remains', in A. Rogerson, 'Excavations on Fuller's Hill, Great Yarmouth', *East Anglian Archaeology, Report no. 2: Norfolk* (Norfolk Archaeological Unit, 1976), 208–26.

Wɪᴅᴍᴏʀᴇ, R., *An Enquiry into the Time of the First Foundation of Westminster Abbey* (London, 1743).

Wɪʟᴋɪɴsᴏɴ, B., 'The Peasants' Revolt of 1381', *Speculum*, xv (1940), 12–35.

Wɪʟʟɪs, R., *The Architectural History of the Conventual Buildings of the Monastery of Christ Church, in Canterbury* (London, 1869).

Wɪʟᴍᴀʀᴛ, A., 'Une riposte de l'ancien monachisme au manifeste de Saint Bernard', *Revue Bénédictine*, xlvi (1934), 296–344.

Wᴏʟʟᴀsᴄʜ, J., 'Les obituaires, témoins de la vie Clunisienne', *Cahiers de Civilisation Médiévale*, xxii (1979), 139–71.

Wᴏᴏᴅ, S. M., *English Monasteries and their Patrons in the Thirteenth Century* (Oxford, 1955).

Wʀɪɢʟᴇʏ, E. A., and Sᴄʜᴏꜰɪᴇʟᴅ, R. S., *The Population History of England, 1541–1871: A Reconstruction* (Cambridge, reprint (1989) with new introduction, of 1st edn. (1981)).

Yᴏᴜɪɴɢs, J., *The Dissolution of the Monasteries* (London, 1971).

## IV. UNPUBLISHED THESES

Bᴇʀʀʏ, N. P., 'The Estates and Privileges of Malmesbury Abbey in the Thirteenth Century' (Ph.D. thesis, University of Reading, 1989).

Tʜᴏᴍᴘsᴏɴ, B. J., 'The Church and the Aristocracy: Lay and Ecclesiastical Land-owning Society in Fourteenth-Century Norfolk' (Ph.D. thesis, University of Cambridge, 1990).

# Index